Intellectuals

Aesthetics
Politics
Academics

CULTURAL ⚘ POLITICS

A series from the Social Text collective

Intellectuals

Aesthetics
Politics
Academics

Bruce Robbins, editor
(for the Social Text collective)

Cultural Politics 2

University of Minnesota Press / Minneapolis

Copyright © 1990 by the Regents of the University of Minnesota
Andrew Ross, "Defenders of the Faith and the New Class," first appeared in
No Respect: Intellectuals and Popular Culture. © Routledge, Chapman & Hall,
1989.

Published by the University of Minnesota Press
2037 University Avenue Southeast, Minneapolis MN 55414
Printed in the United States of America on acid-free paper.

Library of Congress Cataloging-in-Publication Data
Intellectuals : aesthetics, politics, and academics / Bruce Robbins,
   editor.
    p.   cm. — (Cultural politics)
   ISBN 0 – 8166 – 1830 – 5. — ISBN 0 – 8166 – 1831 – 3 (pbk.)
    1. Intellectuals—Political activity. 2. Intellectuals—United
States—Political activity. I. Robbins, Bruce. II. Series:
Cultural politics (Minneapolis, Minn.)
HM213.I5475   1990
305.5'52—dc20
                               90 – 10717
                                CIP

"Is it hubris, *perhaps, to say that if one were to look about at the present from the year 2000—which, after all, is only thirty-four years away—that one could discern, in the second half of the twentieth century, the transformation of the University into the primary institution of the emerging post-industrial society, just as the business firm had been the most important institution in the previous century and a half?*

Daniel Bell (1966)

Faudra-t-il écrire, dans les dictionnaires de l'an 2000: intellectuel, nom masculin, catégorie sociale et culturelle née à Paris au moment de l'affaire Dreyfus, morte à Paris à la fin du XXe siècle; n'a apparamment pas survécu au déclin de l'Universel'?"

Bernard-Henri Lévy (1987)

CONTENTS

INTRODUCTION:
THE GROUNDING OF INTELLECTUALS
Bruce Robbins

*The effective critical apparatus of America has broken
down in matters of urgent national concern.*

William F. Buckley, Jr. (1959)

*The relative decline of unattached intellectuals over the
last thirty or forty years . . . is part of the growing
institutionalization and, more particularly, academization
of intellect.*

Lewis Coser (1965)

*In the third-world situation the intellectual is always
a political intellectual. No third-world lesson is more
timely or more urgent for us today, among whom the very
term "intellectual" has withered away, as though it were
the name for an extinct species.*

Fredric Jameson (1986)

*The near total absorption of intellectual life by the
universities marks the decline, if not the obliteration, of
"the intellectual" as a distinctive social type.*

Jean Bethke Elshtain (1987)

The Reagan-Bush right has performed a public service.

In 1984, former Secretary of Education William Bennett's *To
Reclaim a Legacy* began a counteroffensive against the changes

---

The editor gratefully acknowledges the assistance of a Rutgers University Trustees
Research Fellowship in preparing this book for publication.

wrought in American education and cultural life by or since the 1960s—changes to whose description and defense *Social Text* devoted *The Sixties without Apology*, published by the University of Minnesota Press in the same year. In 1987, when E. D. Hirsch's *Cultural Literacy* and Allan Bloom's *The Closing of the American Mind*[1] made the best-seller lists, the right's demonizing of the decade was broadcast to a much broader public. Since then the attack has continued to swell. But it has had paradoxical results. By lifting the debate out of individual professions and disciplines and carrying it into the "public sphere," the cultural conservatives clearly hoped to rally enough popular and state backing so as to reassert their own claims over a realm that seems more and more to have slipped out of the customary hands. Instead, they inadvertently displayed how much support the programs of the 1960s have little by little won for themselves, even among those who once had (and may still have) some misgivings. By complaining loudly about the left's influence over America's educational and cultural institutions, the right has brought to everyone's attention how *normal* that influence now seems there, both in its basic premises and in its institutional consequences. With all due allowance for the conservatives' penchant for hortatory hyperbole, they seem to have effectively shown that the new center, the broad coalition of views marshaled in response to the so-called killer B's (Mary Louise Pratt's phrase for Bennett, Bloom, and Saul Bellow), is in large part a product of the New Left of the 1960s.

Thanks to the Reaganite backlash, much of the public has thus learned that, for better or worse, the left is a forceful presence in American cultural life. More unexpectedly, the left itself has had to learn the same thing. Enough of the cool but invigorating comforts of pure marginality to which it had become accustomed, the deprived but after all mildly flattering self-image of inner exile, alienation, detached and unencumbered oppositionality. In the face of the right's offensive, it is no longer possible to deny that something palpably grounded in reality, something realized and accomplished, exists for the right to attack, and the left to defend. All this public recognition, however critical, is forcing left intellectuals to acknowledge what they have most often not wanted to acknowledge: their own cultural and institutional *achievements*.

It is this strangely unconscious and uncompleted success story that has put the subject of intellectuals back on the agenda.

As the preceding quotations suggest, the proposition that intellectuals no longer exist is a commonplace shared and passionately declared by left and right alike. This unsettling consensus offers one gloss on the polysemous title, "The Grounding of Intellectuals." In the 1920s Karl Mannheim described intellectuals as "free-floating, unattached."[2] In this sense, they have run aground. Everyone seems to agree that intellectuals today, or their much-diminished remains, are bound to or bound up in institutional circumstance as never before. On behalf of the right, Norman Podhoretz blames the disappearance of intellectuals on the 1960s: "Selfhatred took the form of a repudiation not so much of who as of what they were. To be an intellectual—a scholar, a thinker, an artist, a writer—was not good enough. Not even the 'production of literary masterpieces' was good enough: one had to change the world."[3] For Alan Wald, on the other hand, the "ideology of becoming 'independent critical thinkers,' indeed intellectuals beyond the blinding grip of ideology itself," only masked the New York intellectuals' shift in political allegiance to the right.[4] In order to change the world, intellectuals must ideally be, for leftists like Wald, "engaged" (Sartre) or "organic" (Gramsci) rather than critically independent.[5] That is, they should be grounded in a social constituency, project, or movement. In practice, however, the left tends to accuse intellectuals of being *all too successfully* grounded in reality—a reality of academic jobs and careers, compromised institutions, "selling-out," and "co-optation." It accuses them of changing *into* the world.

In other words, the grounding of intellectuals is no longer in question. It provides the new common basis for debate and analysis.

The issue, then, is what to make of this grounding, what value or inflection it deserves, how to differentiate ethically and politically among grounded actualities. The verb "to ground" includes two logically antithetical but historically coexistent senses: (1) to strand, beach, confine to quarters, restrict the movement of, and (2) to base, establish, serve as foundation of. Both Gramsci's concept of the "organic" intellectual and Foucault's[6] concept of the "specific" intellectual—discussed in R. Radhakrishnan's essay in this volume—would count as modes (continuous and overlapping rather than opposed to one another) of "grounding" in this second sense. The debate at the end of the 1980s and the beginning of the 1990s must set out from the premise that intellectuals can be "grounded" in both senses, and at the same time. It is less a debate over the legacy of the 1960s than a debate over the institutional form the energies of the 1960s have taken: how much has been retained, what has been transformed, what possibilities have opened up, what might have to be jettisoned. In helping to initiate this debate, the contributors to this volume recognize that the phrase "intellectuals in power," the title of a recent book by Paul Bové, can no longer seem a contradiction in terms.[7] They pay attention to power both exercised in and delimited by specific circumstances, power that is morally and politically ambiguous, and power that is also, since the Bennett/Bloom/Bellow onslaught, very much at risk. These essays respond to the task of mapping the specific social sites, situations, and "cases" of intellectuals, analyzing the actual institutions with which intellectuals are "affiliated" (Edward Said's usefully neutral term)[8] and the political valence of their affiliations, and trying to distinguish what is enabling from what is restricting.

More specifically, these essays are largely animated—whatever their topics—by a desire to interrogate the received opinion that the "success" of the left in grounding itself within American educational and cultural institutions since the 1960s must be seen as the "failure," betrayal, decline, or demise of the intellectual. One representative obituary is Russell Jacoby's *The Last Intellectuals: American Culture in the Age of Academe*.[9] In an argument whose symmetries with that of Allan Bloom have often been pointed out, and which is echoed in the special issues of *Salmagundi* (Spring-Summer 1986) and *Telos* (Spring 1987) devoted to intellectuals, Jacoby condemns the rise of "academic Marxism," that is, the left's absorption by academicization, specialization, and professionalization, which robs intellectuals of the public role and the oppositional force that had defined them. "Independent intellectuals, who wrote for the educated reader, are dying out" (6). "Today nonacademic intellectuals are an endangered species'' (7). ''By the 1960s the universities virtually monopolized intellectual work'' (8).

One reason for skepticism about this narrative (which is repeated, though in a very different accent, in Alfons Söllner's account of the Frankfurt School's passage from the OSS to the academy) is the generational allegory implicit in the book's title. The ''last'' intellectuals who have failed to reproduce themselves are centered in, though not restricted to, the New York intellectuals, and the ''missing generation'' (xi) that failed to take over from them is the generation of the 1960s. As Lynn Garafola points out, Jacoby's celebration of the New York intellectuals ''overlooks the abysmal record of their behavior in the 1960s—the fulminations against the counterculture, the denunciations of the New Left, the jeremiads against feminism. If the New York intellectuals left no heirs, the fault is largely their own.''[10] To celebrate them now is to repeat their trashing of the 1960s. More important, this family drama brings out the hidden meanings of Jacoby's plausibly antithetical terms ''public'' and ''academic.'' Philip Rahv's affirmation of ''the alienated modernist as a role model for dissident intellectuals,'' Wald notes, made it impossible for him to join or support ''the counterculture of the 1960s,'' to give just value to the new literature of ''blacks, Chicanos, and Native American Indians'' (221). Blacks, Chicanos, Native Americans, even women—those groups whose new representation in American universities, curricula, conferences, book lists, and so on has drawn so much fire in the antisixties backlash—were not, in appears, ''the public.'' For the New York intellectuals, as for so many others who invoke that potent abstraction, ''the public'' cannot be represented by specific names, faces, or places. As soon as anyone in particular stands up and demands to be counted as *part* of ''the public,'' that necessarily anonymous source of representational legitimacy absents itself, and is then invoked from a distance to thrash away their temerity. This is to say that for Jacoby, the word ''public'' can in practice be translated, on the contrary, as ''alienated'' or ''marginal,'' unconstrained by social specificity. The confusion appears on the first page of his preface. ''Few American intellectuals live in exile,'' he laments. In *exile*? This is, on the same page, what is signified by ''the impoverishment of public culture." To be "public" is to be exiled, ungrounded, hovering somewhere above the messy melee of actual collective and overlapping identities that is society. In the morally weighty name of "the public," Jacoby is in fact protecting the privileged free-floating *independence* of an older and less morally creditable conception of intellectuals.

Another reason for skepticism is that we have heard variations on Jacoby's narrative of decline many times before. When Jacoby complains, for example, that "as intellectuals became academics, they had no need to write in a public prose: they did not, and finally they could not" (7), he reminds one of many similar complaints, equally apocalyptic and equally short-sighted about what might be capable of producing an eventual impact on the "public." Like the response of the Budapest philosophers to Georg Lukács and his "Sunday Circle" in 1919: "We ask of them only one thing: that they take more care to speak clearly, in good Hungarian. Why, for example, do they always have to refer to *das Werk*? If there is no Hungarian word for the concept, it is a waste of time to philosophize about it in Hungarian."[11] It was in the same year that Lukács was to concern himself with culture in the government of the new Hungarian Socialist Republic. Surely "public" enough for the most stringent critic?

Jacoby himself quotes Irving Howe's 1954 attack on Lionel Trilling, in which the "absorption" of intellectuals by universities meant "they not only lose their traditional rebelliousness but to one extent or another they cease to function as intellectuals" (82), followed ten years later by Richard Hofstadter's gleeful references to Howe himself as "Professor Howe." As the accusations of Fall from a Higher State pile up, it becomes clear that the adjectives "public" and "independent" affixed to intellectuals do not refer to states of collective generality or individual autonomy that intellectuals ever actually enjoyed. Rather, they are rhetorical instruments that serve to beat down the private specificities and dependences of others while hiding those of the accuser. The university is only one in a long list of institutions in which it is continually being discovered, with unexhausted and apparently inexhaustible surprise, that intellectuals are grounded, by which they are limited or absorbed, on which they are dependent.

Obituaries for the intellectual, like Jacoby's, are so persistent a genre because intellectuals have never lived the gloriously independent life so often ascribed to them, and thus must always appear, when observed closely, to be on the point of losing it. According to Sartre's definition, "The intellectual is someone who concerns himself with what is none of his business" (12). This definition is self-contradictory. To *make* something your business, either in the sense of deriving a living from it (though "business" in the sense of "making a living" is not suggested by the French original) or simply by devoting a great deal of time and energy to it, is paradoxically to *disqualify* that activity as the basis of your identity as an intellectual. It must be, as it were, a hobby, carried on in leisure time, touched only lightly and glancingly in the course of a life centered elsewhere. Sartre's famous call for "engagement" is simply the other side of this coin. Sartre *has* to indulge in ardent, moralistic voluntarism in order to get intellectuals attached to the world again, for the simple reason that his own definition has assumed their initial detachment from it. Indeed, one might say that such definitions are floated only in order to run aground—that, switching examples and metaphors, Julien Benda's *La trahison des clercs* (1927)[12] names not a violation but the essence of intellectuality thus conceived. If to be an intellectual involves, in Francis Mulhern's paraphrase of Benda, "an unworldly rejection of all national particularism or social partisanship in the name of the disinterested service of humanity as a whole,"[13] then the "clerc" must *always* "betray" from the moment his (I will come shortly to the question of gender) thought assumes any social embodiment. It is at the moment of betrayal—the moment of "grounding"—that the subject comes into existence.

Book titles that link intellectuals to politics, the state, revolution, reform, modernization invariably fail in their attempt to achieve catchy incongruity. The wishful incongruity between intellectuals and politics dissolves into a historic intimacy. If you do a search in a respectable library, you will find that nearly *all* of the (many, many) titles concerning intellectuals also refer to politics, the state, institutions, revolution, and so forth. This is not hard to understand. The term came into usage, during the Dreyfus affair,

as a slogan that assumed both political and occupational situatedness. "By the time the word was coined," as Zygmunt Bauman
points out, "the descendants of *les philosophes* or *la république
des lettres* had already been divided into specialized enclaves with
their partial interests and localized concerns. The word was
hence a rallying call, sounded over the closely guarded frontiers
of professions and artistic *genres*: a call to resuscitate the tradition
(or materialize the collective memory) of 'men of knowledge' em-
bodying and practicing the unity of truth, moral values and aesthetic judgment."[14] "It was intended, so to speak, as an act of
propaganda" (23).

As a piece of political rhetoric rather than an ideal historical past
from which we have sadly fallen, the concept of the intellectual
has to be judged by rhetorical criteria. The rhetorical genre of arguments like Jacoby's is not strictly speaking the obituary but
rather the jeremiad, a denunciation of decline or demise that,
however, leaves open the possibility of moral resuscitation, and
indeed finds its justification in moral revivalism. The problem
with the jeremiad, discussed at length in Sacvan Bercovitch's
book on the subject, is its immodesty.[15] In berating the fallen, it
asserts a very high mission from which they have fallen and to
which they can and should still aspire, which is rightfully theirs.
In blaming intellectuals for something that may be entirely beyond their control—even Jacoby concedes, in a rare departure
from journalistic glibness, that "the demise of public intellectuals
reflects the recomposition of the public itself" (236)—it ascribes
to them marvellous if only latent causative powers. But do intellectuals deserve, as Andrew Ross asks in his essay, a preeminent
claim to "the mantle of resistance?" What is implicitly suggested
about those who are *not* burdened or favored with a mission? Although Jacoby refuses to discuss foreigners, what would he say,
for example, about what George Ross calls "the decline of the left
intellectual in modern France,"[16] where it is of course a socialist
rather than a republican government that has recently controlled
the "public sphere"? Can the jeremiad be dissociated from the arrogance of American (or French) exceptionalism?

Politically speaking, jeremiads in the name of the "autonomous" intellectual are asking for an impossible or sectarian pur-

ism. And jeremiads in the name of the "public" intellectual demand a centrality that can perhaps only be satisfied by forsaking the political left for the political center. Jacoby's list of heroes makes this tendency glaring. The so-called missing generation is largely composed of female, working-class, black, Hispanic, and other groups who simply *were not represented* in the white, male, largely upper-middle-class intelligentsia of the past. (The working-class background of many New York intellectuals should not be allowed to conceal this point.) Many of the figures Jacoby idealizes were *born* to the "public" stance he likewise idealizes. And as a result, many of those he approves as "public" are closer to the American mainstream—in a different vocabulary, organic to a more dominant class or bloc, or simply further to the right—than those he disapproves. But simply to scorn the latter error—the "public" as camouflage for rightist or mainstream politics—would be to fall into the former: a purist fastidiousness with regard to power. Surely it is better to examine with care the necessary ambiguities of such grounding, to specify the possibilities and the entanglements of exercised power—as Jonathan Arac does in the case of Macaulay—than to fall for either of the jeremiad's antithetical simplifications.

One of the foremost reasons to insist that grounding in the university is something other than the betrayal, compromise, or co-optation of the intellectuals is gender. The subject of intellectuals has been about as gender-neutral as pro football. *Men of Ideas*, the title of Lewis Coser's book on the subject (reissued in 1970),[17] is roughly representative of the past record, and among three recent anthologies, all published in 1987, Gagnon's includes one woman out of twelve contributors, the collection by Eyerman, Svensson, and Söderquist has one woman out of thirteen contributors, and Mohan's volume has no women at all.[18] (The present volume, insufficiently exceptional in this regard despite the contributions by Deirdre David, Gayatri Spivak, and Barbara Ehrenreich, demonstrates how far good intentions are from being enough.) If women have not been invited into the conversation about intellectuals, they have also had good cause to feel that the conversation had nothing to offer them. A discussion centered on the ideal of universality without ties, on intellectuals as

unattached and disembodied (Benda himself specified that the
mission of transcendence precluded marriage and family) could
easily appear to occupy a realm of male fantasy. To begin on the
other hand with the grounding of intellectuals, with a recognition
of ties, bodies, situations, is thus a necessary step toward the
demasculinizing of the discourse about intellectuals, the creation
of a conversation that women might have a motive for joining.

The same holds for the recognition that the ground won by intellectuals in the university since the 1960s, including and perhaps preeminently feminist intellectuals, must be seen as an
achievement. In the context of gender politics, it requires no paranoia to see attacks on the inadequate "publicness" of the contemporary academy from left and right as a covert means of undermining the specific (though still fragile) gains scored by
feminism there. Such attacks are understandable enough from the
right, but there is no excuse for anyone else. As if for women,
even getting out of the home and into the labor market (not to
speak of getting into the academy, where so much of the content
of socialization is determined) were not to take even the smallest
step in a "public" direction! Even in the worst instance, professionalization is always partly achievement from below as well as
co-optation from above. And if you devalue all political accom-
plishments (in the name of a purity that is strictly "academic"),
you end by being unable to strive for or even see them, whether
in the academy or out.

To accept that the university is itself a "ground" in both senses,
enabling as well as restricting the activity of intellectuals, is not
necessarily to jump from the "decline" narrative of the cultural
conservatives to the "rising" narrative of "New Class" theorists
like Daniel Bell, Alvin Gouldner, and Ivan Szelenyi.[19] Claiming
that "the University has inevitably begun to move to the center
of the social stage" (3) Bell clearly overstates the case. And he is
not alone. Taking the expansion and aggrandizement of universities as part of a larger shift in the location of power, other New
Class theorists flirt with the possibility that there has occurred or
will soon occur a "rise of intellectuals to a position of dominance
in modern society." "The great expansion of the state and 'public
sector' in Western societies and the stabilization of state socialist

regimes in the East have underpinned new attempts to conceptualize the relationship between intellectuals and political power. The 'sluices' of the state may have opened wide enough and become extensive enough to provide the basis for a new type of ruling class in Eastern socialist and Western capitalist societies" (Eyerman et al., 5).

Barbara and John Ehrenreich's path-breaking essay, "The Professional-Managerial Class,"[20] should, I think, be distinguished both from the "end-of-ideology" complacencies of the right and the self-aggrandizing and naively optimistic varieties on the left. The effort that inspired it, and that has continued through the many discussions it has provoked, was to theorize a resistance that already existed: the student revolts of the 1960s. The issue was not so much how to fit intellectuals into Marx's class analysis, still less whether or not they could be considered a revolutionary substitute for the working class, but rather how to understand the sorts (and limits) of professional oppositionality that followed as students and dissident ideas moved (not without considerable trouble) into positions of social authority. Thus it seems best to interpret the word "class" broadly, as a reminder that no portrait of intellectuals alone, flattering or unflattering, can usefully speak to this issue; what counts are relationships with other social actors and forces. Although the new set of social circumstances and institutions goes by too many totalizing, conflicting, or unconvincing names—"the postindustrial state," "technocracy," "mediocracy," "consumerism," "the service economy," and "the information society," to list a few—even the ideological abuse of such terms should not stop us from asking, with an eye both to political traps and to political openings, what social changes may have occurred *around* intellectuals so as to shift their value, function, and potential for resistance. The essay by Stanley Aronowitz and the interview with Barbara Ehrenreich in this volume both further this project.

The trap to avoid here is to acknowledge such groundings only at the cost of falling back into another narrative of decline. The most brilliant recent instance is Regis Debray's *Le pouvoir intellectuel en France*.[21] In the United States, an important example is Richard Wightman Fox and T. J. Jackson Lears's reading of the "rise" of the professional-managerial class or stratum in terms of "consumerism"—that is, as true democracy's decline and fall.[22] According to Fox and Lears, toward the end of the nineteenth century intellectuals began to produce "professional advice, marketing strategies, government programs, electoral choices, and advertisers' images of happiness" (xii). In selling their own creativity and expertise, however, they were selling goods and services for others, smoothing over capitalism's inner contradictions by way of "reform," and, most important, seeking "to generate needs that only they could fulfill" (xiv). Their services undermined the autonomy of the recipients of those services. Specifically, "they preached a new morality that subordinated the old goal of transcendence to new ideals of self-fulfillment and immediate gratification," both packaged as "liberation" within a "therapeutic worldview." "Leadership by experts and pervasive self-absorption have developed symbiotically in American consumer culture" (xii). The result has been "the decline of autonomous selfhood" and a "sense of unreality" (9).

It would be a pity if this were taken to represent leftist common sense. The narrative by which professionally produced symbols and images replace "reality" and one's own "experience" is exchanged (at a loss) for the "expertise" of others falsely assumes a prior reality that has no need of symbols and images, a prior (self-reliant) selfhood fully in possession of its experience. In so doing, it condemns all intellectual (and artistic) activity to the status of more or less redundant, reprehensible, "undemocratic" imposition upon an otherwise "autonomous" public that needs no advice, no images, no art—that *has* no needs it cannot fulfill itself. Yet the relations between intellectuals and the public are more subtle and diverse than this crude opposition suggests. Surely one can dissent from the "therapeutic worldview" without sinking into a zero-sum game where intellectuals can win their relative autonomy only by stealing away that of the democratic citizenry. The self-interest that of course motivated intellectuals—theorists, reformers, therapists, advertisers, muck-rakers, and so on—need not be identical with, but it also need not be opposed to, the self-interests of the recipients of their images and advice. What is happening is less Manichaean: for better and for worse, social customs that had been considered "nature" or "second nature" are opening up to new consciousness, new alternatives, new choices. The intellectuals who make such matters their business thus acquire new significance and new authority. But no leftist, however skeptical of that authority, can afford to wish us back to a world where intellectuals would be unnecessary.

Plato's banishing of the poets from his ideal republic is more than a parallel here. As protest against the production of symbols and images by the professional-managerial class suggests, another phrase, like "the therapeutic worldview" or "consumerism," for those developments that have made intellectuals more prominent is the aestheticization of society. New Class theory distinguishes between the realm of the practical (where older powers hold sway) and the realm of the symbolic (where the intellectuals exert a new power). The opposition is a weak one—is there ever practice *without* symbolism?—but it does underline the linkage between the increasing prominence of intellectuals and what Stuart Hall calls "the penetration of aesthetics into everyday life."[23] "Culture has ceased to be, if it ever was, a decorative addendum to the 'hard world' of production and things, the icing on the cake of the material world. The word is now as 'material' as the world. Through design, technology, and styling, 'aesthetics' has already penetrated the world of modern production. Through marketing, layout, and style, the 'image' provides the mode of representation of the body on which so much of modern consumption depends" (25). This "deeply *cultural* character of the revolution of our times" is one reason for the existence of a journal called *Social Text*, one reason why the self-definition of the New York intellectuals should have been so bound up with literary and artistic modernism, and one reason, finally, why the present volume should have so high a proportion of contributors (all but three) who are (among other things) literary critics. On the other hand, that criticism feels obliged to make this call is of course no reason for granting its opinion any special authority. Confusion lingers between "literariness" and the intellectual's traditional "autonomy," both of them models of marginality asked to assert an ideal unity against actual fragmentation. It is no accident that Mannheim developed his notion of the free-floating intellectual in the

same Budapest conversations in which Lukács was sorely tempted by the reigning aestheticism. But while this confusion helps explain the fascination of the critics, it also leaves a great deal to be
said about intellectuals by others.

One view of the intellectual that might seem "overliterary" to
some is the poststructuralist-style death announcement of Jean-
François Lyotard's *Tombeau de l'intellectuel*.[24] Dead upon arrival
in a postmodern age that no longer tolerates pretensions to
universality, the intellectual and his oppositional function are
replaced, for Lyotard, by art and the artist, which remain resolutely local in their contestatory ambitions. It is sometimes hard to
take this modesty at face value. The Foucault who offers Bentham's Panopticon as a symbol of the totally administered society
and of the unjustly privileged, oppressive vision of the "universal
intellectual" within it is also the Foucault who famously wishes
to be left "faceless"—a condition that can be realized, in the society he imagines, only by the unseen watcher in the panoptical
tower. Perhaps the success of Foucault's rhetorical ploy can be at-
tributed as much to the continuing imaginative appeal of that
position—the position of the traditional intellectual—as to our
fear of intrusive surveillance.

Poststructuralist suspicions of the intellectual's representativeness, which belong to the general crisis of literary and political
"representation" in recent thought, have the definite advantage
of inhibiting the wild self-assertions that are sometimes concealed
in the rhetoric of "responsibility," of which the jeremiad is one
instance already mentioned. In *The Political Responsibility of the
Critic*, Jim Merod writes: "More than anything else, the other-
worldliness of the classroom obscures, if it does not deny altogether, the possibility that critical activity is (or might be) the
one human force most committed to clarifying the world's structure in order to change it."[25] This is either tautology or megaloma-
nia. We would all like to feel that what we do is important, and
if necessary many of us are prepared to change what we do in order to make it more important. But when strangely exclusive
claims to *lead* the changing of the world insinuate themselves into
calls for the intellectual's "responsibility," a humble, ascetically

antirepresentational localism of the sort Paul Bové champions in *Intellectuals in Power* acquires hidden virtues. Better honest self-interest than hypocritical abuse of a distant or hypothetical constituency.

This is not to say, on the other hand, that all efforts at legitimation on the part of intellectuals can or should be rejected as hypocrisy and self-aggrandizement. Paul Piccone, like Lyotard, argues that in the postmodern age, intellectuals no longer *require* legitimation . "[The 'public'] intellectual gives way, with the collapse of the New Deal-Great Society model, to the professional whose social foundation becomes so stable that it no longer requires any 'public' exposure or even any justification of its broader social role outside bureaucratic-academic enclaves."[26] For Jim Merod, on the contrary, "The one thing that most defines the humanities today is intense competition for critical authority and intellectual legitimacy" (198). After the onslaughts of Bloom, Bennett, and company, Merod seems closer to the truth, both inside the humanities and in their (internalized) dialogue with the public outside. And this is a competition whose loss can have real consequences. Jürgen Habermas, who has done much to sustain and elaborate the language of legitimacy and is also a great living example of an incontrovertibly "public" intellectual, has taken an admirable public role in the German *Historikerstreit* over revisionist readings of Nazism. In that debate, the academic historians who were in effect apologizing for the Nazis could insist that, as a mere philosopher, Habermas lacked appropriate expertise. Their stronger and stranger argument, however, has been a version of the poststructuralist one: suspicion of all claims to legitimacy before a nonacademic public. As John Torpey writes, the German neoconservatives argue that "a 'New Class' of intellectuals wield their 'power of the spoken and written word' (Schumpeter) to obtain greater social rewards and prestige for themselves. This self-aggrandizing 'New Class' allegedly offers lofty, universalistic justifications for social welfare programs that are only covers for their own interest in an expanded state sector. The intelligentsia thus puts its greater capacity for interpretation in the service of its own political and economic ends."[27] At least

for those who take Habermas's side against the revisionist historians, this would seem an argument for intellectuals *not* to forsake
all efforts at legitimation. It is too easy for the right to claim
legitimacy for itself, discrediting its opponents as an elite of
"specific," self-interested outsiders. Again, the current activities
of the American right bear the decisive lesson.

Conor Cruise O'Brien, whose misguided foray into South African politics is discussed here by John Higgins, recently wrote:
"One of the great advantages of this country is that most intellectuals I've met feel they can live quite contented lives without being involved in the political process." If this statement seems as
instantaneously and undoubtedly wrong to the reader as it does
to me, then it supplies additional evidence that the hunger for
legitimation has not yet expired, as well as a personal note on
which to conclude this introduction. By all acocunts, transmission of the cultural heritage—the most powerful conservative
definition of the intellectual's proper activity—is currently inadequate to produce "contented lives" among American intellectuals. That may be because many more of us, reversing Weber, now
live *off* as well as *for* ideas, or because (by the same token) "alienation," which once defined the oppositional intellectual, is now so
general a condition. (This generalizing of perceived marginality,
taking away the intellectual's former badge of honor, would perhaps also explain why intellectuals today can begin to admit their
"grounding.") In any event, on one level the conceptual reloca-
tion of intellectuals *within* rather than outside occupations,
which is an essential step in their grounding, is also an ethical demand to achieve vocationally "contented lives" without sacrific-
ing political consistency. To some this demand may well appear
absurd, even spoiled. But the term "intellectual" began, in Zygmunt Bauman's words, not as a description of an existent category but as "a widely opened invitation."[28] If there exists no single
category today that unites our diverse occupations in a common
oppositionality, the topic is still worth discussing because the invitation is still, in some new wording, worth extending. If the intellectual is a figure of the political imagination, a character who
cannot be separated from the various political narratives in which
he or she appears, grounded in the emergences and declines of

successive oppositional forces and institutions, then we must not call for a return of intellectuals to an illusory state of prior autonomy, but must reconsider the political narratives whose peripeteias and denouements have left the intellectual hanging or unraveling. That is, we must consider the intellectual as a character in search of a narrative.

Addressing themselves to the possibility of a new, perhaps already incipient, politics of intellectuals, the essays that follow set themselves three tasks: first, to reevaulate, in the light of the present conjuncture, the heritage of thinking about intellectuals and politics (for example, the fate of the *Partisan Review*) and those theoretical controversies (for example, between Gramsci's organic-traditional opposition and Foucault's universal specific opposition) that seem most pertinent; second, to explore case studies of particular intellectuals who have been involuntarily embroiled or deliberately engaged in politics under especially revealing circumstances (Edward Said, those members of the Frankfurt School who worked for the Office of Strategic Services during World War II); and third, to investigate emergent institutions like the media, the university, and the "new social movements" that, in transforming the political landscape, have also transformed the nature and political potential of intellectuals. As Andrew Ross and Dana Polan show with regard to the media, and as is manifest in the volume's attention to the new "publicity" of "cases" and "affairs" like those of David Abraham, Colin MacCabe, Paul de Man, and Heidegger, coming to terms with this transformed political landscape and its transformation of "publicness" is indispensable to the effort to reconceptualize political resistance at the end of the twentieth century.

NOTES

1. E. D. Hirsch, Jr., *Cultural Literacy* (Boston: Houghton Mifflin, 1987), and Allan Bloom, *The Closing of the American Mind* (New York: Simon & Schuster, 1987).

2. Karl Mannheim, *Ideology and Utopia*, trans. Louis Wirth and Edward Shils (New York: Harcourt Brace Jovanovich, 1936).

3. Norman Podhoretz, *Breaking Rank: A Political Memoir* (New York: Harper & Row, 1979), p. 362.

4. Alan Wald, *The New York Intellectuals: The Rise and Decline of the Anti-*

Stalinist Left from the 1930s to the 1980s (Chapel Hill: University of North Carolina Press, 1987), 369.

5. Jean-Paul Sartre, *Plaidoyer pour l'intellectuel* (Paris: Gallimard, 1972); Antonio Gramsci, *Selections from the Prison Notebooks*, ed. and trans. Quintin Hoare and Geoffrey Nowell Smith (New York: International Publishers, 1971).

6. Michel Foucault, *Language, Counter-Memory, Practice*, ed. Donald F. Bouchard (Ithaca, N.Y.: Cornell University Press, 1977).

7. Paul A. Bové, *Intellectuals in Power: A Genealogy of Critical Humanism* (New York: Columbia University Press, 1986).

8. Edward Said, *The World, the Text, and the Critic* (Cambridge, Mass.: Harvard University Press, 1983).

9. New York: Basic Books, 1987.

10. Lynn Garafola, Review of *The Last Intellectuals, New Left Review*, 169 (May-June 1988), 126.

11. Mary Gluck, *Georg Lukács and His Generation, 1900–1918* (Cambridge: Cambridge University Press, 1985), 82.

12. Julien Benda, *The Treason of the Intellectuals*, trans. Richard Aldington (New York: Norton, 1969).

13. See Regis Debray, *Teachers, Writers, Celebrities: The Intellectuals of Modern France*, intro. Francis Mulhern; trans. David Macey (London: Verso, 1881), viii.

14. Zygmunt Bauman, *Legislators and Interpreters: On Modernity, Post-Modernity, and Intellectuals* (Cambridge: Polity Press, 1987), 1.

15. Sacvan Bercovitch, *The American Jeremiad* (Madison: University of Wisconsin Press, 1978).

16. George Ross in Alain G. Gagnon (ed.), *Intellectuals in Liberal Democracies: Political Influence and Social Involvement* (New York: Praeger, 1987).

17. Lewis A. Coser, *Men of Ideas: A Sociologist's View* (New York: Free Press, 1970).

18. Gagnon (ed.), *Intellectuals in Liberal Democracies*; Ron Eyerman, Lennart G. Svensson, and Thomas Soderquist (eds.), *Intellectuals, Universities, and the State in Western Modern Societies* (Berkeley: University of California Press, 1987); Raj P. Mohan (ed.), *The Mythmakers: Intellectuals and the Intelligentsia in Perspective*, Contributions in Sociology, vol. 63 (New York: Greenwood, 1987).

19. Daniel Bell, "The Intellectual and the University—An Address" (New York: City College Papers no. 4, 1966); Alvin Gouldner, *The Future of Intellectuals and the Rise of the New Class* (New York: Continuum, 1979); George Konrad and Ivan Szelenyi, *The Intellectuals on the Road to Class Power*, trans. Andrew Arato and Richard E. Allen (New York: Harcourt Brace Jovanovich, 1979).

20. See Ehrenreich and Ehrenreich, in Pat Walker (ed.), *Beyond Labour and Capital* (Montreal: Black Rose Press, 1979).

21. See note 12.

22. Richard Wightman Fox and T. J. Jackson Lears (eds.), *The Culture of Consumption: Critical Essays in American History, 1880–1980* (New York: Pantheon, 1983).

23. Stuart Hall, "Brave New World," *Marxism Today*, October 1988.

24. Paris: Galilée, 1984.

25. Jim Merod, *The Political Responsibility of the Critic* (Ithaca, N.Y.: Cornell University Press, 1987), 1.

26. Paul Piccone, Roundtable in *Telos*, 71 (Spring 1987), 8.

27. John Torpey, "Introduction: Habermas and the Historians," *New German Critique*, 44 (Spring-Summer 1988), special issue on the *Historikerstreit*, 19.

28. Bauman, *Legislators and Intepreters*, 2.

PART I
THEORY

On Intellectuals
Stanley Aronowitz

Since the 1970s a new debate has emerged concerning the social and political significance of intellectuals. For the most part, the discussion has centered on questions raised at various times since the turn of the twentieth century by neo-Marxist theory concerning the emergence of intellectuals as historical agents in both "advanced" and developing societies.[1] The occasion for renewed interest is undoubtedly the palpable refusal and/or inability of the working classes in advanced capitalist countries to engage in revolutionary activity. In the perspective of the last twenty years since the 1968 general strike in France and the Italian "Hot Autumn" of 1969, it has become increasingly evident that, given the restructuring of world capitalism of the 1970s and 1980s (a response, in part, to the wave of militancy that marked the 1960s as well as the emergence of Japan as a major world economic power rivaling both the United States and the combined force of Western Europe), the industrial proletariat has not been merely integrated into the new austerity regime brought about by capital migration and recession; it has been defeated, decomposed, and recomposed. Trade union power on the shop floor has declined corresponding to the weakness of organized labor's social weight. In the most industrially developed countries—notably the United States, the United Kingdom, and Germany—deindustrialization and recession have forced socialist, labor, and democratic parties to seek a decisive shift in their social base, a strategy that has produced tension between the traditional labor

3

and the new middle-class constituencies.[2] It is a story not merely of reduced numbers of union members in basic production industries but of a significant shift in the relationship between the union and nonunion sectors, within a single industry and for the economy as a whole. The internationalization of capital means, among other things, that the regime of capitalist regulation within which union labor occupied a relatively privileged space in comparison to nonunion labor has broken down. On the one hand, especially in the United States and the United Kingdom, capital flight has resulted in massive plant shutdowns and decimated many small and medium-sized cities and towns; on the other hand, free-market ideology has generated deregulation, a measure that has led to the increased concentration of ownership and a renewed employer offensive against wages and working conditions. And, especially in the United States (where state controls over firms were never secure), transnational corporations are virtually free to shift capital resources at will.

Although none of the major capitalist powers matches the United States in the degree to which industrial relations are now driven by the nonunion sectors, with the exception of the Federal Republic of Germany and Sweden, versions of this pattern have afflicted the labor movements of all countries. Socialist electoral victories in Southern Europe, the growing strength of the Socialist Democratic Party in Germany, and the partial comeback of the Democratic Party in the last years of the Reagan administration have not substantially reversed this trend except, perhaps in Canada, where the labor movement has actually grown and, national defeats notwithstanding, the New Democrats have gained strength at the provincial level. On the contrary: the Socialist victory in the May 1988 French presidential elections is not attributable to a leftward movement of the electorate; it was the Socialists who moved to the center, becoming an imprecise analogue to the American Democrats who, since the 1980 Reagan victory, have steadily retreated from their New Deal heritage. On the whole, left political formations have felt obliged to seek new constituencies or else risk permanent minority status. Only in some Northern European countries, especially Germany, has this departure led to a leftward move, chiefly because of the emergence of the Green Party as a viable electoral force.

Thus, the context for the revival of interest in the economic and political positions of intellectuals is rooted, in part, in the apparently definitive passing of the era of proletarian ascendancy, even in its relatively staid social democratic variety. More profoundly, we may no longer speak of the present epoch in terms of "late" capitalism, for the optimism that attended this amendment can no longer be comfortably sustained at a time when state socialism scrambles toward "market" economy and other features of echt modernity that often resemble key elements of capitalist democracies. While world capitalism continues to wallow in one of the longer global economic crises of its 400-year history, it has never been ideologically more powerful; or, to put it more precisely, its key tenets—market, entrepreneurship, private ownership and control of the means of production, and possessive individualism, which is no longer merely an Anglo-American belief—have gripped significant portions of the masses in the East as well as the West. The emergence of these ideas conjoins with the increasingly powerful argument that freedom presupposes a relatively free market, especially for consumer goods.

Some of these conditions were already perceived in the late 1960s and early 1970s when a considerable fraction of the New Left, inspired by the Cuban and Vietnamese revolutions and independence movements, especially in Angola and Mozambique, theorized the Third World as the new collective proletariat and they key site of revolutionary upsurge. However, by the middle of the decade, events in Cambodia, the death of Mao (who may be considered a central architect of this new doctrine) and the violent reversals of economic and political direction by his successors, as well as the progressive accommodation of the Third World to the realities of economic crisis, led to a series of retreats by the new revolutionary regimes. These have evolved into various types of authoritarian power and have subsequently given rise to a new democratic movement in Eastern Europe as well as China, Korea, and Brazil, and more recently in Vietnam, to mention only the most visible. With these changes, we have seen a loss of innocence among their Western supporters. Not even the events in Central America beginning with the Nicaraguan revolution in 1979, the civil wars in El Salvador and Guatemala, and the democratic mass workers movement in Brazil were able to sustain Third World political radicalism in the West. Nor did the strikes in Poland and South Africa of the early 1980s, which were acts by massive legions of workers, save proletarian internationalism. The Solidarity movement is plainly the most important popular challenge to the characteristically authoritarian mode of Eastern European political and economic rule. Its originality consists in the fact that it is a union of a new type, a political party as well as a trade union, a national and international moral agent as well as an agent of economic reform. Further, Solidarity has made an explicit alliance with a considerable fraction of intellectuals. Although supported by many democrats, it suffered until the advent of Gorbachev from the ambivalence of a U.S. far left that has grown to abhor anticommunism for reasons having to do with the cold war environment of the 1950s and 1980s, as well as the widespread belief in these circles that, other problems notwithstanding, the Soviet Union remained a firm ally of independence movements. There is no such ambivalence with respect to the struggle against apartheid in South Africa or for Palestinian rights, especially after the popular uprising that began in December 1987. It must be said, however, that these struggles have failed to inspire new theory or to revive the old one that held the Third World as the most significant of the new social agents.

The debate about intellectuals cannot be separated from these contexts. Its contemporary history emerges from the void left by a working class whose conditions of political strength have largely been surpassed, except in countries of the semiperiphery where working-class struggles in a new form appear as democratic as well as class movements. The compromises by Third World revolutions with capitalist economic hegemonies have not only produced second thoughts among Marxists and other socialists but have also spawned a certain anti-Third Worldism that is, on one hand, a healthy counterpoint to the almost slavish subordination of one part of the left to this doctrine and the movements it "represents"[3] and, on the other, a symptom of the conservative revival in our midst.

The central terms of the new debate are those of agency. To be more specific, most writing about intellectuals addresses questions of a conventional Marxist type: Are intellectuals under capitalism becoming a new class? Or, as Konrad and Szelenyi argue, is this class emergence confined to state socialist societies in which the private ownership of the decisive means of production has been abolished?[4] Second, what are the elements of class formation under transformed conditions, specifically, the emergence of knowledge as the crucial productive force in nearly all societies? The core question is whether the (undeveloped) Marxist theory of class, in which questions of ownership and control define classes, continues to hold, or whether, owing to the new conditions of production and reproduction, new categories of relations now constitute the basis of class formation. In this essay, I want first to sketch the assumptions of class in Marxist theory and review the state of the theory of intellectuals prior to the publication of what has become the seminal work of the new debate, Alvin Gouldner's *Future of Intellectuals and the Rise of the New Class*. Then I will summarize and critique Gouldner's approach and take up some recent developments in the Soviet Union, Western and Southern Europe, and the United States that bear on the question.

I

Needless to say, the burning question of class theory since Marx is not, as is often assumed, the spatial relation of social categories to the mode of production of material existence. The economic identification of social classes—whether they own, control, or are the objects of the production and reproduction of material existence, whether they occupy an intermediate position between the owners and the propertyless—is an interesting sociological question but hardly addresses the politico-historical dimension of class issues. While the elegant simplicity of *The Communist Manifesto* implies historical agency from such structural considerations, Marx and Engels are equally clear that actual historical situations warrant no direct relation between structure and agency. Indeed, as Marx's pamphlet *The 18th Brumaire* argues with respect to the question of whether French peasants form a class, their common relation to the means of production is necessary but not sufficient for class formation. Marx argues that their dispersal into small holdings militates against community, a common culture, and therefore self-representation at the political level. "They must be represented by others,"[5] says Marx. In these passages two further qualifications beyond economic identification emerge: what we might call a discursive community and political-self organization are necessary elements of class formation. In this mode, classes are the outcome of a social process whose result remains indeterminate from the structural perspective. In the same pamphlet Marx argues that historical context is the boundary condition of agency: "Men make their own history but not as they please." They are constrained by circumstances, which, having been produced by the interaction of prior structures and agents, present themselves in a naturalized form to actors and appear to resist change. We might add that, at any moment, the outcome of acts, speech or otherwise, is underdetermined, from the perspective of either structure of agency, by the specificities of the interaction between them.

Note here that by slightly altering the language of this famous passage of Marx's we also alter the significance of his formulations concerning class. Classes come into being under conditions of (1) the occupation of a common structural space; (2) a common discursive (cultural) position that, however, is not presupposed by structural unity; and (3) political organization exemplified by political parties and national trade unions that also function discursively. This last condition need not imply a correspondence between the representatives and constituents on every point, but it does imply a democratic model of participation, that is, that the party be *of* as well as *for* the agents. Since the turn of the century, there has been a developing problem of divergence, especially between the party leadership and the working class. Since Robert Michels made us aware that socialist bureaus, by controlling the apparatus of social action (especially communications), may evolve into elites in a conventional way, political studies of socialist and workers' parties have identified a plurality of organizational models.[6] These studies have correctly thrown into question the theory of representation according to which socialist parties reflect, in broad outlines, working-class interests and elections provide the corrective to the entrenchment of an unresponsive elite. One counterfactual example is the British Labour Party, within which the trades unions have enjoyed since its founding a dominant position, especially at the discursive level. Such dominance notwithstanding, the party is actually a coalition of different social categories with intellectuals and professionals playing important and sometimes divergent roles both in the apparatus and, historically at least, in the constituencies both of the unions and each other. The French Socialists did not enjoy substantial support among union members until the late 1970s, when the communist ideological and political hegemony rapidly began to erode. Working-class votes then went socialist without an appreciable growth of working-class influence over party policy. This pattern of a socialist party that is chiefly a national rather than a class party holds for all Southern European countries. In the north, especially Sweden and Germany, the relation of party to the working masses remains close and has been only partially loosened in the 1980s. I invoke these differences in the composition and orientation of social democratic parties to illustrate heterogeneity in the configuration of representation as well as the relative autonomy of politics from its structural determinants. I want to argue that each level of articulation is underdetermined by the others, at least in advance. This poses the problem of adopting a general rule with a wide application. Although theory must articulate the categories of analysis prior to a concrete, historically specific investigation, the relations among these categories are not a priori determined. In this discussion of intellectuals we are obliged to observe the same rule: whether intellectuals form a class or a social category is always an empirical question once the elements of class formation are stated. As we review the more influential works on intellectuals in the neo-Marxist literature, we will discover changing emphases in different historical periods. We shall try to account for these changes as well as describe them.

II

In 1968, students and other intellectuals presented themselves as new agents not only in Paris, Berlin, and other Western capitals but also in Mexico City, Buenos Aires, and Prague. In the struggle to comprehend the nature of their emergence, Antonio Gramsci, until the 1960s a shadowy figure outside his native Italy, quickly surfaced as a crucial guide. His *Selections from the Prison Notebooks*, published in English in 1971, provided an argument, if not an elaborated theory, that placed intellectuals on the cusp of social transformation in societies where rule by consent replaces rule by force as the primary mode. By the late twentieth century, this describes almost all countries, even those burdened by military and other types of authoritarian and totalitarian rule.[7] For in a historical epoch when democratic ideology, at least as negative freedom (defined here as the absence of constraints on speech, assembly by individuals and groups, and so on), is crucially linked to what used to be called rising economic expectations by the widest strata of all societies, coercion alone can be expected to ensure social order for a brief period, after which democratic awakening appears virtually assured. This formula is based not on an abstract conception of modernity but on the palpable internationalization of culture since the end of the war. The export of Western culture to formerly inchoate areas is linked with market expansion beyond the usual colonial search for raw materials and strategic bases. Now the "Third World" has become a consumer market in proportion to the extent to which its role as a provider of oil, metals, and food is supplemented by industrial production, itself the outcome of international competition and working-class strength in the developed countries.

Under these conditions, discourses capable of legitimating the prevailing order are absolutely necessary for its preservation. Consequently, argues Gramsci, classes wishing to overturn the dominant form of rule are obliged to contend for "intellectual and moral leadership" of society, to wage a war of "position" long before a "war of maneuver" or insurrection can be successfully staged. This struggle for ideological hegemony entails, among other things, imposing a new common sense to replace the prevailing one. In effect, intellectuals acting in behalf of a new rising class become, in Gramsci's argument, a central object as well as a subject of political discourse. Among the tools of displacement in advanced industrial societies, none stands higher than the use of the categories of ideology critique and the identification of a new common sense with science. Science is a term we affix to ideology that wishes to become hegemonic; in turn, "ideology" is the name given to the discourse of the (putative) vanquished. My reading, freely borrowed from Louis Althusser's Gramscian ruminations,[8] emphasizes the intimate link of knowledge and power. It suggests a political theory of intellectuals by showing that science, far from its claim to social neutrality, or in a more political mode, to becoming a technology of freedom, becomes a master discourse and confers legitimate power on its agents and others who subscribe to science as the embodiment of what we mean by truth. Further, in these societies in which the scientific worldview is the measure of all knowledge claims, it becomes the new common sense. In democratic countries hegemonic ideas do not thereby ban others; those ideas that cannot pass muster as scientific are merely consigned to the margins of public discussion. They may be valued in other terms (say, as poetry, myth, or opinion), but they are not taken seriously as knowledge that contributes to the collective goal of progress or to state policy. Therefore, it is virtually incumbent upon the intellectuals who have identified themselves either with the prevailing power or with its opposition to declare ideas scientific and to condemn others as ideology.

In Gramsci's own conception there is no question of intellectuals becoming themselves historical agents; their social weight consists in their ability to link themselves with "real" agents, namely classes, which for Gramsci and all Marxists are the only forces capable of making history. This is precisely the contention I want to explore in what follows. There are two questions here: Can intellectuals as a social category act on their own? That is, do they constitute distinct discursive communities that generate unique subject positions? Not so much by virtue of their critical mass or their growing significance to the prevailing social order (these points are fairly well established by now); in terms of "class" formation, the issue is whether they can represent themselves politically in a manner similar to the great social classes of the bourgeois epoch. Or, are they merely destined to affiliate with classes arising from new production relations already in existence, in which case their role is, as Gramsci specified, to articulate the worldviews of hegemonic or counterhegemonic classes? This formulation brackets the issue of intellectuals as a "class" for reasons that will become evident later in this essay.[9]

The second question concerns the precise circumstances under which intellectuals perform specifically political functions. For however important their work is for various state institutions prior to the modern epoch, intellectuals begin to occupy a unique political position when the question of the "masses" enters political discourse. On the whole, the masses appear in the context of the bourgeois revolutions as a necessary but not central participant and are first articulated in the form of the "social question" at the moment they acquire their own voice, whose first expression coincides with the proclamation of universal rights by their new patrons, the bourgeoisie.

Peter Weiss's dramatic reconstruction of the crowd in the French Revolution may be understood in paradigmatically Gramscian terms. Here is Jean-Paul Marat, the voice of the voiceless, whose declamations are absolutely crucial for the realization of the rights for the poor since the various parties of the bourgeoisie have long since reneged on their promises. *Marat/Sade* raises the question of power between the organic intellectual and the underclasses. Who dominates whom? Marat takes the role of both sadist and masochist in relation to the crowd, which can insert itself into history only through the instrumentality of his voice. He resists their entreaties even as he dominates the space of the organic intellectual. After all, he is a bourgeois man; that is, he could have enjoyed a private life separate from the streets, or at least he craves such a life, a longing that is displaced as illness. De Sade, on the other hand, is the intellectual representing not a political class but desire that languishes on the margins, whose locale is an insane asylum, the menagerie of those imprisoned in the extralinguistic. Desire cannot be reduced to rational discourse—rationality understood as the old common sense. It may be argued that de Sade is the real subversive because he opts out of the official power game and stands opposed to it. He is dangerous to the moral order since he claims only negative freedom, that is, freedom to be left alone. That the state cannot grant this for de Sade declaims against the moral authority of the state to regulate private behavior. In fact, de Sade exposes the cynicism of the liberal state, which professes to defend liberty but recoils from its exercise when the substance slips beyond the bounds of acceptable discourse.

De Sade may be taken as an "antihegemonic" intellectual rather than a counterhegemonic force; his intervention calls into question the power of public authorities in the private sphere, especially the state's power to regulate desire. His transgression consists in suggesting an alternative moral order in which freedom is defined as much by the unfettered exercise of desire as by political rights. Thus, he goes beyond the conventional limits of democratic practices by insisting on the absolute separation of public from private or, to be more adventurous, on pushing the bourgeois idea of freedom to excess. By stretching the limits of individual rights within the revolution, de Sade emerges, albeit ambiguously, as a self-representing voice; the intellectual in this instance is attached to a new kind of universality, the possibility of healing the split between mind and body that the political revolution leaves in place. In Weiss's reprise we may thus infer two contrasting theories of intellectuals: first, as the voice of contending class antagonists, the social category that, however indispensable to the class struggle in the epoch of rule by consent, cannot act for itself in history even as it increasingly occupies the corridors of power as its essential precondition; and second, as the social category that, as the possessor of cultural capital, moves toward self-representation and becomes a contending social force on the basis of knowledge, which in our times is taken as truth. Truth requires no referent outside itself. Unlike politics, whose legitimacy derives from external authority, knowledge is legitimated by its own procedures, even as science claims its referent is really the external world. Intellectuals may retain their role as representatives of others but discover their own power insofar as they conclude their knowledge need no longer be subordinate to economic production or to the prevailing forms of political rule, since relations of dependency in which knowledge was sub-sumed under capital and the state are slowly being reversed.

Beyond the functional elements of knowledge is its critical dimension. Alvin Gouldner's claim for the social power of intellectuals rests on the category of the "culture of critical discourse" (CCD), uniquely situated among knowledge producers and transmitters.[10] The characteristic reflexiveness of critical discourse makes it self-referential; its authority cannot be derived from external sources because their discourse cannot be reduced to functional space. I will now explore CCD as a sufficient explanation for the emergence of intellectuals as a "class." Building on Gouldner, I will argue that Gramsci's understanding of the centrality of intellectuals for the constitution of social relations is incomplete in at least two respects: it does not comprehend the possibility that, under specific historical conditions, intellectuals themselves become political actors, since, despite Gramsci's powerful innovations, economic relations are still accorded primacy. Economic relations in Marxist theory are conceived in the first place as production relations. Consequently, ideas, no matter how significant for reproducing social power, are subordinate, even if now in the strict sense derivative of class relations. Gramsci's thesis of the importance of ideological hegemony (as contrasted to coercion) for reproducing social relations does not mean that he is prepared to go the final mile, that is, to comprehend discursive knowledge as fully constitutive of social structure and therefore of social power. Nor are the purveyors of ideas, in this theory of hegemony, independent agents. Gramsci speaks almost exclusively of the so-called traditional intellectuals, a category historically linked to prevailing power or its opposition. These are literary, philosophical, and scientific intellectuals, including those who study theology, upon which the bourgeois state relied in its struggle against the remnants of feudal social and political power. Gramsci's conception does not include the wider category of technical intellectuals-managers, practical scientists, and technologists directly linked to production and state policy formation.

III

Gouldner's claim for the autonomy of intellectuals is, at the same time, a description of their historicity. Only at a certain stage in capitalism's development, the mid-nineteenth century, does intellectual (as opposed to practical) knowledge become a productive force. It takes another century for intellectual labor to displace manual labor as the primary condition for the reproduction of capital.[11] Since the 1950s, manual labor is displaced not only relatively but absolutely from the labor process. This displacement is not attributable to the internationalization of production but to intensification owing to the application of scientifically based technologies to the labor process. Technological change, which in recent economic theory acts as a spur to economic growth, has not functioned in the 1980s according to this prediction. Technological applications have outstripped real growth in part because the content of these applications is qualitatively different from earlier technologies. The difference between mechanical and electronic technologies has to do with the immense labor-saving features of artificial intelligence, particularly its capacity for memory and self-regulation within specified limits.

In consequence of the centrality of knowledge for social reproduction as well, that is, for both coercive and state activities that serve to obtain consent, only recently have intellectuals begun to assess their own subordination in capitalist and state socialist societies. In some cases, they conclude that their position is untenable. The new rationality of intellectuals entails the demand at least for power sharing, if not for the displacing of the prevailing power group. Of course this question is posed most forcefully in countries where industrial development takes place under state direction, whether nominally socialist or not. This is especially the case in the era when scientific and technologist innovations define the pace and direction of economic growth, the configuration of social policy, and, more broadly, the character of cultural life. Given the rapidity of deindustrialization in some of the more advanced capitalist societies, the question is *when* intellectuals will emerge as new power centers, and whether they will be contending against or in concert with a restructured capitalist class for political hegemony, not *whether* this will occur.

In the past, this question has been posed as the problem of "technocracy"—the conception according to which engineers in the widest meaning of the term constitute, normatively, a group capable of resolving social and economic contradictions. But to the degree the older category of traditional intellectual is transformed into a social engineer (which itself is an ideological legitimation), the two broad strata of independent intellectuals become less pronounced. This position contrasts with that of Andre Gorz, who argued more than a decade ago that the traditional intellectual was dead and only a technical intelligentsia remained—instrumental in its rationality and lacking a large ideological vision extending beyond its function in the social and technical division of labor. While the old political intellectual cum littérateur, philosopher, social critic has all but disappeared in the 1980s (at least in the technologically developed societies), or to be more precise lives on as an academic professional whose public role is severely withered even in comparison to the 1960s, Gorz's formulation seems too dismissive of the real challenges posed by intellectuals, especially in state socialist societies. Moreover, it assumes that, absent a revolutionary working-class movement or movements of systemic opposition from, say, ecologists and feminists, the intelligentsia is ineluctably subsumed under capital or the authoritarian state. Such a judgment is unwarranted if we do not assume that intellectuals, especially the scientific intellectuals, are exclusively a phenomenon of the left. For it is entirely possible, even probable, that the formation of new power centers from these quarters replaces or modifies the existing hierarchies with another based on the domination of intellectual over manual labor and, more generally, explicitly makes the knowledgepower link a new form of social rule. In this instance, intellectuals may constitute a new power center, not on the basis of a culture of critical discourse but on the foundation of the hegemony of scientific and technical knowledge for propelling both the economic and social machine.[12]

Gorz's conclusion was argued after the events of May 1968, when intellectuals, especially in France, appeared to settle down to the pursuit of promising careers in the new technological climate, and when a profound economic crisis was interpreted in Western Europe and North America as a signal to modernize nearly all economic functions by computerization and scientific management. In this regime technical intelligence surely plays a key role: on the one hand, the problems associated with economic restructuring are intimately bound up not only with the internationalization of capital but also with the passing of the technologies of the intermediate range, that is, regimes of production in which the employment of scientific knowledge is only partially effected; on the other hand, intellectuals manage the renovation of the education, health, and other social sectors as well as the production of ideology to articulate with the new economic and technological order. In the first place the cultural idea of the scholar and social critic is replaced by that of the scientist and technician. Moreover, the characterization of these societies changes from industrial to postindustrial, a term that signifies (1) that consumption is considered productive activity and (2) that the metaphor of knowledge production is no longer one of things but of processes, systems, "strings." Replacing the high-modernist "chaos" model of the universe are new totalizations. Or, in other words, the regime of organization describes the now dominant knowledge forms required by the state and the economy. The new society privileges "learning," a concept having nothing to do with its traditional critical connotation. In this context, learning means the capacity of the prevailing order as well as individuals to adapt to new conditions by implementing new production techniques and new organizational modes as well as taking new policies when changed conditions require them. Jürgen Habermas and Gouldner have made sharp criticisms of this perspective, arguing that in the face of qualitatively new conditions and the problems arising from them, only critical knowledge based on new moral precepts is adequate. Postindustrial society is postmodern in this sense: the old ideology was based on a set of principles that, however violated, remained normatively operative. In the new technological game, the terms are "flexibility" and "pragmatism." Ends do not dominate means, as in Weber's notion of instrumental rationality, for this still implies their separation. In the new order, means *become* ends; from the perspective of policy, the technical regime constitutes not only the boundary conditions for human action but its content as well. Of course the recent permutations in the place occupied by knowledge producers in the economic and political order have plenty of historical precedent. For thousands of years intellectuals have presented themselves as mandarins, administrators of empires, the soul of various bureaucracies. Sometimes the literati, who were identical to administration in the earlier period, were distinguished from bureaucrats, who assigned them the task of preventing the identification of culture with bread and circuses, an important distinction for rulers faced with the specter of delegitimation. In Eastern and Third World societies intellectuals have led the struggle for transformed economic and political power, not in their own name, but in the name of workers and peasants. However, as some writers have alleged, their revolutionary nationalist and socialist flags often mask jacobin motives.[13] In question is whether intellectuals have become a power center representing not the mass movement but a new ruling class (themselves) or, alternatively, a military (or more recently a religious) regime swaddled in the garb of a revolutionary guerrilla movement.

In these descriptions the intelligentsia are conceived as part of the prevailing social powers, especially when they proclaim themselves a vanguard, which in many cases has resulted in their reluctance to surrender their sovereignty to those in whose name they have taken action. Their political significance is not in doubt. They occupy crucial positions in social reproduction: as teachers they are charged with the transmission of the prevailing moral norms as well as culture. As ideologists they provide the justifications for the existing system of power, even the revolutionary regimes, producing the ethical strictures that bind human conduct. They are responsible for the organization and maintenance of the justice system, both the law and the courts and, in modern times, the vast social welfare apparatus. And, especially in revolutionary regimes, they have occupied the leading positions in the political party apparatus that frequently controls economic production as well. These modes have always been the dominant spaces of intellectuals in the social order.

IV

The twentieth century adds an entirely new dimension to the role of intellectuals; now the category of scientific and technical intelligentsia is created, as we have seen, by the systematic application of science to the labor process and the elevation of administration to a social principle, rather than a technology for the achievement of predefined ends. For Gorz, the intellectuals, neither part of the working class nor a full partner in the power system, are divorced from history, or more exactly, are understood as a subordinate part of the prevailing capitalist and state socialist systems. Scientists and engineers are servants: they lack genuine autonomy in the performance of their labor and may make decisions only on a narrow range of technical issues. In the labor process they are clearly subordinate to managers, even though they can join their ranks. Thus, they enjoy no independent political expression, nor are they capable of it. Even when they organize unions they are not part of the labor movement, but form separate organizations of cadres that usually are given to pronouncements that place them outside the political and economic ideologies of the working class. It is important to note that in Gorz's theory of intellectuals, the distinction of managers and technicians is retained. Gorz still holds to the separation of means and ends. Clearly, if these are conflated, the scientific and technical cadres are continuous with administration, are actually an arm of it, which accounts for the interchangeability of these categories.

Contrast this state of affairs to the stature of intellectuals during the extended period of the bourgeois revolutions of the eighteenth and nineteenth centuries and, in the twentieth century, national liberation movements in central Europe and later in the Third World—or, indeed, their position in the socialist revolutions immediately following the two world wars. In these situations intellectuals link themselves with class and national movements and are relied on to articulate the movement's goals, devise strategies and programs, and organize propaganda networks through the party and state apparatuses (which they increasingly control). This means that, absent a real bourgeoisie or even autonomous peasant and worker movements with their own ideology, programs, apparatuses, they are, for all practical purposes, the leadership.[14] Left-wing intellectuals become crucial for revolutionary movements precisely because their talents, traditionally cultivated in the service of the established order, are indispensable for any project of transformation of state power. They direct economic development under conditions where the market is marked by petty commodity production and exchange. They impose a new common sense on the underlying population without which the struggle for political and economic transformation is impossible. This new common sense often entails the imposition of national over regional and sectoral goals and consequently demands the integration of whatever independent movements have affiliated with the national revolution. For, more often than not, these movements tend to cling to their "parochial" class or ethnic interests, which, from the perspective of the revolutionary center, often constitute a barrier to fulfilling national objectives. Where the movements do not voluntarily surrender autonomy, they are frequently repressed by bourgeois, socialist, or nationalist intelligentsias.

In this reprise, intellectuals are more than functionaries of power held by others; they are, in all circumstances, the core of the movement. Their utopias form the political imaginary of social transformation, and their organizational and literary skills provide the sinews of administration without which revolutionary wars and states founder or die. What makes the bourgeois intellect so valuable is "his" training as a universal intellectual, a trait that is part of the scientific and cosmopolitan ideology according to which intellectual knowledge is equivalent to reason.[15]

Lenin may be understood as the most significant theorist of intellectuals as historical agents. Although he retains the view that in the final instance their political effectiveness depends on the development of a mass working-class movement, the final instance may have never come. For the history of the Russian Revolution may be told, in part, as the struggle for the integration of that working-class movement into the national movement led by intellectuals organized as the Communist Party. That integration occurred both ideologically and coercively, but the outcome of the struggle was painful, albeit classic in its dimensions: the independent movements of workers and peasants were destroyed by force as much as persuasion, along with the movements of opposition intellectuals.

That political intellectuals have come to power in nearly all revolutions in the twentieth century testifies to the tenuousness of the Gramscian notion of the organic intellectual, which posits the formation of intellectuals within the hegemonic or counterhegemonic classes and the fusion of traditional intellectuals with sovereign political formations of and by (as well as for) the class in question. This model is drawn from the early stages of the revolutions of the eighteenth and nineteenth centuries under conditions of a fairly well developed bourgeois class that, as often as not, recruited intellectuals from its own ranks as much as it attracted the traditional literati. However, notwithstanding the immense educational apparatus the Bolsheviks organized in the wake of the revolution, the Soviet Union did not give birth to a new category of worker-intellectuals, except at the level of the technical expertise, an event that reached fruition only after the Second World War. The proletarian dictatorship was for the workers, at least rhetorically, but was never by them. Eastern European and Asian regimes that have come to power in the name of communism are fundamental instances of rule by intellectuals who monopolize both the means of legitimate violence and the means of ideology production. Moreover, they constitute a state oligarchy that determines what counts as science and more broadly legitimate knowledge.

In state socialist societies political, but not scientific and technical, intellectuals have come to power. For, even if knowledge is a productive force, the concentration of power in the hands of the party hierarchies (which are composed, almost entirely, of political intellectuals, whatever technical or professional training they may have had) creates new problems for regimes plagued by serious economic difficulties. In addition, they are facing mass disaffection from a considerable fraction of the scientific and technical intelligentsia. In Eastern Europe and China it is no longer enough to provide a relatively sumptuous living standard for scientific and managerial categories or, as in the case of natural sciences, to lift constraints on the production of knowledge that is not (yet) officially sanctioned. The blatant imbalance of social power between the party and the cadres upon which the viability of the system increasingly depends creates tensions between them that have mushroomed in the 1980s into contradictions. To put the matter more graphically, a widening gap has been opened between the possessors of human capital and the relatively impoverished possessors of symbolic or cultural capital, whom the regime does not reward by offering shares of concomitant political power. To be sure, many scientists and engineers are party members, but they rarely attain high or influential positions, a measure of which would be the social composition of the political bureaus and the leading ministries. Of course one finds a fair representation of individuals of working-class origin, but this does not signify that the party is a working-class party, only that the hierarchy feels compelled, given the official political ideology, to represent those of working-class origin on its leading committees even if these individuals have served for many years as functionaries and have lost, for the most part, their concrete links with the workers.

On the other hand, neither the Soviet Communist Party's adoption of the slogans of the scientific-technological revolution as quasi-official ideology nor its proclamations in the Gorbachev era for free discussion and political restructuration have yet resulted in a major reconciliation between the party and its cultural and scientific intellectuals. Even though Konrad and Szelenyi may have been mistaken in announcing the rise of these intellectuals to class power in the mid-1970s, the error proved to be one of timing rather than concept. For it is still not clear whether in state socialist societies intellectuals can be integrated without the rulers' sharing power with them. This crisis becomes increasingly apparent the more economic and cultural life is organized around technical rather than ideological discourse, which is the traditional province of the political intelligentsia.

The recent moves toward reform in the Soviet Union and China refer to three areas. First, they assure the scientific and technical cadres of their secure place in the future of the society. Recently, this promise has included recognizing the candidacy for the Supreme Soviet of a dissident figure such as Sakharov on the official slate of the Academy of Sciences. The official reformers hope to enlist dissident intellectuals in the struggle for modernization of production and cultural life.

Second, the new party and state leadership is desperate to raise worker productivity, a reform that entails more than persuading workers to produce more in the same time. What is involved is nothing less than a proposal to abrogate the long-time social contract in which many, if not most, workers observe only loosely the rigors of industrial discipline—in short, do not work hard by western or Japanese standards. The most reliable method of addressing worker resistance to higher work norms is, of course, to eliminate manual labor. This strategy means, invariably, intensifying the application of scientific knowledge in the workplace in all economic sectors. Intellectuals seem enthusiastic to support the regime's effort to decentralize economic decisions by introducing some market criteria for determining what is produced, by what means, and how much; this innovation implies offering incentives to managers to accelerate worker performance (which would not exclude technologically induced redundancy), as well as dismissing those who refuse to meet production norms. For the present, many cultural intellectuals are pleased with the reforms and take issue only with the relatively slow pace at which they occur. On the other side, a substantial section of the party and perhaps an even greater portion of the industrial working class remains suspicious and, in some cases, openly hostile to the reforms.

Third, it is clear that the degree to which scientific and technical intelligence is recuperated by the new regime will depend on its capacity to share genuine power over decision making at all levels, including the party. The call for more democracy, responds to widespread disaffection by many in the politically active population.

One cannot assume, however, that Soviet intellectuals intend to speak for more than themselves. Indeed, all indications are that their definition of cultural and scientific freedom does not necessarily extend to workers and peasants or to those whose opposition is globally directed at the regime itself rather than its specific weaknesses. Andrei Shakharov has made clear he has no contact with other disaffected social forces within the Soviet Union, least of all workers. Gorbachev speaks of openness in the context of the party's program for restructuring economic, cultural, and political life but is not yet prepared to overhaul political life to abolish the one-party state or the official ideology, despite the recent electoral reforms that permit individuals to run for elective office against the party's candidates.[16] Recent local elections in the Soviet Union have witnessed the end of the party monopolies over city and town councils. At this writing (April 1990) *natural* alternative parties have not yet emerged as they have in most of Eastern Europe. The intellectuals want more power in areas that go beyond their work. They want to share control over the *results* of their work, such as a voice in determining nuclear weapons and energy policy, ecology, and the migration of Jews (who have frequently been refused exit visas) and want educational reform reflecting the cultural and intellectual changes of the past decades). I would not want to deprecate the significance of either the electoral reforms or the emergence of scientific and independent political intellectuals such as Sakharov and Yeltsin in gaining public office against the party's candidates.[17] These highly visible and significant victories are symptomatic of the depth of discontent in the country and indicative of the relative boldness of the Gorbachev faction. Nevertheless, the term "democracy" lacks universal meaning, even if its invocation has become a universal signifier. Soviet intellectuals, in the current conjuncture, want to share power with the ruling elite, want a voice within (and not against) the prevailing party and state order. With the exception of the organic intellectuals of the growing nationalist movements against what Lenin called "Great Russian chauvinism," who have articulated a panoply of demands ranging from greater autonomy to independence from the Soviet Union, most cosmopolitan intellectuals have not demanded a pluralist political system in the Western sense, a term that implies a multiple party system and legalization of nonofficial newspapers and other publications, both of which entail a participatory democratic model. Rather, they have contented themselves with negative democratic demands, that is, freedom from the state, with respect to individual rights, including speech, and greater participation in state policy. The limits of intellectuals' dissent (except for a small fraction of participatory democrats) reflect two features of Soviet dissent: much of it remains a demand for inner-party democracy (or at least a greater openness at the level of elites), and intellectuals perceive the severe boundaries of tolerated opposition. In short, many intellectuals are loyal party members despite their dissent from its policies, and others remain skeptical about the extent to which opposition may safely be expressed. The nationalist intelligentsia, on the other hand, have intensified their campaigns against the inequalities between Russia and the other republics, both at the more "advanced" western borders of the country and in the semirural east and south. These movements, concentrated among various intellectual strata, propose either a separation from the state socialist system in favor of a Western democratic state (presumably with a welfare mixed-market economy) or an indeterminate economic and political system independent of the Soviet Union, as in the cases of Georgia and Armenia. In these struggles are revealed the limits of perestroika: it does not extend to the traditional Leninist dictum of the right of nations to self-determination.[18]

V

In the West, Gorz's post-1968 contention that the technical intelligentsia has refused to constitute itself as a new class remains a fair judgment of the current situation. The cultural intellectuals who until the mid-1970s were asserting their independence of the state (especially with respect to policies affecting the environment, the size and content of defense spending, and the conduct of foreign affairs) have during the past fifteen years steadily retreated from positions of political independence.[19] This is not to say that debate on these and other questions has entirely ended or that some scientists (e.g., the recent dissent of a substantial fraction of the American physics establishment over the "Star Wars" defense system), artists, and other intellectuals speak out on specific issues. More recently, Exxon's near-criminal neglect (resulting in the massive Alaska oil spill) and the fierce debate over stricter environmental controls in the wake of the thinning of the ozone layer and the so-called greenhouse effect are among the events that have rekindled the embers of what was once, however briefly, a hearty fire.

Yet, whatever these developments may portend, until now the drift has been away from social responsibility among intellectuals and toward a position of subordination to capital and the state. At MIT a leading group of biologists and engineers have agreed to surrender ownership of patents for bioengineering discoveries in return for substantial corporate funding for their research. Although the scientists did not initiate the collaboration, they have approved such arrangements by large majorities wherever these questions have been put on the academic agenda. On the one side, this indicates the still powerful pull of capital's subordination of knowledge; on the other hand, the steady decline of state support for basic research has shifted the scene of research to applied, commercially oriented areas.

After three decades during which the technical intelligentsia has played a dominant role in the crucial sectors of world capitalist production, American scientists and technical intellectuals remain professional-managerial servants of the corporate capitalist order, despite some indications that this situation has begun to change at the corporate level, particularly in computer-mediated industries and the state.

It would be a serious mistake to judge various theoretical formulations that posit the relative autonomy of knowledge from capital, and thus the possibility of intellectuals occupying the subject positions of social agents without organic links to other classes, by the inconclusive historical evidence at the political level outside Eastern Europe. For just as a weak bourgeois class expanded its ideological and political horizons slowly, even though its economic position had already overshadowed feudal relations, so the role of the technical intellectual in production, the fundamental importance of basic research for technological innovation, the crucial and expanded role of the cultural intellectuals in the reproduction of discursive legitimations for the prevailing order, their domination over state policy, and so on, may prefigure new forms of political self-representation within the capitalist order. While Gouldner's theory of the culture of critical discourse as the foundation for intellectuals' autonomy is a necessary ingredient of an adequate theory, it is insufficient because, despite Gouldner's criticism of orthodox versions, it remains ensconced in the Marxist framework; that is, it is crucially tied to class analysis for comprehending agency.

Norbert Elias's theory of power may provide a more adquate basis for developing a theory of intellectuals.[20] Elias proposes four spheres in which power is exercised in any society: control or monopolies over the means of economic production; control over the means and norms of violence; knowledge; and the civilizing process. Elias refuses the primacy of the economic; his major concern is to investigate the conditions for the constitution of mutual relations and finds that four determinate sets obtain in social formations in which the state plays the crucial organizing role. The development of classes articulates with these spheres. Feudal and bourgeois economic relations are not presumed in Elias's theory to determine other relations, a presumption already rejected by one of his progenitors, Max Weber. On the contrary. The warriors (or in modern times, the military) actively intervene on their own terms in many societies. Similarly, priests, the conventional bearers of knowledge, and their successors, the ideological and scientific intellectuals, are among the controlling interests, regardless of whether they own productive property. Although Elias is silent on the issue, one would have to infer that in modern social formations, the technical intelligentsia, which includes the scientists, would be part of the complex state in which power is routinely exercised in all spheres of social life.

Of course Marx recognizes the power of knowledge; the "ruling ideas of every epoch are the ideas of the ruling class," he states in The Germany Ideology. But this formulation acknowledges the function of ideas only as superstructure; however crucial to class rule, they play no genuinely independent role. As industrial production becomes characteristically based upon scientific rather than traditional craft knowledge, Marx deepens his conception of the degree to which knowledge becomes a productive force and thereby acquires a place within the infrastructure as well as the ideological superstructure. Since at the time of writing the notebooks for *Capital*, this development is still in its early stages, Marx does not theorize intellectuals as social actors. Yet, despite his statement that the industrial stage of capitalist development is marked by the subsumption of science under capital, the crucial role of knowledge and its embodiment in a new social category are tacitly asserted. That is, Marx sets the agenda for further investigation, even if his conception of knowledge does not explicitly address its bearers as new social agents.

It may be argued that a theory of intellectuals awaited the full development of industrial capitalism, the maturation of parliamentary regimes, and especially the rise of labor, socialist, and other parties and movements that signified the political aspirations of the working class. This political expression was not confined to participation in legislatures of executive organs of democratic states; it also manifested itself in direct action: the Italian factory council movement that replaced trade unions during 1919–20; "the great U.S. Steel strike of 1919; the 1926 general strike in Britain; and, of course, the crucial significance of 1905, the year of the first Russian revolution, which, among other things, gave birth to the Soviets. Inspired in part by the Paris Commune as well as the ineffectiveness of the Duma (the czarist-sponsored legislature), Russian workers conceived of popular assemblies and "delegates" were directly accountable to them as an alternative to traditional bodies where parties mediate the relationship between the state and the masses. And it was precisely this example that prompted the debate concerning intellectuals that became an important theme of socialist theory in the first decades of the twentieth century.

Neo-Marxists such as the Austrian school of Max Adler and especially Otto Bauer, as well as Luxemburg, Lenin, and Gramsci, were contrained to ponder the differences between leaders and the led. In her review of Lenin's pamphlet "One Step Forward, Two Steps Back," which calls for a highly centralized all-Russian social democratic party to replace the panoply of small groups (e.g., study circles and locally based political clubs), Luxemburg argues that his Jacobin and even Blanquist model of organization, according to which a central organization literally dictates to lower bodies, violates the specifically socialist character of the movement. According to Luxemburg, social democracy is a movement of a new type: "It is the movement of the working class" in which "self-centralism," "the rule of the majority," replaces the rule of an elite both in society and in the party organization.[21] Therefore, centralism becomes necessary not for the purpose of working out tactics but for coordinating the actions of a whole class. But coordination is not the same as command.

Against Lenin's ultracentralism in which the party directs revolutionary activity, Luxemburg insists that the role of the social democratic leadership "is of an essentially conservative character." As the proletariat gains new terrain on the basis of spontaneous mass actions, such as the strike that began in Russia with a student movement in St. Petersburg in 1901 and culminated in a workers' strike shortly thereafter in Rostov-on-Don ("[which] the boldest Social Democratic daredevil would not have dared to imagine only a few years before"), the party's tendency is to consolidate the gains on the basis of compromise and reforms such as parliamentarianism. In this way, parties often reverse the creativity of the masses. For these reasons, Luxemburg argues for the tactical freedom of the movement at the base, leaving to party congresses the determination of broad policies. Lenin's error, according to Lutemburg, is to see only the anarchistic decentralist tendencies among intellectuals that must be remedied by powerful proletarian-minded central control. He does not understand that over centralization is also the product of an intellectual faction within social democracy that would stifle working-class initiative in the name of revolutionary discipline. Although persuaded, against anarchism and other libertarian ideologies, that the party is necessary to provide a "framework" for conscious activity, Luxemburg emphasizes the struggle against bureaucratism and elitism rather than being primarily concerned with the possibility of opportunism through centralized leadership.

Thus, in political terms, the debate concerning intellectuals appears for turn-of-the-century Marxism as a debate about the relationships between the leaders and the led, the role of the party versus the role of the masses under revolutionary and prerevolutionary conditions, and the relation between strategy and tactics. Lenin's position remains that of Karl Kautsky, for whom the working class could not itself produce more than trade unions as opposed to revolutionary consciousness. Therefore, especially under conditions of the absolutist state, a revolutionary vanguard composed primarily, if not exclusively of uprooted intellectuals (most of whom would be "class traitors"), is necessary, not only to safeguard the integrity of the organization against the police, but to ensure systematic struggle against the opportunists who would settle for reforms. Lenin sees "localism" as the preferred organizational form of bourgeois intellectuals within the movement who, lacking the working class's discipline (gained largely from the regimen of factory labor), sow the seeds of opportunism while resisting the power of the center.

In this debate, both sides express serious reservations about intellectuals. Despite his ultimate reliance on their education and economically wrought freedom from bourgeois obligation, Lenin is deeply suspicious of intellectuals' demands for autonomy and their resistance to party discipline. Luxemburg understands the socialist revolution to consist precisely in the emergence of the working class itself as the apparatus as well as the soul of the movement, the first oppressed class in human history capable of self-liberation. In her discourse, intellectuals, as the possessors of the party apparatus, are inherently conservative forces retarding creativity, a characteristic reserved for the mass movement. Intellectuals are the masters of maneuver and compromise within a relatively complex parliamentary system. She praises German Social Democracy, ironically, for having "adapted itself wonderfully, in the smallest detail to the parliamentary system. . . . At the same time, however, this specific tactical form so thoroughly covers the further horizons that, to a great degree, the inclinations to eternalize, to consider to consider the parliamentary tactic as purely and simply the tactic of Social Democracy makes itself felt."[22]

Thus it is not the localism of intellectuals that leads to reformism and opportunism in relation to the revolutionary goal; it is, implicitly, the passion for winning within the rules of the prevailing game, which are made by the political and bureaucratic intellectuals of the bourgeois regime, that constitutes this conservatism. For Luxemburg the logjam cannot be freed from above or purely by discussion in leading bodies. The "inertia" of current parliamentary tactics inhibits a debate concerning an imagined future whose contours are still vague. But the movement must keep itself responsive to innovations from below in which local organizations addressing changed conditions attempt to invent new tactics on the way to establishing a new terrain of struggle. In a word, the party must assist these local organizations or get out of the way. So the concept of "spontaneous" action always refers to the initiatives of existing party or workers' collectivities and not to some idea that movements contain no preconditions in the organized experiences of prior generations of actors.

In this dialogue, we can see the distance between the two speakers. It is not enough, as some commentators are wont to do, to ascribe Lenin's theory of the intellectual vanguard to absolutist conditions, especially in the light of its reliance on Kautsky's formulations concerning class consciousness. More to the point are Lenin's jacobin assumptions, that is, the idea that the revolution, whose aims are universal, is conducted by a dedicated minority on behalf of the majority. Needless to say, the tradition emanating from Luxemburg and the democratic and libertarian councilist movements of this century harbors, like Lenin, ambivalence regarding intellectuals. Yet, with the exception of Marx himself the problem of knowledge itself remains unexamined until Gramsci. To be sure, within the political discourse of Marxism, intellectuals are taken in their traditional significance, as possessors of high culture—writers, artists, philosophers, priests. Marxism takes them as objects of controversy in relation to their participation in the working-class movement, an issue that perhaps refers more to the problem of the capacity of workers for self-emancipation than to the intellectuals themselves. This tradition is preserved in Gramsci's theory of hegemony, which, however much light it sheds on the space intellectuals occupy in the class struggle, regards knowledge and its bearers within social formations defined by the older paradigm of classical political economy.

Elias, by positing, on the contrary, the independence of knowledge from social formations, makes possible the development of a theory in which the history of knowledge itself, as much as its relations with other components of social power, provides us with a framework for a theory of intellectuals. For even if Marxism has recognized the historical significance of science and ideology in the processes of production and reproduction, it holds that these are in the final instance subordinate to economic relations. Elias argues that the monopoly over knowledge and control of the means of violence are the two spheres that constitute contemporary state formation. This argument changes the social conception of the state. It cannot be understood merely as the expression of the interest of the dominant economic class or, in later neo-Marxist theories, as a field within which classes contest. As the holder of a virtual monopoly over the exercise of violence, it establishes the boundary conditions for economic and political combat. Within this framework, one may measure democracy in terms of whether these boundaries are wide or narrow, whether the transfer of power entails the necessity of a group transgressing boundaries or is a "peaceful process." Marxism insists that such a peaceful transfer of power can occur only on condition that economic relations remain intact, that any intention to change these relations entails breaking the rule that only the state may use the means of violence.

Within these boundaries the rule of law, a complex of reified codes governing both public and private behavior, is supreme, at least normatively. Although laws express the changing nature of the economic, political, and ideological compromise among contending forces, they also have their own history. If Elias's theory of the civilizing process holds, this history becomes transsituational. In other words, although the historicity of the constitution (whether tacit as in the United Kingdom or explicit as in the United States) must be acknowledged, it is mediated by norms that often span historical epochs. These norms are not, therefore, merely functional justifications of the existing state of affairs. They regulate, in large measure, the given state of affairs and have their basis in legal and ethical intellectuals (priests, teachers), their knowledge, and the systems they administer. As scholars and experts, intellectuals are the repositors of the accumulated knowledge of law and, in this sense, have more than legitimating status. Legal expertise, as we have recently seen in the confirmation hearings for U.S. Supreme Court justices, plays an important role for determining who is qualified to arbitrate contending interests in accordance with acceptable interpretation of constitutional law. Thus, the statement that members of this body read the newspapers signifies that interpretation is subject to political hegemony and counterhegemonies. But this maxim does not exhaust explanation for court rulings. Accumulated knowledge configured by the doctrine of legal precedent controls a considerable measure of adjudication. While the specific form of this knowledge is overdetermined, it is surely underdetermined by both conjunctural political struggles and interests and by the letter of the law. Knowledge itself, of which legal ideologies are constitutive, acts autonomously within the multiplicity of determinations whose outcome is a legal decision.

Each institutional sphere of the state has its own history, which is controlled by intellectuals. Of course the idea that science has an internal history that can be traced through the various disputes among competing paradigms is widely acknowledged. That modern science, law, and other discourses live out this history in the context of economic, political, and ideological struggles has also been amply demonstrated by both historians and sociologists (although Elias accepts the methodology of modern science as axiomatic to his work). Nevertheless, the degree to which knowledge is an independent social force is expressed in the claim of science to value neutrality, exempt from the propositions of the sociology of knowledge, the heart of which is the idea that knowledge (except science) is interested inquiry and therefore partial. Consequently, we may trace the social interest that underlies ordinary nonscientific knowledge but not science because it is held to be situated outside the ideological system. This claim is grounded in its self-critical methodology, whose procedures are meant to screen out interests.

Two ideas—that science has a purely internal history in which discoveries are built on others without social mediation, and that scientific knowledge and art are not subject to ideological influence except perhaps the metaphysics of the age, which themselves have internal histories (Koyré)—form the major claims of intellectuals to stand outside the class system.[23] For Karl Mannheim's declaration that the problem of truth could be solved only by a social category that was "free floating" is based on the concept that society requires a sphere of knowledge that cannot be relativized in order to dominate nature and to manage human affairs.[24]

In the terms in which Jürgen Habermas frames the question, a society's survival depends on its capacity to learn, that is, to adapt its rules for communicative action to new conditions, especially those not subject to purposively rational solutions such as are found in the sphere of production.[25] Where "problem-solving" mechanisms no longer suffice because the rules of the game do not encompass the class of actions in question, society tends to reduce the problem to manageable proportions, thus ineluctably occluding or excluding issues that cry out for collective address. The intellectuals, whose main activity can be described as producing noninstrumental knowledge through the invention of new language games, ought to be able to intervene in the affairs of both state and civil society to represent the new questions as well as their solution, even as class-based or work-based knowledge remains ensconced in particular interests. Habermas has no explicit theory of intellectuals and society, but privileges the new bearers of critical communications as catalysts for change. In this "reconstruction" of historical materialism, he implicitly condemns the tendency of all social formations to subordinate intellectuals to the game of technical rationality or, to be more exact, to set too restrictive boundary conditions over legitimate intellectual activity without condemning it to a marginal existence. The real criterion of a dynamic society is whether new, noninstrumental knowledge is genuinely valued not only as art, but as the basis for social decisions. Where critical intelligence is shunted to the margins, even in democratic societies, the social formation is destined for decline. For while there is no law of social determination that can predict that a given society will rely on its own critics (tacit or overt) to set its directions, the critics remain the only learning class precisely because of their distance from economic and social reproduction. Consequently, a society that narrows the space for critical discourse risks oblivion or at least stagnation and decline.

We can see the process at work in the nearly thirty years of effort in the Soviet Union and Eastern Europe to reform archaic institutions such as central economic planning and state control over knowledge, the arts, and political dissent. A fraction of the ruling bureaucracy, perceiving stagnation and decline, has attempted to save the system by integrating scientific, cultural, and dissident political intellectuals into the state as partners rather than subordinates. On the one hand, reforms such as introducing a limited market, especially for agricultural goods, and genuine elections for some high offices are implemented for the practical interest of assuring cooperation among peasants and intellectuals in the face of severe economic hardship. The provision of consumer goods and recruiting scientists and engineers to participate in technologically driven growth are measures designed to legitimate the Soviet system among an increasingly disaffected young and an educated middle class frustrated by the system's rigidities. On the other hand, a substantial fraction of hegemonic intellectuals who occupy key party, state, and economic positions have grasped the possibility that the "legitimation" problems of the regime do not exhaust the necessary reasons for reform. While change from above may in the end prove chimerical because of the inherent conservatism of party and state apparatuses, the social forces set in motion by the reform are beginning to go beyond the limits proposed by these authorities in Poland, China, and Hungary. In Poland and China, intellectuals have reached beyond their own social category toward a new discursive basis for social rules—democracy, a term that is not defined exclusively by its conventional parliamentary connotation but embraces conceptions of negative freedom such as human rights, recognizing independent trade unions, and, more broadly, a new egalitarian morality. Some of these tenets have not reached the Soviet Union, especially the ideas of trade union autonomy and multiple political parties, which have already been recognized in Hungary and other Eastern European countries. Yet despite two generations of ideological monologism, ideas of genuine social renovation are ascendant in these societies. And with the stunning exception of

Poland, democratic ideology is an emanation of scientific and political intellectuals, and signifies their emergence as new social agents. Yet, it is still not clear that, without the strength of alliances with other social categories, the intellectuals can pull it off. It is not clear whether the Soviet Union's policy of partially freeing intellectuals from strict ideological censorship—but within a state-approved framework—can do the trick of unleashing the desired scientific and cultural creativity. For if intellectuals require genuine independence to make a radical contribution to society's self-knowledge, if something like the alienation effect is necessary, then integration may be "counterproductive"; it may substitute a "velvet prison" for the iron bars of overt repression.

In Western societies scientists and artists enjoy considerable autonomy, but those holding dissenting or avant-garde ideas are not always invited to contribute. Those who dissent from normatively approved paradigms of scientific or artistic culture may form groups, publish their work (in marginal journals), and agitate for them without overt interference from the authorities, who hold the means of violence. On the other hand, the press is free for those who own one; major print and visual media may not publish or broadcast the work of those too far outside the mainstream. Still, small alternative presses may publish marginal and subaltern discourses, although radio and television access for these views is severely restricted by financial and ideological forms of censorship.

For scientists the pressure to conform is more severe. Dominant paradigms exercise both intellectual and institutional power and demand that those who would perform scientific work establish the validity of their discoveries within approved frameworks. The consequences for those who refuse may not entail imprisonment, as in totalitarian regimes, but they are nonetheless serious. Laboratory facilities may not be made available by government-funded corporate or university administrations; the leading journals may decline to publish the findings of those whose adherence to the prevailing wisdom, much less the dominant paradigm, is in doubt.

Paradigms have two aspects: most important is the method of discovery, the imperative that hypotheses be subject to repeatable tests, and then the agreement of the tested hypothesis with the dominant paradigm at any specified time. For, even if method is observed, the leading presuppositions upon which experimental science is based must themselves conform to the central metaphors of hegemonic science. As Thomas Kuhn argues, even if both conditions are fulfilled (or if the paradigm is under attack from the investigator), the acceptance of new knowledge depends on persuading key members of the scientific community. In this respect the history of science paints an extremely ambiguous picture. Canonical theories are frequently overturned, but often the scientific community holds dogmatically to already established knowledge even in the wake of substantial evidence, by its own criteria, to the contrary. The "democratic" norms to which the scientific community is supposed to adhere are observed as much in their breach as by their exercise. Dogma in science as well as statecraft inhibits the effectiveness of critical discourse, even when it does not use violence to prevent it from happening. The West has its velvet prisons too.

This raises the question of the status of scientific and cultural communities, East and West. Clearly the term "community" signifies collective work and decision making. While the sociology of science has found that such activity occurs, investigation reveals that these "communities" are also power systems that guard their particular knowledge and its forms jealously and frequently repel challenges with considerable ferocity. This tradition undoubtedly owes its virulence to the powerful opposition enlightenment science encountered from the established church during the Renaissance and Reformation, and the equally repressive encounters with Soviet and Eastern European regimes in the Stalin era. But it cannot be said that Western science is genuinely autonomous, especially in the late twentieth century when its alliance with (and reliance on) the state and large corporations has been established (and verified by a large body of literature). The close relationship of intellectuals in sciences and the arts (except for the avant-garde) with the state carries a price for society's collective capacity to adapt to new conditions. Here I want to cite only two examples (although others can be mentioned): nuclear weapons proliferation and the ecological crisis. While a relatively small fraction of scientists have opposed nuclear production and a somewhat larger group have advised against proliferation, U.S., Soviet, and French scientists are tied to the defense establishments. In the United States, when an influential group wrote a secret (and repressed) report against President Reagan's plan for the Strategic Defense Initiative, their arguments were framed entirely in terms of technical feasibility rather than addressing the moral and strategic issues. One can infer that a technical discourse invites wider reception among policymakers while to challenge U.S. strategy places the alliance of science and the state in jeopardy. But this is precisely the point. The claim of science in Western societies to autonomy is ideological; only the *forms* of constraint differ from those of Eastern Europe.

The case is equally powerful in relation to the ecological consequences of industrial pollution for water, air, and food. In this regard the scientific community has entered the debates as technicians, but has as yet refused to raise the larger issues: Should society continue to pursue policies of economic growth that result in poisoned waters, air that contains carcinogens? Should public policy sanction the production and use of industrial herbicides on the basis of economic necessity? Scientists and engineers often demur from addressing these questions on the grounds that they are really political, not scientific, issues. Thus, the separation of science from its political consequences preserves the moral right of scientists to engage in research that may be harmful to public health.

Perhaps the questions raised by the introduction of bioengineering are most revealing in this respect. At issue is the use of technologies that alter genes in order to produce new varieties of grain, make organisms resistant to viruses and other infections, and, more broadly, alter the functions of nervous systems, especially the brain. Many, including some molecular biologists (from whose science the technology derives), have challenged the potentially harmful effects of releasing new organisms into the environment. But few if any have declared that the further production of these organisms may be inimical to human survival. Instead, one often hears from scientists the refrain that bioengineering is "here" and therefore cannot be subject to either a moratorium on further production pending investigation or a reversal of the practice of gene splicing. Here, the facticity of a science and its technical applications bears heavily upon the scientific community, which cannot imagine halting a particular scientific practice as a remedy to the dangers engendered by its activities.

It would be too simple to claim that the reluctance of even the most active critics of the uses of biotechnologies to call for suspending the technology itself bears on their dependence, for the performance of scientific work, on the patronage of those who provide funds. This is surely an important element for explaining the limits of criticism within the scientific community, but is, in the end, insufficient. The power of science consists in its claim to both common sense and to the space of truth. Molecular biology is today received in most quarters as what counts as legitimate biological knowledge. The validity of its applications, which are intimately bound up with its theoretical presuppositions, is taken as self-evident, subject only to the self-regulation of the scientific community. This scrutiny is directed in most cases by scientists themselves under the not too close supervision of public bodies. On the one hand, the ideology of scientific autonomy fits nicely with the current practice of deregulation; on the other hand, molecular science's dispassion is undermined by its virtual subsumption under commercially linked technology.

The reluctance of science to submit to public control contrasts sharply with its willing subordination to state and corporate institutions who assure the resources for research. In the latter instance, collaboration between science and industry is considered legitimate because science enters the arrangement voluntarily. In the former, oversight prescribed by law is equated with the heavy hand of church and crown against modern science in the sixteenth and seventeenth centuries. The traditional stance of science since the sixteenth century is autonomy; in the contemporary context, scientists resist arguments that show the economic and social constitution of scientific knowledge and that the relation of scientific knowledge to interest is no less intimate than any other social practice.

In this brief discussion I have focused on the importance of the emergence of scientific and technical intellectuals in contemporary society because social theory has only begun to recognize these sites. In the main, the focus has been on the literary intelligentsia, especially in the period beginning with the First World War and ending with the close of the 1950s. This attention may be explained by the consensual judgment that the close of this era also concludes a much longer span of time during which intellectuals constituted a public sphere of critical discourse.

This discourse was by no means confined to criticism of industrial capitalism. It included a broad range of public issues bearing on the civilizing process in America, the nature of artistic and scientific culture, and the character of U.S. foreign affairs at a time of this country's world ascendancy. In this endeavor, literary intellectuals of the left play an important part, out of proportion to their number. In fact, the small network of literary and political magazines from the turn of the century to about 1960 embodied the avant-garde of political and artistic dissent, and were the channels through which modernisms of all sorts received their most ardent defense and aesthetic and theoretical articulation. It may also be argued that the literary left, described recently in a veritable cascade of books and articles, memoirs and biographies by and about key actors in these circles, and collective (mostly literary/political) studies of institutions of the intellectual left, have bequeathed a legacy to which current and future intellectual generations must respond. For the overwhelming portrait is that of the past as cornucopia—if not an integrated civilization, at least a spiritual community that succeeded in producing high intellectual voices in a predominantly yahoo culture. In this view, the present signifies retreat, intellectuals have left public spaces for the academy, which for Russell Jacoby and others is a space of impotence. I want to offer an alternative view of the present: the university has become a knowledge factory, but also a center of a cultural explosion whose impact is as great as that of the independent intellectuals of the "golden" age. We may mourn its passing, but only the most myopic vision can speak seriously of the intellectuals of that bygone era as the "last." Indeed, I want to show that the passing of the public intellectual of the old type does not signify the passing of the public intellectual as such. The forms and the issues are different, and it may be that we have lost the capacity for master discourses. Today the left intellectual is a feminist, an ecologist, a critic of science and technology, a person of color. Right-wing intellectuals still occupy those universal spaces once the province of the left and liberals. And, in an era where science and technology are forms of power, its organic intellectuals are far more powerful than ever.

VI

Gouldner contends that intellectuals are rapidly constituting themselves as a new class capable of contending for a political power corresponding to their already formidable economic and cultural position. For Gouldner, the fundamental contradiction of their contemporary situation in late capitalist and state socialist societies consists precisely in the disparity between the considerable autonomy they already enjoy owing to the culture of critical discourse and their political subordination. Gouldner insists that the old "moneyed" class is dying, but even more that the old base of capitalist social relations is being eclipsed, not by a revolutionary proletariat, but by the new class of knowledge holders. Although he criticizes Marxism's dogmatic assertions of the persistence of the class struggle in the old terms, he has not advanced too far beyond some crucial features of Marxist class analysis: with Pierre Bourdieu he offers a fairly mechanical analogy between material and cultural capital.[26] Even though the new class is salaried and therefore does not own the material means of production, its power derives from its centrality in production, its possession of knowledge and the discourse that derives from it. Thus since the new class possesses the means of material production through its monopoly over the means of intellectual production, its "blocked ascendancy" at the political level must result in social contradictions that have historical consequences.

Despite the evident economism of these propositions, Gouldner has advanced the debate beyond Gramsci's theory of hegemony in which, it will be recalled, intellectuals derive their social weight from the characteristic classes of a given mode of production. By insisting that intellectuals are self-legitimating, his new class theory relies, in the last instance, on the idea of postindustrial society. The chief characteristic of societies in which the old capital-labor relation no longer dominates is that cultural capital has displaced material capital as their leading dynamic. Cultural capital is understood not as a property of superstructure, where the struggle over accumulation would be the infrastructure, but as a new universal signifier for the system as a whole. If knowledge has displaced manual labor as the crucial component of capital formation, a thesis that can be quantitatively as well as theoretically substantiated,[27] its bearers must constitute not only a new and increasingly significant social category but also a class challenge to the prevailing bases of power that are rooted in the old production relations.

Thus, Gouldner's provocative suggestion of intellectuals as a new class parallels Elias's theory of knowledge as independent of the productive forces. More exactly, he argues for the autonomy from capital, at least in the present conjunction of knowledge. The difference between the two is that Elias posits knowledge as a structural feature of the constitution of any civilization, whereas Gouldner, retaining a historical materialist framework, argues temporally. The Marxist categorical scaffolding remains in place, but the actors, corresponding to new "higher" production relations, have changed. The "class" struggle is depicted in terms consonant with the transition from feudalism to capitalism: a rising new class, having established the domination of the production relations of which it is the bearer, confronts old political and social powers. From this premise, the old regime is "more or less rapidly" transformed into new, higher relations of production. The crucial move is to abolish the machinery of the state and replace it with new class power.

At the same time Gouldner borrows a major theme from the sociology of science: those who participate in the culture of critical discourse, a norm of the scientific community, want free communication in the dissemination of knowledge, an objective frustrated by corporate and state bureaucracies, which value knowledge only as a commodity and wish, therefore, to hold it as property. This notion was advanced in the late 1930s by Gouldner's mentor Robert Merton, who posited "communism" as an inherent feature of science.[28] For Merton the conflict of science and society arises when society imposes, for any reason, restrictions on the free flow of information among scientists. Therefore, free science requires a democratic society.

The subversive side of this theory is its tacit critique of the private ownership of knowledge; on the other hand, Merton has constructed an ideal type whose correspondence to the actual social relations of science, both the internal power structure of the scientific communities and their links with the larger social nexus, is not only imprecise but tends to justify the social relations of science under conditions of Western capitalism—indeed to justify a kind of democratic pluralist state as the only context sympathetic to the flowering of scientific knowledge. Gouldner accepts this framework as a basis of his own theory of intellectuals, and this borrowing results in a series of fundamental lacunae. He identifies capitalist and state socialist states as inimical to the underlying values of the knowledge communities that, he assumes, are "interested" in critical discourse. This assertion is made without the benefit of argument; that knowledge communities constitute a culture of critical discourse is taken as axiomatic and combined with well-known sociological insights to form a thesis of class formation. Indeed, the idea of science as critical inquiry is precisely what is in contention. Far from accepting Merton's theses regarding the normative content of scientific communities, a new generation of sociologists of science have shown, with considerable theoretical and empirical acumen, that science is ordinary discourse; that is, its supposed character as self-reflexive, self-correcting inquiry belongs to the mythology on which its social power is based.[29]

If this view is right, then we may not uncritically include scientists in the cohort of critical intellectuals. Yet, by relying on the notion of knowledge as a productive force to justify his theory. Merton's concept of intellectuals not only includes scientific and technological workers, but is crucially dependent on them. One might argue, especially in revolutionary societies, for the idea of cultural intellectuals as a new source of class power; certainly the humanistic intellectuals in China, the Soviet Union, and Poland have played important roles in the democratic movement. But this is not what Gouldner means. Although he has not explicitly acknowledged the origin of CCD in the scientific and technological communities, the ninth thesis of his *Future of Intellectuals*, which concerns their conflict with bureaucratic and political elites, reveals his belief that the interest of the new class is not constrained by conventional ideologies or, more to the point, that it refuses the authorization of established institutions. Instead, the obstacles to their political ascendancy and enhanced status appear increasingly irrational from the perspective of the actual movement of the productive forces. The new class appears, at least to itself, as the legitimate inheritor of political authority because it holds scientific and technical knowledge and, moreover, constitutes a culture that finds itself at odds with the still dominant culture.

Gouldner ignores the mounting evidence, already available prior to 1979 when his book was published, that the norms of freedom that purportedly inform the scientific community are evident as much in their breach as in their observance. The fact is, established scientific knowledge is frequently defended against new knowledge by those who possess the means of its production, means that no longer embody the intellect. For the modern laboratory, no less than the university, is a knowledge factory controlled by those whose power to pronounce truth is held as private property against others who might challenge their hegemony.[30] Far from conforming to the culture of critical discourse, much of modern science and technology is constituted as dogma. In short, if the scientific community is taken as a model of CCD, there is reason to believe that its invocation is seriously flawed as the presupposition for the thesis of a new class. Both those engaged in "pure" science and the so-called technical intelligentsia are paradigm bound. Those challenging the dominant paradigm are consigned to the margins of the communities or, more routinely, completed excluded. As Ludvik Fleck, Bruno Latour, and others have forcefully argued, scientific paradigms are forms of power that go beyond intellectual authority in the narrow meaning of the phrase. The displacement of a given paradigm entails the overthrow not only of intellectual orientations but also leading institutions and groups within the community, methods of production, types of capital investment, and so on. In turn, this struggle is implicated with larger social forces in other ways: the scientific community may enjoy relative autonomy, and its exercise of power confronts the old moneyed classes and state bureaucrats as both opponents and allies.

To shift a paradigm entails, therefore, more than Kuhn allows: it is not only a group of leading scientists that must be persuaded, but corporate leaders and politicians as well. Moreover, the internal content of the paradigm is not independent of the ideologies and discourses of the dominant social formation. In short, the culture of science and technology is a subset of hegemonic rationalities from which knowledge communities are not free. For the thesis of a new class formation among intellectuals would have to demonstrate that knowledge is independent of its social context with respect to both its methods of inquiry as well as its results and their form in order to contravene the idea that its place within the prevailing division of labor does not set boundary conditions for its range of action. Gouldner's new class theory falls on his acceptance of the internal history of scientific knowledge as an adequate basis for class formation under determinate, historically constituted conditions.

Having said this, there is growing evidence that scientific and technical intellectuals are seeking an independent role in state formations, even as they are subordinate to capital and bureaucratic states. I have argued that this is particularly relevant to state socialist societies, but there is a second sign of nascent class formation in the emergence of the French Socialist Party (SP) under Mitterrand after 1968. In contrast to the Communist Party, which was a mass party whose cadres were recruited largely from the industrial working class, the traditional, cultural intellectuals, and a fraction of local professional politicos, the Socialists, once derisively described as a party of provincial teachers, were rebuilt mostly under Mitterrand's leadership as a party of technical and managerial intellectuals. To be sure, the French bureaucracy has always had a strong grip on the state, owing to the centralization of crucial economic and social institutions under its aegis. The technocratic class is by no means a new phenomenon associated solely with the Socialists. However, the originality of the new configuration consists in the fact that the party leadership is recruited almost exclusively from this social category, a development highlighted by its ostentatious and obligatory fronting of figures of proletarian or trade union origin in a sea of leaders whose careers have been made as high bureaucrats or professors.

Faced with the post-de Gaulle, post-1968 disarray of the grande bourgeoisie and the breakup of the right Gaullist hegemony over the old political class, the Socialists have become the party of government of the 1980s, a party whose relation to traditional constituencies of the old capitalist regime is extremely tenuous. The postwar SP was rife with factions and experienced several splits in the 1950s, most notably from a left-wing formation called the Unified Socialist Party (PSU), which built some ties to trade union activists, especially within the Democratic Confederation of Labor, France's second largest labor federation. Under the leadership of Jean Pierre Chévénement, the CRES, another left faction, played an important role in forging the SP alliance with the Communists, which lasted from 1972 to 1986 and which, Daniel Singer and others have argued, was the linchpin of the new socialist ascendancy.[31] But this group virtually disappeared as an independent party force in the years since Mitterand took presidential power and won a parliamentary majority in 1981. With the reintegration of the majority of the PSU, the left of the party, which, at least in tendency, was oriented toward building a mass, democratically-based party, no longer plays a real role in policy formation; nor is the traditional socialist "right"particularly strong except in the south of France, where Socialists capture important local offices in and around Marseilles with the help of the staunch anticommunist Catholic center. These forces have never enjoyed significant national influence in the reconstituted PS and remain content to support the technocratic leadership of Mitterrand and former PSU leader Michel Rocard, who has been a major force in transforming the party from one of opposition (and therefore faction ridden) to one of government (and consequently unified under the leadership of technical intellectuals). As a party of government it has felt obliged to move even more to the center, replicating its traditional alliance with the moderate right in the 1950s at the local level. This opening persuaded many disaffected Communist voters to return home in the 1988 legislative elections when the PS ran a campaign to win a bare parliamentary majority on the basis of a de facto coalition with the center-right in preference to achieving a clear left majority.

After his decisive victory over Jacques Chirac, Mitterrand's strategy was to hold down the legislative victory so that workers, immigrants and intellectuals could not reasonably demand, as they did in 1981, a new wave of social reform such as dramatic rises in minimum wage, voting rights for immigrants, and other major redistributive measures.

The PS objective, to administer economic austerity with a human face, is based upon growth-oriented politics. According to the conventional technocratic wisdom of which the PS more than the traditional political class, is the supreme expression in contemporary France, the key to growth is scientific and technological investment, especially in the new industries such as genetic engineering, computers, electronics, arms, and nuclear energy. Further, the Socialists have made political modernization one of their top priorities. It is aimed at reducing the importance of both extreme right-wing parties and those of the extreme left to the electoral vanishing point, to weaken the fighting capacity of the labor movement and the Communist Party (which, to a considerable degree, still dominates it, although with reduced strength) and, concomitantly, to take ideological considerations out of politics, at least those ideologies emanating indirectly from the unfinished business of the French revolutions of 1789 and 1871. In short, the PS program amounts to the politics of aggregation rather than social movements, new or old; it is heavily electorally oriented, which implies the conflation of democracy, republicanism, and a conception of socialist responsibility identical to the welfare state. Even the PS democratic promise of decentralized, locally based authority, so boldly announced in the wake of its victory in 1981, has been quietly relegated to the back burner. Notwithstanding Lenin's fear that intellectuals favor reformist localism, decentralization is really anathema to new class technocratic intellectuals for whom effective planning requires a greater concentration of power at the top.

This is a politics profoundly suspicious of organized constituencies and social movements that insist on retaining their own voices. The Socialists have amassed something more than a third of the vote, but their coherence is defined by the broad and increasingly ambiguous concept of the "left" alliance under the hegemony, both ideologically and organizationally, of the state bureaucracy. Even in violation of its own party, the PS, this bureaucracy constitutes a relatively autonomous force in French state politics. Thus, in contrast to Germany and Sweden, where a specific social democratic movement has dominated the left since the turn of the century, the French Socialists constitute a significant fraction of graduates of the Grandes (literary and administrative) Ecoles. For example, one of Mitterrand's closest political advisers and his undisputed confidant, Jacques Attali, historian and critic, is representative of the social category that has affiliated with the new PS; Michel Rocard, a Grande Ecole-trained civil servant, is typical of a second and increasingly dominant group of intellectuals, the technical and administrative stratum. Taken together with the significant French scientific establishment, which is largely part of the civil service, these categories constitute a new political class sharing the same or similar social backgrounds, educational formation, and occupational identities. That these categories form the core cadre of the dominant party in contemporary French politics may be attributable to the three-way ideological split on the right, but also to the deep left divisions that are unable to choose between opposition and power. The unflinching characteristic of the PS is its taste for power at nearly all costs. The burning questions of the old socialist movements (e.g., whether to take state power within a capitalist framework and, if so, the degree of socialization of ownership that may be imposed without revolutionary transformation) fail to detain mainline socialist leaders even for a second: these are men for whom power calls out its own demands. Since their social base is at once diverse and massified, and their ties with the traditional party, its discipline, and its ideology have been severed, they are not constrained except by the rituals of political campaigns. To a large extent, the PS is, like American political parties, a child of the new media and the polling organizations to which it is subordinate for both style and policy. Statistics may not have completely replaced live persons, but the effects are as if this displacement defines the political terrain.

Among the new political principles is that socialism signifies left-Gaullism—left insofar as Mitterrand and his associates recognize that France may not pursue a national strategy apart from the European interest to become an economic and political force independent of the two superpowers, and Gaullist in that even this European internationalism takes second place to nationalism. The Socialists have supported a strong military establishment, including a substantial nuclear capability, just as did de Gaulle. Thus, the French have led the way for other European Socialist parties (particularly those in Italy, Spain, and Greece). As national parties the Socialists can do no more than initiate or carry over elements of the welfare state, ensure trade union freedom to organize and bargain collectively, and safeguard the infrastructures of parliamentary democracy. The southern European Socialists feel constrained by the world economic crisis, which has impacted heavily on their national economies. Hence they move steadily rightward, inviting the rebirth of a new left whose contours remain unclear.

In all of these countries the intellectuals, far from remaining professional servants or organically tied to traditional classes, have forged political vehicles in which they hold the reins of power, even as they are obliged to recognize, but only tactically, some of the demands of movements whose support they seek or, more pertinently, wish to divert from entering politics on an autonomous plane. For example, the Greens, who are weak everywhere in southern Europe except Italy, have nevertheless evoked a cynical, but superficially sympathetic, response from Mitterrand. He named their former leader minister of the environment only to defund and ultimately embarrass him. Moreover, the leading party group regards ecological concerns as inimical to growth politics. As the economic crisis wears on in Europe, the Socialists (as the party of state managers) grow in proportion as the right, whose rise to power was propelled by postwar economic "miracles," loses legitimacy in its echt conservative manifestation, but not in its populist mode. The communist left struggles to gain a new lease on political life after deindustrialization. Each of these partially discredited parties was constituted once by great social movements that intervened in making history. The Socialists, on the other hand, betray the tendencies normally associated with hegemonic ideologies and parties: their "movement" roots lie far in the past and today resemble contemporary Western progressivism; that is, they are agents of modernity. They disclaim interest in structural reform, but instead present themselves in the garb of honest and efficient government. The New Class seeks to make of its métiers a set of new political principles by signifying that effective administration, scientific and technological progress, and cultural dissemination includes social justice as a by-product. Far from representing the CCD, the New Class dedicates itself to government as a process of puzzle solving, just like normal science in Kuhn's reprise; its gasp of the economy is drawn from neoliberal economics, and its understanding of the social question is purely instrumental and disinterested.

The vision of the New Class is one where technologies of administration and economic growth replace ideology as the stuff of social rule. As in the United States, social justice is a signifier whose meaning has shifted to compassion. Now compassion implies noblesse oblige, in this case the largesse of a government and the classes that constitute its power constellation. The compassionate state is an image shared by the center left and the center right, which have agreed that the old democratic slogan of self-management first advanced before 1968 by the PSU and adopted briefly as the common PS-PC program in the 1970s is infantile or worse, disruptive in the quest for the smooth society.

Yet this shift in socialist ideology remains unchallenged on the French and other lefts. It has become hegemonic precisely because of the decline of the working class and the traditional intellectuals who took the action critique of factory occupations and generalized it to a new antibureaucratic principle, not only an antidote to corporate and state bureaucracies but those of the labor movement itself. The New Class emerges from the void produced by the demobilization of these social categories, but also from the weight of technicism in modern life whose legitimating characteristic is its claim to neutrality, that is, the idea of bureaucratic administration as an instrument of rather than barrier to democratic process.

This raises the problem of the avant-garde in contemporary society. For the common features of artistic and political vanguards is their marginality or, put another way, the possibility of margin in technocratic regimes. While the thesis of total administration advanced by the late Frankfurt School is not only excessive in its empirical claim but theoretically forecloses the emergence of new agents and fails to account for the persistence of the opposition even in darkest times, the valid core of the theory emerges with special poignancy in periods of retrenchment such as we have collectively experienced since 1968. The explosion of that year, today celebrated as nostalgia as well as legacy by left remnants everywhere, reminds us that nothing is forever, that today's upsurge is tomorrow's museum piece. But it is also important to remember Weber's hesitation before Marx's sweeping historical judgment about the permanence of class formations within the capitalist mode of production. Weber argued that classes and class struggle could only be posited in concrete contexts; in one language, they consolidate around problematics whose historicity constitutes their boundaries. Thus, the industrial working class is a crucial social actor in the epoch of machine production, the struggle for universal male suffrage, the formation of powerful trade unions based on craft and industry, and so forth. The end of this epoch, which lasted more than a century in the United States and longer in Britain, produces a profound shift in class structure even as capitalist social relations prevail. The new epoch is marked by the domination of intellectual over manual labor to the extent that scientific knowledge becomes the major productive force.

But beyond production cultural hegemony is the condition for reproducing the system as a whole, particularly popular consent for the prevailing order, especially when force cannot even be used as a last resort without the ruling group's suffering serious consequences. In the transition from one regime to another, Laclau and Mouffe have argued that class is replaced by discourse and the concept of the social itself disappears.[32] Such judgments cannot be examined here, except to note that those who claim privilege of discourse over class formation may unintentionally signify the dominance of knowledge. Gouldner's theory of the New Class may have misidentified the source of the power of intellectuals. Provisionally I want to argue that in these societies in which the knowledge mode of production prevails and culture is an ineluctable feature of social rule, intellectuals may become the only genuine political class. Thus, the political avant-garde can no longer imitate the old professional revolutionary, for whom the conquest of state power by the class-conscious proletariat was ideological cant. Such a proletariat no longer exists in these societies, even as it emerges in state socialist and peripheral capitalist regimes.

The new avant-gardes must today challenge the democratic claims of the bureaucratic state of which the new class has become the soul. To be sure, the new class cannot be theorized as an inevitable consequence of the passing of the powers of the old working class. It comes into being when the old ruling class reveals its incapacity for political rule. This crisis is expressed not so much in terms of the economic displacements currently afflicting workers in advanced capitalist countries and, tendentially, in state socialist societies. The mechanisms of the welfare state do not, on the whole, permit these societies to replicate the mass suffering of the last great depression. Rather, the crisis is one of legitimation of the entire political and cultural order, including the old left parties that were an integral part of it. Lacking Keynesian solutions or socialist alternatives to the economic crisis, the terms of political debate turn on questions of administration. Elections are fought on the proposition that administration must replace the old ideological debates, on the consensus that these are times when there are no real answers that go beyond considerations of policy. The victory of the right over the left in the 1980s is in the process of being superseded by a new class hegemony speaking in the name of the "left," but resembling it in only the threadbare remnants of Keynesianism, a framework it adopts only opportunistically for the purposes of capturing office without power, but in which it has no confidence. The new avant-garde must be utopian even as it takes into account the drift of utopias to authoritarianism and no longer in the technological sense followed by intellectuals since Saint-Simon and Fourier. It can only prevail as an educational force by engaging the signifiers of power—democracy, management, justice—in a new way that systematically delegitimates the claims of the New Class to own the images associated with these signs.

In the United States, the Jackson campaign succeeded in addressing justice, removing its signifying power from New Class representations. But his campaign lacked a language to extend the debate beyond its Keynesian connotations to questions of management, that is, to a new conception of democracy. In this respect, Jackson follows the myopia of the conventional left progressives, who lacked even a democratic rhetorical practice except that derived from the Popular Front slogans of the 1930s. These signs, taken together with the elusive ideas of freedom and pleasure that have always been the palpable enemies of total administration and work-oriented societies, constitute in their totality the elements of a new utopian discourse. To be sure, their constituencies are, for now, defeated and dispersed in the West, taking shelter in the underground of the dominant culture. In their intellectual manifestation they do constitute a culture of critical discourse in that they challenge the scientifically based technocratic culture that is emblematic of the New Class. In germ, this is the basis of the doctrines of radical feminism and social ecology, discourses that have, until recently, lacked a language of social justice and thereby often cut themselves off from crucial political interventions. Green politics is today an important component of a new, not yet emergent political culture. Its class basis shifts contextually but comprises strong currents of disaffected New Class members. Similarly, feminism, often disparaged by the conventional left for its middle-class basis, may be read as another crucial indicator of the power of the new social categories of knowledge producers and may signify, together with the ecology and gay movements, a countervailing weight to the still dominant technological discourse within the professional-managerial "class" (here the quotation marks are meant to indicate the still indeterminate character of these categories). Whatever the outcome of the struggle, there is simply no doubt that new agents have emerged whose histories are in the process of shifting from subordination to social power.

NOTES

1. See especially Alvin Gouldner, *The Future of Intellectuals and the Rise of the New Class* (New York: Seabury Press, 1978); Andre Gorz "Technology, Technicians and Class Struggle," in Andre Gorz (ed.), *The Division of Labour* (London: Harvester Press, 1976); Antonio Gramsci, "On Intellectuals," in *Selections from the Prison Notebooks*, trans. Quintin Hoare (New York: International, 1971).

2. This problem is most pronounced in the United States and United Kingdom where the Democratic and Labour parties have been caught in the contradictions between trade union support for welfare state expansion and the fear among managers and professionals of a rising tax burden as well as the growth of neoliberalism in the middle strata.

3. I am referring particularly to Maoist and some Trotskyist tendencies and groups in France and the United States in the 1970s.

4. George Konrad and Ivan Szelenyi, *The Intellectuals on the Road to Class Power* (New York: Harcourt Brace Javovich, 1979).

5. Karl Marx, "18th Brumaire of Louis Bonaparte," in Karl Marx Selected Works vol. 2 (New York: International, n.d.).

6. Robert Michels, *Political Parties* (Glencoe, Ill.: Free Press, 1955).

7. Witness the rapid transformations in Brazil, Chile, and Argentina since the end of the 1970s, although the Philippines is surely a more ambiguous instance.

8. Louis Althusser, "Ideology and Ideological State Apparatuses," in Althusser, *Lenin and Philsophy* (London: New Left Books, 1971).

9. The chief reason for bracketing the term "class" is that is belongs to the discourse about capital/labor/power. If one adopts the knowledge/power discourse the category of class becomes severely attenuated. A similar fate awaits ideology. As I shall argue, it is possible to hold both discourses, in which case one must specify which framework is employed.

10. Gouldner, *The Future of Intellectuals*.

11. From this description some—notably Daniel Bell—have derived a theory according to which capitalist production relations have been superseded by the new knowledge/managerial control over many of the key operational decisions of the international economy. Consequently, the class struggle either disappears or is relegated to a subordinate place in a new regime of technologically led problem solving. On the contrary, there is no logical progression from the older capital/labor antagonism to the world Bell would have us believe has come into being. Knowledge-based productive forces do not imply the end of history; they only open up possibilities for new forms of capital domination and especially new social actors. The thesis of the knowledge/power link does not entail displacing the class/power relation.

12. Karl Marx, *Grundrisse* (New York: Vintage Books, 1973).

13. This thesis is advanced with particular force by David Rousset, *The Legacy of the Bolshevik Revolution*, vol. 1 (London: Allison & Busby, 1982).

14. Rousset, ibid., chapter 5.

15. V. I. Lenin, *What Is to Be Done?* (New York: International, 1934).

16. There is no question of technological determinism, only the relatively independent role played by knowledge in the social process, relatively independent because capital still configures the choice of knowledge object. In this framework, intellectuals derive their power from their discursive positions.

17. Or the measured response of the regime to the widespread strike movements in 1989, especially the mass miners' strikes, which contained contradictory elements. On the one side, miners demanded the regime make more consumer goods available in stores. On the other miners joined the prodemocracy movement asking for wider decision making over workplace practices, a clear signal that they are heading for confrontation with the technical intelligentsia.

18. V. I. Lenin, *The Right of Nations to Self-Determination* (New York: International, n.d.); Joseph Stalin; *Marxism and the National Question* (New York: New Century, 1945).

19. Although scientists' organizations effectively reduced the Reagan administration's Star Wars program, ecology and feminist movements whose key activists are recruited from professional strata are important exceptions to the general drift away from independent political interventions among intellectuals.

20. Norbert Elias, *Power and Civility* (New York: Pantheon, 1982).

21. Rosa Luxemburg, "Organizational Questions of Russian Social Democracy," in Dick Howard (ed.), *Rosa Luxemburg: Selected Political Writings* (New York: Monthly Review Press, 1971).

22. Ibid, 294.

23. Alexandre Koyré, *From the Closed World to the Infinite Universe* (Baltimore: Johns Hopkins University Press, 1957), chapter 1.

24. Karl Mannheim, *Ideology and Utopia* (London: Routledge & Kegan Paul, 1936).

25. Jürgen Habermas, "Historical Materialism and the Development of Normative Structures," in Habermas, *Communication and the Evolution of Society* (Boston: Beacon Press, 1979).

26. Gouldner, *The Future of Intellectuals*; Pierre Bourdieu, *Reproduction in Education and Society and Culture* (Los Angeles and London: Sage, 1977).

27. See Fritz Machlup, *The Production and Distribution of Knowledge in the United States* (Princeton: Princeton University Press, 1969), for a nearly exhaustive analysis of the position of knowledge production in terms of major economic indicators. His data have been updated in Machlup, *Knowledge: Its Creation, Distribution, and Economic Significance*, 3 vols. (Princeton: Princeton University press, 1980, 1982, 1984.

28. Robert Merton, *The Sociology of Science* (Chicago: University of Chicago Press, 1970).

29. The literature is vast. For a good sample see Karin Knorr-Cetina and Michael Mulkey (eds.), *Science Observed* (Los Angeles and London: Sage, 1983), and Michael Mulkey, *Science and the Sociology of Knowledge* (London: Allen & Unwin, 1979).

30. Bruno Latour, *Science in Action* (Cambridge, Mass: Harvard University Press, 1987).

31. Daniel Singer, *Is Socialism Doomed?* (New York: Oxford University Press, 1988).

32. Ernesto Laclau and Chantal Mouffe, *Hegemony and Socialist Strategy* (London: Verso Books, 1985).

Toward an Effective Intellectual:
Foucault or Gramsci?

R. Radhakrishnan

Any attempt at theorizing politics in the poststructuralist context is immediately caught up in a contradiction. On the one hand we experience, more urgently than ever before, the need to posit a common and solidary humanity that faces global threats of unprecedented magnitude. On the other hand, our situation is characterized by an unbounded heterogeneity of subject positions, each of which is a world unto itself insofar as it is informed and semanticized by its own macropolitics. These subject positions are indeed so diverse and, as instances of a nonsynchronous global development, so hopelessly out of sync with one another, as to resist the kind of collective totalization implicit in such formations as "our world" and "our problems." In the domain of critical theory, the very use of the word "we" has become profoundly problematic. Meanwhile, in the "real world," a number of coalitions of oppressed, marginal, and minority groups have developed under common and collective principles with the objective of empowering themselves in a variety of political arenas. Yet another example of the theory-reality disjuncture is the fact that even as an avant-garde and postrepresentational theory rages against Identity, the Voice, and the Self, myriad groups are voicing themselves with conviction into Self and Identity. It is quite an anomalous scenario in which the best of progressive theory seems bereft of objects of explanation, while emerging historical realities seem oblivious of high theory. Is this really the case?

I do not think so, and to elaborate my conviction I turn to the

57

all too real phenomenon of the Rainbow Coalition, its achievements in the 1984 and the 1988 campaigns, and in particular to some of the crucial pronouncements made by the Reverend Jesse Jackson. For it seems to me that the coalition is taking place at that very juncture where theory and reality are finding each other within a shared axis. After a selective discussion of some of the themes of the Rainbow Coalition, I will attempt to demonstrate how these very themes have exercised the political and critical intelligence of Antonio Gramsci and Michel Foucault, each of whom in different but related ways had sought to give new meaning to the agency of the political intellectual.

During the course of the 1988 campaign, Jackson made the point emphatically that it is imperative for individuals and constituencies to feel, think, and identify themselves beyond the irreducible immediacy of their own regional rationale. Stated in theoretical terms, Jackson's message has been that the contents and causes of disparate and seemingly unrelated regions are indeed subtended by a common structure and etiology, and that every position is characterized both by a regional and a global structure.[1] The political ethic, then, of the coalition is to honor and do justice to the specificity of subject positions such as black, Chicano, feminist, immigrant, ethnic, gay, and lesbian, and at the same time, to enable structurally homologous and isomorphic readings of one situation in terms of the other. This is the change in direction that Jackson explains in response to Stuart Hall's questions in the pages of *Marxism Today*:

> So it became patently clear to me that our drive for self-respect and self-determination would have to be led by us and that we had to change the direction. There's a broad body of people in this country across lines of race, religion, region and sex who desperately want that new direction within this country and new connections with other people and forms of government in the world.[2]

Jackson asserts that the "rainbow is not so much about race as a direction, because all colours are in the rainbow,"[3] and goes on to argue that within the overarching context of the coalition, "the black vote is not a selfish and isolated vote, it is the trigger vote, the catalytic vote, for the entire progressive coalition."[4] Jackson's claim here on behalf of the coalition is both representational and postrepresentational, just as the valence of the black vote within the rainbow spectrum is both "itself" and more/less than "itself." Jackson's model, in moving beyond the canonical mode of representation and its insistence on a one-to-one correspondence between "identity" and "representation," reaches out toward a postrepresentational politics, but in doing so enriches the meaning of political representation. In other words, each constituency within the spectrum goes beyond and outside itself (the postrepresentational move), but only to reclaim the significance of representation within a more inclusive and collective organicity. Each constituency is representative not of itself but of a constitutive relationality that can only be eccentric to the givenness of any one of the components of the coalition. The resemblance between this model and the notion of hegemonic articulation developed by Ernesto Laclau and Chantal Mouffe is indeed very striking. In both cases, given identities are articulated within a relational field whose differential disposition brings Identity and Difference into relationships of mutual accountability.

Jackson's rhetoric at the 1988 Democratic convention pointed up the necessity of dealing with "identity in difference" and "difference in identity." For example, his statement that he and Michael Dukakis had come to the United States of America on different ships, but were now "in the same boat," vivifies the reality of a common but unequally and asymmetrically shared history.[5] In the same spirit, Jackson insisted on the need for a new and different "equation." The term "equation" covers a lot of significant ground. With its connotations of equality, it carries the moral urgency of affirmative action and the need to redress existing imbalances and asymmetries. As an algebraic trope, it establishes the valence of any given variable within the equation as a function of a collectively negotiable reality. In other words, given the operational logic of the equation, no variable within it can remain aloof, isolated, and unaffected by the equational process. Even as he develops the idea of the coalition representing itself from within its own space, Jackson is vigilant about the dangers of being represented and exploited by the dominant ideology. To state this differently, the burden of the coalition is both specific and transcendent in its specificity. It articulates "universal" themes even as it commits this universality to the contingencies of specific perspectives. (I shall return to this theme later in this essay in the context of Foucault and Gramsci, where I will be discussing the nature of the relationship between "what" is being said and "who" is saying it.) Thus, in his conversation with Stuart Hall, Jackson comments that "differences have been exaggerated for the purposes of exploitation."[6] This critical capacity of Jackson to situate or coordinate the *locus* of the coalition both in terms of itself and in relation to the dominant ideology calls to mind a Gramscian hegemonic politics that makes rigorous distinctions between allies and opponents. Equally Gramscian is the emphasis on "interests" and "interestedness." For example, Jackson has this to say about some of his political positions: "I would call them the most moral as opposed to the most radical positions, because radical has the connotation that you are out of step with reality, or out of step with our interests."[7] In preferring the "moral" to the "radical" (a term used by Stuart Hall in his question), Jackson seems to be (1) stressing the pragmatic and felt nature of the entire enterprise, (2) asserting very strongly that one cannot have a politics that is out of step with present-day interests, and (3) distancing himself from the elitist language of academic theory. As a matter of fact, at one point in the interview Jackson responds to Hall's question with the following disclaimer: "Well, I am not sophisticated enough to understand all the labels you made up. I just try to use the natural reasoning process."[8] I will not get into an analysis of what "natural reason" might mean in the context of Jackson's politics, but I will merely observe in passing that Jackson's category is not all that different from the notion of "common sense" in Gramsci's political theory. I shall reserve for a later section of the essay a more detailed analysis of the relationship of natural and commonsensical worldviews to professionally theoretical worldviews; there I will also take up the question of whether professional intellectuality denaturalizes and therefore steps beyond its organic solidarity with the commonsensical and the natural.

Having delineated some of the trajectories of the Rainbow Coalition, I would now like to connect these trajectories with a number of theoretical issues that constitute the space where Michel

Foucault and Antonio Gramsci may be said to address each other in critical dialogue.

I

Who or what is an intellectual? Who or what is the intellectual accountable to? How does the *topos* of the intellectual remain true to its own relatively autonomous specificity while continuing to perform a more collective, organic, and representational function? Are we still within a world-historical conjuncture where there are the "leaders" and the "led"—a situation that necessitates the avant-gardism of the intellectual? Or, have we reached a stage where the very category of "the intellectual" has become historically obsolescent? And indeed, when we talk about "our" world-historical conjuncture, what particular world or worlds are we taking about: First, Second, or Third World, dominant subject positions or subaltern? If there are multiple worlds subtended unequally and asymmetrically within a more inclusive coeval history, is it even worthwhile to think of the intellectual as a global and/or universal figure? Will not each situation produce its own kind of intellectual formation, in response to its own specific agendas and priorities? But conversely, since no place is an island, how does any given location carry simultaneously both a global and a regional valence, and moreover, by what authority does any location work out a satisfactory, effective, and progressive equilibrium of the regional with the global? Given the multiplicity of intellectual and political models, how do these models communicate with one another, and in the name of what global assumption is such communication carried out? What is the nature of the very category of the "political"? Is it still caught up within a representational *episteme* or has it gone beyond representation toward the phantasmal areas of a postrepresentational, heterogeneous, and differential politics? Are our theoretical representations of the world somehow out of sync with our political representations of the world? In other words, as Jackson's disapproval of the term "radical" points out, does theory all too easily leave the world behind to indulge in a contentless utopianism? How do critical negativity and the need for affirmation negotiate with each other under the aegis of the "political"? Is it still possible, or desirable, to think in global terms when so much recent history seems to warrant a critique of globalness? Do our times insist that "thick politics" be replaced by "thin politics" and the "macropolitical" by the "micropolitical"?[9] Has the necessity to practice an acutely subject-positional politics deferred and/or problematized the need for an alliance politics that intends to recover global connections along different lines and directions?

These themes and questions have occupied center stage in Michel Foucault's theater of thought. In a different though related way, Antonio Gramsci has elaborated these problems from within the prison walls of Mussolini's Italy. My purpose here is to highlight aspects of the models of resistance that these two theorists of praxis have to offer, compare and contrast some of their crucial formulations, and eventually, through a process of mutual exposure and interrogation, account for the specificity as well as the finitude of each model. It is to Foucault I turn first.

There is something constitutively contradictory about Foucault's location as a political intellectual. He has been a privileged, empowered, and "sane" thinker who has sought fraternal membership among the insane, the marginal, and the powerless. He has even become their theoretical representative, even as his very thought thematizes the duplicity of his location vis-à-vis that of the insane, the marginal, and the powerless. As a rigorous and honest thinker, Foucault has quite thoroughly foregrounded the irrelevance and the untenability of his own theoretical authority even as he has transformed the course of Western historiography by rendering it fundamentally vulnerable and accountable to what it has systematically repressed. In his own brilliant and probing ways he has tried to think the "unthinkable," but from a subject position that has been assigned by the dominant ideologies of Western thought. The valence of his critical thought is then by very definition "always already" homeless and marginal: on the one hand it lies "outside" the contours of official Eurocentric thought, but on the other hand, it cannot and will not be part of an emerging order interested in establishing its own hegemonic articulations. In short, his is a highly attenuated but diagnostic politics that will not affirm a new axiology: a politics that paradoxically achieves its interventionary effects within a macrological vacuum. It is an orphaned politics that cannot be "in the name of" any principle or cause. His appreciation and endorsement of what he calls "subjugated knowledges" are held in position within a genealogical practice that is constrained to posit the dominant knowledge as the primary point of departure. Ergo, we have Foucault identifying subjugated knowledges as "those blocs of historical knowledge which were present but disguised within the body of functionalist and systematising theory and which criticism— which obviously draws upon scholarship—has been able to reveal."[10]

It is by enacting an oppositional relationship between "historical contents" and a certain kind of theory that Foucault opens up a space where subjugated knowledges can announce and pursue their insurrection. He is pointing to two kinds of narrative: that of historical contents characterized by ruptures and struggles, and that of a totalizing and systematizing theory that defuses and reconciles ruptures and discontinuities in the name of a theoretical and systemic unity. In this respect Foucault's critique is not unlike Gramsci's, which makes a similar distinction between a traditional intellectuality that seeks to be timeless and unitary and an organic intellectuality that posits historical contingency and conflictuality. Foucault's critique is also aimed more generally and fundamentally at the very algorithm of representation that, in "speaking for" historically discontinuous and different events, deregionalizes these events and denies them their legitimacy as local and autochthonous articulations. Grand theory may be said to represent "historical contents" through an act of epistemic violence. How can these events and contents be enabled to speak "for and from within" themselves as subjugated knowledges? How does one and who should be the one to speak on behalf of the authentic location of these knowledges?

This raises a profound question concerning the historical reality of subjugated realities and knowledges. These blocs are characterized by a contradictory formation: they have always existed in history, but in the domain of theory they have been written out of effective existence. Within the auspices of the dominant theory their very historical and material reality has been dehistoricized and rendered nonexistent. Situated as absences within a theoretical historiography not their own, these knowledges are faced with a problem at the moment of their insurrection. Where will they speak from: rupturally from within the hegemonic body or from a position "without" that is not complicitous with the mandates of the official body of knowledge? Foucault's reading is that these blocs "were present but disguised" *within* the body of the dominant or master theoretical discourse. And it is here, I believe, that notwithstanding his theoretical rigor and political sensitivity Foucault's "subject position" vis-à-vis the locus of these subjugated knowledges falters and acknowledges its own limits. For the positional status of Foucault's own discourse *about* these knowledges is not clear. Does it speak from within the legality of these emergent spaces, is it the voice of the official discourse critically deconstructing itself and thus speaking as *its own other*; or is it the expression of a tertiary and disinterested space that functions at a "panoptic" remove from its object of criticism?[11] Stated in world historical terms, who or what is speaking here? What "subject" is making these attributions about subjugated knowledges and from what perspective? My argument is that the choice of the "in/out" figurality is not merely rhetorical, not is it coincidental. Contemporary theorists of subjugated subject positions (feminists, ethnic theorists, critics of colonialism and imperialism) have contested the necessity to conceive of their positions as "lacks" and "absences" within the dominant structure. Why not "think" these spaces as separate and disjuncted from the official body and therefore capable of engendering their own theories? The choice to locate these insurrectionary spaces within the hegemonic totality forecloses possibilities of "separatist" and "alternative" historiographies that may have nothing to do with the lacks and insufficiencies of the hegemonic model. Besides, this way of looking at these events exclusively as "insurrections" foists on them an eternally "transgressive" and "reactive" identity that is forced to feed parasitically on what it should effectively forget and "prehistoricize." The ability of these constituencies to historicize themselves remains the obverse of the capacity of the "official lack" to identify itself. In psychoanalytic terms, the realities of "others" are essentialized into a grand alterity (the capitalized Other), which in itself is nothing "other" than the ruling ideology in an antithetical or "reverse narcissistic" contemplation of itself.

In spite of these shortcomings or blind spots, Foucault's critical articulation retains its diagnostic acuity. Foucault is eminently successful in turning the tables on established "regimes of thought" and in securing possibilities for "local criticism" and a "noncentralised kind of theoretical production." In the name of what, then, does he position himself alongside these local criticisms, and how does he valorize the impulses that shape and inform local criticism? Foucault is very clear in his appreciation of the polemical trajectories of local criticism:

> It is here that we touch upon another feature of these events that has become manifest for some time now: it seems to me that this local criticism has proceeded by means of what one might term "a return to knowledge." What I mean by that phrase is this: it is a fact that we have repeatedly encountered, at least superficially at a superficial level, in the course of the most recent times, an entire thematic to the effect that it is not theory but life that matters, not knowledge but reality, not books but money etc.; but it also seems to me that over and above, and arising out of this thematic, there is something else to which we are witness, and which we might describe as an *insurrection of subjugated knowledges.*[12]

The keynote here is the "return to knowledge," life, and, eventually, life knowledge. Here again the theme is the occlusion of reality and knowledge by theory. If theory suffocates differences, discontinuities, the heterogeneities and polyvalences of reality (what Bakhtin has termed the "dialectic of real life"), then it is clear that an effective articulation of real knowledge has to look elsewhere for fulfillment. And it is here that Foucault introduces the notion of people, of populism, and of singular lived realities that are their own meaning-events. He gives the name "genealogy" to "the union of erudite knowledge and local memories which allows us to establish a historical knowledge of struggles and to make use of this knowledge tactically today.[13] Genealogical researches, he says, are also "anti-sciences" that seek to eliminate "the tyranny of globalising discourses with their hierarchy and all the privileging of a theoretical *avant-garde.*"[14] (It is interesting to note that

Foucault cites Marxism and psychoanalysis as examples of global theories and therefore parts company with them, but only after acknowledging that they have indeed provided and "continue to provide in a fairly consistent fashion useful tools for local research." More of this in my discussion of Gramsci's Marxism.) Theory-political knowledge (the people as a collective) and the intellectual as a residual avant-garde—that is the nexus I turn to next, for the question of the status of subjugated knowledges cannot be sufficiently probed unless we also simultaneously raise the question of the intellectual/masses relationship and the underlying ideology of the individual/society paradigm. The challenge that Foucauldian thought has to take up is that of postrepresentational politics and of accounting for the politics of intellectuality in a different way. And sure enough, Foucault has a lot to say about this.

In a conversation with each other, subsequently published in English as "Intellectuals and Power," Foucault and Gilles Deleuze announce the death of representation and the total obsolescence of the cadre known as the "intellectual." Both Foucault and Deleuze are interested in "lateral connections" and "networks of relays" that go beyond the representational paradigm and its dyadic (the spokesperson and his or her constituency) structure. In the words of Deleuze, "a theorising intellectual, for us, is no longer a subject, a representing or representative consciousness," and "those who act and struggle are no longer represented, either by a group or a union that appropriates the right to stand as their conscience." The upshot of it all is that "representation no longer exists."[15] This is an insight with which Foucault is in enthusiastic agreement.

How do we understand the claim that representation no longer exists? Are we to understand that in our contemporary world there are no more representational models to be found, no more leaders and constituencies, no more delegated/parliamentarian/democratic forms of government, but only and exclusively "groupuscules" *being* and legitimizing themselves in total freedom? Clearly this is a bizarre scenario that has nothing to do with the way the world is running. We must then interpret the statement to mean that although the world is rife with forms of representation, theory has proved that "representation" is defunct; that is, in the avant-garde and futuristic world of theory, "representation is no more." But would not such an interpretation revalorize that very forwardness of theory that Foucault finds so irrelevant and indefensible? The difficulty here is that of "routing" and historicizing the progressive temporality of theory through the actualities of the given situation. It is clearly not evident (if anything, it is quite the contrary), given France's current national and international politics, either that representation is dead or that intellectuals like Foucault and Deleuze and their several regional and nomadic projects (however laudable their regional efficacy, and here I am thinking of Foucault's groundbreaking work on the prison system) are even remotely influential in shaping France's domestic and foreign policy. What we have instead is a intellectual fringe, both marginal and marginalizing of itself, that has debilitated itself for lack of "pure" means and a fear of complicity in existing forms of political struggle. As a result, the adumbration of a daring and different future finds itself completely severed from the world "as it is." The question of how to get "there" from "here" is bracketed indefintely in favor of an aporetic thinking that monumentalizes the gap between forms of current history and practices that are utopian. As a result, the "unthinkable" is removed from its dialectical implication with the determinacy of historical thinking. We are left with an anarchist version of a permanent revolution.

What is particularly significant in the conversation between Deleuze and Foucault is the necessary connection between the "end of representation" and the celebration of the knowledge that the masses produce without the help of the intellectual. Clearly the events of May 1968 in Paris provide the underlying logic of this connection. Those events have taught intellectuals like Foucault and Deleuze the disquieting lesson that there exists a profound asymmetry, within society, between the perspectivity of the intellectual and that of the masses. The May events become that transformed space where the masses *are* their own protagonists fully capable of empowering themselves and speaking for themselves without the mediation of the intellectual. Is there then a role in this unfolding drama for intellectuals like Foucault?

The answer seems to be no. Foucault's symptomological reading of the intellectual in this context is quite unsparing in its honesty. For not only does he celebrate the masses who "no longer need him to gain knowledge," he also fiercely decelebrates the intellectuals who "are themselves agents" of a repressive system of power that "blocks, prohibits, and invalidates" the discourse of the masses. The intellectual's role, Foucault declares, "is no longer to place himself somewhat ahead and to the side"[16] in order to express the stifled truth of the collectivity; rather, it is to struggle against the forms of power that transform him into its object and instrument in the sphere of "knowledge," "truth," "consciousness," and "discourse."

This self-critical and deconstructive rhetoric certainly sounds correct and politically wholesome except for one little problem: it is not clear "who" is speaking here, and "why," and "about whom," and from what point of view. If it is really the case that the movement of the masses has definitively superannuated the agency of intellectuals like Foucault and Deleuze, surely the question then arises: why are Foucault and Deleuze even saying anything at all about the movement? If it is true that the people have found their voice, and furthermore, that Foucault and Deleuze are "in the way" of the people's movement, how then do we understand and interpret the "representations" that Foucault and Deleuze are compulsively producing about the nature of the movement? Do these representations have any validity at all? Are these representations capable of making any cognitive truth claims at all, that is, given the poverty and irrelevance of their perspective in relation to whatever is really happening out there? How are we to receive and valorize a point of view that persists in articulating itself on the assumption that it has nothing worthwhile to say? How are we to read these pronouncements of a totally contentless critical negativity against the emergence of an affirmation by the masses? Are intellectuals like Foucault and Deleuze on the one hand, and the masses on the other, citizens of the same world, or is it the case that in spite of their best intentions, Foucault and Deleuze are guilty of creating an Us-Them divide?

The problem here is that Foucault's (and Deleuze's) protocols of self-problematization do not go far enough, a point Edward W. Said makes in his appreciative critique of Foucault's political imagination:

> We may finally believe with Foucault and Lyotard that the great narratives of emancipation and enlightenment are over, but I think *we must remember more seriously what Foucault himself teaches* [my italics], that in this case, as in many others, it is sometimes of paramount importance not so much *what* is said, but *who* speaks. So that it can hardly pass muster that having declared the "assujetissement du discours," the same source that does so erases any opportunity for adversarial responses to this process of subjugation, *declaring it accomplished and done with at the start* [my italics].[17]

Said's quarrel in this passage is not with Foucault's intentions but with the reality of Foucault's practices: they do not go far enough. In spite of Foucault's intentions, his discourse ends up privileging "what is said" without raising the question of "who is speaking." In other words, in active transgression of his wonted exhortations in behalf of specificity and contingency, Foucault does end up making a number of representational truth claims. No one has made this criticism with more force and rigor than Gayatri Chakravorty Spivak, whose critical epistemology, I must add, is in many ways quite Foucauldian, but whose politics are quite different. Commenting on the conversation between Deleuze and Foucault, Spivak acknowledges "the most important contributions of French poststructuralist theory: first, that the networks of power/desire/interest are so heterogeneous that their reduction to a coherent narrative is counterproductive—a persistent critique is needed: and second, that intellectuals must attempt to disclose and know the discourse of society's Other."[18] But at the same time, she criticizes Deleuze and Foucault because they "systematically ignore the question of ideology and their own implication in intellectual and economic history." She goes on to say that "neither Deleuze nor Foucault seems aware that the intellectual within socialized capital, brandishing concrete experience, can help consolidate the international division of labor."[19]

I have already made the claim that Foucault's critical-intellectual practice does not go far enough. I would now like to elaborate the specific ways in which it does not go far enough. It is quite astonishing that Foucault, the thinker of specificity, does not identify himself problematically as a European and Eurocentric intellectual who has gone on to make sweeping generalizations about power, discourse, subjectivity, disciplinary societies, and micropolitics, on the basis of limited and exiguous french empiricities. Of course Foucault's criticism of all that has been harmful and oppressive in global emancipatory programs has to be lauded for its honesty and polemical specificity. But my point is that Foucault's critique of global strategies does not in itself invalidate the global dimension or the historical fact that all "differences" and "local subject positions" are part of a given global reality. By merely expunging the term "global" from his world of reference the mighty philosopher cannot be said to have gotten rid of the world itself. It is one thing to opt for a strategy (for whatever reasons) that is local rather than global and quite another to maintain or believe that in the choice of the "local" one has somehow abolished the "global." I would rather argue that the "global" controls and articulates Foucault in ways that he is not aware of. In a super-Nietzschean move on behalf of a local and discontinuous perspectivity, Foucault forgets that even the most disjunct perspective is globally subtended and that the very local perspectivity he champions against the claims of universality envisions its "own world" and thereby sneaks in through the backdoor the authoritarianism of global thinking into the terrain of the local. In other words, the local perspective itself is symptomatic of a certain choice on behalf of a certain world. Moreover, the will to power that resides within even the most local perspective shores up certain priorities and agendas, thus providing for that location the authority of a "world." It is also ironic that Foucault, the theorist of constituted subjectivities and assigned subject positions, suddenly "chooses" freely and joyously to be a specific, deglobalized, local, and countermnemonic intellectual. What gives him the right to make that choice, that is, given his historical proximity to the regimes and narratives of colonialism and imperialism? By what mandate, global or regional, does Foucault assume a statute of limitation on the long *dureé* of colonialism and imperialism so as to inaugurate his local and countermnemonic discourses?

To understand this contradiction in Foucault's politics, a word is in order here about the absolute and axiomatic prominence given to the events of May 1968 by French poststructuralist thought. Without at all questioning the significance of those events, I would like to suggest that their idealization confers on them a kind of pure and autotelic significance. It is as though May 1968 had occurred as a singular event in defiance of all preexisting histories and historiographies. The impassioned valorization of May 1968 as a "break" results in a willed loss of memory: a forgetfulness of the generation of Sartre, Camus, Merleau-Ponty, and de Beauvoir who had all been embroiled in the "macro" discourses of French colonialism, international communism, and Stalinism. We cannot, for example, forget the strong Algerian connection in the philosophico-political fiction of Sartre and Camus, the moral-political-existential enervation of a Roquentin and a Meursault whose "world" and "center" fell apart as a microcosmic symptom of the bankruptcy of Western/French colonialism. We also need to remember that the highly individualistic philosophy of the absurd, as propounded by Camus, was at the expense of an Arab who had to be bumped off meaninglessly so as to provide the European individual with the negative ontology of "an indifferent universe." Nor can we forget the resurgence of racism and xenophobia in France today. My point is that the West has had and continues to have global investments, and it is not up to anyone's intentional choice to declare a sudden and dramatic deglobalization. If anything, such historically "innocent" moves only serve to conceal the connectedness of the world's problems. Whereas in the macropolitics of the Marxists one perceives a sense of accountability to the past, we see in the countermnemonic Foucault an all too felicitous willingness to "forget" his genealogical determinations. Yes, indeed, it is a strength of Foucault's genealogy effectively to combat and break with the past; but no break can ever be "pure." Impressive as the achievements of French poststructuralism may be, it would be quite erroneous and harmful to assume that the "present" juncture is radically different. To put it slightly differently, the Foucauldian task of writing the history of the present in all its willed discontinuity has to renegotiate with the received past and its many ramifications.

A pure European countermemory is suspect and disingenuous, for it would seem to exonerate Europe's past all too easily and thereby forfeit the lessons to be learned from the past. A contemporary Europe that will not negotiate with the moral authority of its erstwhile "Other," Africa and Asia, is a Europe that will not pay a price or atone for its colonialism. More generally, any dominant subject position that is in the process of deconstructing or calling itself into question cannot do so in solipsistic isolation, but must do so rather in a participatory dialogue with the subaltern positions.

We can detect a clear difference between Foucault's local and specific politics (a politics that will resist possibilities of coalitional articulation) and Jackson's call for "common ground," or for that matter, Edward Said's emphasis on the need for a cooperative thinking across and beyond existing asymmetries. Foucault's practices remain incapable of generating a positive politics; for he has foreclosed those possibilities: as one of the European "Us" haunted by Stalinism, the failure of Western Marxism, and the nightmare of the Gulag, he cannot have a macropolitics, and by virtue of his assigned subject position he cannot be one of "Them": the masses, and a whole range of subaltern positions. There is something wrong with this way of positing the choices, for it does away with the very possibility of influence and dialogism. I will now try to demonstrate how Foucault's (and Deleuze's) reading of the revolution of the masses reinstates the Us-Them divide.

The basic thesis that Foucault and Deleuze propose in their conversation is that the masses are "at one" with their reality and that they have no need for theories of mediation. Reality just happens in factories, asylums, and prison houses; and the expressions that emanate from these sites are not "about" (as in the false panoptic mode of representation) experiences: they *are* those unmediated meaning-events that are expressive in their very intransigent concreteness. The assumption here is that the collective purity of the people's movement in the very moment of its praxis translates itself into its own theory, and therefore, every member of the collective is already a living demonstration of a freedom that theory can only distort or destroy. Here is a reality that has transcended the need for theory: "they" do not need theory, for "they" are theory in practice. Such a characterization is incredibly romantic, for now the masses have been reified as a pure form of alterity. Here again we can see that what underlies this romanticism is a lack of specificity. In the guise of retiring the "universal intellectual," Foucault retires the entire cadre of the intellectual and the many typologies that comprise that cadre. Of course we are left with the specific intellectual, but this intellectual is "always already" dispossessed of macropolitical intentions. We need only contrast Foucault's strong denial (ironically, on behalf of the people) of the masses' need for an intellectual with the very different historical emergences of recent movements, to see how mutually exclusive the two models are. Ethnic, feminist, anticolonialist, and independence movements assume an authentic organicity of constituency where leaders are delegated to lead and the people accept and empower the leaders as *theirs*. Martin Luther King, Mohandas Gandhi, Jesse Jackson, W. E. B. Du Bois, and many many others were not coercive leaders, nor did they usurp the sovereignty of the people they spoke (and speak) for. Between the leaders and the people there can be a sense of an active political community that makes the act of representation genuine and historically real. These leaders seek confirmation with the people and proceed to elaborate programs of action that take into account questions and details of organization. Within the movement, there are many different mediations and many different layers of structure and organization. The people and the leaders together discuss ways and means of historicizing the revolution through political, institutional, and administrative processes. These movements create their own leaders and intellectuals who are interested in making sure that the revolution does not peter out into an "eternally displaced present," or the intransitivity of *jouissance* as an anarchist nirvana. Here, as in other areas, Foucault fails to make crucial distinctions between forms of representation that are legitimate and those that are coercive, between leaders and intellectuals who are organic with the movement and those that are traitors, between forms of power that are repressive and those are libertarian, ameliorative, and emancipatory.

The troubling aspect in all of these pronoucements is that the masses continue being "spoken for" by Foucault. What are the masses themselves saying? Have they designated their leaders? Will the masses, for example, claim that an ideal reality has already occurred and that there is no need for further elaborations and representations? Is the revolution beyond all ideology, and if not, is it not important for the masses to find ways of expressing and historicizing the revolution in terms of its own ideology? How can this ideology be embodied if not through a whole range of carefully orchestrated mediations and political, intellectual, and institutional thresholds? The phenomenological privileging of concrete experience, argues Spivak, forecloses "the necessity of the difficult task of counterhegemonic ideological production." What follows is a telling diagnosis: "It has helped positivist empiricism—the justifying foundation of advanced capitalist neocolonialism—to define its own arena as 'concrete experience,' " as "what actually happens." Indeed, the concrete experience that is the guarantor of the political appeal of prisoners, soldiers, and schoolchildren is disclosed through the concrete experience of the intellectual, *the one who diagnoses the episteme*" (my italics).[20] Spivak's analysis forces Foucauldian thought out into a global space: a space that it is unwilling to acknowledge. The point to be made here is that the discovery of "concrete reality" in a particular region is in itself symptomatic of a larger and more inclusive location, that of advanced capitalist neocolonialism. I read Spivak as saying that local regions in France (or Europe) cannot be treated as disjunct epiphanies that are rid of a "global before and after." Speaking of them as "concrete reality" confers on them an unquestionable transparency that radiates "with the historical sun of theory, the Subject of Europe." Spivak's reading also stresses that the concrete intellectual continues to be the custodian and interpreter of the truth of the *episteme*. The specific intellectual may be less absolutely oriented than the universal intellectual; but he is still the mouthpiece through which the *episteme* declares itself.

To sum up this part of my argument, Foucault's ambivalent rhetoric vis-á-vis the masses lands him in a dilemma he will resolutely not resolve. Having begun to "speak about them," he cannot but employ the categories of his own intellectual formation.

Once he mobilizes these categories and protocols of analysis, he is paralyzed by the insight that these procedures do not apply to "them," and so, for fear of doing epistemic violence to "them," he forecloses his own analysis, thus denying "them" the historical materiality of "representation." His predicament is rather similar to that of Samuel Beckett, who "cannot go on, but must go on." Having disarmed "representation" universally, Foucault denies "them" the perspectivity of their particular form of representation. This universal and unsituated delegitimation of "representation" does away with distinctions between "who" is saying and "what" is being said, and also between forms of representation that are organic and coercive—in other words, insider/outsider differentiations are entirely dismantled. Since "representation as such" is a "speaking for," and since "speaking for" is an act of violence, all representations are inauthentic and/or culpable. At a rarefied structural level, a feminist speaking on behalf of women, the African National Congress representing black South Africans, and Foucault speaking on behalf of the masses are all one and the same, notwithstanding the historical and macrological density of each of these situations within its own "organic space." To put it perhaps a little too harshly, European intellectuals, having lost their sense of "organicity," ordain that "organicity as such" is dead. The reason for this slippage, as Spivak demonstrates, is that "two senses of representation are being run together: representation as 'speaking for,' as in politics, and representation as 're-presentation,' as in art or philosophy."[21]

Unfortunately, from my point of view, Foucault's not going far enough has the following results. He will not allow his agenda to be interrogated, transformed, and recontextualized by the agenda of the "masses." I will argue that such a macropolitical change is indeed possible, that it is possible for Foucault to be one of "them," provided he makes room for a certain kind of "self-consciencization" in the context of the emerging subaltern realities. It is possible for the specific intellectual of a certain formation to declare solidarity with a revolutionary politics, but on the condition that this intellectual allow himself to be represented and reparsed within the syntax of the emerging subaltern politics. I am not suggesting that the revolutionary politics of the oppressed does away with the extreme differences in subject positions, but rather that self-reflexivity concerning one's own subject position does not have to deny the possibility that different subject positions negotiate with one another in the name of a certain globalness. But any declaration of solidarity becomes impossible to Foucauldian epistemology, for, with its insistence on "difference," this epistemology completely undermines the collectivist assumptions that underlie the notion of solidarity. To Foucault (after the gulags, after Stalinism, etc.), collectivity connotes organization, and organization connotes totalization, and totalization spells tyranny and oppression. Hence, the reference to the masses remains undifferentiated. There is the individual and there are the masses, and there is the additional understanding that each individual is a "groupuscule" that cannot be represented. So to what or whom can solidarity be declared? Unless of course it be to "difference." But what would a solidarity in "difference" mean except a contradiction?

For lack of a clear theory of ideology (whether it be that of class, gender, sexuality, nationality, or a heterogeneously crosshatched interpellation), "the freeing of difference" is at best redolent of an idealist thinking devoted to the bohemianization of all that is singular and exceptional and a near-solipsistic aestheticization of the political. The presiding principle of a difference that "requires thought without contradiction, without dialectics, without negation," a difference that expresses itself through the "thought of the multiple—of nomadic and dispersed multiplicity that is not limited or confined by constraints—of similarity,"[22] is the ideology of a privatized self in search of rarer and rarer thresholds of uniqueness in transgression of social limits and commonalities. Such an insurrection of difference is in many ways a throwback to the Sartre of *Being and Nothingness* and to the artist in Camus, in *Exile and the Kingdom*, in search of the solit/d/ary. The quarrel with the individual and the unified self eventuates not in a more complex understanding of the dialectically mediated relationship between individuality and collectivity but rather in the apotheosis of multiplicities or "groupuscules" that are *intraindividual*. The shattering of the unity of the individual Self takes the form of an *implosion*, that is, a fallout "within." It is still a world where "liberation" is a banner that the "individual as multiple"waves against society.

I am well aware that Foucauldian enthusiasts might find me guilty of locating Foucault in an altogether erroneous context, and thereby of misreading him. The historical and historiographic question concerning Foucault's location could be stated quite simply: does Foucault still operate within the Marxist *durée*, or is his thought post-Marxist? Foucault himself never, except in passing and in polemical asides, deals with this question seriously. But even these minimal confrontations tell us something. So, let us hear Foucault on Marxism.

As the advocate of difference and the singular "meaning-event,"[23] Foucault cannot (and rightly so) allow any one model of opposition officially to install itself as *the Set* of all oppositional subsets and thus naturalize its right to vanguardism. As a result, his approval of proletarian and class-specific politics has at best been provisional. The reality of each individual and local resistance, in Foucault's view, is in danger of being betrayed by the univocity of the proletarian revolution. His apprehension is that "as soon as we struggle against exploitation, the proletariat not only leads the struggle but also defines its targets, its methods, and the places and instruments for confrontation; and to ally oneself with the proletariat is to accept its positions, ideology, and its motives for combat."[24] He argues against such a total identification and suggests instead that "if the fight were directed against power, then all those on whom power is exercised to their detriment, all who find it intolerable, can begin the struggle on their own terrain and on the basis of their proper activity (or passivity)."[25] This is vintage Foucault. It is difficult to argue with Foucault here, for in our own times the danger of one oppositional perspective becoming *the* perspective is all too real. Given the multiple determinations of gender, class, race, sexuality, nationality, and so forth, Foucault is absolutely right to warn us against monolithic, monological, and monothetic opposition. Each group has to enter the revolutionary process in its "ownmost" way. We must also remind ourselves that Foucault does acknowledge that "these movements are linked to the revolutionary movement of the proletariat to the extent that they fight against the controls and constraints which serve the same system of power." His interest in "the fight directed against power" leads him, understandably and significantly, to the problem of understanding *power in general*—its omnihistorical ontology and its omnipresent microphysics. Foucault asks, "Isn't this difficulty of finding adequate forms of struggle a result of the fact that we continue to ignore the problem of power?"[26] He then goes on to speculate that "it may be that Marx and Freud cannot satisfy our desire for understanding this enigmatic thing which we call power, which is at once visible and invisible, present and hidden, ubiquitous."[27]

Equally important is Foucault's critique of Marxian scientificity. Having declared that the theoretical and methodological task is to effect "the union of erudite knowledges and local memories which allows us to establish a historical knowledge of struggles and to make use of this knowledge tactically today," Foucault asks "what types of knowledge" might be disqualified when something becomes a science. He is fearful that in the name of science a number of speaking, discoursing subjects will get discounted. Arguing against a certain kind of theoretical professionalism, Foucault accuses the theoretical avant-garde of isolating itself "from all the discontinuous forms of knowledge that circulate about it." But even here, we must take heed that as he takes theoretical avant-gardism to task, he does so in the name of popular knowledges that are *discontinuous*. In Foucault's scheme of things, "discontinuity" is the empowering principle, that is, the articulation and empowerment of discontinuity *qua* discontinuity.

A number of interesting and contradictory themes are at play here. First, there is the critique of Marxist universality and the attempt to empower each resistance in "its difference." There is then the interest in "power" as something both transitive and intransitive—power in determinate forms that are subservient to particular ideologies, and *P*ower as an "in-itself" that is transcendent of particular instantiations of itself. Finally, there is the investigation into knowledge as practice, tactic, and intervention. In each of these inquiries there is a persistent tension between the "historical" and the "utopian." The historical need to unpack and pluralize a monolithic Marxism correctly and crucially identifies the heterogeneity of subject positions; but, having done so, rather than attempt to articulate these multiple positions within a relational field, Foucault's rhetoric leaps away into the realm of pure difference. Analogously, having identified the realities and affects of both power (lowercase) and Power (capitalized), Foucault's thought is attracted more toward the transideological and transhistorical phenomenology of Power. Finally, and in a similar manner, having empowered local knowledges against theoretical professional theory, Foucault's agenda privileges the local and discontinuous knowledges *as discontinuity*, rather than pressure these knowledges to form new and different alliances among themselves. In every instance, the utopianist impulse to deterritorialize turns into a ceaseless anarchism for lack of mediation with determinate history. Foucault's project turns out to be very different from Jackson's "common ground" coalition or Laclau and Mouffe's "hegemonically articulatory practices."[28] Laclau and Mouffe are as much aware and solicitous of differences and discontinuities as Foucault, but their plan of action, from within Marxism, is radically different. Their interpretation of the situation is that "the problem of Marxism has been to *think these discontinuities* and, at the same time, to find *forms reconstituting* the unity of scattered and heterogeneous elements."[29] Their concern is with "the relational moment" (among the elements) "whose importance increases to the extent that its nature becomes less evident."[30]

As I move toward my discussion of Gramsci, I would like, by way of Barry Smart, to reask the question concerning Foucault's post-Marxian politics. For clearly there are a number of similarities between Foucault's notions of intellectuality and Gramsci's, and yet the terrains on which they operate are vitally different. Of course there is also the more specific question of whether or not a number of Gramscian elaborations anticipate a number of Foucauldian practices. Here too there is the question of the "before" and the "after." Furthermore, there is a certain amount of undecidability about the status of the "after": does the "post-" do away with the regime of the "before," or does it unpack the "before" within its own macrology?

Focusing on the categories of "the intellectual" and "hegemony,'' Barry Smart claims that a case can be made for reading Foucault's work "as providing a radically different approach and a new set of concepts through which to develop analysis and understanding of the exercise of power and the associated effects of hegemony in modern societies.''[31] Foucault is also said to have critically stepped away from the Gramscian and Marxist problematic of ideology so as to discover how "truth" and "power" constitute hegemony. Eschewing global analysis, Foucault's genealogical approach "is directed towards the multiple processes through which events are constituted, in particular to the study of technologies of power, their strategic deployment, and effect(s) respectively.'' Smart also advances the thesis that "Foucault's work can be considered to provide a reconceptualization of the problem of hegemony, shifting it away from the essentially humanist philosophy of action to be found in Gramsci's work to an examination of the production, transformation, and effects of the true/false distinction which has been at the centre of processes of government in modern Western societies.''[32] Lastly (to limit my agenda to just a few of the interesting intersections between Foucault's and Gramsci's theories), there is the Foucauldian "specific intellectual" (in opposition to the universal intellectual), who works "within specific sectors at the precise points where [the specific intellectual's] own conditions of life or work situate" him or her. The specific intellectual is intended in demystification of the universal intellectual just as the Gramscian organic intellectual exposes the ideological underpinnings of the traditional intellectual. But there the similarity ends, for the agencies of the two intellectuals have very different orientations.

The putative post-Marxist articulations are, first, an attempt to account for hegemony not in terms of "interest" or "ideology," but in terms of the truth-power network; second, a move away from discourses of interiority and temporality to those of spatiality and externality whereby technologies and bodies constitute themselves as meanings rather than be in a symptomatic relationship to "meaning"; third, the emphasis on processes that postpone or render untenable the very notion of "intentional meaning" and the consequent denaturalization of "human agency" (whatever the ontological nature of the "human"); and fourth, the casting of the intellectual in a thin or micrological matrix whereby he or she is (a) neither a representative nor a revolutionary consciousness and (b) is merely a nodal point within an elaborately specialized system that cannot be available to any consciousness in its plenitude—furthermore, the specificity of each node commits it to purely local imaginings and operations. Which is to say, there is no Subject, nor are there subjects—only operations, practices, and deployments. If these practices of truth power are constitutive (i.e., are not merely epiphenomenal) of human subjectivity, how is this subjectivity to seek control over and direct these processes? How is "history" to be thought of except in technological forms? As we discuss the question of whether these problems are post-Marxist or not, let us turn to Antonio Gramsci and see to what extent his political theory of praxis is aware of these issues as autonomous issues. Perhaps, in his context, these are not all that autonomous after all.

II

From Foucault to Gramsci is both a predictable and a farfetched connection. The themes and the anxieties that concern the two are very similar, and yet their intellectual formations are very different. They did not live and theorize in the same world: Gramsci precedes Foucault, and unlike the latter, works on Marxist terrain even as he fundamentally transforms it. Between Gramsci's Italy and Foucault's France, a number of crucial and decisive events, both regional and global, have taken place. The meanings of terms such as "Marxism," "international communism," "nationalism," "internationalism," and "class" have undergone great changes. And finally, if Gramsci seems to represent a historical conjuncture that is hopefully expectant of the triumph of international communism, Foucault represents a moment that has been disillusioned of the very dreams that animated Gramsci's world. One could even say that poststructuralist pessimism is the expression of what was unconsciously inherent in Marxist thought: its potential to failure. In spite of all these differences, some questions seem to have survived from Gramsci to Foucault.

I begin with Gramsci's essay "What Is Man?", with the intention of opening up a significant area of disagreement between Foucault and Gramsci. In this essay, Gramsci contends passionately that "it is essential to conceive of man as a series of active relationships (a process) in which individuality, while of the greatest importance, is not the sole element to be considered." According to Gramsci, "The individual does not enter into relations with other men in opposition to them but through an organic unity with them, because he becomes part of social organisms of all kinds from the simplest to the most complex."[33] These relationships that man enters into "are not mechanical"but "active and conscious," so much so indeed that man changes or modifies himself "to the same extent that he changes and modifies the whole complex of relationships of which he is the nexus." Gramsci concludes resoundingly that "if individuality is the whole mass of these relationships, the acquiring of a personality means the acquiring of consciousness of these relationships, and changing the personality means changing the whole mass of these relationships."[34]

It must be quite clear by now how different Gramsci's enterprise is from Foucault's. First of all, well before the agency of the intellectual comes under discussion, Gramsci's critical anthropology takes on an even more fundamental obsession of Western thought: the binary opposition between individuality and collectivity. The intellectual/masses opposition is but the exacerbation of a more basic binary antagonism: group versus individual. Given this basic valorization in Western thought of "individuality," the figure of the intellectual is also drawn up in the image of the preeminent individual who will resist homogenization (by the masses) and thus be in control of "quality" (as against quantity and numbers) in cultural intellectual life. Even Foucault, who is brilliant in his deconstruction of the "identical and self-same subject," remains trapped within the ideology of Western individualism: hence his valorization of "difference" as discrete and singular. Foucault's destabilization of the univocal subject remains philosophical; that is, it does not become political. More generally, a philosophically subversive move does not automatically and simultaneously translate into a politically subversive strategy simply because, given the relative autonomy of the philosophical and the political, the two realms are often (even within the *episteme*) out of sync with each other. The way out of this contradiction (a way Foucault does not take) is to make philosophical thought accountable to political practice. And this is what Gramsci does ceaselessly: the "superstructural" shoring up of individuality is perennially dialogized within a constitutive organicity.

To unpack Gramsci's position further, the individual is seen as a function of the collective that in itself is perceived as the expression of a mobile and ever-changing system of relationships. Nowhere in Gramsci's thought is "collectivity" imposed as an apriorism; the collective dimension itself is historically produced in response to changing situations and crises. In arguing for a "change in the conception of man," Gramsci historicizes "man" through and through by declaring the "human" to be a process. Is Gramsci guilty of "humanism" here just because he privileges the term "man"? Has not poststructuralist and structuralist thought thoroughly and radically denaturalized and desubjectified the "human," and has not Foucault's discourse on archaeology banned forever not merely forms of essentialism but also notions of unilateral human agency? Yes, all this is certainly true, but what seems even truer is that Gramsci is well aware of these so-called post-Marxist wrinkles. I would even claim that not only is Gramsci not a humanist, but that he is well ahead of his time, a structuralist thinker who anticipates Althusserian Marxism. But there is a difference. Even as Gramsci *commits* (a term I use very deliberately in thematic opposition to that Nietzschean-Foucauldian word, "sacrifice": I have in mind the thesis of the "sacrifice of the subject" to the processes of knowledge) "man" to a field of relationships (and to what after Hayden White we might call the "history of forms," and the "forms of historical contents"), he insists that these relationships are not "mechanical." In other words, to Gramsci the issue of agency is a valid and live one. There might not be "agency" except in terms of these relationships that are "external and exterior" to "agency," but this does not result in the complete collapse or immanentization of agency. Gramsci keeps this question alive: how, why, and *in the name of what* do these relationships change? In denying the purely mechanical model, Gramsci revives the issue of historical human intentionality, and its corollary, the issue of the instrumentality of "process." On the one hand, process may be considered "subjectless," but this long view of process has to be dialectically instantiated in and through specific histories of affirmation and consolidation. In other words, the road to utopia is not a fortuitous or aleatory path, but rather a determinate path with determinate signposts that can tell us whether we are really on our way to utopia or merely on a trip to an eternally anarchist "anomie." (As a matter of fact, in the works of such post-Marxists as Baudrillard and his many postmodern and postpolitical and postsocial epigones, not only we find that "anomie" is accepted on the basis of its immanence, but we also realize that we are not going anywhere at all: we are already "there.") Hence, the insistence in Gramsci on the interplay between "man as structure" and "man as intentionality." It is of paramount importance to Gramsci that even as these relationships historicize the "human," they continue to "be" and bear the signature of the "human." Gramsci would have no difficulty with a systemic or Foucauldian interpretation of the "nodal" situatedness of the "human," but he would go on to say that the human being, by entering the relationships, constitutes a nexus agentially and intentionally. The "constituted" nature of "man as node" does not preempt the possibility of man functioning as an agent in relatively and historically constituted freedom. The "relationships" are a means to an end; they are not the end in themselves. It is no wonder then that the emphasis in Gramsci's discourse is on "change." Change is to be produce through a critical consciousness and a critical knowledge of these relationships. There is a relationship of transitivity between the "relationships" and the "human" whereby when the complex of relationships is modified, man is modified too. The point to make here is that "man" is not passively identical or synonymous with the complex of relationships, for Gramsci is not interested in generating a tautologous identity that is timelessly true and therefore invulnerable to historical criteria. To Gramsci, "man" *is* what man *does*, and what man *does* is the active realization of changing complexes of relationships. The "is" and the "does" are not transfixed within a mutural identity; they indicate a relational non-coincidence that is essential to the intentional production of the future from and by the present based on its knowledge of itself and its past.

Superficially, it would seem that Gramsci's conception of individuality as "the whole mass of these relationships" is a forerunner of the individual as "groupuscule" (in Foucault and Deleuze), but a closer analysis reveals irreconcilable differences. In Gramsci's context, there is always an emphasis on "relationships," relationships that can be thematized, understood, problematized, and modified. To be located within a relationship does not mean the same thing as being condemned to that complex of relationships in a spirit of passive acceptance. Through a synthetic consciousness of these relations, knowledge can be produced as change and as a theory of change. Unlike in the Foucauldian scenario, (1) questions concerning totality and organicity can be raised from the specificity of one's position because one's position is always already both *specific* and *specific relationally* to the whole complex of relationships; and (2) the internally dialogized and heterogeneous individuality is mediated by the heterogeneity of the entire field. There is therefore no need to protect the "individual as groupuscule" from the so-called violence of a collective representation. Gramsci's questions have to do with generating a programmatic agenda from change based on theoretical knowledge. How to organize, persuade, and represent were concerns that were always uppermost in Gramsci's theory. And it is in response to these concerns that Gramsci raises the question of the "organic intellectual" and his or her capacity to elaborate "hegemony."

In elaborating his notion of the "organic intellectual," Gramsci "established a particular framework," explains Anne Showstack Sassoon, "for the discussion of the intellectuals in order to highlight the mystification of their role by such thinkers as Croce, who, he [Gramsci] argued, contained a tradition going back to Plato and culminating in Hegel."[35] "Every social group, coming into existence on the original terrain of an essential function," writes Gramsci, "creates together with itself, organically, one or more strata of intellectuals which give it homogeneity and an awareness of its own function not only in the economic but also in the social and political fields."[36] As Sassoon observes, Gramsci's concept of the intellectual fulfills a number of tasks. It critiques the idealist view that intellectuals "exist above and outside the relations of production." It determines intellectual activity as "a very real but also a very mediated relationship," while it is also "aimed against the lack of comprehension in the socialist movement, based on an economistic interpretation of reality, of the social and political role of intellectuals."[37] Sassoon concludes convincingly that on the one hand "Gramsci attempts to demystify intellectual activity *per se* and on the other he assigns it a specific place and importance within the complex of social relations, thus arguing both against an idealist tradition and an economistic one." Gramsci's theory of the intellectual is coextensive with his theory of mediations, and since there are multiple mediations within any given society, there are multiple modes of intellectual activity, each of which is mediated in its very organicity. In Gramsci's theory, mediations enhance unpack, and elaborate organicity into a multidimensional reality, whereas to Foucault, "mediations" as "specificities" are not "mediations of" an organic and inclusive reality. In Gramsci's world picture, the relationship between intellectuals and the world of production is " 'mediated' by the whole fabric of society and by the complex of superstructures, of which the intellectuals are, precisely, the 'functionaries.' "

The telling insight in the last passage is that intellectuals are "functionaries" *of the whole complex and the social fabric.* In other words, they are not "intransitive" Kafkaesque functionaries cut off from their representative and, if you will, synecdochic relationship to the totality. Of course, we must acknowledge, against Gramsci's theoretical lucidity, that in our own times the autonomous logic as well as material circumstantiality of mediations (as technologies, apparatus, practices, local applications, bureaucratic and governmental protocols, institutional and disciplinary codes, etc.) has become so dauntingly autonomous that we are tempted to conclude that this realm signifies nothing but itself. We experience great difficulty in moving from these formal significations to that "ideological reality" *of which* they are the significations. We are tempted, in our enervation, to call the search off and be contented with *mediations as such* that are no longer *mediations of*, and with a "simulacral" reality that frustrates and mocks our every attempt to achieve what Edward Said (after Gramsci) calls "worldliness." But here again, as Said has memorably and persistently contended, the fact that we as intellectuals are having great difficulty deciphering our "worldliness" does not mean that we are "not had" by the world. Whether intellectuals are aware of it or not, they are functionaries of an inclusive macropolitical logic, whether it be that of the state or capital or nationality or whatever. Said's complaint is not that people in contemporary Western societies do not have a politics, but that these very people seem not to know what it is to be political *as intellectuals*. Meritocracies, professional tags, membership in esoteric discourses and practices, and in general, various forms of professional specialization deracinate the intellectual from a total and "primitive" sense of constituency.

It is within this sense of organic constituency that Gramsci asserts that although "all men are intellectuals, all men do not have the function of intellectuals in society." For, to Gramsci, "the 'organic' intellectuals which every new class creates alongside itself and elaborates in the course of its development, are for the most part 'specialisations' of partial aspects of the primitive activity of the new social type which the new class has brought into prominence." As Sassoon points out, "Organic intellectuals are specialists who fulfill technical, directive, organisational needs." The specialist and superstructural autonomy of the intellectual is always relative to a "primary" organicity, and *ergo* its commitment to organizational tasks is valorized, not in the name of the specialist activity, but in the name of a primary organicity. It is interesting to note that Gramsci's "new intellectual," from the point of view of poststructuralist thought, is guilty of avant-gardism, but this avant-gardism, in Gramsci, is not bereft of a sense of constituency; if anything its forwardness is undertaken in the name of the entire constituency. A representational politics underwrites the whole program. And this is how Gramsci describes the new intellectual, in terms that are purposeful, agential, and organizational.

The mode of being of the new intellectual can no longer consist in eloquence, which is an exterior and momentary power of feelings and passions, but in active participation in practical life, as constructor, organiser, "permanent persuader" and not just a simple orator (but superior at the same time to the abstract mathematical spirit); from technique-as-work one proceeds to technique-as-science and to the humanistic conception of history, without which one remains "specialised" and does not become "directive" (specialised and political).[38]

We can see Gramsci attempting here to effect, through processes and history, a number of transformations, transformations Foucault would seem to take for granted as part of an "always already" revolution. First, there is the move from the mere tropological or rhetorical "exteriority" of "pure eloquence" to the "internalized" solidarity of "persuasion." As persuader, the intellectual cannot afford to be idealist, nor can he or she remain bereft of a sense of constituency. As "persuader," the intellectual is inserted into historical participation whereby his or her eloquence is given terms of purpose. Someone is being persuaded by somebody toward some determinate purpose: the persuader is thus made accountable historically and politically. Second, the activity of persuasion as construction and organization allows for the analytic discreteness of the superstructure and infrastructure while at the same time it binds the two as one historical bloc. Third, the task of persuasion is "permanent," which is to say that it is terminable (as in the achievement of specific historical objectives), but it is also interminable as process (i.e., as the expression of a long revolution). Fourth, the intellectual activity is neither merely visceral and impassioned nor purely abstract and formal but a judicious and successful synthesis of thought and feelings. Fifth, *technique-as-work* and *technique-as-science* are related by a progressive movement; they are not two isolated activities. Gramsci makes room for the autonomization of specialist and professional spheres of activity, but insists that the autonomization has a prior and more inclusive placement within the totality. In doing this, he also moves decisively away from the ironclad determinism of the base/superstructure model. To Gramsci, superstructural activities are a form of praxis that are in effective mediation with the total structure. And finally, in Gramsci's humanism (and we must remember that his humanism has nothing to do with the humanism that has been so ably trashed by thinkers starting from Martin Heidegger up to the contemporary poststructuralists), the category of the "directive" is an inalienable constituent of the "political." What is at stake here, in the difference between Gramsci and Foucault, is the very meaning of the term "political." Gramsci will not entertain a politics without direction: not for him the "politics of abandon or abandonment," or the "politics of the specific" without relation to the general. Not having lost the vision of a total (and not totalized) historical bloc collective, it is still meaningful for Gramsci to take into account the imbalances and inequalities within the same society; hence his didactic and pedagogical anxiety on behalf of the entire constituency. His aim is to cure and rectify these imbalances through the critical-theoretical practice of a dialectical relationship between the masses and "its" intellectuals. As he puts it with characteristic rigor:

> The process of development is bound by an intellectuals-mass dialectic; the stratum of intellectuals develops quantitatively and qualitatively, but every leap towards a new "fullness" and complexity on the part of the intellectuals is tied to an analogous movement of the mass of simple people, who raise themselves to higher levels of culture and at the same time broaden their circle of influence with thrusts forward by more or less important individuals or groups toward the level of specialised intellectuals. But in the process, times continually occur when a separation takes place between the mass and the intellectuals (either certain individuals or a group of them), a loss of contact, and hence the impression [or theory] as a complementary, subordinate "accessory."[39]

First of all, unlike Foucault, Gramsci is interested in telling a story, in producing a developmental narrative. The production of narrative is also the production of unevenness and contradictions, and one such contradiction as the mass/intellectual contradiction. Unlike much poststructuralist thought that shies away from contradiction either in the name of "difference," or an acategorical thought or the singular event or an all-enveloping and undifferentiated heterogeneity, Gramsci's theory takes on contradictions substantively even as it anticipates, in utopian fashion, the disappearance, in and by and through history, of contradiction. (The dissappearance of "contradiction," we know, would signify the end of the "political" itself.) Also, in the preceding passage, the loss of contact between the mass and the intellectuals is perceived as a problem. The seeming separateness of theory is diagnosed and demystified, and not celebrated or merely recorded as an event in its own right. Surely it is obvious from all this that Gramsci does take for granted the "leader-led, the rulers and the ruled" division. But it most be noted that his belief in this division is based on historical reality; it does not mean that he wishes for the perpetuation of this division. He does raise the question whether one wishes "there always to be rulers and ruled, or does one wish to create the conditions where the necessity for the existence of this division disappears?" And yet, he asserts that "it needs to be understood that the division of the rulers and the ruled, though in the last analysis it does go back to divisions between social groups, does in fact exist, *given things as they are, even inside the bosom of each separate group, even a socially homogeneous one* [my italics]."[40] Unlike Foucault and Deleuze, who speak about subaltern reality from *without*, Gramsci voices this reality from within. These are very different forms of representation and their messages are very different too. By conflating the two meanings of *representation* (a criticism made persuasively by Spivak), Foucault and Deleuze romanticize the subaltern and arrive at the conclusion that "theory is practice," whereas Gramsci states that "a human mass does not 'distinguish' itself and does not become independent 'by itself' " without organization by intellectuals. It is extremely significant that post-structuralist admirers of subaltern reality glibly do away with the theory-practice distinction whereas Gramsci, the subaltern practitioner of subaltern reality, asserts that "there is no organisation without intellectuals, that is, without organisers and leaders, *without the theoretical* aspect of the theory-practice nexus distinguishing itself concretely in a stratum of people who 'specialise' in its conceptual and philosophical elaboration."[41] In terms of my polemical interest, the "who" that speaks here is of critical importance.

Our situation now is not post-Gramscian. The problem faced by an entire range of emerging groups is indeed one of organization. Decolonized independent nations are looking for nationally organic leaders and an intelligentsia that is of the people as against the metropolitan intelligentsia that is all too easily drained away into a deracinated international continuum. Within feminism, there are active concerns regarding the political valence of the more academic and university-based elaborations of feminism. Minority intellectuals and minority activists worry constantly about the problem of depoliticization by institutionalization and superstructural validation. A point in question is the relationship of the black intellectual to black schools, black ghettos, black modes of pedagogy, culture, and so on. In the context of the civil rights movement and the battle against racism, questions of leadership, delegation, representation, the creation of broad and democratic bases, the articulation of a common identity characterized by multiple mediations, and so on, were active during the days of Martin Luther King and they are active now as the Rainbow Coalition seeks to politicize itself over increasingly broader and crosshatched constituencies. But all these programmatic and organizational commitments, from Foucault's point of view, would seem erroneous or unwarranted. Who is right, Foucault or Gramsci? This is surely a vulgar and reductive way of posing options, and I am doing so only to drive home the point that on a certain level there is a mutually exclusive relationship here that has to do with the location of each politics: on the one hand, the "outsider" politics of Foucault that in spite of its best intentions of "letting the masses be," ends up in a prescriptive mode telling the masses what they should know, and on the other, the solidarity politics of the insider Gramsci who has no difficulty giving his politics a name from "within."

I have been suggesting all along that what makes Gramsci's politics more real and worldly than Foucault's is that it carries with it a strong sense of hegemonic agency. Now let us look at the concept of hegemony in Gramsci and examine how and in the name of what positivity (economic, social, political, or moral) hegemony is exercised. It would seem that a poststructuralist politics of heterogeneous subject positions (and the poststructuralist deconstructions of a univocal, positive, full, and representable social reality) would escape easy marking by the notion of hegemony. Hegemony as the expression of a collective will and poststructuralism with its emphasis on pure difference would seem to escape mutual influence.

What does Gramsci have to say on hegemony? Here again, typically, he gives us not a definition but the growth of a process. Hegemony has a history and a developmental process. "The first and most primitive moment," in Sassoon's reading, "the economic corporative one, is when members of the same category feel a certain solidarity toward each other but not with other categories of the same class."[42] "A second moment," in Gramsci's words, "is that in which consciousness is reached of the solidarity of interests among all the members of a social class—but still purely in the economic field."[43] The third moment, which Gramsci calls "the most purely political phase," marks the transcendence of the "corporate limits of the purely economic class," and the inauguration of broader, coalitional sympathies that reach out to "the interests of other subordinate groups too." This moment is also the passage from a union "of political and economic aims" to possibilities of "intellectual and moral unity."[44] (It is not coincidental that Jesse Jackson's rhetoric also strongly rings the moral bell even as it does full justice to themes of economic and political enfranchisement.) According to Laclau and Mouffe, it is in the movement from the "political" to the intellectual and moral plane "that the decisive transition takes place toward a concept of hegemony beyond 'class alliances.' "[45] Since I find Laclau and Mouffe particularly convincing on this point, I will quote from them extensively:

> For, whereas political leadership can be grounded upon a conjunctural coincidence of interests in which the participating sectors retain their separate identity, moral and intellectual leadership requires that an ensemble of "ideas" and "values" be shared by a number of sectors—or, to use our own terminology, that certain subject positions traverse a number of class sectors. Intellectual and moral leadership constitutes, according to Gramsci, a higher synthesis, a "collective will," which, through ideology, becomes the organic cement unifying a "historical bloc." All these are new concepts having an effect of displacement with regard to the Leninist perspective: the relational specificity of the hegemonic link is no longer concealed, but on the contrary becomes entirely visible and theorized.[46]

I am aware that there is a problem with this reading: is this a Gramscian reading of Gramsci, or is it a poststructuralist extension or adaptation of Gramsci? For my purposes, this is a convincingly strategic reading; and as for its fidelity to Gramsci, I would say that there is no tendency in his elaboration of alliances that resists this reading. The manner in which Laclau and Mouffe import their terminology of "subject positions" into Gramsci's discourse is highly suggestive. It raises the question of whether or not "class specificity" is adequate to the task of orchestrating and organizing the hegemonic link. If class is not, as Spivak has argued deconstructively, an "inalienable aspect of reality," but a useful and powerful category that cannot escape the contingency of its own historicity, what is its relational position within the hegemonic link? Is it one among many determinants, or is it, as a construct, *primus inter pares*, first among a number of equal determinants, such as gender, race, and sexuality? What is its hierarchical space within the arrangement of the historical bloc? While unpacking hegemony into a differential link, Laclau and Mouffe still hold on to the "collective will" in Gramsci. In other words, the explicit thematization of the relational specificity of the hegemonic link does not, as it does for Foucault, retire the notion of collective will. On the contrary, a politics of collective and relational difference, to Laclau and Mouffe, is predicated on the fact that "hegemony" alludes to "an absent totality." If "hegemony" is an allusion to an absent totality, and if furthermore there is no effective way of arbitrating among the elements that comprise the historical bloc, how will the bloc speak on its own behalf? Are we back to Foucault's apprehension that one element within the bloc will set the pace for all others and for the entire formation?

The concept of the historical bloc works quite complexly in Gramsci and it is important not to simplify it. The bloc is the political expression of what I have called, in the context of the Rainbow Coalition, "difference in identity" and "identity in difference." The bloc functions both as a descriptive category and as a didactic/interventionary/organizational principle. As a descriptive category, it makes sure that our description of the socialpolitical field is adequate to the complexity of the field. It looks for multiple positionings and multiple determinations and multiple alliances rather than for a single unifying principle or essence, say, *class* in the context of orthodox Marxism. As Laclau and Mouffe have demonstrated, "hegemony" and the "historical bloc" have been responses to a crisis, namely, the fracture of the social sphere and the irruption of contingency within the category of "historical necessity."[47] In other words, any description of the world, after the failure of orthodox Marxism, has to thematize, within its own descriptive space, the contingency of its own categories. If we keep in mind that political (and in particular, Marxist) descriptions are not merely descriptions, but also predictive, interpretive statements that set the stage for a certain kind of transformation of society, then it turns out that political descriptions are accountable to history in very specific ways. The Marxian category of class thus predicts a certain kind of narrative and a certain kind of unpacking of world history; and if in reality, this narrative does not work, or is superseded by other forms of narrative (each with its own axiology), then it is time to let this particular narrative be historicized by its own failure and inadequacy. An honest Marxist then will not hold on to "class" as the only key to the essence of the historical process, but will rather look for alliances among other emerging categories such as gender, race, and sexuality. The failure to relativize *class* in light of multiple subject positions and determinations can only result in poor and inaccurate descriptions of the world. In other words, the "identity of the world" and the "identity of our model of the world" will have lost contact with each other.

The "bloc" as a concept is the description of a space and not of a thing or an essence. The bloc can only be made up of heterogeneous elements, but elements that seek common cause. In this sense, the formation of the bloc is the expression of a contradiction: on the one hand it announces the death of classical notions of identity, and on the other, it forges together a strategic identity effect that is the result or function of a constitutive relationality among the elements that comprise the bloc. The hegemonic articulation of the bloc (and here I am paraphrasing Laclau and Mouffe's theory as it covers and goes beyond Gramsci's praxis) is the possibility of a perennially political displacement. The emphasis, I must add, is both on *political* and *displacement*: political, insofar as the question of change and agency has to be posed strongly and programmatically, and displacement, since in "our times," the political in itself is constituted by the shifting nature of subject positions in relation to one another. Given the "built-in-ness" of displacement, the hegemonic bloc is capable of responding to Foucault's valid critique. Yes, it is certainly possible that at any given world-historical conjuncture or its locally inflected conjuncture, a particular constituent of the bloc will play the dominant role or cast the trigger vote. But there is nothing to be alarmed about since (1) the trigger vote will be cast on behalf of the bloc with the consent of the bloc and (2) the structuration of the bloc is not a constant through history: the positions within the bloc will be in a state of constant change. Thus at a certain time, the black vote will be the trigger vote, while at another, this function may be performed by the feminist vote. The superiority of the hegemonic articulation lies in the fact that the dominant constituent (or constituents or even a subrelational alliance within the bloc) is made to be both itself and more (or less) than itself. In being the trigger vote, the dominant element is made to sacrifice some of its specificity (a sacrifice it can afford historically, i.e., relative to a number of "even more minority" elements within the bloc) in the name of a wider and more inclusive commonality. In poststructuralist terms, the "other" is being perennially acknowledged "within" and "without." Extending Gramsci in a Bakhtinian direction, I would say that this constitutive exotopy of the field makes for a practice that is always undertaken in the name of the weakest (the most oppressed) element within the formation.

What Gramsci achieved with the conceptualization of hegemony may be likened to Althusser's formalization of structuralist Marxism. Both theorists returned to Marx and, in the very process of speaking for Marxism, articulated it as radical difference from itself. In developing, with the help of structuralism, a critical reading of *reading as such*, Althusser radicalized the orthodox macrology of Marxism toward relatively autonomous micrological processes without forfeiting the Marxist horizon. Gramsci, in his theory of hegemony, employs class specificity but only to discover that the nature of alliances transcends the category of class.

"Class" is thus both preserved within the Marxist terrain and generalized beyond an exclusively Marxist determination. In a sense it is not all surprising that "class" becomes the basis for the political expression of *identity in difference* and *difference in identity*. For do we not have Marx describing "class" in the following way: "In so far as millions of families live under economic conditions of existence that cut off their mode of life, their interest, and their formation from those of the other classes and place them in inimical confrontation, they form a class," and, insofar as "the identity of their interests fails to produce a feeling of community . . . they do not form a class"?[48] The Gramscian themes of alliance and opposition are both adumbrated here. The emphasis on economic-corporative interests marks class in a certain specific way, but at the same time the motif of finding commonality across forced separation paves the way from economic and political alliances to moral-intellectual alliances. The insistence on transforming separateness into connectedness is both class specific and transcendent of class specificity. The awareness that it is only by creating "common ground" from a seemingly "disparate" scenario that human beings effect their own hegemony is not the sole prerogative of class specificity. It is only by progressively deconstructing itself in the name of whatever has been suppressed within it, that any specific model achieves hegemonic politicization. Thus, paradoxically, the generalization of an insight that is specific to a particular model (in this instance, class) results in the deprivileging of that very model. In other words, how can "class" (and analogously, Marxism) disallow to "gender" and to "sexuality" the sense of political agency that it had discovered for itself? Is "class" the trendsetter, or should "race" or "gender" take that place? These are indeed questions that need to be asked. But it seems to me that the more productive question is: how can we read each history or category in terms of the other? (Merely bemoaning the fact that Marxism has been the most recent global theory seems pointless and counterproductive. For one thing, we cannot change that fact, and second, there is much to be learned from Marxian revolutions—lessons that can be modified and questioned as they "travel" from one context to another.) My anticipation is toward a hegemonic future where "class" will be genderized, "race" discussed in terms of class, and so forth. While this would be taking place within the hegemonic formation, it is to be hoped that the hegemonic ensemble as the articulation of subaltern realities will be achieving a related but discontinuous effect on the "enemy," that is, the dominant formations. I am persuaded that this effect "without" should be one of the progressive *subalternization of the dominant discourses.* Is this a Gramscian vision? Yes and no: yes, insofar as Gramsci is always interested in critically generating a utopian future from present history; and no, insofar as Gramsci's historical need for a certain kind of affirmation and consolidation would not allow him to take on questions of the "post-" in their own right. My critical position is that there is great need to inmix Gramsci with Foucault: to cultivate and elaborate "postpolitical" practices but with reference to the reality of particular histories, and to thematize with increasing complexity the asymmetry of what it means to be global in these "our regional times."

NOTES

1. For a significant discussion of regional and global structures, see Louis Althusser and Etienne Balibar, *Reading Capital*, trans. Ben Brewster (London: New Left Books, 1970).

2. "Jesse Jackson: Stuart Hall Interviews America's Leading Black Politician," *Marxism Today*, March 1986, 6.

3. Ibid., 7.

4. Ibid., 8.

5. Edward W. Said articulates this asymmetry between the colonizer and the colonized in his essay "Intellectuals in the Post-colonial World," *Salmagundi*, 70–71 (Spring-Summer 1986, 44–81).

6. "Jesse Jackson," *Marxism Today*, 8.

7. Ibid., 11.

8. Ibid., 11.

9. See "Interview with Cornel West," in Andrew Ross (ed.), *Universal Abandon? The Politics of Postmodernism* (Minneapolis: University of Minnesota Press, 1988), 268–86.

10. Michel Foucault, "Two Lectures," in *Power/Knowledge: Selected Interviews and Other Writings, 1972–77*, ed. Colin Gordon; trans. Colin Gordon, Leo Marshall, John Mepham, Kate Soper (New York: Pantheon Random House, 1980), 81–82.

11. My use of the term "panoptic" is derived from Foucault's powerful critique of Bentham's Panopticon. I have also been influenced by the inclusively critical manner in which William V. Spanos uses this term to interrogate the "overlooking" capacities of dominant discourses.

98   R. Radhakrishnan

12. Foucault, "Two Lectures," 81.

13. Ibid., 83.

14. Ibid., 85.

15. See "Intellectuals and Power," in Foucault, *Language, Counter-Memory, Practice: Selected Essays and Interviews* (Ithaca, N.Y.: Cornell University Press, 1980), 206.

16. Ibid., 207–8.

17. Edward W. Said, "Foucault and the Imagination of Power," in *Foucault: A Critical Reader*, ed. David Couzens Hoy (Oxford: Blackwell, 1986), 153.

18. Gayatri Chakravorty Spivak, "Can the Subaltern Speak?" in *Marxism and the Interpretation of Culture*, ed. Cary Nelson and Lawrence Grossberg (Urbana: University of Illinois Press, 1988); 272.

19. Ibid., 275.

20. Ibid.

21. Ibid.

22. Foucault, "Theatrum Philosophicum," in *Language, Counter-Memory, Practice*, 185.

23. Ibid., 174–76.

24. Foucault, "Intellectuals and Power," 216.

25. Ibid.

26. Ibid., 212.

27. Ibid., 213.

28. See Ernesto Laclau and Chantal Mouffe, *Hegemony and Socialist Strategy: Towards a Radical Democratic Politics*, p. 105–44.

29. Ibid., 18.

30. Ibid., 19.

31. Barry Smart, "The Politics of Truth and the Problem of Hegemony," in *Foucault: A Critical Reader*, 158–59.

32. Ibid., 164.

33. Antonio Gramsci, "What Is Man?" In *The Modern Prince and Other Writings*, trans. Louis Marks (New York: International Publishers, 1959), 77.

34. Ibid.

35. Anne Showstack Sassoon, *Gramsci's Politics* Minneapolis: University of Minnesota Press, 1988), 135.

36. Antonio Gramsci, "The Formation of Intellectuals," in *The Modern Prince and Other Writings*, 118.

37. Sassoon, *Gramsci's Politics*, 135.

38. Ibid., 122.

39. Antonio Gramsci, "The Study of Philosophy," in *The Modern Prince and Other Writings*, 68.

40. *The Modern Prince*, 143.

41. "The Study of Philosophy," 67.

42. Sassoon, *Gramsci's Politics*, 117.

43. Antonio Gramsci, *Selections from the Prison Notebooks*, trans. Quintin Hoare and Geoffrey Nowell Smith (New York: International Publishers, 1971), 181.

44. Ibid.

45. Laclau and Mouffe, *Hegemony*, 66.
46. Ibid., 66–67.
47. Ibid., 7–8.
48. Karl Marx, *Surveys from Exile*, trans. David Fernbach (New York: Vintage Books, 1974), 239.

Defenders of the Faith and the New Class
Andrew Ross

We alumni and alumnae of the colleges are the only permanent presence that corresponds to the aristocracy in older countries. We have continuous traditions, as they have; our motto, too, is noblesse oblige; and, unlike them, we stand for ideal interests solely, for we have no corporate selfishness and wield no powers of corruption. We ought to have our own class-consciousness. "Les Intellectuels!" What prouder clubname could there be than this one.

William James, addressing the Association of
American Alumnae at Radcliffe College (1907)

What we often find is that the intellectuals, the educated classes, are the most indoctrinated, most ignorant, most stupid part of the population, and there are very good reasons for that. Basically two reasons. First of all, as the literate part of the population, they are subjected to the mass of propaganda. There is a second, more important and more subtle reason. Namely, they are the ideological managers. Therefore, they must internalize the propaganda and believe it. And part of the propaganda they have developed is that they are the natural leaders of the masses.

Noam Chomsky, at the Universidad Centroamericano in
Managua, Nicaragua (1986)

There has long been, and still is, an unlikely consensus among certain voices from the right and the left about the intrinsic evils of new technologies and the monstrous mass cultures to which they give birth. For the right, this demonology takes the form of a brutally mechanical possession of the last cultural outposts of

101

high civilization. For the left, the specter of hypercapitalism is omnipresent, looming up behind the cretinizing, stupor-inducing cultural forms produced by a dying system in the last desperate throes of economic and ideological reorganization. Both strains of thought share a generally pessimistic view of cultural decline hurried on by the forces of technological rationality or determinism. As the reign of cybernetics sets in, and an information society is installed as the latest answer to the crisis of overproduction, there is little sign of that conservative-radical consensus weakening, and, in fact, every indication that it will make for stranger bedfellows yet. It should be clear by now that such a consensus works against the kind of engaged contestation of popular meanings that inspires attempts to go beyond these legacies of contempt. In fact, it is a consensus that alienates those who are most likely to be involved in mounting this kind of contest: intellectuals, whose sense of political persuasion and action is not Platonically discrete and is thus not divorced from the daily contradictions of life in a technologically advanced, consumer culture; and second, public consumers of culture (which must also include the former) who are self-consciously active in their pursuit of popular options, and creative in their uses of them.

Today, as the cult of knowledge and expertise presides over the internationalization of the information revolution, and the universities absorb all forms of intellectual activity, it is equally clear that the mantle of opposition no longer rests upon the shoulders of an autonomous avant-garde: neither the elite metropolitan intellectuals who formed the traditional corpus of public taste makers or opinion makers; nor the romantic neobohemians who shaped the heroic Nietzschean image of the unattached dissenter, committed to the lonely articulation of social truths; nor the organic party cadres whom Lenin modeled after the "professional revolutionary." Social movements on the semiperiphery of the multinational economy have, for some time, been organizing their own efforts to change history, thus rejecting the traditional Leninist role of leading intellectuals.[1] In addition, it has been argued, most cogently by Foucault, that "technical" or "specific" intellectuals, whose purview of political action is linked to specific struggles that demand their specific knowledge and expertise, must increasingly form the basis of decentralized opposition. From the time of the first postwar pressure groups against the development of the hydrogen bomb, it has been scientific intellectuals rather than humanists who have been at the forefront of this professional activism.

But for professional humanists, to whose number I belong, and whose services are more marginal than those of scientists, the stakes are no less crucial. Our specialist influence over the production of ethical knowledge and the education of taste has become an important area of contestation within the academy, the number one site of credentialism and legitimation. As a result of developments in the new "social history," the humanist curriculum is increasingly open to popular histories and popular culture, while expanding its critical attention to cultural forms based on the experience of women, people of color, gays and lesbians. Pragmatic histories of the oppression, survival, and struggle for legitimation of marginal groups have begun to erode the massive cultural power generated by the traditional idealist histories, histories that depict the moral struggles waged by heroic individuals in order to save Western civilization from successive "barbarisms." The decline of that version of traditional humanist "idealism" means, of course, that the student upheavals of the sixties will not happen again, at least not in the same way. For many of the students who participated in the culture of dissent, it was the high idealism of a bourgeois, humanist education—with its preachy disdain for technology, popular culture, and everyday materialism—that directly inspired their resistance to taking up what they saw as largely predetermined roles in the technostructure. The balance of a humanist education has shifted in the wake of, and largely because of, the developments of the sixties, just as the left has gained a foothold in university faculties everywhere. What was once exclusively thought of as the education of taste now draws upon many different schools of ethical action, informed not by "universal" (i.e., Western) humanist values but by the specific agendas of the new social movements against racism, sexism, homophobia, pollution, and militarism. All too often, the achievements of this new specialism have run up against the same reactionary consensus of left and right, each unswervingly loyal to their respective narratives of decline: charges of postsixties fragmentation and academification from unreconstructed voices on the left, and warnings of doom and moral degeneracy from the Cassandras of the right.[2]

As humanists and social scientists, we have also begun to recognize that the often esoteric knowledge we impart is a form of symbolic capital that is readily converted into social capital in the new technocratic power structures. Social differences are everywhere "explained" and justified by differences in education. In a socially unequal world that is classified hierarchically by categories of taste, it is the cultural capital accumulated through an institutional education that legitimizes these categories and systematically invests this pathologically stratified spectrum of taste with an ineluctable power not unlike that conferred by natural religion.[3] What is our most available guarantee of challenging this *system* of cultural power? One of the answers lies in a thoroughgoing classroom critique of taste that draws upon forms of popular and minority-marginal culture in ways that explode the "objective" canons of aesthetic taste rather than simply reinforcing or expanding them by appropriating, as a new colony of legitimate attention, cultural terrain that was hitherto off-limits—an exotic source of fresh texts to be submitted to yet another round of clever formalist "readings." This means challenging the categorical function of canons rather than simply changing the nature of their contents. It involves cutting across the pathological spectrum of socially coded tastes and desires, rather than merely arguing that there is more room on the boat for newly legitimate ones. In short, it requires the kind of intervention that overtly exposes the role that is functionally allotted to taste within the system of the academic production of knowledge, prestige, and privilege.

In addition to the need for such a critique of taste, we must also recognize that technology today offers itself to the student adept in the form of a clean machine; it does not carry the smoky taint of "trade" that once earned the reproachful scorn of bourgeois idealism and which governed the antitechnologist ethos of the humanistic heritage. On the contrary, the new danger presented by a cybernetic culture is that its apprentices see the gleaming

Panglossian promise of technological supremacy as their naturally inherited realm of power. Those who doubt this promise will do so because they may judge their inheritance to be at odds with the conditions of its production, perhaps through their recognition of the conditions of chip-making female labor in Asia. Or they will come to resent the sublimation, into the command-control-intelligence structure of the corporate-military hierarchy, of a power that they consider to be the privileged domain of their own expertise. Or they will recognize how the libertarian vision of shared information survives today alongside the endlessly integrative use of the new technology for monitoring and surveilling the everyday activities and transactions of mass populations—in short, the capacity to turn information into intelligence. Or they will have seen how their bodies are contracted and pledged, as McLuhan put it, in "servomechanistic fidelity" to the new technology. Either way, the new cyberpunk youth countercultures of the nineties are already being constructed out of the *folklore of technology* and not, as was the case in the sixties, out of the *technology of folklore*. Not out of Orientalist fantasies and agrarianist nostalgia, or from the faded wardrobes of preindustrial laborers, gypsies, or peasants, but rather, out of the postpunk landscapes of the new science fiction, the vestigial romances of the hacker ethic, and the fluid, makeshift vitality of fanzine culture and electronic bulletin boards.[4] From the technofunk street rhythms generated by the master DJs of scratching, mixing, and matching, to the neurochemical sublime of body-machine interfaces, the new appropriation cultures everywhere feed off the "leaky" hegemony of information technology—a technology that must always seek out ways of simulating prestige for its owners because, in its component architecture, it does not recognize the concept of unique ownership of "electronic property."

Today a code of intellectual activism that is not grounded in the vernacular of information technology and the discourses and images of popular culture will have as much leverage over the new nomination of modern social movements as the spells of medieval witches or consultations of the *I Ching*. The risk of any direct rapprochement with technology and popular culture, of course, is that intellectuals will stop worrying and learn to love whatever IBM and CBS throw at them—a scenario that has already been staged in the debate about postmodernism, and which conventionally goes under the description of "throwing the baby out with the bathwater."[5] But moments of change and reinvestment of cultural energy, especially those ushered in by new cultural technologies, are never just moments of replication, reproduction, and further domination. They are also moments of reformation, when opportunities exist to weaken hegemony and to contest, reconstruct, and redefine existing terms and relations of power as part of the task of modernizing cultural resistance.[6] To enter into that process demands a working familiarity with what Donna Haraway, in her "Manifesto for Cyborgs," refers to as "the informatics of domination" that is now in place everywhere: the home, the workplace, the market, the public media, and the body.[7] Among other things, cyborg politics denies us the assurance of a tidy division between the utopian, unalienated organic body and the oppressively rationalizing regime of technology. Rather, it is a contest for that new impure space that is neither organic nor mechanical, neither manual nor mental. So too, the growth of a "smart" information culture necessitates a politics of knowledge in which the contest is often to know who or what is being outsmarted, why, for what reasons, and by whom. As always, popular culture is the source for most people of the "common sense" that ideologically absorbs and demystifies the specialist discourses that saturate these new technologies of knowledge. Intellectuals who see their task as encouraging and developing that side of "common sense" that harbors structures of disrespect and resistance to privilege and authority are faced today with a new set of contradictions—in encouraging resistance to the privileges of "smartness," they find themselves lined up against the order of cultural capital that is the basis of their own authority as contestants in the social world. This is where the historical confinement to the (left) political margins of the fraught relationship between intellectuals and popular culture now moves onto center stage, in a social order increasingly answerable to the authority of knowledge and increasingly administered by knowledge castes.

Autonomy in Question

In order more fully to represent the grounds of intellectual activism today, it is necessary to look briefly at some of the history of the various intellectuals' traditions in the West. Due to lack of space, what follows is a condensed outline of that history, focused on an often crude characterization of the ideologies that have sustained that history.

By the sixties, U.S. Cold War liberals who had cut their political teeth in the thirties were being charged with accommodationism in their role as legitimists for the anticommunist posture of the National Security state. How could this legitimist role be reconciled with the "intellectuals' tradition" of an independent elite engaged in the disinterested pursuit of social truths? In a discussion of his famous notion of an "adversary culture," in the preface to *Beyond Culture* (1965), Lionel Trilling points to some of the contradictions that had arisen out of this historical mutation. Responding to a reviewer's criticisms of the "we" that he frequently employed as his essayistic personality, Trilling claimed that this "we" did not refer exclusively to the New York intellectuals, as had been suggested in the review, nor should it be taken to simply represent "the temper of the age." For the most part, it reflected the taste and assumptions of a "populous group whose members take for granted the idea of an adversary culture" that stands "beyond" and "against" the cultural conditioning of the larger society. If this *transcendent* position seems to be part and parcel of the tradition of intellectual autonomy in the West, Trilling nonetheless suggests that his "populous group," conceived in sheer numerical terms, may now have a social structure that is different from the traditionally powerful-because-powerless intellectual elites. So populous is this group, he claims, that it is a "class" with its own "internal contradictions." Although he does not use the term, Trilling is nonetheless referring to what neoconservatives, at that time, were beginning to label as the "New Class," rising up in the new university-based knowledge society. From his own point of view, as a humanist intellectual committed to the critical ideal of "autonomy of perception and judgement," the contradictions arise out of the way in which this new class raised itself upon the ideal of autonomy, and yet now, as a class *qua* class, has developed common and "characteristic habitual responses." It even seeks to aggrandize itself by perpetuating these shared, characteristic responses and interests, thus putting in question the relation of its individual members to the important role played by the ideal of autonomy "in the history of its ideology."[8]

While the studiously cautious Trilling was less willing to address these contradictions head-on, it is important, at least, that he names the game here, in acknowledging the problems of massification facing the "adversary culture" in the mid-sixties. In fact, the internal contradictions of Trilling's "new class" can be seen as the result or *confluence* of at least three different theories or traditions of thinking about intellectuals—what I shall refer to, in turn, as the doctrine of defenders of the faith, the doctrine of the responsibility of intellectuals, and the theory of the new class itself. To initiate discussion of these theories, we might ask three questions of Trilling's position. First; if the criteria for establishing "autonomy of perception and judgement" are not socially determined, then to what higher authority do they appeal? Second; is an adversary culture incompatible with the idea of a "populous" or nonvanguardist constituency? Third; is a class that raises itself on the ideal of autonomy not also an imaginary class that lifts itself (the Münchhausen effect) by pulling on its own hair?

Defenders of the Faith

The first question, about autonomy from socially determined criteria, relates to what I will call the doctrine of "defenders of the faith." Edward Shils, Talcott Parsons, and Regis Debray have all described, albeit with different aims and emphases, how the social functions of the medieval clerisy are still vestigially present in the modern idea of the intellectual.[9] As a relatively unattached, classless stratum (to cite Karl Mannheim's enduring but ever contested definition), confined to the "pure," as distinct from the "applied," branches of the humanist and technical intelligentsia, the quasi-religious function of defenders of the faith is to eschew all partisan involvement in the name of a devotional commitment to higher principles—God, Art, Science, and other "institutions of truth." If their work and thought happens to have concrete political effects, this is because it is genuinely prophetic, and not because it bends under pragmatic pressure from a secular, institutional patron. This is not to say that intellectuals ought never to voice political sentiments or opinions, but that they should only do so in their capacity as citizens and not as ex officio intellectuals. Breaching this contract with the sacred results in what Julien Benda famously called the *trahison des clercs*, a treason that was higher, of course, and thus more serious than treason committed toward a country or a lay power. But Benda's largely negative definition of the disinterested pursuit of the ideal ("my kingdom is not of this world") constitutes the weak argument for the defense of the faith. The strong argument emerges at moments when intellectual speech is compromised in the face of outright repression—Zhdanovism, McCarthyism, Maoism. The doctrine begins to blur at the edges when it is invoked in debates about quasi-institutional issues like academic freedom, where the mythology of intellectual freedom is clearly influenced by the more worldly codes of professional *esprit de corps*.

In general, those who subscribe to this doctrine accept that the intellectual is not a "universal intellectual" in the sense in which he or she acts as the conscience/consciousness of society as a whole, but rather that the existence of the intellectual is universal, in other words, that every society has and, presumably, must have intellectuals, whether they are perceived as acting in an oracular, priestly capacity, or, as Rolf Dahrendorf suggests, as "fools," or court jesters, who are allowed to speak the truth in a "society of submissive courtiers."[10] Gramsci's description of "traditional intellectuals," whose onetime organic ties to a rising class have long since been severed, is a category that includes most of those who are in a position to present themselves as defenders of the faith.

The claim of loyalty to a higher, objective code of truth is, of course, the oldest and most expedient disguise for serving the interests of the powerful.

The Responsibility of Intellectuals

Trilling's notion of an "adversary culture" derives from the doctrine of the "responsibility of intellectuals," which, in many ways, is a historically and politically specific version of the defense of the faith. At a particular point in history, "free" intellectuals began to recognize themselves as a self-conscious collectivity —the intelligentsia—cognizant of their influence upon political opinion and events. The emergence of this group as an oppositional elite of necessary dissenters, most notably in the nineteenth-century Russian intelligentsia (and, more important for the West, in the *Manifeste des intellectuels* issued by the Dreyfusards), underlies the assumption that an intellectual will necessarily be oppositional or left-wing, an article of faith later consecrated in Sartre's theory of the artist as *engagé*.

The perceived "responsibility" of the Russian intelligentsia would soon be institutionalized in the form of an avant-garde revolutionary consciousness. Lenin's *What Is to Be Done?* initiated what was to be the doctrine of the vanguardist Party elite in calling for intellectuals to become "professional revolutionaries" and systematically to train themselves for the task of fusing theory and consciousness with the spontaneous labor movement. Much earlier, anarchists like Bakunin had been issuing dire warnings about the consequences of institutionalizing the intelligentsia into a new ruling class; it would produce "the most aristocratic, despotic, arrogant and elitist of all regimes." For when a class rules in the name of knowledge and intelligence, the uneducated majority, he thought, would suffer more oppression than ever before, a prognosis repeated and fleshed out by the experience of the Yugoslav dissident Milovan Djilas in his influential *The New Class* (1957). By the thirties, Soviet scientists and engineers had long since displaced the humanistic intelligentsia as the vanguard of postrevolutionary development, and so we find Gorky berating his fellow writers for not experiencing the new technological advances first-hand, and for not writing about "the thousands of workers engaged in the construction of the Volga-Moscow Canal."[11] Forty years later, in line with Alex Nove's contention that today's "working intellectuals" of the Soviet state bear as little resemblance to the Stalinist apparatchik as that historical specimen did to his revolutionary predecessor, Noam Chomsky was to find little difference at all between the centralized Soviet state bureaucracy and the ruling technostructure of U.S. society, exercising its power through universities, government, research foundations, management, and big law firms.[12]

It was the idea, however, of a *noninstitutionalized* avant-garde that shaped the Western and particularly the American history of thinking about the "responsibility of intellectuals." The four most significant moments of this U.S. history that I shall consider briefly are the progressivism of the prewar and postwar years, the radicalism of the thirties, Cold War liberalism, and the New Left of the sixties.

The assault, in the years before the Great War, on the genteel tradition of the Boston Brahmins saw the formation of a progressivist intelligentsia—Herbert Croly, Van Wyck Brooks, Randolph Bourne, Lewis Mumford, Waldo Frank—around journals like *The New Republic*, *The Seven Arts*, and *The Masses*. Pledged to protest the bigness of monopoly capitalism, and to resist the logic of industrialization, their independently responsible brand of cultural criticism was based upon an organic, preindustrial ethic, and, with the exception of Bourne's interest in socialism and internationalism, their sense of a "usable past" looked to hopes of a revival of cultural nationalism that would unite the divided sensibility of "highbrow" and "lowbrow," Brooks's terms for "culture" and "trade." Bourne, in particular, lambasted the pragmatism of liberals who had eschewed their responsibility as independent intellectuals by "directing" public support for the war effort: "[They] have learned all too literally the instrumental attitude towards life, and . . . are making themselves efficient instruments of the war technique."[13]

By the thirties, the tradition of "intellectuals' responsibility" was sufficiently established for its core element—the desire actively to promote historical change—to have been supplemented by a sense of duty to respond to the cause of an adversarial politics. The appeal of organized socialist initiatives across a wide spectrum of U.S. intellectual life should never be understated. An early high point of the cause was the open letter endorsed by fifty-two intellectuals, some Communists, some Socialists, and most independents, which announced their intention to vote for the Communist candidates, Foster and Ford, in the 1932 election. A robustly written pamphlet entitled "Culture and the Crisis" was addressed to all writers, artists, intellectuals, and professionals who believed that the political system was "hopelessly corrupt," and was cosigned, among many others, by Sherwood Anderson, Erskine Caldwell, Malcolm Cowley, Lewis Corey, Waldo Frank, Granville Hicks, Sidney Hook, Langston Hughes, Matthew Josephson, John Dos Passos, James Rorty, Lincoln Steffens, and Edmund Wilson. Antifascism, from 1933, was a decisive recruiting factor for intellectuals born again as literary shock troops or as cultural technicians for the Party. For many key intellectuals, however, the moment of solidarity with the Communists lasted no more than a matter of months, and had fallen away long before the nationally organized League of American Writers replaced the local John Reed Clubs in 1935, and the Writers' Congresses convened in 1935 and 1937. While the Popular Front organizations won widespread middle-class support, and attracted active membership among writers and media and culture industry professionals in the later thirties and throughout the war years, the more glorified trajectory of cultural critics was one of apostasy, or involvement with the various Trotskyist opposition groups and parties, and thus of critical and increasingly hostile independence from the Communist core of the radical movements. The official dissociation and estrangement of the influential *Partisan Review* critics (Philip Rahv, William Phillips, Dwight MacDonald, F. W. Dupee, Mary McCarthy, Lionel Trilling, Sidney Hook, Meyer Shapiro, Clement Greenberg, Harold Rosenberg, Lionel Abel, among others) from the Party in 1937 is most often cited as the model for responsible intellectuals, mindful of their autonomy and their vocation to stand in opposition, especially within the left itself. More important, the anti-Stalinist and, especially, the Trotskyist left was the natural home for intellectuals with a penchant for high culture and cosmopolitan taste (Trotsky himself was a highly cultivated and cosmopolitan literary critic who had long been skeptical about the potential of a "proletarian culture"). In contrast with the *Partisan*'s endorsement of the brilliant spirit of the European avant-garde, the Popular Front agenda for a people's culture was made to appear parochial and small-minded, a middlebrow version of cultural nationalism that seemed second rate when set beside the impressive pantheon of high modernists espoused by the anti-Stalinist left. This high-mindedness on the part of the anti-Stalinists was underscored by a deep suspicion of the native radical tradition, with its roots in rural populism and its rhetoric of democratic values that the "Americanized" Communist Party was trying to cultivate. During the war years, the *Partisan* group increasingly saw themselves as an isolated elect, solely responsible for the preservation of cultural value, holding the line between civilization and barbarism. Although they were Marxists, their code of responsibility was less and less to a political cause, and more to the redeeming source of high literary tradition in the West at the moment when the European home of that tradition had either come under, or was threatened with, Nazi occupation.[14] Many of those who were disdained or attacked by this self-celebrating elite (Rahv's private comment is not untypical: "We're half dead. Most of the people today are all dead")[15] saw the *Partisan*'s trajectory as one of retrenchment. Yet it clearly grew out of the contradiction between the vanguardist prescriptions of orthodox Marxism and the ideology of intellectual freedom espoused by defencers of the faith, between the revolutionary model of party leadership and the independent ideal of devotion to art as a haven of autonomy.

The intensive courting of celebrity intellectuals by the Party was often caricatured as a demand that intellectuals should deintellectualize and submerge themselves in the service of a mass revolutionary movement, an imperative that seemed to push up against the very limits of the doctrine of intellectual "responsibility." After the famous Waldorf conference of 1949, probably the last attempt to revive Communist support among American intellectuals, Irving Howe asked: "What are the drives to self-destruction that can lead a serious intellectual to support a movement whose victory could mean only the end of free intellectual life?"[16] Howe's target is obvious, but behind his question lies certain assumptions about what it means to be a "free intellectual." Increasingly, the anti-Stalinists' acid test of the serious intellectual life was the capacity to choose an independent path that transcended all ideological alignment. This tendency went hand in hand with their espousal of the enduring premise of classical Marxist aesthetics, which holds that the best or the most genuine high culture creates a space that is relatively free of ideology, and can thus transcend the determining influence of social forces felt in lesser or inferior kinds of intellectual production. Transcendental autonomy then becomes the only guarantee of critical or negative art, just as the intellectual's independence is the only guarantee of critical integrity in dissent. "Freedom," "independence," and "autonomy" all become lofty fetishes in a new defense of the faith, while organic ties to other social communities and movements are abandoned.

Consequently, *responsibility* became redefined as the protection of an intellectual's "freedom" at all costs. The extent to which this redefinition lent itself to more accommodationist positions was made quite clear in the postwar years, when many figures on the anti-Stalinist left became increasingly responsive to the Cold War cause of protecting "freedom" in the West. Anti-Stalinism mutated into Stalinophobia, and the anticommunism of onetime revolutionary Marxists laid the basis of future careers, for many, as professional anticommunists.[17] In the transformed political climate of the Cold War and the National Security state, this shift in alignment helped to legitimize domestic repression before and during the McCarthy years. As for foreign policy, the CIA-funded Congress for Cultural Freedom and its U.S. affiliate, the American Committee for Cultural Freedom, were founded as quasi-official organizations for intellectuals to engage indirectly in what became known as Cultural Cold War, responsible for protecting "free" Western intellectuals from the contagion of socialist ideas. With publishing organs in many different countries— *Der Monat, Preuves, Encounter*, and *Tempo Presente*—and with a host of sympathetic journals at home, including *Partisan Review* and *Commentary*, the anticommunist Congress enlisted the services of many of the well-known liberals of the day. While there were some anti-Stalinists like Howe and MacDonald who resisted the dismantling of class politics, the prevailing mood was such that the domestic "responsibility" of Cold War liberalism was directed toward cementing the postwar settlement between capital and labor and promoting the climate of consensus that rested upon the ideology of liberal pluralism.

Many reasons have been cited for this accommodationist shift of intellectuals: the new prosperity, greater ethnic tolerance, the rewards and recognition of academe, preservation of civil liberties, an intimacy with the state that had begun with Rexford Tugwell's Brains Trust (the "Phi Beta Kappa revolutionaries" of Roosevelt's first administration).[18] Moreover, the Cold War was, after all, an *adversarial* cause, and no doubt this made it easier to recognize as an intellectual's cause. The vocabulary of opposition remained intact, the sense of a militant critique was preserved, even if its target had been switched from capitalism to communism. Intellectuals were still being *responsible*, and the elective heroism of their own individual choices was upheld with the ceremonial importance to which they had become accustomed. Thus, the public "confessions" and "defections" of recalcitrant radicals in the Cold War were periodically reported as events of great significance: from Dwight MacDonald's "I Choose the West" in 1952 to Susan Sontag's public recantation in 1982. Whether one saw it as apostasy or enlightenment, the practice of choosing between mutually opposed positions may have been the most exalted component of the old doctrine of responsibility, and it served the perpetuation of Cold War doctrine in no less obvious ways. In fact, the doctrine's emphasis on the imperative of making such heroic choices and shifts of commitment fitted the Manichaean mold of the Cold War perfectly: revolution or reform? autonomy or accommodation? good or evil? bolshevism or menshevism? us or them? freedom or slavery? In other respects, it is what could be called a macho tradition, mobilizing the hardboiled rhetoric of virility that opposes militancy to sentimentalism, "hard" to "soft," realism to utopianism, and where capitalism/communism can be lined up on either side, depending on the speaker and context. Typical among the memoirs of the Old Left are descriptions, like this one by Daniel Bell, of the struggle of good men and true in the thirties, when all the irons were in the fire: "In some the iron became brittle, in some it became hard; others cast the iron away, and still others were crushed" (the "iron," of course, signifies a commitment to Stalin, man of steel).[19]

For the most part, the New Left set out to willfully disassociate intellectual radicalism from such masculinist *rites de passage*. This did not mean eschewing militancy, of course. In fact, putting one's body on the line for SNCC (the Student Nonviolent Coordinating Committee) became the model, for the next decade, of personal commitment to direct action and the politics of confrontation. Nor, ironically enough, did this tactic guarantee any immediate refinement of the level of sexual politics, for the increasingly pronounced emphasis on generational difference meant that much of sixties activism played out the masculine Oedipal spectacle of the politics of parricide. Nonetheless, the organic social movements that arose at the tail end of the sixties, organized around gender, ethnicity, sexual orientation, and ecology, were directly predicated upon the values of community, liberation, and personal empowerment that had been learned in the initial civil rights phase of the New Left. This attention to personal, liberatory values was a major element in redefining responsibility in terms that either addressed the body directly, or else enlisted the mind and psyche as media of self-transformation rather than as tools to be harnessed to objective political causes.

When its founding ethic of participatory democracy later came to coexist with anarchism, student syndicalism, native utopianism, "progressive" Leninist workerism, and the whole rainbow of countercultural crusades, the New Left was no more unified than the Old Left, with its bewildering spectrum of sectarian groups and parties, had ever been. What was quite different, however, was the new attention to micropolitics—the pervasiveness of political choices and decisions to be made at the level of everyday life.[20] A revolution in style, sexuality, and personal expression characterized the new grammar of dissent and the new modes of political action in ways that did not appeal to the lofty sense of *cultural authority* that had sustained Old Left intellectuals. To the latter, this new ethic of responsibility was an abdication of responsible behavior; the new spirit of civil disobedience was, more often than not, loutish disrespect; and the "politics of the personal" represented a lack of the discipline necessary for taking on and making sense of the burden of history. Irving Howe gives a mandarin outline of the new culture, founded, as he put it, upon the "psychology of unobstructed need":

> The new sensitivity is impatient with ideas. It is impatient with literary structures of complexity and coherence, only yesterday the catchwords of our criticism. It wants instead works of literature—though literature may be the wrong word—that will be as absolute as the sun, as unarguable as orgasm, and as delicious as a lollipop. It schemes to throw off the weight of nuance and ambiguity, legacies of high consciousness and tired blood. It is weary of the habit of reflection, the making of distinctions, the squareness of dialectic, the tarnished gold of inherited wisdom.[21]

Howe's caricature of fast-and-loose irreverence was a typical generational response to a culture self-consciously devoted to liberatory or utopian moments grounded in the bodily present as opposed to the hard, guilt-ridden school of cultural maturity that was equated in youth politics with atrophy. More important, however, the appearance of an adversary culture that was not an elite or minority culture, tied to a movement that was trying to eschew vanguardist structures of political authority, proved too much of a paradox for the older liberal elite that, for twenty-five years, had jealously guarded its territorial purchase on the adversary tradition, and who had excoriated all other competitors in the field.

As I have suggested, the doctrine of the "responsibility" of intellectuals is, in many ways, a more worldly and secular expression of the doctrine of "defenders of the faith'; it has a specific history and is tied to a specific politics of opposition, while the nonpartisan "defenders" are expected to keep the faith universally throughout the ages. Like the latter, however, its strongest arguments emerge in moments of ultimate crisis when the faith itself is under threat of compromise, perhaps most conspicuously over the issue of support for the cause of war. Breaking with his mentor Dewey, and the *New Republic* progressives who had decided to actively support the war effort, Randolph Bourne bitterly accused his fellow intellectuals of facilitating the decision to enter an imperialist war, "a war," he melodramatically proclaimed, "made deliberately by the intellectuals!"[22] In 1940, Archibald MacLeish censured "the irresponsibles" for not rallying quickly and activity enough behind the antifascist Popular Front cause, bolstering, as a result, the climate of appeasement for Hitler.[23] Debate about the Cold War crystallized around the sins of McCarthy—the anti-Stalinists again being guilty of appeasing this monstrous inquistor—and was revived in full by the publication of *Scoundrel Time* (1976), Lillian Hellman's memoirs. Most recently, the charge that the Cold War rhetoric of liberal anticommunism was "responsible" for the American intervention in Vietnam has issued from a chorus of voices, most volubly that of Noam Chomsky.[24]

As the scene of responsibility has shifted from Vietnam to low-intensity conflicts in Central America, Chomsky has remained the most prominent advocate of the code of the responsibility of intellectuals, which, for him, distinguishes truly critical speech from the realm of merely pragmatic judgments. Consequently he is the most vociferous critic of the expert and professional specialist whose knowledge and opinion are everywhere compromised by links with credentialist institutions and foundations. His, by contrast, is the voice of the independent—somewhat romantic, even anarchistic, deeply moralistic, and exemplary of the model of the free-floating intellectual who can sacrifice all ties to class and body and institutional affiliation in order to speak the truth. Where the right to speak out is a form of power denied to most people, then, he maintains, "it is the responsibility of intellectuals to speak the truth and to expose lies."

The New Class

Where the "responsibility of intellectuals" could be said to describe their social function, as opposed to their institutional position, the theory of the "New Class" is directly concerned with the institutionalization of knowledge as power. This theory comprises a number of competing ideologies since there are several versions, each drawing upon a contested history of the middle-class strata recruited and trained at the end of the nineteenth century to manage the increasingly antagonistic relation between capital and labor.

At the heart of the pejorative neoconservative critique of the

"New Class" was the fear born of the spectacle of student radicalism in the sixties, the fear that the adversary culture had far exceeded its habitual function as a necessary "stimulant" for what
Joseph Schumpeter called capitalism's "vested interest in social
unrest."[25] Norman Podhoretz's response to the widely circulated
sixties pamphlet, *The Student as Nigger*, is quite symptomatic;
"In what intelligible sense could these young scions of the American upper classes be compared to a group at the bottom of the
American heap?"[26] Podhoretz's explanation of student radicalism
accepted the terms of the discourse of "status anxiety" that had
become the new religion and a substitute for class politics among
the consensus historians and sociologists of the fifties. Far from
having been killed off by "kindness," he opines that student disaffiliation was a direct result of a revolution of rising expectations
fomented by the post-Sputnik promise to place the expertise of
cultural capital above the rule of inherited wealth and property.
Victims of their own resentment, however, students were "trying
to tell us" that they were being denied their "fair share" of this
promised power, and were therefore refusing to take up their allotted roles in the technostructure. In offering this explanation,
Podhoretz, as always, was probably saying more about his own
personal resentment vis-à-vis power sharing than anything else,
but he prefigures a response that has become typical of
neoconservatism—the inability to understand how and why
those who are in a position to be rewarded by a system would
want to challenge it. In fact, the "poverty of student life" (a Situa-
tionst phrase) was to be theorized in all sorts of unorthodox ways
in the course of the sixties, not least in the perception that the
multiversity was in the business of the assembly-line production
of a "new working class," or servant class of middle-level,
knowledgeable labor trained for the new technostructure. Theories of proletarianization aside, it should hardly have come as a
surprise to Podhoretz, as a student of intellectual traditions, to
recognize that intellectuals romantically express their sense of
ideological subjection (Bourdieu sees them as the dominated fraction of a ruling class) and spiritual poverty by imaginary identification with those who are physically dominated and materially impoverished.

No more useful, however, was Bell's comparison of the New Left indentification with black militants with "the young middle-class rebels of the 1930s ap[ing] the Revolutionary Proletariat."[27] It tells us nothing about the specific conditions under which *racial* oppression came to be a privileged metaphorical vehicle not only for white, liberal guilt—a major source of reexamination of class privilege on the part of the New Left—but also for other forms of cultural oppression, as in the later slogan "Woman Is the Nigger of the World." These identificatory affiliations, and others, like the active identification of gay men with feminist struggles by dressing up in Radical, or "hairy," Drag, were the symptoms of complex and shifting alliances, different in kind from the leading, directive influence of vanguard intellectuals over a "universal" mass movement that had been the activist model of the thirties. So too, they have to be read as responses to the legitimation crisis of masculinity, for which the "virility" of the black militant and the "drag" of the gay male feminist represent the extreme limits. Besides, the diversity of the student movements cannot be profitably compared (at least not until the last violently elitist and sectarian days of SDS) with the more or less unified workerist cause of the thirties. These movements were a critique of (at least) three different areas of social injustice: first, antiwar, the most traditional area of dissent, and the agenda that attracted the support of an increasing number of traditional intellectuals (from Dwight MacDonald, Mary McCarthy, and the *New York Review of Books* community, to policy intellectuals like Senator Fulbright) before it achieved massive popular support; second, civil rights, the most newly legitimate and successful politics, and which increasingly lost the support of traditional intellectuals as the militant black liberation movements rose to prominence; and third, the politics of the university, the least understood of all, because it was the site of a new *politics of knowledge*, waged within the institutions that governed the production of knowledge. This last was a politics that comprised not only a structural critique of assembly-line education and preprofessionalism, but also a more general critique of the privileges of education, expertise, knowledge, and skill; and thus it was the one that most deeply challenged the sensibility of traditional intellectuals whose cultural authority and identity was raised on these privileges.

For those aligned with the liberal tradition, the concept of the "new class" meant something different from either the new, spiritually impoverished, middle-class "proletariat," C. Wright Mills's student "revolutionariat," or the neoconservative conspiracy picture of media and education institutions infiltrated and dominated by a fully credentialed party of opposition. Capitalism's overwhelming efficiency in recruiting and absorbing the adversary intelligentsia (viz. yuppies, New Age adherents, postfeminists) had found enthusiastic backers among liberals like Bell and Galbraith, who described the "new class," by contrast, as a benign technocracy of competently trained and institutionally proficient leaders, the beneficiaries of an orderly transfer of power to the rule of cultural capital. In their version of the new class as a functional elite risen to power in the transition from a production-oriented economy to a postindustrial service economy, the primacy of theoretical knowledge is seen as both *just* and *justified*—just, because a trained technical elite ought to be more rational in its management of power than a hereditary elite; and justified, not only because it distributes more evenly the share of access to power, but also because it simply promotes efficiency. The reign of the professional or expert, at least since the post-Sputnik drive to create a fully educated technocracy, had ceded its highest privileges to a technical intelligentsia. Because they believe that democratic capitalism has already accomplished, for the most part, its mission of safeguarding individual freedoms, and guaranteeing a minimum of social welfare, postindustrialists like Bell tend to describe the new technocratic class as a simple response to the benign needs of capitalism. A more diagnostic commentator might hold that government by experts keeps power in the hands of those with access to esoteric knowledge, and reduces the "excesses" of democratic accountability.

Any properly historical account of what is called the "New Class," or the professional-managerial class (a term more broadly accepted on the left), raises question about its respective proponents' claims for coherence of class position or social function.[28] Such a history would reveal, for example, a common vision of rational, centralized planning, whether in the form of the "engineering of consent" espoused by the client capitalism of early advertising managers, committed to smoothing the way for a social contract between labor and capital, or in the form of the "engineering of ideas" embraced by technocratic radicals, committed to outright social emancipation.[29] But it would also reveal the contradictory political interests of such a "class": self-grounded in the autonomy of its claims to plan and rule by reason and expertise, but also answerable to the historical need of monopoly capitalism for mediators or managers of class conflict; elitist in its protection of the guild privileges secured by cultural capital, but also egalitarian in its positivist vision of social emancipation for all; anticapitalist in its technocratic challenge to the rule of capital, but also contemptuous of the "conservative," anti-intellectual disrespect of the popular classes; and lastly, of course, internally divided by antagonisms between administrative-managerial fractions and those aligned in some way with the value-oriented, antipragmatic codes of action and belief associated with liberal or radical humanism. Any full consideration of these contradictions would undercut accounts of the smooth, inevitable rise of the new class that see the role of the intelligentsia, on the one hand, as a benign, managerial function of the modern state's affairs and needs (Bell, Bazelon, Galbraith) or, on the other, as a private vassalage of a corporate-state bureaucracy (Ewen, Chomsky)—or, yet another, as neutral technocratic inheritors, according to the "iron law of oligarchy," of a vast degree of concentrated power.[30]

In *The Future of Intellectuals and the Rise of the New Class*, Alvin Gouldner presents a relatively uncluttered analysis of intellectuals as historical agents in a struggle with the old capitalist class for dominance and rule on the basis of knowledge, reason, and expertise. Does the new class bear any resemblance to what we would recognize as a ruling class? Not yet, says Gouldner, who sees the new class as a "flawed universal class" that is on the ascendant, and which "holds a mortgage on at least *one* historical future."[31] If it ever comes to be a ruling class, then it will be over the course of centuries, like the historical rise of the bourgeoisie. If, at present, it is a servant class, then that is because all classes are so before they achieve power. From Gouldner's perspective, then, Chomsky's contempt for the intellectuals' subservience to the power elites is a judgment of the intellectuals that is ahead of its time, because it invokes moral standards that lie in the future, and which the intellectuals will one day be in a position to recognize and obey. For the present, their task is to establish and legitimize their own authority as groups who share symbolic capital, and who police the discursive rules that safeguard the property value of their knowledge-power.

While Gouldner's analysis makes it quite clear that the interests of this new class are tied to a will to power, it has less to say about the new forms of domination that the knowledge-power of intellectuals have come to exact upon those at the lower end of the hierarchy of knowledge. As the information society proceeds apace, and the expansion of databases and memory banks everywhere furthers the commodification of knowledge, there is a good deal of concern about the new class polarization between "knows" and "know-nots": one-third of U.S. citizens are functionally illiterate. These new forms of "knowledge" domination supplement, if they do not entirely displace, traditional capitalist modes of appropriation and exploitation. The increasing symbolic domination of the information-rich over the information-poor is not at all confined to merely "symbolic" effects; this structural domination is increasingly programmed into the new "smart" technologies.

For over fifty years new, the discourses specific to symbolic domination have been most evident in the debates among intellectuals about popular culture, or mass culture as it is termed by dystopian critics. For the earlier part of that period, the balance sheet, which records a history of paternalism, containment, and even allergic reaction, does not read well, even when considered in the context of the *dialectical* antagonism that surely governs this relationship at a number of levels. More often than not, it shows a failure to recognize what is at stake in the so-called anti-intellectualism of popular culture, and a reluctance to acknowledge the affective world of popular taste, unless romantically to celebrate the bodily innocence and exuberance of the popular, but more likely to lampoon its audience's victimization and stupefaction in the face of commercial logic. With the onset, since the sixties, of a more pluralistic picture of cultural politics, the authority of the old binary model of struggle has receded even as its explanatory power has been dispersed over the uneven range of a number of other oppositions not reducible to class; as a result, the responsibility of universal intellectuals to speak paternalistically in the name of the popular has been contested and displaced. But the exercise of cultural taste, wherever it is applied today, remains one of the most efficient guarantors of antidemocratic power relations, and, when augmented by the newly stratified privileges of a knowledge society, gives rise to new kinds of subordination.

For some time now, this exercise of symbolic power has been rearticulated through the popular science fictions that have grown up around the new technologies of information processing and artificial intelligence (AI). Such fictions show quite clearly how and why the debate about artificial intelligence itself harbors a story about the imagined autonomous rule of a knowledge elite; the historical antagonism between the intellectual and the popular is seen to be *objective* now that the rule of knowledge is exercised by machines rather than humans. On the one hand, "smart" machines embody all of the rational efficiency of the noble, technocratic tradition envisaged by Saint-Simon and Veblen. On the other hand, the notoriously clinical "inhumanity" of AI machines comes to represent the dark side of the sovereignty of calculation. In postapocalyptic science fiction versions of this story, the "revolt of the machines" ushers in a regime of efficiency that is more despotic than any imaginable form of human domination. This picture of a revolution succeeded by unrelieved oppression conflates capitalism's two most historically familiar phobias: the revolt of the slaves, threatened by the proletariat, and the rule of rational intelligence, proposed by the "new class." But it also enlists and expresses the deeply grounded fears and resentment of the popular classes, whose access to information culture is limited and circumscribed by financial or by institutional exclusion, and whose knowledge and skills have been expropriated by experts and smart machinery. In these stories, the information-poor are typically represented either as survivors, living off morsels scavenged at the margins of the high-tech core culture, or as drones, held in druglike suspension of their emotional lives by the sleep of reason until their resistant spirit is raised out of its hibernation by the example of a lone, dissenting hero. Like intellectuals, the machines are programmed to know all the right answers, and for this they become objects of hatred, especially when they get to be too smart—when their authority is self-grounded in the privileges of legitimate knowledge and intelligence. It is they who draw the most ire, and not the decadent, pleasure-loving, fantasy-building capitalist class that owns them. In these fictions, then, the embryonic will to power of the "intelligent" class (humanity as a memory bank and decision-making machine), steeped in the ethic of public service, inexorably feeds a technobureaucratic nightmare. Such fictions take it for granted that high-tech is already the high culture of new masters.

New Intellectuals

Despite their tendency to commit all outcomes to the benevolence of liberal capitalism (Bell) or History (Gouldner), theories of the new class, or the professional-managerial class, have taken their toll on those intellectuals' traditions that rest upon the codes of alienated dissent or social disaffiliation. Humanists and social critics, especially, have always been loath to share the term "intellectual" with less bona fide word brokers, and with number workers. Increasingly positioned by the contractual discourses of their institutions and professions, they have had to forsake the high ground and recognize the professional conditions they share, for the most part, with millions of other knowledge workers. The loss of this high ground has been much lamented, especially when linked to romantic left narratives about the "decline of the public intellectual," who, in the classical version, is a heroicized white male, and who, if he is like C. Wright Mills, still rides a Harley-Davidson to his university workplace.

Professional intellectuals who are not self-loathing have come to insist that it is necessary to examine their institutional affiliations in order to understand and transform the codes of power that are historically specific to their disciplinary discourses. In this respect, members of the recent generation of poststructuralist thinkers have each applied themselves, in ways unavailable to the classical Marxist tradition, to the kinds of critique necessary for examining and redefining the intellectual's relation to the institution. Most pertinent are Foucault's commentaries on the disciplinary nature of "regimes of truth," and his call for micropolitical actions in place of the grand tradition of autonomous dissent. So too, Derrida's ongoing deconstruction of the universal/university institution, Lacan's challenge to the rationality of science and its relation to the analytic institution, and Bourdieu's critical studies of symbolic capital can all be used in this context. Inside and outside the academy, intellectuals of the new social movements have fostered cultural agendas specific to the politics of gender, race, ethnicity, and sexual preference. The critique of essentialist notions of sexuality and sexual identity on the part of feminists, gays, and lesbians, and of race and ethnic identity on the part of minority intellectuals, has been addressed primarily to discursive or representational categories, but also in the full knowledge of the effects of these categories upon real, persecuted bodies.

With the withering away of the universal intellectual, the political activism of intellectuals today is determined as much by their *position* as intellectuals as by the *function* of intellectuals in general. But this is not to say that the discourse, on the one hand, of the heroic, unaffiliated intellectual who "speaks the truth and exposes lies," and that of the specific intellectual who locally applies his or her technical knowledge and expertise, are *mutually exclusive.*[32] Nor does it mean, more importantly, that the same individual cannot invoke either of these discourses, and others, at different times and places, for that, surely, is a prerogative of the postmodern "citizen." What it does mean, however, is that the *prevalent* image of the intellectual, immune to the contagions of technological rationality, bureaucratism, consumerism, and professionalism, is an image that belongs to recent history, an image that, today, is only to be invoked among many others.

New intellectuals, in fact, are uneven participants on several fronts. They are likely to belong to different social groups and have loyalties to different social movements. They will possess specific professional or occupational skills and knowledges that can be applied within institutions but also in different public

spheres and communities. Their sense of strategy will shift from
context to context, whether it involves the use of specialized
knowledge in an occupational field or the use of generalized persuasion in speaking through the popular media; whether it involves confrontational action with police and other agents of
coercion or everyday interaction with nonintellectuals. In the
face of today's uneven plurality of often conflicting radicals interests, it is quite possible that they will be leading spokespersons,
diffident supporters and reactionaries at one and the same time—
that is, legitimists in some areas of political discourse and action,
and contesters in others. Their ethical sense of the personal as a
liberatory sphere means that their responsibility to "objective"
political causes will be experientially inflected by a deeply subjective psychohistory. Their relation to daily life will not be guilt-
ridden by correctional codes of political behavior, especially in
the cultural marketplace of consumer options and choices; it will
be informed by the matrix of power, pleasure, and desire experienced by all other consumers. Their sense of a usable past will
include more than the always idealized narratives of monolinear
decline—the fall from *Gemeinschaft* to *Gesellschaft*, the loss of
premodernist bourgeois publics, of folk populism, of bohemia, of
a clear-cut class politics and so on; it will also be informed by the
pragmatic, democratizing possibilities ushered in by new technologies and new popular cultures in a hegemonic capitalist society.
And their working sense of a better world will not be remote, utopian, compensatory, or authoritatively deferred until all struggles
are over; it will have to be accessible, in however an impure or
compromised form, in the daily micropolitical round of lived
pleasures and fantasies—in other words, it will have to be articulated along with forms of experience that are not always seen to
be conducive to egalitarian or progressive aims and desires.

   This postmodern picture of multiple and uneven activities,
loyalties, obligations, desires, and responsibilities does not preclude, however, the continued effect of traditional antagonisms,
those that are marked by a dialectic of what I call *disrespect*—
popular "anti-intellectualism," on the one hand, and educated
"disdain" on the other. Even with today's renewed interest in a
common culture, at once demotic and informed (a culture that is

undeniably part of the postmodernist agenda), the dialectical character of the relationship between intellectuals and the popular retains its organizing power over our daily cultural experience. In fact, in a society that is increasingly stratified by levels and orders of *knowledge*, the powerful antagonisms traditionally generated out of the wars of cultural taste are likely to be sharpened by new kinds of disrespect even as they multiply to reflect the endlessly flexible and fissionable creation of new hip categories of taste.

What is the relation, in such a culture, between being "in the know" and the deeply felt popular complaint about the antidemocratic use of expert knowledge? The two are surely interdependent. And the complaint, especially, is one that applies not just to the stratified world of public dialogue, but also to the frictions experienced in daily life when ordinary people brush up against technobureaucratic privilege and arrogance (a more likely everyday encounter than with the owners of capital, or with the ghostly, abstract logic of capital itself). It is a complaint that is felt, like all effects of power, across the body, in structures of feelings that draw upon hostility, resentment, and insubordination, as well as deference, consent, and respect. And it is in many of the more successful fictions of popular culture, however indirectly articulated and however commodified, that these contradictory feelings about knowledge and authority are transformed into pleasure that is often more immediately satisfying than it is "politically correct." Intellectuals today are unlikely to recognize, for example, what is fully at stake in the new *politics of knowledge* if they fail to understand why so many cultural forms, devoted to horror and porn, and steeped in chauvinism and other bad attitudes, draw their popular appeal from expressions of disrespect for the lessons of educated taste. The sexism, racism, and militarism that pervade these genres are never expressed in a pure form (whatever that might be); they are articulated through and alongside social resentments born of subordination and exclusion. A politics that only preaches about the sexism, racism, and militarism while neglecting to rearticulate the popular, resistant appeal of the disrespect will not be a popular politics, and will lose ground in any contest with the authoritarian populist languages that we have experienced under Reaganism and Thatcherism. For many intellectuals, such a politics has always been and still is difficult to imagine, let alone accept, because of its necessary engagement with aggressively indifferent attitudes toward the life of the mind and the protocols of knowledge; because it appeals to the body in ways that cannot always be trusted; and because it trades on pleasures that a training in political rationality encourages us to devalue. But the challenge of such a politics is greater than ever because in an age of expert rule, the popular is perhaps the one field in which intellectuals are least likely to be experts. And in an age of radical pluralism where the politically unified guarantees of past intellectuals' traditions no longer hold sway, the need to search for *common ground* from which to contest the existing definitions of a popular-democratic culture has never been more urgent.

NOTES

1. See Stanley Aronowitz, "Postmodernism and Politics," (ed.), *Universal Abandon? The Politics of Postmodernism* (Minneapolis: University of Minnesota Press, 1988).

2. Two recent and notorious examples are, from the left, Russell Jacoby, *The Last Intellectuals: American Culture in the Age of Academe* (New York: Basic Books, 1987); and, from the right, Allan Bloom, *The Closing of the American Mind* (New York: Simon & Schuster, 1987).

3. See Magali Sarfatti Larson, "The Production of Expertise and the Constitution of Expert Power," in Thomas Haskell (ed.), *The Authority of Experts: Studies in History and Theory*, (Bloomington: Indiana University Press, 1984), 28–83; and Pierre Bourdieu, "Cultural Reproduction and Social Reproduction," in Jerome Korabel and A. H. Halsey (eds.), *Power and Ideology in Education* (New York: Oxford University Press, 1977), 487–511.

4. See Bruce Sterling's cyberpunk "manifesto" in Sterling (ed.), *Mirrorshades: The Cyberpunk Anthology* (New York: Arbor House, 1986).

5. John Clarke comments on this tendency in "Enter the Cybernauts: Problems in Post-Modernism," *Communication*, 10 (1988), 383–401.

6. Nicholas Garnham and Raymond Williams make this distinction between "replication" and "reformation" in order to take issue with Pierre Bourdieu's analyses of cultural "reproduction." The question they ask is an important one: "Can the structure of the symbolic field produce contradictions such that they no longer tend to reproduce the given set of class relations?" Garnham and Williams, "Pierre Bourdieu and the Sociology of Culture," in Richard Collins et al. (eds.), *Media, Culture and Society* (Beverly Hills, Calif: Sage, 1986), 116–30. Stuart Hall has insisted that the answer to that question is to be found in Gramsci:

There is nothing more crucial, in this respect, than Gramsci's recognition that every crisis is also a moment of reconstruction; that there is no destruction which is not also, reconstruction; that historically nothing is dismantled without also attempting to put something new in its place; that every form of power not only excludes but produces something.

That is an entirely new conception of crisis—and of power. When the Left talks about crisis, all we see is capitalism disintegrating, and us marching in and taking over. We don't understand that the disruption of the normal functioning of the old economic, social, cultural order, provides the opportunity to reorganize it in new ways, to restructure and refashion, to modernize, and move ahead."

Stuart Hall, "Gramsci and Us," *Marxism Today*, June 1987, 19.

7. Donna Haraway, "A Manifesto for Cyborgs: Science, Technology and Socialist Feminism in the 1980s," *Socialist Reveiw*, 80 (March/April 1985), 65–107.

8. Lionel Trilling, preface, *Beyond Culture: Essays on Literature and Learning* (New York: Harcourt Brace Jovanovich, 1965)

9. Edward Shils, "The Intellectuals and the Powers: Some Perspectives for Comparative Analyses," *The Intellectuals and the Powers and Other Essays* (Chicago: University of Chicago Press, 1972), 3–23; "Intellectuals and the Center of Society in the United States," *The Constitution of Society* (Chicago: University of Chicago Press, 1982), 224–74; Talcott Parsons, "The Intellectual: A Social Role Category," in Philip Rieff (ed.), *On Intellectuals* (Garden City, N.Y.: Doubleday, 1969), 3–24. One of the classic sources of this view can be found in Karl Mannheim, *Ideology and Utopia* (New York: Harcourt, Brace, 1936). Daniel Bell has different but related things to say about "the sacred" in *The Cultural Contradictions of Capitalism* (New York: Basic Books, 1978), 146–71, and in "The Return of the Sacred," *The Winding Passage: Essays and Sociological Journeys; 1960–1980* (New York: Basic Books, 1980).

Regis Debray presents a more critical view in his account of the French historical trajectory from the clerisy to the new celebrity media intellectuals, in *Teachers, Writers, Celebrities: The Intellectuals of Modern France*, trans. David Macey (London: New Left Books, 1981).

10. Rolf Dahrendorf, "The Intellectual and Society: The Social Function of the Fool' in the Twentieth-Century," in Rieff, *On Intellectuals, 51.*

11. Maxim Gorky, *"The Responsibility of Soviet Intellectuals," in George B. de Huszar (ed.), The Intellectuals: A Controversial Portrait* (Glencoe, Ill.: Free Press, 1960), 237.

12. Noam Chomsky, *Towards A New Cold War: Essays on the Current Crisis and How We Got There* (New York: Pantheon, 1982), 62.

13. Cited by Chomsky in *American Power and the New Mandarins* (New York: Pantheon, 1969), 6.

14. Of the many books about and by the intellectuals associated with the *Partisan Review*, I have found that Terry Cooney most clearly describes the political contradictions of their cosmopolitan taste in culture, in *The Rise of the New York Intellectuals: Partisan Review and Its Circle, 1934–1945* (Madison: University of Wisconsin Press, 1986).

15. Cited by Cooney, *Rise of the New York Intellectuals*, 200.

16. Irving Howe, *A Margin of Hope: An Intellectual Autobiography* (New York:

Harcourt Brace Jovanovich, 1982), 158. Howe was referring, in particular, to the great literary critic and fellow traveler F. O. Matthiessen.

17. Alan Wald makes a strong case for the political and intellectual integrity of the anti-Stalinist left that preexisted the phase of Stalinophobia. *The New York Intellectuals: The Rise and Fall of the AntiStalinist Left* (Chapel Hill: University of North Carolina Press, 1986).

18. For the most level-headed history of this period, see Richard Pells, *The Liberal Mind in a Conservative Age: American Intellectuals in the 1940s & 1950s* (New York: Harper & Row, 1985).

19. Daniel Bell, "The Mood of Three Generations," in *The End of Ideology* (New York: Collier, 1961), 303.

20. Recently published histories of the sixties that emphasize this difference of style include Ronald Fraser (ed.), *1968: A Student Generation in Revolt* (New York: Pantheon, 1988); Todd Gitlin, *The Sixties: Years of Hope, Days of Rage* (New York: Bantam, 1987); and James Miller, *"Democracy Is in the Streets": From Port Huron to the Seige of Chicago* (New York: Simon & Schuster, 1987).

21. Irving Howe, *The Decline of the New* (New York: Harcourt, Brace, 1970), 255.

22. Randolph Bourne, *War and the Intellectuals: Collected Essays 1915–1919*, ed. Carl Resek (New York: Harper & Row, 1964), 3–15.

23. Archibald MacLeish, "The Irresponsibles," in de Huszar, *The Intellectuals*, 239–46.

24. Some of the most damning evidence was provided by Charles Kadushin's polling of the reactions of a chosen, elite group of intellectuals to the war in Vietnam. The results showed that a majority opposed American foreign policy in Southeast Asia, but mostly on pragmatic rather than on moral grounds. *The American Intellectual Elite* (Boston: Little, Brown, 1974).

25. Joseph Schumpeter, *Capitalism, Socialism, and Democracy* (New York: Harper, 1942), 145.

26. Norman Podhoretz, "The Adversary Culture and the New Class," *The Bloody Crossroads: Where Literature and Politics Meet* (New York: Simon & Schuster, 1986), 116.

27. Quoted by Alexander Bloom, *Prodigal Sons: The New York Intellectuals and Their World* (New York: Oxford University Press, 1986), 353.

28. B. Bruce-Biggs (ed.), *The New Class?* (New York: McGraw-Hill, 1981), presents a range of primarily neoconservative perspectives. Pat Walker (ed.), *Between Labor and Capital* (Boston: South End Press, 1979), includes Barbara and John Ehrenreich's "The Professional-Managerial Class," followed by a range of left responses.

29. The phrase "engineering of consent" belongs to Edward Bernays (a nephew of Freud), who fathered the science of public relations in the twenties in books like *Crystallizing Public Opinion* (1923) and *Propaganda* (1925), each of which advocated the application of knowledge about mass psychology to the rhythms of the marketplace. In the *New Republic* of 1932 (March 23, p. 145), Edmund Wilson called for his fellow intellectuals to become "engineers of ideas." Wilson is addressing would-be vanguardist intelligentsia, encouraging them to openly work at creating a mass revolutionary consciousness. Bernays's appeal to fellow professionals is equally vanguardist; their task is to create a consumerist consciousness

for society as a whole. Both discourses assume the technobureaucratic process of rationalization as a benign and necessary fact, invoking its virtues for the "soft" science of persuasion through the "hard" metaphor of engineering (the efficiency methods of Fordism and Taylorization—more efficient than laissez-faireism—had long been unequivocally recognized and appropriated by both Soviet planners and European dreamers, like Gramsci, of a communist state).

30. For a liberal overview, see David Bazelon, *Power in America: The Politics of the New Class* (New York: New American Library, 1967). For a more radical view, see Stuart Ewen, *Captains of Consciousness: Advertising and the Social Roots of Consumer Culture* (New York: McGraw-Hill, 1976). The phrase "iron law of oligarchy" is Robert Michel's and is used to describe how all large-scale organizations must, by their very nature, degenerate into oligarchies ruled by the few. Robert Michel, *Political Parties: A Sociological Study of the Oligarchical Tendencies of Modern Democracy*, trans. E. and C. Paul (New York: Free Press, 1962). For a set of arguments that rejects Michels's position see Robert J. Brym, *intellectuals and Politics* (London: Allen & Unwin, 1980), 35–53.

31. Alvin Gouldner, *The Future of Intellectuals and the Rise of the New Class* (New York: Seabury Press, 1979), 6.

32. Paul Bové poses a related opposition in comparing the leading or representative intellectual type (Edward Said) who, in his view, perpetuates the competitive, will-to-power image of traditional male intellectuals, with the skeptical and nonutopian genealogist (Michel Foucault) who refuses the privilege of intellectuals to speak for others, for the "truth," and for alternative futures. Bové, *Intellectuals: A Genealogy of Critical Humanism* (New York: Columbia University Press, 1986), 209–37. For an extended discussion of the implications of this kind of comparison, see Jim Merod, *The Political Responsibility of the Critic* (Ithaca, N.Y.: Cornell University Press, 1987).

PART II
INTERVIEWS

American Intellectuals and
Middle East Politics
Edward W. Said

The following interview took place in New York City on February 14, 1988, shortly after Verso's publication of *Blaming the Victims: Spurious Scholarship and the Palestinian Question* (coauthored by Edward Said and Christopher Hitchens) and the beginning of the Palestinian uprising (the intifida) in the Occupied Territories. The interviewer is Bruce Robbins.

BR: In *Blaming the Victims* and elsewhere, you have spoken about how the media tend to organize the story of the Palestinians in terms of the "agony" of the local Jewish lobby, in other words as a way of bringing home to an American public events which it seemingly can register only if they *are* "brought home." It strikes me that there's some connection here with the way in which *you* bring this material home to people, especially on the American left but also to Americans generally. Events like the intifada seem to come to us often from very far away. Part of the force of this book for American intellectuals, and one of the reasons why your work has generated so much excitement, is in its contention that something like "scholarship"—I'm thinking of your subtitle—actually *matters* in things like this, that there is a battle also and significantly fought out on the terrain of information, vocabulary, imagery, and so on, that is on our home turf.

ES: To my mind it's a unique case: the support for Israel in the West and especially in the U.S. among the left in particular. Don't forget that in the early days, in the post-1948 period, the cause of Israel was in the case of Britain, essentially a Labour cause, and in the U.S. of the Democratic Party, and large segments of the independent American left. The International League for Human Rights, Roger Baldwin, Reinhold Niebuhr, Norman Thomas, later Martin Luther King, all these people were very powerful advocates of a Jewish state. In time, the way discourse works, through the accumulation of information and sheer density of material, it was possible for the case to be built in such a way as to completely obscure the existence of a Palestinian presence. Dispossessed in the case of the refugees, oppressed and kept under in the case of the Palestinians who remained. Of course with 1967 the splits began to appear. Israel could no longer claim that it was a beleaguered state. And you get the famous rifts within the New University Politics, amongst left intellectuals, and the Blacks who are trying to draw analogies between what was happening in Africa and what was happening in the Middle East. And this has persisted in one way or another. But the most interesting thing is that the beginnings of a kind of revisionist scholarship in Israel, after 1982 I think, have really received very little attention in this country: the work of people like Benni Morris, Tom Segev, and Simha Flapan, and so on. These are works by Israelis, works that it's possible to publish in this country. Take the case of Simha Flapan's book *The Birth of Israel*, or Bennie Beit Hallehmi's book on the Israeli arms connections with various dictatorships in the Third World. These books have scarcely been reviewed or paid much attention to. Whereas it seems to me that they provide extraordinarily interesting ways of extending what we already know about the Third World and the network of arms. Take also the case of Iran-contragate where the Israeli role was completely suppressed with the connivance of Senator Inouye and Michael Ledeen and others. Now I find it particularly fraught because any piece of information that comes out inevitably adds force to the picture of an Israel that has been in deliberate and one might even say programmatic violation of virtually everything that has been said either by or about Israel in the years after 1948. For example, Israel was thought always to have been in need of and wanting and waiting for an Arab interlocutor. We now have evidence provided by Israeli scholars that the Israelis received assurances from the major states, after 1948—Egypt, Jordan, Syria—that they wanted to conclude a peàce with it, but the peace was turned down by Ben-Gurion programmatically. That the Palestinians were forced to leave, that they were not asked to stay, that the various efforts to restore some kind of *modus vivendi* in Israel for the Palestinians and Israel in the region—all these have been positions taken routinely by the Israelis, but suppressed in the U.S. And of course there's also been a systematic cover-up of the horrific things that have been done to Palestinians in the intervening years. What I'm trying to say is that it's not just the information, which is plentifully available now, both from the Israeli press, from the alternative scholars in this country, like Chomsky and Jane Hunter and others. The interesting thing is how little of this gets into circulation. As you read reports in the press, you keep trying to tell the reporter, journalist, or commentator, why not connect this with this other material that's there? That connection has never been made.

BR: There's an extraordinary irony that comes out in the book about the difference between Israel and the United States. Take the famous case of "the broadcasts" [Arab radio broadcasts supposedly urging Palestinians to flee their homes in 1948], according to the Kidron article: that is a myth that has been *abandoned* in Israel and is still going strong in the U.S.! Or the Joan Peters case, exactly the same thing. One thing I wanted to ask you about is the irony that these things should be abandoned in Israel and still going strong in the U.S.; the other is what does it say about the standards of responsible scholarship in the U.S., that in these cases people have not even looked at the evidence—that one elementary act of what one thinks of as scholarship?

ES: One thing that comes to mind is that people have often been stopped not by the first step but by what they believe to be the second step. That is to say, let us say that we discover that these broadcasts never took place, or that Israel has systematically refused to make peace in the region, principally because it wanted to expand its boundaries—it never really had an interest in defining its international boundaries and therefore turned away any peace offers; there's plentiful evidence for that. The problem has always been, if we find that out, what follows from it politically? It's somehow thought to be unacceptable because it would mean less support for Israel, that is to say amongst the American left, who feel that they are committed to it, as Jews if they happen to be Jewish or as people who feel something about the need for reparations to the Jews after World War II. And then the next question is, supposing it's true, what are we supposed to do about it? Can we deal with the cumulative history of injustice and hypocrisy that has in fact been there? It becomes very, very difficult, because there's so much that needs to be not only reexcavated but has to be forsworn. You have to say I was wrong, I lied, I connived, I was complicit. And that's a step that's very hard to take because, as we show in this book, so massive is the scale of lying and disinformation, or at least deliberately partial information, that people are often stopped. Whereas it would seem to me, speaking for myself, that there are a number of quite concrete gestures that could be made at this point that are much simpler than renouncing the whole past, and those include recognizing the need immediately for a restoration to the Palestinians of a fairly massive sort.

BR: One conclusion you might draw is that, as Hayden White remarked a few years ago, the Palestinians need better narratives. I don't know whether this has been a consideration of yours, or whether it's a consideration that informs *Blaming the Victims*, but when you see absolute neglect of empirical evidence in the way that you've just mentioned, because it can't be fit into a larger narrative, it makes you think that if critique is a negative model for intellectual activity, there might be a need for this alternative positive model, providing narratives that people could fit the information into.

ES: The narratives have been there. They're of a different sort. I don't think there's a kind of "grand narrative": it's essentially not a Western narrative. The model of wandering and exile is available; I. F. Stone always says the Palestinians have become "the Jews of the Middle East." But that's a borrowed narrative. There's the problem that it's after all an alien culture; it doesn't speak English, it doesn't resonate with Western myths. I've become aware of this as I've gotten older. There's a kind of stubborn and somehow uninformed refusal on the part of the Palestinians to accommodate easily. It's certainly been true in the Arab world;

that's become symptomatic of the Palestinians. It's difficult to describe; it's almost epitomized in the appearance of Arafat; he doesn't correspond to any known notion of what a national leader should look like.

BR: Isn't that creative rather than a refusal . . . ?

ES: You could say that it's creative. That's one way of looking at it. But that's at least a way of explaining the absence of an easily manageable narrative. After all, this is a narrative that always has to compete with a very powerful, already existent narrative of resurgent nationalism of the retributive kind, of the sort that one associates with Zionism. So on a lot of fronts there are formal problems. Then there's the tactical problem of where's this narrative to be formed? Because the Palestinians are locked into the Arab (so-called) narrative, and that's usually tied into oil, and the *Arabian Nights*, and a whole set of other myths, on the one hand. And on the other, in the West it's virtually impossible for the narrative to be located hospitably in any set of allied or counternarratives. Because it keeps coming up against these problems we've mentioned. The only place where it's now appeared of course is in television news—the rock thrower, without a history, without a name, without a face . . . Just like the man who came over in the hang glider, you remember, who killed six Israeli soldiers. He was never even named. Most of these kids are never given names. Although we Palestinians publish them and they're perfectly available. The list of the dead in Gaza, killed by the Israelis, the hands broken, are never published in the West because they don't have a place here.

A third alternative for a narrative emerges here and there in the strangest places, like Peter Wollen's film *Friendship's Death*. Or in a remarkable new Palestinian film *Wedding in Galilee* by Michel Khleifi. They're so programmatically eccentric and alternative that you can't think of them as partaking in the general economy of the grand narratives that we live by. And fourth and probably most important, the notion of Palestinian liberation is still unclear in the minds of many, even the Palestinians themselves, who want to be recognized, but recognized for what? This is self-criticism. The question of how we accommodate with the Jews of Israel is still uncertain. There's no formula for this. It can obviously only be done with the Jews, who have so far shown, with few exceptions, little interest in it. It's the teleology that's both missing here, and is difficult to imagine. Hence the attenuation of the narrative.

BR: One of the book's most striking examples of the battle on the home turf of intellectuals, a battle over vocabulary, is its polemic in pieces both by you and by Noam Chomsky, against the abusive concept of terrorism. The lack of any critical reaction in the United States to, say, the Israeli bombing of Tunis or the U.S. bombing of Libya, to take two examples among many, suggests that this is an uphill fight. How do you win acceptance for a counterterm like "state terrorism"? What are your ideas on this?

ES: That's where I disagree with Chomsky. I find the use of the word *terrorism* in almost any context, whether you use it as the media and the apologists have used it—as a way of creating and then attacking foreign devils—or as a label to apply to the state violence of the United States, Israel, et cetera, to be a largely self-defeating tactic.

BR: It's an "ism" we should just get rid of?

ES: I think so. I think Hitchens has been right about this. The use of the word "terrorism" is usually unfocused, it usually has all kinds of implicit validations of one's own brand of violence, it's highly selective. If you accept it as a norm, then it becomes so universally applicable that it loses any force whatever. I think it's simply better to drop it. I prefer the use of the word "violence," which allows for notions of *different types* of violence. What I've tried to do in a piece I've done since this book appeared is to look at terrorism, as well as the discourse and rhetoric and tropes of terrorism, as part of what I call the "politics of identity." These emanate out of the various identitarian forces in the nationalist world where patriotism, to be seen for example in the reinforcement of the curriculum in America all this about "Western values," "Judaeo-Christian values," are part of the economy that creates the limitlessly expanding discourse of terrorism, by which things "we" do not like are identified with terrorism. Therefore I think it's better not to talk about terrorism and show that we're really not the terrorists or "they" really are the terrorists; rather it is better to show terrorism as having a historical semantics which connects it with other processes in society with which we can interact oppositionally, so as to prevent violence against unarmed civilians and to eliminate the causes of desperate and irrational terror. Terrorism today is so nebulous a concept, has become so infected—almost as a business concept: there are, after all, terrorism experts, handbooks on terrorism, many many books, courses on terrorism, programs. It's a situation I don't think one ought to encourage by entering the fray. Rather, give alternatives to the notion and locate it in something else: violence as part of the politics of identity.

BR: While we're on the subject of terrorism: as an intellectual who's also active in a cause branded by many as terrorist by definition, I wonder whether you've ever felt that there's some affinity between the two terms in the American consciousness, that is, between the intellectual and the terrorist, two alien figures which, at least in the terms of American anti-intellectualism, seem to blend into one another.

ES: Partly because of the affinity you mention between the two terms, which is obviously a hidden affinity though an affinity nonetheless, I've noticed that among the *left* the use of the word "intellectual" has fallen into disrepute and disuse. And what instead has appeared are words like "professional" and "scholar" and "academic." And the use of the word "intellectual" has been relegated to some premodern realm, partly because "intellectual" suggests something rather more general. If you want to keep Foucault's use of the word—he distinguishes between a general and a specific intellectual—then it might come back into currency. But it hasn't. And people have been much happier, I think, with the notion of a technical expert or the academic or the professional or the critic—a word with much more positive valences than the intellectual. I think it's partly because of the general refusal of American Left intellectuals to accept their political role.

BR: It's been, of course, deliberate state policy in Israel both to expel local leaders from the Occupied Territories and to deny the representativeness of the PLO. Lately in this country you've had something very similar with the effort to close the PLO mission at the United Nations . . .

ES: . . . and the information office in Washington.

BR: One could take this as an attack on the idea of the representative intellectual, in fact, a kind of undermining of the notion of the intellectual by deliberate state policy. One wonders, when you also have within the academy, or that part of the academy that's influenced by so-called literary theory, an erosion of the concept of the representative intellectual, whether these two movements are not in some way related to one another, and whether we might have to draw some kind of conclusion: to put it schematically, whether this concept needs to be defended a lot more than it needs to be undermined right now.

ES: It probably ought to be looked at within the context of the general suspicion of representation, the whole problematic of representation. It is assumed that there's a kind of, not so much inauthenticity, but ideological deformation taking place whenever representation is at issue. Thus the notion of the representative intellectual strikes a chord of antipathy because there's assumed to be something constitutively false and deconstructible in it, so that nobody wants to venture into that place. If you refuse to occupy the position of representative intellectual, that makes it possible to occupy the kind of Archimedean position of the critic, who's always outside the group, who doesn't represent anything, but is a force for skepticism. I wouldn't want necessarily to leave aside from our discussion the profound effect on all of this of people like Derrida and de Man, who have contributed very much to the disrespect and distrust for the discourse of politics as something by which people live, constitute themselves, fight, die, et cetera. This kind of suspicion, this hovering on the margins, this infatuation with the undecideable and the ironic, it's all part of this. One can only look at it as a formation of late capitalism in the American academy.

BR: Before we get too far away from terrorism I just want to ask you one more question. I know that when the Reverend Benjamin Weir was a hostage in Lebanon he read some of your works, in Arabic I think . . .

ES: No, it was in English.

BR: And he appreciated them very much, as he has said. I wonder, if you can put your modesty aside for a minute, if you think there's any message in this experience—exactly the sort of thing one doesn't hear about hostages in the American media—for those who are interested in deconstructing the discourse of terrorism.

ES: Well, it's not only Weir and his story, which you repeated, but also Jeremy Levin of CNN, who was a hostage and escaped. He has become an active partisan of the Palestinians, but also of the general adversarial attitude to U.S. policy in the region. Of course it could be put down as just an example of the "Stockholm syndrome," the man who's fallen in love with his captors. But these are people who underwent not a "conversion" but a really quite dramatic change in their perception and have become rather active in trying to understand the ramifications and unforeseen results of U.S. policy as a policy which is not benign and altruistic but which has far-reaching effects on the lives of ordinary people. There are others, too. Take Pauline Cutting, this remarkable British physician who went to Beirut and worked in the camps of Sabra and Shatila as a physician. During the war of the camps (1985–88), she would be broadcasting from Sabra and Shatila when they were besieged by the Amal militia, and she said, "They are now eating cats and dogs. They are on the verge of cannibalism." So horrific were conditions during the siege. This is a British physician who volunteered to go in; she knew nothing about Palestine. It was through a Malaysian friend, I think, that she went. She came back and she wrote this book called *Children of the Siege* which is the number two best-seller in Britain. She cannot find an American publisher for the book. So there are cases like that. The question is how little effect their voices have had on the general discourse of terrorism, which continues to characterize Palestinians and others as terrorists.

BR: A question about Foucault and Gramsci as providing paradigms of the intellectual. You've written about both, and I know both of them have been quite important to you. I wonder whether you find both oppositions—that is, between the specific and the universal intellectual in Foucault and between the organic and the traditional intellectual in Gramsci—equally useful, and whether in your own thinking you find they contradict or complement each other.

ES: Insofar as a lot of people have taken those to be absolute distinctions between two kinds of intellectuals in both cases, intellectuals who are more or less reified in their position, I think they're not very useful. If they're conceded to be only analytic distinctions, then I think they're interesting in a kind of momentary way, especially the general-specific distinction made by Foucault. The organic-traditional duality proposed by Gramsci I think is interesting only in one way. I think it's perfectly possible—and I think Gramsci intended it this way, as a close reading of the *Notebooks* suggests—that the traditional intellectual was once an organic intellectual. The cycle is what is interesting about it. All classes have intellectuals who organize their interests. Once the class has achieved a certain stability, whether power or adjacence to power, then the conversion of the organic intellectual into the traditional intellectual is almost a foregone conclusion. But Gramsci leaves open the possibility that the traditional intellectual can also become an organic intellectual once again. He gives an instance in his essay on the Southern Question of the writer and editor Goletti, you may remember, who was a traditional intellectual who turned himself into an organic intellectual. So I think that's a very central and important set of distinctions and dynamic relationships.

To go back to Foucault: the specific-general distinction he makes is interesting except in the light of his later work when one begins to see that perhaps what he had intended as a legitimization of the specific intellectual turns into a kind of antecedent for his (to my mind) exclusive interest in the constitution of the self and subjectivity. If you look carefully at his analysis of specific intellectuals, it isn't that the specific intellectual only masters a particular field and has a discrete competence, but also that the specific intellectual has a particular subjectivity which is constructed as part of his or her selfhood and therefore legitimates the notion of selfhood in a particular context or setting. That is to say, Foucault already seems to be moving towards the politics of subjectivity, which becomes of course the subject of his later work, and which I find a falling off of interest. Insofar as the specific intellectual is a retreat from the world of the general, of the historical, of the social, it's an antipolitical position for Foucault to be supporting, and an invidious distinction. Most often it isn't perceived that way, of course; Foucault has achieved the status of a classic and remains an extraordinary figure.

BR: One of your own very influential coinages has been the term "affiliation," which proposes a possible model for the intellectual's relation to a constituency or collectivity. Another term which has had an equal effect is "worldliness." I wonder whether these two terms say the same thing in different ways, or whether there are significant differences in emphasis.

ES: Worldliness orginally meant to me, at any rate, some location of oneself or one's work, or the work itself, the literary work, the text, and so on, in the world, as opposed to some extra worldly, private, ethereal context. Worldliness was meant to be a rather crude and bludgeon-like term to enforce the location of cultural practices back in the mundane, the quotidian, and the secular. "Affiliation" is a rather more subtle term that has to do with mapping and drawing connections *in* the world between practices, individuals, classes, formations—that whole range of structures that Raymond Williams has studied so well in books like *The Long Revolution* and *The Country and the City*. Above all affiliation is a dynamic concept; it's not meant to circumscribe but rather to make explicit all kinds of connections that we tend to forget and that have to be made explicit and even dramatic in order for political change to take place.

BR: Since you mention Raymond Williams, he makes an interesting distinction, as I'm sure you know, between alignment and commitment, the latter being more intentional. Alignment is what you're stuck with. I wonder whether you could locate "affiliation" in relation to that distinction.

ES: The point is, of course, about intention. If you want to put it in a Freudian context, it's the move from unaware alignment to active commitment that he's interested in, the bringing of social relationships to consciousness.

BR: I didn't ask my question well. I guess I always wondered how much intention there *was* in affiliation, how close it was to alignment and how close it was to commitment.

ES: Oh, I see. That's a tough one. Well, I suppose it's closer to the notion of alignment than it is to commitment. It has also to

do with larger degrees of involuntary association and unconscious or hypocritically concealed association, complicity, and so
forth than it does with active commitment. The problem of commitment is a very difficult one. It's not difficult in England, where
there's a settled political tradition. Here, the notion of commitment is necessarily tactical. There is really no discourse of the left
here. There is no left formation of any sort, unless you think the
Democratic Party is the left. So the notion of commitment becomes a very difficult one to use. That's why it struck me as not
possible to employ it in the American context, except within a
very limited compass.

BR: In your critique of Michael Walzer in *Blaming the Victims*,
you demonstrate the political cost of his notion of belonging,
and you also suggest that "critical distance and intimacy with
one's people" need not be "mutually exclusive." It seems to me
that this suggestion answers those critics who've accused you of
erecting marginality and exile into an exclusive principle of intellectual activity. In the U.S., some leftists may be more willing
to tolerate Walzer's emphasis than they should be because
there's a sort of perceived relative deprivation of community.
We feel that we *need* this more than countries like England. I
wonder whether you yourself see the struggle to change American policy toward Palestine as requiring the building of new
solidarities, as well as the critique of old ones.

ES: There are two very important issues here. I'll start with the
end. The changing of our policy toward Palestine doesn't necessarily involve, in my opinion, building new forms of solidarity. All
I'm asking for at this point is honesty—to apply a rigorously
honest and international standard to discourse about the Middle
East, the same standard that one would like to apply to writing
about Central America. That's where the big gap has been. People
who find it very easy to support the Sandinista revolution or to
support the ANC in South Africa have said absolutely nothing
about the parallel case of the Palestinians in the Middle East. So
that's one very important point. The second point is that I think,
unless I'm forgetting here, that I attack Walzer on this point about
intimacy and belonging because of *where he got it from*. He got
it from the Algerian connection. It was an attempt to revalorize,

as he said, Camus's choice of his mother over "terrorism." What I found wrong with this—as most of the time when justifications for morally fallible and hypocritical choices are advanced—is that there's a factual inaccuracy at the base of it (I have no trouble talking about the factual). He was making it seem as if all of his life, Camus considered himself an Algerian and supported the demands of Algerian independence, and it was only when he was asked to choose between the terrorism of the FLN and his mother's life, that he in the end chose the community of the *pieds noirs*. That's a factual lie. I've studied it—the whole case of Algeria is a very interesting one—and it's true that in his early writings on Algeria Camus condemned French colonialism. But he condemned colonialism the same way Conrad condemned colonialism in Africa. Conrad condemned the abuses of the Belgians, and he condemned a little bit the excesses and the pretensions of the English, but he saw no alternative to colonialism. He said that this is the fate of this continent and this people, to be colonized by— I'm putting it crudely—their betters. And in fact when it came to writing about the existence of an Algerian nation, a separate Algerian nation that should *not* be colonized by France, of an Algerian-Muslim people, Camus always denied its existence, in exactly the way, in fact, Walzer and his cohorts have denied the existence of a Palestinian nation. Camus is explicit on this point. If you look at his *Chroniques algériennes*, he says, "Il ný a pas de nation algérienne. Ça n'existe pas." Which is to say that this entire nation, which has been "underdeveloped," to say the least, milked, abused, exploited by France for 130 years, didn't constitute a nation in the eyes of this Frenchman of Algiers. And therefore he chose his mother. All of this background Walzer removes from the account. So to say it's a matter of belonging is simply to overlook what kind of belonging it is. There's belonging, and then there's belonging. One can certainly belong to communities in ways that don't always involve rapacity, exploitation, and the denial of equal rights to other communities.

That's the second point. The third point I want to make is that I never said anything about rootlessness and exilic marginality as excluding the possibility of, shall we say, sympathetic—I'm using a very simple word—sympathetic identification with a people suffering oppression. Especially when the oppression is caused by one's own community or one's own polity. The example I always give is the example of a comparatist. You and I have comparatist backgrounds. The credo of Auerbach, this exiled German Jew in Istanbul during World War II, citing Hugo of Saint Victor, strikes me as a very different thing from saying, on the other hand, one must celebrate wandering exilic marginality. There's a kind of exilic existence which involves the crossing of barriers, the traversing of borders, the accommodation with various cultures, not so much in order to belong to them but at least so as to be able to feel the accents and inflections of their experience. As the antithesis of Camus in Algiers, take the case of Genet. Genet was the man who was able, in fact, to rise above this French identity, to identify in *Les paravents* with the Algerians and in his last and, some say, his greatest work, *Le captif amoureux*, with the Palestinians. This was a remarkable act of self-exile and repatriation in another's homeland. That's the point. Walzer seems to have missed all of that.

BR: To some extent the discourse of exile seems to stand in the way of articulating the Palestinian problem as a problem specifically *for Americans*, even though of course as you were saying a few minutes ago Israel depends so absolutely on American support. I'm thinking of what I call the "Little Drummer Girl" syndrome. In the film that was made of the Le Carré novel both sides of the Middle East conflict, Israeli and Palestinian, can be respected as "authentic," while the European or American, the Diane Keaton figure, in the film, who affiliates herself with a foreign cause, someone else's cause, is judged to be transgressing and is systematically broken and humiliated by the movie. In your experience trying to win a place on the leftist agenda for the Palestinian people, have you found any such "jargon of authenticity" to function as an obstacle? Is the fact that action presents itself to the American left as a sort of shopping list of foreign causes (South Africa, El Salvador, Nicaragua, and so on) an issue that can or should be tackled explicitly?

ES: What I think you're saying is that, whereas it's okay for the Palestinians and the Israelis on the one hand to feel strongly about what they stand for, the problem with Diane Keaton, with the little drummer girl, is that she feels she can identify with one *or* the other and thereby transgresses her own identity . . . right?

BR: That's the way the film represents anyone who would, not being Palestinian or Israeli, affiliate him or herself with such a cause: that person is inauthentic. In other words, there's no room for the *articulation*, which is so necessary to this particular case.

ES: I see your point. There are two things to be said—both of them about the Le Carré novel, which I read at the time it appeared (I didn't see the film). One is that the novel conceals what is, in fact, an ideology of the outside observer who can negotiate the claims of the two people. It is the prerogative of the Western white overlord who could stand outside and see and adjudicate the conflicts between these two warring rabbits, the two small parties. Of course Charlie's mistake is to go from one camp to the other in whole solidarity with one at the expense of the other. The critique of that is that one should stand above those camps: that is proper role of the Western referee/umpire. I felt at the time that this book was in fact a vindication of Western imperialism. Whereas of course by many Israelis it was taken—given of course Le Carré's writing about the war in 1982, when he wrote for The *Observer*, in sympathy with the Palestinians—it was taken to be a sympathetic account of the Palestinians. But in fact, in the structure of the book and its epistemology, there really is a legitimization of the outside disinterested observer who could only be white, Western, and WASP, and who is entitled to this perspective.

Number two: the other side of it is that there is assumed to be a kind of symmetry here, which "we" on the outside can perceive. Whereas from my point of view, I see the artificiality of the perspective of symmetry and balance which you find in Le Carré, in the "MacNeil/Lehrer Report," in the use of words like "objective" and "balanced" and all the rest of it, that people adopt in the discourse of American political science and governmental expertise. It's fundamentally flawed because in any conflict, it seems to me—and this is another problem that I have with Walzer—there's a question of justice, of right and wrong, comparatively speaking, of course. The major task—I say this actually without any qualification whatever—the major task of the American or the Palestinian or the Israeli intellectual of the left is to *reveal* the disparity between the so-called two sides, which appear rhetorically and ideologically to be in perfect balance but are not in fact. To reveal that there *is* an oppressed and an oppressor, a victim and a victimizer—unless we recognize *that*, we're nowhere. We'll endlessly be going around looking for formulas the way the United Nations and American diplomats are always looking for the right formula.

BR: One idea that has been much repeated in conversations about intellectuals and their relation to collectivity, especially among feminists, is the necessity to accept "the risk of essence," a phrase associated with Gayatri Spivak and Stephen Heath. Does that formulation have any resonance for you? Does it seem at all generalizable or useful in the case of the Palestinians?

ES: As I understand "the risk of essence," it means the insistence on the nativist essence in a national or gender struggle. There's a very good point here. The history of modern and indeed premodern nationalism suggests that the telos of nationalism is the fundamental reinforcement of a kind of native identity which becomes tyrannical in the end and of course dissolves or occludes important questions as well as issues of class, race, gender, and property. In my opinion, on the other hand, there is no way around the fact that struggles such as those of the Palestinians and other oppressed people, struggles that have to do with the attempt on the part of their oppressors to exterminate them—I don't mean physically only, but in an ethnic sense, to destroy the essence of the Palestinian, to make the Palestinian an "Arab" again or to drive them out, or any of these things associated not merely with Kahane but with elements of the Labor left, who say the Palestinians can go somewhere else—in this context, there's no substitute therefore for the struggle for identity. But I think that the struggle for nativist identity must always be linked to a further perspective leading to liberation, the perspective offered by people like C. L. R. James and other anti-nativist critics like him for whom I have great respect. On the one hand you want the right to represent yourself, to have your own ethos and ethnos, but unless they are linked, on the other hand, to a wider practice which I would call liberation, beyond national independence—liberation that would include attacking the question of the relationships between classes, between other "tribes" if you like—then I'm totally against it. It seems to me a violently dangerous and awful trap. Nowhere is this more evident than in the Israeli case. And to a lesser degree, in the case of the Lebanese Christians.

Criticism, Feminism, and the Institution
Gayatri Chakravorty Spivak

Gayatri Chakravorty Spivak came to Australia as one of the guest speakers of the Futur*Fall Conference—a conference on postmodernity held in Sydney July 26–29, 1984. The following interview was recorded in Sydney on August 17, 1984, by Elizabeth Gross, and was first published in *Thesis Eleven,* no. 10/11 (1984–85).

GROSS: Questions of writing, textuality, and discourse seem a major preoccupation in your published works. Could you outline what relations you see between problems of textuality and the field of politics, given that, for many theorists, these seem two disparate domains roughly divided along the lines of a theory-practice split?

SPIVAK: I think that this split is a symptomatic one. To define textuality in such a way that it would go in the direction of theory, with practice on the other side, is an example of how the institution and also rivalries between and among major intellectuals actually reduce the usefulness of a concept by giving it a minimal explanation. I think the notion of textuality was broached precisely to question the kind of thing that it is today seen to be, that is, the verbal text, a preoccupation with being in the library rather than being on the street. As far as I understand it, the notion of textuality should be related to the notion of the worlding of a world on a supposedly uninscribed territory. When I say this, I am thinking basically about the imperialist project, which had to assume that the earth it territorialized was in fact previously uninscribed. So then a world, on a simple level of cartography, inscribed what was presumed to be uninscribed. Now this worlding actually is also a texting, textualizing, a making into art, a making into an object to be understood. From this point of view the notion of textuality within the Western European/Anglo-U.S./international context tries also to situate the emergence of language as a model from the second decade of the twentieth century to see how the location of language or semiosis as a model was in itself part of a certain kind of worlding. Textuality is tied to discourse itself in an oblique way. Classical discourse analysis is not psychological largely because it tries to get away from the problem of language production by a subject. Textuality in its own way marks the place where the production of discourse, or the location of language as a model, escapes the person or the collectivity that engages in practice, so that even textuality itself might simply be an uneven clenching of a space of dissemination which may or may not be random. From this point of view, what a notion of textuality in general does is to see that what is defined over against "The Text" as "fact" or "life" or even "practice" is to an extent worlded in a certain way so that practice can take place. Of course you don't think this through at the moment of practice, but a notion of generalized textuality would say that practice is, as it were, the "blank part" of the text but it is surrounded by an interpretable text. It allows a check on the inevitable power dispersal within practice because it notices that the privileging of practice is in fact no less dangerous than the vanguardism of theory. When one says "writing," it means this kind of structuring of the limits of the power of practice, knowing that what is beyond practice is always organizing practice.

The best model for it is something woven but beyond control. Since practice is an irreducible theoretical moment, no practice takes place without presupposing itself as an example of some more or less powerful theory. The notion of writing in this sense actually sees that moment as itself situatable. It is not the notion of writing in the narrow sense so that one looks at everything as if it is written by some sort of a subject and can be deciphered by the reading subject. I would also like to say that the fact that words like "writing" and "text" have a certain paleonymy—that is to say, they are charged within the institution and they can be given the minimal interpretation of being nothing but library-mongering—itself marks the fact that the intellectual or anti-intellectual who can choose to privilege practice and then create a practice-theory split within a sort of theory, in fact, is also capable, because he or she is produced by the institution, of giving a minimal explanation of words like writing and text and forgetting that they mark the fact that we are, as we privilege practice, produced within an institution.

GROSS: You mention the intellectual. There has been much discussion in Marxist and leftist circles since 1968 about the role of the intellectual in political struggles. Althusser, for example, in his article "Lenin and Philosophy" has claimed that, in general at least, intellectuals are embroiled in ruling ideologies and act as their unwitting proponents. More recently, Foucault has suggested that the function of the intellectual is "no longer to place himself 'somewhat ahead and to the side' in order to express the truth of the collectivity; rather, it is to struggle against the forms of power that transform him into its object and instrument in the sphere of 'knowledge,' 'truth,' 'consciousness' and 'discourse' " ("The Intellectuals and Power." *Language, Counter-Memory, Practice*, 207–8). There seems, in other words, to be a debate between the role of the universal or the specific intellectual. What are your thoughts on this debate?

SPIVAK: I want to ask the question—the rhetorical question really—does the intellectual, *the* intellectual, have the same role in social production in Australia as in France? It seems to me that one of the problems here is that even as the intellectual is being defined as specific, there is at work the figure of an intellectual who seems not to be production-specific at all. The notion of the different place of the intellectual since May 1968—May 1968 does not have the same impact outside of a certain sort of Anglo-U.S.-French context—I am not at all denigrating the importance of May 1968 within the French context. In fact, as a result of reading the material that came out in France about May 1968 ten years later, I was able to see how important the event was. But, even within the U.S. in fact, there isn't something that can be called "an intellectual." There isn't, in fact, a group that can be called "a group of intellectuals," that exercises the same sort of role or indeed power within social production. I mean, a figure like Noam Chomsky, for example, seems very much an oddity. There isn't the same sort of niche for him. It is a much larger, more dispersed place which is racially, ethnically, historically, more heterogenous. There, one doesn't think about May 1968 in the same way unless it is within certain kinds of coterie groups. Having lived in the United States for some time, I would say that Berkeley 1967 makes more sense to me. Then if you think about Asia, and I notice you didn't mention that I am an Asian in your introduction—now let me say that I am one—there are intellectuals in Asia but there are no Asian intellectuals. I would stand by this rather cryptic remark. From this point of view I think the first question—the first task of intellectuals, as indeed we are—as to who asks the questions about *the* intellectual and *the* specific intellectual, *the* universal intellectual—is to see that the specific intellectual is being defined in reaction to the universal intellectual who seems to have no particular nation-state-provenance. Foucault himself, when he talks about the universal intellectual, speaks most directly about the fact that in France, in his own time, there was no distinction between the intellectual of the left and the intellectual. Now this particular absence of a distinction would make very little sense if one went a little further afield. Having said this let's look for a moment at Althusser.

I myself find safety in locating myself completely within my workplace. Althusser's notion of disciplinary practice in the essay called "Lenin and Philosophy" says that disciplines are constructed in terms of denegation. Disciplines are histories of denegation and what in fact disciplinary practice should be redefined as by the intellectual is a savage practice—a wild practice—so that the point was to transform the denegating disciplinary practice as a person within a discipline—*une pratique sauvage*.

This is the specific practice of the intellectual within his institutionality—and within it the question and text of science and ideology must be, as Althusser says, asked and opened repeatedly. It seems to me sometimes because of the historical constraints upon the figure of Althusser we tend to forget his moment and tend to locate ourselves on the text that is particularly named "theoretical practice." I would say that the tendency not to look at the margins, at what escapes the things with proper titles, is in itself caught up in this definition of the intellectual.

Foucault, on the other hand, is not really looking at, though I think he is practicing, this kind of wild disciplinary practice; he is looking more insistently at the disciplinarization of the discipline itself. There I think the student movement was then recuperated within the construction of what Mike Davis has called late American imperialism, that is to say 1953 to 1978; very slowly the notion of power, the specific power that the intellectual must confront, is conflated into power as the same system. I am narrativizing a complicated itinerary, so clearly I will be doing some injustice to Foucault, who remains a very important figure for me, but it seems to me that at that time when this matricial concept of power as the same system begins to emerge is at that point that the intellectual defined in this *very* situation specific way, which is then seen as "universal," and against that, the intellectual begins to declare and claim a sort of specificity, that's the moment when the intellectual begins to abdicate. We would say that that claim for specificity which is in reaction against a universality which is itself specific but cannot be given this specificity that it has—that claim for abdication is not a refusal, but a disavowal. We don't think that the intellectual placed in that situation is free to abdicate. I think this is why the discipleship of these great figures in fact transforms them immediately into the kind of watershed intellectual, universal intellectual that they would like not to be. It's almost as if their desire is being given back to them and defined by the fact that the way they are taken up, the way they're defended, the way they're nervously followed, shows that the intellectual is imprisoned—the Anglo-U.S.-Western European intellectual—is imprisoned within an institutional discourse which says what is universal is universal without noticing that it is specific too—so that its own claim to specificity is doubly displaced. It seems to me that their desire is being defined by their discipleship which is very quickly transforming them into universal intellectuals.

GROSS: **This raises the question that if the intellectual is in part defined by the position he or she occupies within an institution,** what do you think the relationship between that institution and the noninstitutional environment in which it is situated should be?

SPIVAK: Here, in fact, I say something which I have learnt from Foucault. I don't think there is a noninstitutional environment. I think the institution, whichever institution you are isolating for the moment, does not exist in isolation, so that what you actually are obliged to look at is more and more framing. And from that point of view, let me add a digression here. It seems to me that if one looks at institutionalization within the West since the seventeenth century without looking at the fact that those kinds of institutionalizations are being produced by something that is being perpetrated outside of the West—precisely during these years—then the story of institutionalization, disciplinarization of the definition of the man within the West—remains itself caught . . . within the institutionalization of the West as West, or the West as the world—that is something that needs to be said too—I don't think there is an extrainstitutional space. In a moment we might want to talk about how even paraperipheral space in terms of the Centre-Periphery definition is not outside of the institution.

GROSS: **There are institutions whose definition is such that they are supposedly defined as places of "pure learning," and since May '68 in France, since '67 in America, and around '69 in Australia as a result of the Vietnam War a number of academics have attempted to espouse their political commitments in places beyond the institutions in which they work. This raises possible problems. I wonder if you see any problems with this.**

SPIVAK: I myself see the step beyond the institution sometimes, not always, as capable of recuperation in a way that confronting the institution is not. It seems to me that within a cultural politics, and this is a phrase I will use over and over again, within a permissible cultural politics which allows enchanted spaces to be created, sometimes alternate institutions which might define themselves as "beyond the institution" are allowed to flourish so that the work of the production of cultural explanations within the institution can go on undisturbed. Let me take a *very* specific example relating again to my own workplace. I have found over the years that whereas the whole notion of interdisciplinary work has been allowed to flourish so that it can slowly degenerate into pretentious internationalism, if one confronts questions like distribution requirements, curricula requirements, *within* the structure of the institution, one meets with much more solid and serious opposition. So many more vested interests are at work within a society where repressive tolerance plays a very important function that in some ways it's almost easier to give space for alternative activity. I am not dismissing them, but it seems to me that the whole deglamourized inside of the institution defines our stepping beyond this.

As an academic myself I would say that if one begins to take a whack at shaking that structure up, one sees how much more consolidated the opposition is. I will go a step further: it seems to me that the definition of the institution as a place of pure learning is itself almost like a definition of the universal against which to become specific. I said a moment ago that when the Western European intellectual defines the universal intellectual and then says I am specific as opposed to that universal, what he doesn't see is that the definition of that universal is itself contaminated by a nonrecognition of a specific production. In the same way if one looks at—of course the system of education is different here from the United States—if one looks at how things like fiscal policy, foreign policy, the international division of labor, the multinational globe, the rate of interest, actually conduct the allocation of resources to institutions which take on a defining role in terms of what goes on in the institution, I think to create a straw institution which is a place of pure learning, so that we can then step beyond it, has almost the same morphology as creating a straw universal intellectual so that we can become specific.

GROSS: While you were in Australia you gave a number of lectures on the work of Derrida that were rather controversial. How would you situate Derrida's work in the context of this debate?

SPIVAK: Perhaps by the accident of my birth and my production —being born British-Indian and then becoming a sort of participant in the decolonization without a particular choice in the matter and then working in the United States, floating about in Europe, Africa, Saudi Arabia, Britain, and now Australia, I think I avoided in some ways becoming someone who takes on a master

discourse and I am always amused to see that I am, as you say, perhaps best known as a translator and commentator of Derrida, because the deconstructive establishment, I think, finds me an uncomfortable person. So I will say to begin with that I am not
particularly interested in defending Derrida as a master figure and
from that point of view I find it just by accident interesting that
it is not possible for me to follow Derrida in his substantive
projects. Within the *enthusiastic* Foucauldianism in the United
States there is a lot of that sort of following through on substantive projects. Having said this, what I like about Derrida's work
is that he focuses his glance very specifically at his own situation
as an intellectual who questions his own disciplinary production.
He tries in his latest work to see in what way, in every specific situation where he is in fact *being* an intellectual—being interviewed,
being asked to lecture, being asked to write—being asked to do
all of these things which an intellectual continues to do whether
he wants to do or not. He sees in what way he is defined as a foreign body. This has led to some very interesting work, because
it focuses not on what one's own desire is to be specific, rather
than universal—nonrepresenting, rather than a spokesperson, it
focuses on the perception of the institutionalized other as you as
an intellectual are asked to opine, to critique, even to grace and
to perform. He notices then specific situational contracts. He will
not allow us to forget the fact that the production of theory is in
fact a very important practice that is worlding the world in a certain way. At the moment his project is deeply concerned with the
problem that, within hegemonic practice, a method is identified
with a proper name. In spite of all the efforts to dismantle the notion of watershed or universal intellectuals within the Western
context, what is happening to the work done by the powerful intellectuals against that theory is in fact a transformation of that critique into the celebration of these figures as universal intellectuals. And I find it quite useful that Derrida focuses so strongly on
the problems that make a method identical with a proper name,
in our historical moment. I must say something else too. Where
I was brought up—when I first read Derrida I didn't know who
he was, I was very interested to see that he was actually dismantling the philosophical tradition from *inside* rather than from

outside because of course we were brought up in an education system in India where the name of the hero of that philosophical system was the universal human being, and we were taught that if we could begin to approach an internalization of that universal human being, then we would be human. When I saw that in France someone was actually trying to dismantle the tradition which had told us what would make us human, that seemed rather interesting too.

GROSS: You have argued that "French theorists such as Derrida, Lyotard, Deleuze and the like, have at one time or another been interested in reaching out to all that is not the West, because they have, in one way or another, questioned the millennially cherished excellence of Western metaphysics: the sovereignty of the subject's intention, the power of prediction and so on" ("French Feminism in an International Frame," *Yale French Studies*, no. 62, p. 157). In what ways do you see such French theory influencing your work on the critique of imperialism. (I ask the question partly because such examples of French theory have, at least occasionally, been labeled esoteric, elitist, and self-preoccupied, in which case, it may be hard to see their relevance in tackling the questions of exploitation and oppression.) What do you think about this?

SPIVAK: Now, I am not going to talk about the critique of the French intellectual's desire to do this; I am going to focus on the other side of your question—how it relates to my own kind of work on the critique of imperialism. I think wherever I have spoken about this desire on the part of intellectuals in the West, I have seen it as commemorating and marking a repeated crisis of European consciousness—and when I use the word "crisis" I am thinking not only of a crisis of conscience in a limited sense, but also in the broader perspective of crisis theory, the broader perspective of the theory of the management of crisis. If one reverses the direction, and here I am working within a very established deconstructive model of reversal and displacement, what does it say? That you reverse the direction of a binary opposition and you discover the violence. If one reverses the direction of this binary opposition the Western intellectual's longing for all that is not West, our turn toward the West—the so-called non-West's turn toward the West is a *command*. That turn was not in order to fulfill some longing to consolidate a pure space for ourselves; that turn was a command. Without that turn we would not in fact have been able to make out a life for ourselves as intellectuals. One has to reverse the binary opposition, and today of course since there is now a longing once again for the pure other of the West, we postcolonial intellectuals are told that we are *too* Western, and what goes completely unnoticed is our turn to the West is in response to a command, whereas the other is to an extent a desire marking the place of the management of a crisis. Now my critique of imperialism is not a principled production. I found as I was working through my own disciplinary production, the influences that I was working with, where Marxism itself must be included, I found that there was nothing else that I could do. To an extent I want to say that I am caught *within* the desire of the European consciousness to turn toward the East because that is my production. But I am also trying to lever it off—once again this is a deconstructive project if you like—to raise the lid of this desire to turn toward what is not the West, which in my case could very easily be transformed into just wanting to be the "true native." I could easily construct then, a sort of "pure East" as a "pure universal" or as a "pure institution" so that I could then define myself as the Easterner, as the marginal or as specific, or as the parainstitutional. But I am trying to see how much in fact I am caught within the European desire to turn toward the East; but how it has become doubly displaced. I think my present work is to show how in fact the limits of the theories of interpretation that I am working with are revealed through the encounter of what can be defined as "non-Western material."

GROSS: Perhaps we could move away from the question of the intellectual per se to look at the role of the feminist intellectual. You have accused First World academic feminists of a double standard: of ignoring, reducing, or explaining away the otherness of other women (e.g., "When we speak for ourselves [as academic feminists] we urge with conviction: the personal is the political. For the rest of the world's women, the sense of whose personal micrology is difficult (though not impossible) for us to acquire, we fall back on a colonialist theory of the most efficient information retrieval. We will not be able to speak to women out there if we depend completely on conferences and anthologies by Western-trained informants''; '' 'Draupadi' by Mahasveta Devi,'' *Critical Inquiry*, Winter 1981, p. 382). How is it possible to avoid a politics of representation, speaking for or on behalf of other women, retaining their specificity, their difference, while not giving up our own?

SPIVAK: My project is the careful project of unlearning our privilege as our loss. I think it is impossible to forget that anyone who is able to speak in the interests of the privileging of practice against the privileging of theory has been enabled by a certain kind of production. To my students in the United States, I talk about the "instant soup syndrome"—just add the euphoria of hot water and you have soup, and you don't have to question yourself as to how the power was produced and to an extent all of us who can ask the question of specificity, all of us who can make public the question of feminist practice in fact have been enabled by a long history to be in that position, however personally disadvantaged we might be, and from that point of view I would say just in answer to a specific question, the project is more of unlearning that privilege as a loss and it will not come through benevolence, it has to be charted out very carefully step by step. One of the things I am doing which seems, from the outside very complicated and intellectual indeed, is to search out psychobiographies, regulative psychobiographies for the constitution of the sexed subject which would be outside of psychoanalysis or counterpsychoanalysis. It seems to me that when one thinks about the question of women or women specifically as sexed subject either in terms of psychoanalysis or in terms of counterpsychoanalysis, what it leaves out is the constitution of women as sexed subject outside of the arena of psychoanalysis. This is one of the things I am trying to search out. Then you begin to see how *completely* heterogeneous the field of the woman elsewhere is because there you have to focus on regulative psychobiographies which are *very* situation-culture specific indeed and that effort is one way of using our disciplinary expertise, to see that the constitution of the sexed subject in terms of the discourse of castration was in fact, something that came into being through the imposition of imperialism, so that the discourse of antipsychoanalysis is in itself the working within a field which leaves out the constitution of the female subject elsewhere. That's one of my projects of unlearning my privilege, because in fact what is being done is that this kind of psychoanalytic discourse is being imposed upon the woman elsewhere. Also it seems to me what's being imposed on the woman elsewhere upon the other side of her more privileged ethnic sisters is a sort of glorification of sexual division of labor in other kinds of patriarchal/patrilinear/patrilocal societies, in opposition to the kind of space we inhabit. So from this point of view I would say that the major project for me is to unlearn our privilege as our loss; however personally disadvantaged we might be, we are still able to specify the problems of female specificity and that is the beginning—there is much more to say on this issue but that will be the beginning of my answer.

GROSS: **In a number of published texts you have discussed the "universal" oppression of women under patriarchy in terms of the effacement of the clitoris, of women's sexual pleasure whereby clitoridectomy can be considered a metonymy of women's social and legal status. Could you elaborate on this?**

SPIVAK: I was talking, of course, not only about clitoridectomies as such but also about symbolic clitoridectomies as marking the place of women's desire; but I should also say that the choice of universality there was a sort of strategic choice. I spoke of universality because universality was in the air on the other side in the talk of female discourse. What was happening was a universal solution was being looked for and since I believe that one shouldn't throw away things but use them, strategically I suggested that perhaps rather than woman inhabiting the spaces of absence, perhaps here was an item which could be used as a universal signifier. I was asking myself the question . . . how can the unexamined universalizing discourse of a certain sort of feminism become useful for us since this is the hegemonic space of feminist discourse. I chose that one and tried to scrupulously work it through in terms not just of actual clitoridectomies but symbolic ones. My own interest, on the other hand, as I have just indicated, is in working out the heterogeneous production of sexed subjects. It is also, to move the question outside of subject-constitution—in terms of recognizing the international division of labor. There I think one looks not only at the construction of the urban subproletariat, since most specifically since 1971, after capitalism in the West became postmodern—not only at the construction of the paraperipheral woman, unorganized peasant labor among women and so on, but also such questions as tribality, aboriginality and in fact if I can throw in an aside since you are an expert on Kristeva, I would say that for me the question of the abject is very closely tied to the question of being *ab*-original, rather than a reinscription of the object, it is a question of the reinscription of the subject. Now it seems to me it is very useful if one can think of female subject constitution as well, because one doesn't usually. The kind of discourse you get when you speak of the constitution of the urban subproletariat or the paraperipheral woman, or tribality, aboriginality, et cetera: either a very hard, classical Marxist fundamentalist kind of talk or a sort of celebration of the other. In terms of those psychobiographies I am interested in looking at these women who are being shafted by postmodern capitalism. I am interested in looking at them also in terms of their subject constitution which would throw a challenge to being caught within psychoanalysis or counterpsychoanalysis. This is what I meant when I said in answer to your question of how my critique of imperialism relates to the French intellectual's gaze toward the other of the West I said that I find that the limits of their theories are disclosed by an encounter with the materiality of that other of the West—that is one of the limits. So, I am fundamentally concerned with that heterogeneity, but I chose a universal discourse in that moment because I felt that rather than define myself as repudiating universality, because universalization, finalization, is an irreducible moment in any discourse—rather than define myself as specific rather than universal—I should see what in the universalizing discourse could be useful and then go on to see where that discourse meets its limits and its challenge within that field. I think we have to choose again strategically, not universal discourse but essentialist discourse. I think that since as a deconstructivist—see, I just took a label upon myself—I cannot in fact clean my hands and say I'm specific. In fact, I must say I am an essentialist from time to time.

There is, for example, the strategic choice of a genitalist essentialism in antisexist work today. How it relates to all of this other work I am talking about—I don't know, but my search is not a search for coherence, so that is how I would answer that question about the discourse of the clitoris.

GROSS: I don't know exactly how to follow up this question, but I am interested in how to *use* universalism, essentialism, et cetera, strategically, without necessarily making an overall commitment to these kinds of concepts.

SPIVAK: You see, you *are* committed to these concepts, whether you acknowledge it or not. I think it's absolutely on target not to be rhetorically committed to it, and I think it's absolutely on target to take a stand against the discourses of essentialism, universalism as it comes in terms of the universal—of classical German philosophy or the universal as the white upper-class male, et cetera. But *strategically* we cannot. Even as we talk about *feminist* practice, or privileging practice over theory, we are universalizing—not only generalizing but universalizing. Since the moment of essentializing, universalizing, saying yes to the ontophenomenological question, is irreducible, let us at least situate it at the moment; let us become vigilant about our own practice and use it as much as we can rather than make the totally counterproductive gesture of repudiating it. One thing that comes out is that you jettison your own purity as a theorist. When you do this you can no longer say my theory is going to stand against anyone else's because in this sense the practice really norms the theory, because you are an essentialist from time to time. So, from that point of view the universal that one chooses in terms of the usefulness of Western high feminism is the clitoris. The universalism that one chooses in terms of antisexism is what the other side gives us, defining us genitally. You pick up the universal that will give you the power to fight against the other side and what you are throwing away by doing that is your theoretical purity. Whereas the great custodians of the antiuniversal are obliged therefore simply to act in the interest of a great narrative, the narrative of exploitation, while they keep themselves clean by not committing themselves to anything. In fact, they are actually run by a great narrative even as they are busy protecting their theoret-

ical purity by repudiating essentialism. This is how I would describe that situation.

GROSS: You have just made a distinction between feminism
and antisexism. Antisexism, I take it, is a negative, critical gesture
toward dominant forms of patriarchy, whereas feminism seems
to be much more positive. Would you like to elaborate on this?

SPIVAK: Yes. Antisexism is reactive in the face of where we are
thrown. I am sure you wouldn't agree that notions of feminism
could in fact be located in terms of sexual difference understood
as genital difference. That is a total reduction of feminism, but as
antisexism is reactive, it seems to me that there one has to produce a reverse legitimization of sexism itself. If you just define
yourself as antisexist you are indeed legitimizing sexism. I don't
care, as I said I am not interested in being pure even as I remain
an antiessentialist. It seems to me that that kind of contamination
of my own possible theoretical excellence is how situational practice norms my theory. Because if I chose to be pure in that sense,
you know, displacing the question of sexual difference rather
than legitimizing it by acting to confront the discourse of the sexist, it seems to me that all I would gain is theoretical purity, which
in itself I question in every way. So antisexist work is work on every level, not just the tenuring of women, but the work that goes
on in battered women's clinics, of paralegal work in the women's
sections of unions; this is as much antisexist as the tenuring of
women or structuring a conference so that there is equal
representation. In the United States I think this kind of affirmative
action is deeply in hock to corporate feminism. So what is one
supposed to do, withdraw? And if one doesn't withdraw, this is
not just a revisionary argument. This is a practical argument since
it seems to me that antirevisionary arguments have become
fetishized in the context of postmodern capitalism. So from that
point of view one can't choose to be a purist as opposed to a revisionist. It seems to me that in that context one contaminates one's
virtues by becoming an antisexist rather than a feminist in the
sense of looking at subject constitution—distinguishing between
and among women and so on.

GROSS: A feminism which didn't address the question of antisexism is in danger of utopianism.

SPIVAK: I think it's happening—in fact the example I gave here which is troubling me a great deal, when I was in Urbino at the conference on deconstruction just a couple of weeks ago and I stood up to speak about the foreclosing of the importance of the question of sexual difference or the law of genre in Derrida . . . , the people who were most uneasy were the card-carrying female deconstructivists because they wouldn't touch antisexist work because that would only prove once again that they were not being theoretically pure deconstructivists and what was most marked was the unease—talk about civilization and its discontents—you know that in the German version of the Freud text the word is actually unease, rather than discontent, and that is what you saw—they were sitting in front and you know from your adolescent days how hard it is to keep up a nervous giggle for like, 30 minutes. These women were just sitting and giggling because they felt the inclusion of some vulgar antisexist person. I wasn't being a "vulgar antisexist" there because I was not talking about body counts; I was talking about what was being foreclosed in the deconstructive establishment, but they were redefining their other, which was *vulgar* antisexism—the word is gynegogy —they were defining that as their other, so that they could be the pure deconstructive feminists. That was happening—the moment antisexism was let go.

GROSS: This relates rather neatly to my next question. You have argued in two texts, "Displacement and the Discourse of Women" in *Displacement—Derrida and After* (ed. M. Krupnick), and "French Feminism in an International Frame," *Yale French Studies*, no. 62, that, and I quote, "I . . . find in deconstruction a 'feminization' of the practice of philosophy, and I do not regard it as just another example of the masculine use of woman as instrument of self-assertion. I learn from Derrida's critique of phallocentrism—but I must then go somewhere else with it?" ("Displacement and the Discourse of Women," p. 173). Where is this "somewhere else"?

SPIVAK: It's a question that in part I have answered as I have been responding to your other questions. But let us bring the bits and pieces together so this will be a sort of repetitive answer. But perhaps it should be said first that the product of the feminization of philosophy has changed within Derrida's own work. It didn't go in the direction of *"devenir-femme"* in Derrida. I should also point out that the critique of phallocentrism has itself changed within the context of what Derrida calls affirmative deconstruction—it is more a critique of anthropomorphism. There one can either go in the direction of saying that when a text is purged of anthropomorphism, what one should look for is how the text constitutes the narrative of its own production. This is the way that dominant deconstruction is going—there *anthropos* is defined as human. But the direction in Derrida's later work is to see that *anthropos* is defined as "man" as a sign that has no history. So Derrida then begins to worry about the history of the sign "woman." And he goes to the question of the establishment of philosophy or theory as the repeated refinding of the lost subject, and here with all due respect I would say that some of this symptomaticity is seen in *The History of Sexuality*, the repeated refinding of the lost object. This is confused with the question of women so that the Derridean scene changed. But my "somewhere else" is—I don't know quite what it is—but let me just give an account: one of my somewhere else's is this kind of antisexism which is against a sort of purity of the deconstructive approach. Derrida himself is very careful to distinguish woman in some genitalist description from the figure of woman, the question of woman, the law of genre, et cetera. There I part company. I think it is important to be an antisexist. My second way has been not only to see how remaining within a Freudian discourse one can identify the production of philosophy of the refinding of the lost objects but to find some place outside where the regulative psychobiographies construct women in another way. Thirdly, this business about the international division of labor does not exist within deconstructive considerations at all. Not that it exists elsewhere. One of the points that I have made repeatedly is that because the moment of the epistemic violence of imperialism in the seventeenth and eighteenth centuries is not really considered, the international division of labor today is allegorized into the situation of the "guest workers" or the Third World people in First World arenas, which has really very little to do with the larger problem. So looking at the constitution of class structure, the new reconstitution of the class structure within and among women, even as that constitution has to be confused by the question of subject constitution, has no place within the deconstructive arena. And the final task, which is the unlearning of one's own privilege as a loss, Derrida does it, but it is another privilege that he is dealing with. I think since one can't know where one's "somewhere else" is because one is also caught within this place, which is, in the context of this question, Derrida's discourse, I can only give shadowy repetitive indications of what that is.

GROSS: **One final question. Your work can be considered both deconstructionist, Marxist, and feminist. Given that these three fields maintain something of an awkward, if not tense relationship, do you think some reconciliation between them is possible?**

SPIVAK: In a recent interview Foucault has disclaimed his commitment to the notion of discontinuity and has suggested that it was a misreading of *Les mots et les choses* to define him as a philosopher of discontinuity—I *am* going to use the term here because I am really thinking of—to use a very old-fashioned grid—I am thinking of it now synchronically. I really think that given all that I have said about strategic choices of essentialism and so on, the irreducible but impossible task is to preserve the discontinuities within the discourses of feminism, Marxism, and deconstruction. I have seen already here how in questions and answers it can be effaced by the name "Marxist" and how it can be effaced of course by the imposition of the name "deconstructivist." If I have learned anything it is that one must not go in the direction of a Unification Church, which is too deeply marked by the moment of the colonialist influence, creating global solutions that are coherent. On the other hand, it seems to me that one must also avoid as much as possible in the interests of practical effectiveness, a sort of continuist definition of the differences so that all you get is hostility. On one side you get a sort of identification of Marxism in the U.S. left in the sixties, or with what has been happening since the British New Left in Britain, or the party structure in France or other Eurocommunist countries, and the slogan "Marxist is sexist" bears this hostility, not understanding that it is a method that is used in very different ways. On the other side you get declarations by figures as powerful as Samir Amin, not to mention figures less powerful like Paul Piccone from *Telos*, in the United States, that feminism has been the movement that has been most against the interests of social justice in our time. Of course deconstruction, we have already rehearsed some of those in your questions, is only textualist, it is only esoteric, concerned with self-aggrandizement, nihilist, et cetera. It seems to me that the role of the person, or persons, the collectivity, interested in using the immense resources of feminism, Marxism, the much more recent deconstructive morphology is in the field of work to preserve the discontinuities, and I say ultimately it is an impossible task for finalization is itself impossible but irreducible. To preserve these discontinuties in that sort of sense, rather than either wanting to look for an elegant coherence or producing a continuist discourse which will then result in hostility—I think that is what I want to do.

GROSS: **Do you have any final remarks?**

SPIVAK: In fact I've been wanting to say something all through this. I believe that many of these answers would have been impossible if my experience in Australia—and I have given sixteen lectures in two weeks—had not almost obliged me to think through the implications of what I have been doing, and in a sense the place of Australia on the map is so problematic, the way in which it relates to and is going to relate to Asia in the coming years, the place in which it seems to construct itself in relation to Western Europe and Anglo-U.S. It seems to me that if, as someone of Asian provenance working in the United States with a certain *carte d'identitie* in Western Europe and Britain, I think I have been really pushed to the extreme—of having to take stock and having to see exactly what it was that I was up to, so thank you.

The Professional-Managerial Class Revisited
Barbara Ehrenreich

The following interview was conducted in November 1988 as Barbara Ehrenreich was completing *Fear of Falling* (forthcoming from Pantheon), which explores further the topic of her enormously influential essay (co-authored in 1976 with John Ehrenreich) "The Professional-Managerial Class." The interviewer is Bruce Robbins.

BR: Most twentieth-century discussions of intellectuals and politics seem to ignore gender completely. It's as if, even while intellectuals were treated as a "universal," the category was assumed to apply only to men. How do you think feminism's reflections on gender have already modified or ought to modify the ongoing debate over intellectuals? Is the category one that you feel at home in and with yourself? Do you think women have a stake in the discussion, or really need not feel particularly concerned by it?

One special reason for asking these questions is the following: in several responses to Russell Jacoby's *The Last Intellectuals*, you have been offered as a conspicuous example of one stubbornly independent intellectual who has resisted the flight into the universities. For Jacoby, this flight foreshadows the end of intellectuals as such. With what feelings do you greet such narratives (which of course emanate as much from the right as from the left) of academicization as the decline and fall of the formerly public-spirited intellectual? Does your own career as a writer and activist seem to you exceptional in this regard? Is the institutionalization of the so-called New York Intellectuals and then of much of the oppositional culture of the sixties something to be regretted? Should the strong presence of feminism within the academy today be seen more as the academy's co-optation or as feminism's achievement?

BE: First, I want to be sure we are not mixing up "intellectuals" and the New Class—professional-managerial class, or, as I now call it, only slightly more euphoniously, the professional middle class. One of the biggest problems in left discussions of the PMC or new class is the failure to distinguish between "intellectuals" and the larger class. This is one of the weaknesses of Gouldner's otherwise incisive book, *The Future of Intellectuals and the Rise of the New Class*. The PMC contains many people who are not intellectuals in any sense of the word, and, conversely, people who ought truly to be regarded as "intellectuals" are scattered throughout all social classes.

Actually, Gouldner—like John Ehrenreich and myself—defines the New Class broadly to include white-collar, at least college-educated, professional and managerial people. So we have a group whose members include not only "intellectuals" (e.g., professors of lit, et cetera, but chemical engineers, corporate lawyers, executives (below the level, wherever it is exactly, where stock options, et cetera, put one into the capitalist class or corporate elite). Some of these people are "intellectuals" in their reading habits, conversational expectations, et cetera. Some of them are incurious, ill-informed dopes.

To digress for a moment into definitional matters: I know that members of the more intellectual professions bridle at being lumped in the same class as chemical engineers, et cetera. This was the source of much of the criticism John and I encountered for the PMC essay in 1976. Intellectuals want to be in a class of their own, and actually would prefer to be "classless" if possible —disembodied minds. There are at least two good reasons for defining the PMC more broadly:

One: There is an occupational commonality between professionals and managerial personnel. Both are in the business of what could roughly be called conceptualization and command. The engineer's design defines the labor of many lower-level workers; the professor's idea may (if it is a very successful idea) define the labor of students and others. This similarity is, I must say, much more visible from outside the class than from within—as numerous interviews with working-class people demonstrate. Also, individuals routinely move between the two types of occupations, or between the profit and nonprofit sectors, without experiencing upward or downward mobility.

Two: a group is not a "class" unless it has some kind of internal social cohesion (or at least cohesion within racial or ethnic subgroups). Professors and chemical engineers (just to stick to those examples) do not occupy different social worlds. They live in the same neighborhoods, go to the same social events, marry each other, and hope that their children turn out to have similar occupations. (The professor of lit may be mildly disappointed if his or her child turns out to be an engineer, and vice versa; both however, would be devastated if the child becomes a forklift operator). Much of what is interesting about a class derives from its *social* existence, and its hopes for reproducing itself, in castelike fashion, from one generation to the next.

But to return to the intellectuals: one reason I am so insistent on distinguishing intellectuals from the PMC is that I come from a family that contained a good sprinkling of *working class intellectuals*: people who did not have much formal education, but who read widely and loved a hot discussion. Television has no doubt reduced the ranks of working-class intellectuals—and intellectuals in general—but I still know plenty of them. In fact, looking back, I would say that one reason I was sensitive to the existence of a PMC in the first place was that I was not inclined to see the division of labor—and the distribution of intellectual skills implied by it—as just or "natural."

All of this to get to women as intellectuals. I don't know what the "debate over intellectuals" is, aside from Jacoby's book—the general point of which I agree with. But there are no women to speak of in his book—certainly not me. In fact, I am quite flattered that he has been criticized for ignoring *me* (and other women and people of color). Maybe women are still invisible. But it is also possible that Jacoby's thesis is all too true, and that *nonacademics* are invisible—even to him.

I would love to see a good study of feminist intellectuals and the academy. Personally, I am very ambivalent about the academicization of feminism—and perhaps, especially, socialist feminism. On the one hand, I'm glad to see all these feminists stably employed, and employed in a manner which allows them to influence younger women—and hence to help reproduce the feminist movement. Women's studies has become a major reproductive organ, if you will forgive the anatomical analogy, of feminism. We couldn't do the same thing, or perhaps have the same intensive effect, if we were all scattered in our basement offices, as I am, hustling to make a living.

On the other hand, the academicization of feminism has meant the end of the exciting feminist intellectual milieu I once moved in. Where once feminist thinkers of all sorts (variously employed, unemployed, and so forth) gathered for conferences and study groups, now the academics have their own world. They have to give papers in academic settings because that is where the career points are. But worst of all, they have to give *papers*. There is no setting, or very few settings, that allows for wild speculation and unrestrained curiosity. Ideas, in the PMC, are property. People hesitate to overstep the boundaries of their field, or to be caught saying anything reckless. There is caution. There is anxiety.

It seems to me also that academicization has brought some isolation of (academic) feminist intellectuals from the left. Not long ago I was talking to some of the organizers of the annual Socialist Scholars' Conference about how to beef up the feminist presence at this event. No small part of the problem is that the kinds of socialist feminist academics they would like to attract to the SSC are not really disposed anymore to fly halfway across the country and address a somewhat heterogeneous audience in a context that offers little or no professional recognition. The same women do speak at universities and at professional meetings, to smaller audiences and often for no pay, but the idea of mixing it up with left intellectuals of all sorts no longer seems to appeal.

I feel lucky to still have a toehold in the academic world. I get invited to speak at professional meetings, women's studies' conferences, and I occasionally get offered an academic job. But I do sometimes feel that the gulf between me and the academic world is widening. Here's a tiny example: a couple of months ago I got a letter from the new journal associated with the National Women's Studies Association, asking me to submit an article based on a speech I had given. The article, I was warned, would have to be in "appropriate" form, meaning, I suppose, footnotes and a laborious style. Then it would be critically reviewed—and of course, possibly rejected—by a panel of "experts in your field."

Well, of course I have no "field," nor do I have a job which allows me to write academic-style articles for no remuneration. I think the sisters at NWSA are becoming a little insular. And I worry that, if I can't cross the cultural barrier that walls off academia —and I can write an academic article if I have to—then who can?

So we are well into your third question here. Would I say my career has been exceptional, meaning unusual? Not really. At this point, most of my close friends are not academics, but are writers, journalists, media people, union personnel, public-interest activists of one sort or another. Few of these people have followed very orderly career trajectories; few of them specialize in any one intellectual "field." If there is an occupational group I belong in, it is free-lance writers. They are a motley crowd, living mostly from hand to mouth, interested in everything. Sometimes I envy my friends in academia because they get paid *even if they don't think of something new*, even if they teach or write the same thing over and over for months at a time. But, like most free-lancers I know, I am congenitally incapable of specialization. After I am done with what I am writing now about the new class, or PMC, I will probably do a lot more reading about history—or cosmology.

As for being a "public" intellectual: writers seek to be published—that's how we get paid—and this makes us "public" whether we are interested in influencing opinion or not. I am a little afraid that Jacoby's "public intellectual" is really a *famous* intellectual. Many, many fine thinkers strive to have a political impact through their writing and do not ever become as visible as, say, Irving Kristol. The important thing, to me, is being a *political* intellectual: trying to "shift the discourse" through every available medium and, equally important, keeping in touch with all kinds of streams of protest and dissent so as to know what's important to say. And I would really emphasize the latter because of the class insularity of so much intellectual culture. Being a political intellectual means keeping abreast of all kinds of struggles, trends, ideas, people. Then you have something to be "public" about.

BR: Your influential essay "The Professional-Managerial Class" has occasionally been seen as a possibly overoptimistic adaptation of earlier "New Class" arguments to the specific (and now vanished) headiness of the sixties. Looking back, how do you see the context that essay came out of? How have subsequent events affected your view of the political potential of the "PMC"?

I'll tack on a somewhat related question. In some of your writing, the political target seems to be the new "expertise" that increasingly and authoritatively defines women to themselves. In what organizational form, under what banner or banners do you imagine the resistance to such expertise taking shape? Should expertise *as such* be contested (for example, in the name of the preexisting knowledge that the experts expropriated and/or defeated), or is expertise neutral in itself, but only exploitative as practiced?

BE: The PMC essay was hardly an "overoptimistic" adaptation of new class arguments. In fact, most of the critics in the midseventies found it too negative. It was widely taken as an *attack* on the PMC, and there was often a tone of personal umbrage in the criticisms. Yet the essay was pointedly ambivalent, which is in keeping with the politics of the class itself.

As far as I can see, all left or liberal assessments of the new class in the sixties and seventies were "overoptimistic." This is because the new class, or PMC, called attention to itself principally through the student movement of the sixties. People who studied the class saw its radical side—its capacity to stand up against capital and fight for greater autonomy for the class, or to fight on behalf of others—the poor, blacks, the Vietnamese. There was a tendency to see the class as inherently radical, or at least liberal, and this tendency reaches an extreme with the neoconservatives, who see the new class as deeply and permanently hostile to capitalism, "traditional values," et cetera, and caricature it as the "liberal elite."

I think John and I were fairly unique in seeing the conservative side of the PMC at that time. No one else (on the left) emphasized its elite status relative to the working class. No one else pointed out its uneasy and often antagonistic relationship to the working class. No one else talked about the possibilities for the use of "expertise" as an instrument of domination, and in defense of class status. This got us into a lot of trouble at the time, and you might want to read the essays in *Between Labor and Capital* to get the flavor of the responses.

The context our essay came out of was an activist one. By the seventies, many of us from the New Left were trying to create a more class-diverse kind of movement. Former student activists were going into factories to "proletarianize" themselves. Organizations like New American Movement, of which we were members, were seeking to attract blue- and pink-collar recruits. Tragically, many of these experiments with a multiclass, non-university-based left were disastrous, and they were disastrous principally because of the unconscious class insularity and class arrogance of leftists from the PMC. John Welch's essay in *Between Labor and Capital* gives you an idea of how the left looked from *outside* the PMC, and it wasn't good.

We tried to figure out what was going on. Marxism gave us the idea of class, but no idea of the "new class." We might have saved a lot of head scratching if we'd known then about the work of David Bazelon, a refreshingly nonacademic, former Trotskyist who had written (pretty optimistically) about the new class in the mid-sixties. But we had no clue as to the prior intellectual existence of a "new class" and had to invent it for ourselves. Naturally our view of the class was ambivalent: we had seen, in parts of the student left and the feminist movement, the PMC at its best—defiant of capital and hierarchy in general, eagerly reaching out to others. We had also seen it at its worst, for example, in the responses of white professionals to the black-led "community control" movement in New York City in the mid-sixties.

So, no, I haven't changed my mind. We were critical, not optimistic. And if we hadn't been critical, we wouldn't have had any way of understanding how the same class could have generated the New Left in the sixties and the yuppies in the eighties. For *that* story, you will have to wait for the book [*Fear of Falling*] I am working on now.

About "expertise": it's a great thing. There are just two problems: one, often it's wrong. Deirdre English's and my book *For Her Own Good* is all about expert ideas being bent out of shape to serve the purposes of gender domination, so I won't say any more about that. Women's collective experience has led us to be very wary of "experts" telling us how to live, et cetera. Two, often it's *stretched* out of shape to become "generalized expertise," which is about the same thing as class ideology. For example, you can get on a TV talk show if you've written a book, have a Ph.D., or similar credential. Then you can say just about anything on any subject. This is great for those of us who aim to be "public intellectuals," but it also deeply offends my populist instincts.

I don't know about "organizational forms" for battling misuses of expertise. Usually antiexpertise tends to become anti-intellectual. The trick is to battle ideology-disguised-as-expertise in a *pro*-intellectual manner, that is, to insist that truth matters, that ideas matter, and that truth is *everyone's* responsibility.

BR: **Where do you locate the intellectual roots of the so-called New Class? What theorists were important to you as you began to explore it? What were its relations to the student movement of the sixties?**

BE: There was no great media "discovery" of the class which had generated the student movement. But there was, both here and in Europe, a surge of intellectual interest in the social group —"class," "stratum," or whatever—that had generated this surprising rebellion. They were like any other workers, in that they possessed no great material assets and made their livings as hirelings to others. But they were *educated* workers, and this set them off as a kind of intelligentsia above the average person who labors, often at quite menial tasks, for his or her subsistence. The challenge—to theorists of the left, right, and center—was to explain the political proclivities of this white-collar intelligentsia, or middle class, and particularly its unexpected appetite for rebellion.

On the left and liberal side of the spectrum, theorizing about the middle class—or, as it was more often called in intellectual circles, the "new class"—predated the student movement by more than a decade. Two rather disparate developments spurred this early, and often obscure, interests in the subject. One was the evident failure of the Soviet Union as a model for democratic socialism, which suggested that a new kind of class domination had arisen within the communist world. The other was the rapid growth, brilliantly documented by C. Wright Mills, of the white-collar workforce within the United States. This suggested that a new class, an educated, white-collar middle class, was gaining strength within the capitalist world.

The problem of what had gone wrong with the Russian Revolution consumed left-wing, but anti-Stalinist (i.e., Trotskyist) intellectuals throughout the forties and fifties. The Soviet Union obviously wasn't capitalist, but neither was it a "dictatorship of the proletariet," if that unfortunate phrase was supposed to mean that the working class was running things. So who exactly was in charge? Evidently, the bureaucrats and something that could be called the intelligentsia were on top, but who, in rigorous Marxist class terms, were *they*?

The Trotskyists' eventual answer was that the Soviet bureaucracy, which ran the state and hence just about everything, represented an entirely new, and generally unforeseen, social class. This idea was convincingly seconded by the Yugoslav dissident Milovan Djilas, whose book *The New Class* appeared in English in 1957. Djilas had been second in command to Tito during the Yugoslav revolution: now he declared that the revolution had been betrayed by a "new class" rooted in the "political bureaucracy." All communist revolutions, he argued, had run the same course: declaring themselves victories of the working class, they had succeeded only in replacing the old capitalist elite with a new managerial and bureaucratic elite.

It was not obvious, to left-wing intellectuals in the fifties, that there might be a parallel class within capitalist societies like the United States. But to John Kenneth Galbraith, who was probably aware of Djilas's book, but had the advantage of not being seeped in the tight, claustrophobic, reasoning of the Trotskyist left, the American parallel seemed self-evident. In his best-selling 1958 book, *The Affluent Society*, he unapologetically introduced an American "new class" of professional and managerial workers. It was not sinister and power-hungry like its socialist counterparts, but nevertheless struggling "energetically to perpetuate itself."

Unburdened by the need to "prove" that this new middle class existed in a doctrinaire, Marxist sense, Galbraith instead raised the interesting question of why its existence had gone so long unnoted. The explanation, he argued, lay in "one of the oldest and most effective obfuscations in the field of social science." This was the idea that "all work—physical, mental, artistic, or managerial—is essentially the same." In fact, for most people, work is "fatiguing or monotonous or, at a minimum, a source of no particular pleasure." Only in the New Class is work seen, and often experienced, as intrinsically rewarding, creative, and important. But to admit the difference would be to acknowledge a deep and disquieting inequality: "In both [capitalist and communist] societies it servesthe democratic conscience of the more favored groups to identify themselves with those who do hard physical labor. A lurking sense of guilt over a more pleasant, agreeable, and remunerative life can often be assuaged by the observation 'I am worker too.' "

Aside from this apparently minor deception, Galbraith found little to fault in the New Class or its ambitions. If its work was more pleasurable and rewarding than that of the working class, then more power to it. The New Class had no particular political ax to grind, in Galbraith's account, and represented the estate that most people would attain if they could. The humane thing to do was to let the old dirty and exhausting forms of toil wither away —presumably through automation—and let the New Class expand until it had absorbed nearly everyone.

Once the sixties were under way, and with them the student rebellion, no one could imagine that America's educated middle class, or "New Class," was politically neutral. It seemed to most liberal and left-leaning intellectuals to represent a fresh force for change—inclined to be at least liberal in its views if not actually radical. No one imagined that it would move, in a few years, to the right; the problem was to explain and interpret its leftward momentum. One of the best and most accessible analyses of the

American "New Class" was David Bazelon's delightfully written 1967 book, *Power in America.*

While Galbraith had stressed the comforts and privileges enjoyed by the new middle class, Bazelon stressed its subordinate status as employees of the truly powerful. In Bazelon's view—and my own—real power rested with those who owned vast resources—land, factories, capital. People in the "New Class," or educated middle class, owned little beyond their "intellectual capital"—the knowledge and skills they had acquired through education. Hence in relation to the real powers-that-be, New Class people were mere hirelings, with ultimately only limited control over their own work and careers.

Bazelon agreed with Galbraith, however, that the personnel of the new middle class were not "just workers." Because they had their intellectual capital to trade on, they were in a far better situation than their fellow wage earners in the traditional working class. They got paid more—enough to enable them to have settled the suburbs in force—and they got far more respect, both on the job and off.

But were they a *class*? Bazelon's acknowledged that his definition of the New Class covered the whole range from "a prize student in physics at Cal Tech to a recent squeak-through graduate of a local college in South Carolina." But, he argued, "if this seems bizarre, please recall that in the past we somehow managed to become accustomed to lumping together Henry Fords and candy store operators as 'capitalists.' " Particularly since the New Class "is new" and a still-emergent historic phenomenon, Bazelon argued that it made sense to cast the definitional net as broadly as possible, to include "anyone whose economic position is based on education, and any non-owner with a superior position within an organization each receiving a better income thereby."

With a definition that included, in Bazelon's words, "a professor at Harvard, Herman Kahn [the nuclear war strategist] . . . a corporate executive, a government bureaucrat, William Kunstler, an engineer, Tom Hayden, and me," there was no reason to expect much political harmony within the New Class. In fact, according to Bazelon, the New Class had provided the personnel for

both the left-liberal reform-Democratic movement in the early
sixties and the right-wing Goldwater campaign in 1964.

But, as Bazelon saw it, the liberal impulse was more natural to
the New Class, for reasons which were rooted in its occupational
role. Educated to expect autonomy in their work and even a
touch of idealism, New Class members too often found themselves lost in the corporate hierarchy, and forced to subordinate
their professional concerns to the priorities of the property-
owning class. It made sense for the New Class to resist the corporate domination of society and attempt to expand its own
decision-making domain. The liberal, he concluded, "although
an acute minority of the New Class, is the most fully achieved and
conscious form of it, to date."

While the student movement grew—and, in France, touched
off a near revolution involving masses of white-collar, middle-
class *adults*—left intellectuals debated, fiercely and often arcane-
ly, whether it represented a new class or simply the educated
wing of the old working class. But there was general, underlying
agreement that whatever it was exactly, it was ushering in an entirely new era of social activism. The "old" working class had
fought for its livelihood, usually around bread-and-butter, trade-
unionist issues. But the class that generated the student movement had already achieved material comfort; it was free, apparently, to fight for loftier things—for peace, for gender equality,
for the liberation of the world's downtrodden. Michael Harring-
ton summarized the left consensus when, in an essay based on
Bazelon's book, he described the New Class as a potential "constituency of conscience," bringing moral leavening to the age-old
struggle for social justice.

But even at the height of the student movement, a very different assessment of the middle class and its political inclinations
was taking form. Not everyone among the established intellectuals who took it upon themselves to interpret the movement was
cheered by this upsurge of radicalism. In fact, for a large and influential faction of the nation's leading intellectuals and opinion
makers, the student movement of the sixties was the signal for a
sudden ideological reassessment, leading rightward.

The rightward-turning intellectuals, some of whom had been

Trotskyists in the thirties and many of whom were to become the "neoconservatives" of the seventies and eighties, recalled and drew on the disquieting role of the "new class" in communist societies. If the educated middle class had used the momentum of socialist revolution to gain power in other societies, why not here? This suspicion threw a sinister light on the middle-class radicals'—and even liberals'—apparent sympathy for the poor and downtrodden. What looked like disinterested concern might disguise a strategy for a "New Class" takeover, in which the role of the hapless poor was simply to provide the numbers that the "new," or middle, class lacked.

These rightward turning critics of the student movement could not see any redeeming moral impulse in the radicalism of the young. Rather, they saw only the vanity and bad temper of a generation—and, by implication—a class that had *too much*: affluence, power, and ambition. In the conservative view, the middle class did not suffer from thwarted desires for autonomy and creativity, but from its own self-indulgence, or—in what became the verbal bludgeon for so many conservative attacks on liberalism—"permissiveness."

PART III
HISTORICAL CASES

Peculiarities of (the) English in the Metanarrative(s) of Knowledge and Power
Jonathan Arac

My title echoes a riposte by E. P. Thompson to Perry Anderson some two decades ago,[1] and it signals my intention to take a relatively particularistic position in this tale-telling contest to which we have been invited.[2] Among the most valuable narratives of the history of theory, I believe, are those organized around the careers of individual intellectuals. As in some of the chapters of *Critical Genealogies*,[3] I will emphasize an English figure, and even more particularly, the study of English literature—thus my title's fancy parentheses.

One starting point for these reflections is the *Times Literary Supplement* review of Allan Bloom's *The Closing of the American Mind*, done by Kenneth Minogue, director of the London School of Economics. He concludes by observing that Bloom has effectively limited himself to the impact of French and German thought—I might add, that Bloom is but does not in his book acknowledge himself the editor of the English abridgment of Kojève's lectures on Hegel[4]—and that Bloom's account might have been quite different had he concerned himself with the distinctively British contribution to recent thought.

What is that distinctive British contribution? Where does it show up, for instance, in the synoptic polemic of Jean-François Lyotard, *The Postmodern Condition*, which seems, like Bloom, devoted to the French and Germans? You will remember that the *grands récits*, the universalistic tall tales of legitimation, on which Lyotard focuses are the narrative of Emancipation that springs from the French Revolution and the narrative of Speculation that finds its institutional embodiment in the German university. These two stories, most closely connected with the names of Rousseau and Hegel, produce a third in the totalizing tale of Marxism. Lyotard omits the British contribution to Marxism—whether the tradition of economic analysis that Marx sought to terminate or the working-class history that he hoped to consummate.

Where, then, is the distinctively British contribution to modern thought in Lyotard? As in Poe's "Purloined Letter," where one overlooks the name EUROPE because it stretches across a map in such large letters so widely spaced, so here "Britain" is writ large yet not remarked. The basic conceptual tools that Lyotard uses to develop his alternatives to the universalizing metanarratives are those of postwar British philosophy: Wittgenstein's notion of "language games" and Austin's notion of speech acts and the "performative" function of language. To the extent that these notions are put to use without themselves being subjected to test or analysis, they suggest that Lyotard has "gone over" from the Continent to Britain—not that he has been warmly or easily received within the Anglo-American analytic conversation.

This function of British thought within Lyotard's work, not in his narrative but in his apparatus, may suggest the question, "Is there some respect in which British thought has been always already postmodern?" Against the world-historical schemes of the metanarratives of Emancipation or Speculation, think of the famous remark of John Maynard Keynes, "In the long run we are all dead." Against the totalizing powers of nationalism, think of E. M. Forster's commitment to individual relations: he would sooner betray his country than his friend. It is significant that these iceberg tips of Bloomsbury are anecdotal rather than systematic; it would contradict my point if Keynes had grounded the economics of his *General Theory* on an explicit theory of human nature, or if Forster had written a treatise on political ethics.

Bloomsbury still possesses the power of scandal for contemporary conservative intellectuals like Gertrude Himmelfarb, who has targeted Keynes's remark in order to attack at once his liberal economics and the sexual permissiveness that does not set the reproduction of the human race as its highest goal.[5] But Bloomsbury no less affronts even so flexible a Marxist as Raymond Williams, whose antagonism to this "fraction" may be seen in his contrast between their privileged "conscience" and the "consciousness" he imputes to a "self-organizing subordinate class."[6] Nonetheless, an American socialist feminist like Jane Marcus finds in Virginia Woolf a powerful resource.[7]

This particularist, antitotalizing feature of British thought, which Lyotard uses but does not analyze or challenge, was polemically featured in Perry Anderson's remarkable essay "Components of the National Culture"—a document of "1968," published in the Penguin special entitled *Student Power*, and an important reminder that even in its heyday on the streets the New Left was never all agitation and no thought.[8] Surveying postwar British intellectual life, Anderson grimly reported that there was no place where "the category of the totality" (p. 226) was being developed, even in so relatively inert and conservative a form as that of Talcott Parsons's sociology in the United States. Anderson observed that even in the British reception of Continental émigrés this same pattern was at work: the exemplary intellectually influential émigré to England was Karl Popper, whose critique of "Historicism" from Plato to Marx first widely established his name.[9]

This overall lack of totalizing social thought, Anderson argued, accounted for the peculiarly powerful role of literary criticism in British cultural life, for the work of F. R. Leavis and his associates at *Scrutiny* was the one place in British culture where questions of wholeness were under live consideration. I would emphasize here something Anderson did not, but that has become more important in the light of developments since his essay: namely, that this emphasis on "wholeness" in the British, and to some extent the American, traditions of literary criticism distinguishes them from the German tradition of aesthetics, which sharply delimits a particular "sphere" in which it is valid. For Coleridge, Arnold, Leavis—or Emerson and Lionel Trilling—such a delimitation would abdicate all that is important or valuable in literary study.[10] If there is something distinctively, and precociously, "postmodern" in the British contribution to modern thought, then, it is not in literary criticism as we know it. (And thus Leavis was no more positive about Bloomsbury than are Williams and Himmelfarb.)

Spurred by my own original ambitions in Victorian studies, an interdisciplinarily oriented historical field that has been largely eclipsed as an active force by the emergence of "theory," including women's studies, I look back to a figure who powerfully represents a function of criticism, and a conception of "English," that has been largely eclipsed but that takes on newly provocative force in our current situation. This provocation is powerfully ambivalent, for this figure represents a road not taken, and not necessarily one that should have been taken, but one that should not be forgotten. He seems to combine literature with politics, achievement in writing and in action such as many critics now yearn for, and against which Richard Rorty warns of the necessary disconnection between cultural "sublimity" and political "decency."[11] My chosen figure is Thomas Babington Macaulay, most likely to be recognized as "Lord" Macaulay. The suggestions of the title, however, are as misleading as those that arise from calling Samuel Johnson "Doctor." What is important in each case is the social *ascent* marked by the honorific title. Johnson was so humiliated by his charity scholarship that he left Oxford after fourteen months, and Macaulay was the first person *raised* to the peerage for his literary achievements.

Born in 1800, Macaulay arose from the cluster of evangelical activists, the "Clapham Sect," that included Virginia Woolf's grandfather Sir James Stephen and Forster's great-aunt Marianne Thornton. He was once himself centrally canonized as a literary figure —for example, in the *History of English Literature* by his French contemporary Hyppolite Taine (arguably still the best such performance by any single person)—and remained so certainly into the 1930s. Matthew Arnold considered Macaulay so formidable an opponent that Arnold used his biggest guns, his great totalizing figures of culture and the state, in order to deprecate Macaulay as the "great Apostle of the Philistines."[12] And Macaulay in fact stood resolutely against the "Lake School," the group around Wordsworth and Coleridge from which so many of Arnold's, and our, deepest and most problematic literary—and cultural-political—bearings derive. Macaulay loved Coleridge's poetry but he hated Coleridge's Tory politics; and one of his most forcible essays attacks Robert Southey's *Colloquies on Society* for their evocation of a preformation wholeness. Macaulay's liberalism had no patience with right-wing anticapitalism.

Macaulay is still known, and condemned, as the great practitioner of "Whig" history writing, but he was also a pioneer of a new social history. Scornfully rejecting the "dignity of history,"[13] he drew on lowly ballads and pamphlets, and he sought out manuscript diaries and private correspondence by people in middling conditions of life especially in order to document the lives of women, the half of humanity that traditional emphases on state politics had ignored. Moreover, it is worth noting from the perspective of postmodernism that Sir Herbert Butterfield's famous critique of Whig historiography faults it for being insufficiently dialectical, and thus we may claim in its defense that if it is not total, it at least has the virtue of being deliberately partial. Macaulay did not write with the assurance of a single triumphant march of history. He was famous for imagining a future elegiac figure, a far-traveled New Zealander who contemplates the ruins of London.[14] He knew that the side to which he was partial was itself not the whole story; "improvement" was his key value: a necessarily endless process, with no metanarrative apocalypse.

Despite lending his assistance to his father's campaign against slavery in the British Empire, Macaulay was not in Lyotard's sense fundamentally "emancipationist" in his thought.[15] The figure in intellectual history he most admired was the seventeenth-century English jurist, courtier, essayist, and philosopher Francis Bacon; and of Bacon his praise was that he had given direction to an age already "freed, yet not knowing how to use their freedom."[16] Macaulay in his political activity was a progressive in order to prevent revolution, to diminish the contradictions that if exacerbated would become explosive. No more was he in Lyotard's terms "speculative" in his intellectual or historical outlook. Bacon was his hero because he judged Bacon the greatest anti-Platonist; it pleased him that Bacon preferred Democritus to "the revolution which Socrates effected in philosophy" (p. 367). If the "aim of the

Platonic philosophy was to exalt man into a god," the better aim of Bacon was to "provide man with what he requires while he continues to be man" (382). Resolutely local in his thought, Macaulay insisted that "an acre in Middlesex is better than a principality in Utopia" (383). Bacon's gifts were not logical or theoretical, according to Macaulay, but rhetorical: he furnished not "rules" but a "motive" (398). He was what we would call an antifoundationalist; he denied that there was any "common ground" on which he could controversialize with other approaches. Therefore, he did not "arm his philosophy with the weapons of logic" but instead "adorned her profusely with all the richest decorations of rhetoric" (401). His influence stemmed from "his love of the vulgar useful, his strong sympathy with the popular notions of good and evil, and the openness with which he avowed that sympathy" (385). Macaulay thus figures in Bacon an exemplary precursor of Richard Rorty's postmodern civic pragmatist: all decency, and leaving sublimity to the philosophers and others with nothing important to do.

Macaulay himself fulfills certain roles that have once again taken a high place among our desiderata. He was a literary essayist deeply engaged in politics. He won early fame in 1825 with an essay on John Milton in the *Edinburgh Review*. In the earler pages of the essay there is an extended comparison between Milton and Dante with regard to their figurative strategies: one is like the "hieroglyphs of Egypt," the other like the "picture-writing of Mexico."[17] But Macaulay knew that any judgment of Milton had to confront his politics, and before the essay has concluded it has taken a very strong position on the politics of the English Civil War. In the generation before Macaulay, in opposing the revolution in France, Edmund Burke had considered it essential to distinguish the Glorious Revolution of 1688 from the Civil War of the 1640s (what is now often spoken of as the Puritan Revolution), but Macaulay, writing after nearly three decades of intensely repressive domestic politics, nonetheless insists on the continuity between the two, and he goes further in defense of revolution than we might have imagined, for this figure who now seems to embody Victorian bourgeois hegemony was at this pre-Victorian moment part of a still-emergent opposition: "We deplore the outrages which accompany revolutions. But the more violent the outrages, the more assured we feel that a revolution was necessary" (33). This essay made him famous, and gained him the attention that soon led to his being nominated to a "pocket borough" seat in Parliament. There his speeches further enhanced his reputation, beginning with one in support of political rights for Jews, culminating in his speeches on behalf of the Reform Bill—even though it would abolish the seat in which he sat.

Macaulay became one of the most publicly powerful literary intellectuals that one can readily imagine. In 1834, he was named "legal member" of the Supreme Council of India. Thus he became one of the five men responsible for ruling British India, at an annual salary of £10,000. In those days before the growth of the professional-managerial class, that was perhaps the highest salary received by anyone in Britain and certainly worth over a quarter of a million current dollars. He wanted that money because it would allow him to build a nest egg to assure his independence: he would not have to rely on government office when he returned from India but would be free to take positions on his own judgment, and perhaps even to withdraw entirely from politics in order to write his planned history of England from the Restoration to the Reform Bill.

In India Macaulay enacted such improvements as freeing the press from licensing restrictions and passing what was stigmatized as the "Black Act" because it denied the British in India access to special courts that were not available to the native inhabitants. The British whose privileges he was restricting opposed him by asserting their English "liberties," but Macaulay maintained a scrupulously local and contingent analysis of the situation: "The political phraseology of the English in India is the same as the political phraseology of our countrymen at home. But it is never to be forgotten that the same words stand for very different things in London and at Calcutta. We hear much about public opinion, the love of liberty, the influence of the press. But we must remember that public opinion means the opinion of five hundred persons who have no interest, feeling or taste in common with the fifty millions among whom they live; that the love of liberty means the strong objection which the five hundred feel to every measure which can prevent them from acting as they choose towards the fifty millions, that the press is altogether supported by the five hundred and has no motive to plead the cause of the fifty millions." If we thrill to the realistic vigor of this analysis, how do we respond to the conclusion of Macaulay's argument?: "We know that India cannot have a free Government. But she may have the next best thing—a firm and impartial despotism."[18]

Macaulay in India seems a perfect icon of the "good orator" of classical rhetoric, the deeply learned and vitally active public figure that Renaissance humanism had aimed to reproduce and who still figures in the case for humanities courses in "the Western tradition." While drawing up the arrangements that helped make the English language as culturally important as it became within India's educational system, and while almost single-handedly accomplishing a digest of Indian law into a single, uniform penal code—which still has much consequence in the independent nation—he read massively in classical and modern literature: "I read much, and particularly Greek. . . . I read, however, not as I read at College, but like a man of the world. If I do not know a word, I pass it by unless it is important to the sense. If I find . . . a passage which refuses to give up its meaning at the second reading, I let it alone."[19] (The substance of the letters from which this excerpt is drawn makes clear that there was plenty, down to very fine details, that he did grasp.)

In the Indian climate, he found the best hours of the day those of the early morning, and it was from the hours of "five to nine" A.M. (413) that he read classics: "During the last thirteen months, I have read Aeschylus twice; Sophocles twice; Euripides once; Pindar twice; Callimachus; Apollonius Rhodius; Quintus Calaber; Theocritus twice; Herodotus; Thucydides; almost all Xenophon's works; almost all Plato; Aristotle's Politics, and a good deal of his Organon, besides dipping elsewhere in him; the whole of Plutarch's Lives; about half of Lucian; two or three books of Athenaeus; Plautus twice; Terence twice; Lucretius twice; Catullus, Tibullus; Propertius; Lucan; Statius; Silius Italicus; Livy; Velleius Paterculus; Sallust; Caesar; and, lastly, Cicero" (410). In the evenings, after his day's work, he read "a great deal of English, French, and Italian; and a little Spanish. I have picked up Por-

tuguese enough to read Camoens with care; and I want no more"
(416). As I read Macaulay, I think of our times. It was part of the
archaic grandeur of Charles de Gaulle that even while president
of the Fifth Republic he would still at times read Thucydides in
Greek; and it was part of what we grudgingly admired in Henry
Kissinger that at least he sometimes read Thucydides, even in English. I imagine that nowadays it would be grounds for impeach-
ment to reveal that a public official spent so much time reading
classics.

Yet this very astonishing strength of Macaulay points also to the
features that make him so painfully ambivalent an exemplar for
contemporary intellectuals. On the one hand, his local, partial—
in Rorty's term, "ethnocentric"—Western learning was part of
what we would now condemn as a program of domination. In
drawing up plans for Indian education, he wrote, "I have no
knowledge of either Sanscrit or Arabic.—But I have done what I
could to form a correct estimate of their value. I have read transla-
tions of the most celebrated Arabic and Sanscrit works. I have
conversed both here and at home with men distinguished by their
proficiency in the Eastern tongues. I am quite ready to take the
Oriental learning at the valuation of the Orientalists [NB: not the
"Orientals"!] themselves. I have never found one among them
who could deny that a single shelf of a good European library was
worth the whole native literature of India and Arabia."[20] And on
the other hand, this archaic cultural icon was also a modern, individual subject. His reading was not part of a flourishing wholeness; rather it was desperate compensation for the loss of his two
dearest loves, one sister dead in England shortly after he left, and
the other married in India shortly after arriving with him. As he
explained, "That I have not utterly sunk under this blow I owe
chiefly to literature. What a blessing it is to love books as I love
them;—to be able to converse with the dead, and to live amidst
the unreal!" (398); and in another letter months later, "Literature
has saved my life and my reason. Even now, I dare [!] not, in the
intervals of business, remain alone for a minute without a book
in my hand" (408). The sublimity of his cultural life seems more
fragile and defensive, while the decency of his public life seems
more narrow-minded than we can readily admire.

Yet if we consider Macaulay overall, the possibilities he represents seem sufficiently cogent that we may find some loss in his eclipse. This process began already in the 1840s when Thomas De Quincey, Tory political economist and fellow-traveler of the Lake School, developed from Wordsworth's critical language a distinction between "the literature of *knowledge*" and the "literature of *power*." In asking, "What is it that we mean by *literature?*" De Quincey gave all the power to "literature properly so called," which moves the human soul.[21] This dissociation of Macaulay's Baconian pair of knowledge and power marked a further step toward the paradoxical dilemma of the English tradition of English studies, its all-encompassing claims to value combined with its intense practical isolation, left and right agreed in shunning local improvement as insufficiently radical or comprehensive. Against this, there may remain some virtue in Macaulay's worldly definition of the "true philosophical temperament": "much hope, little faith."[22] I gloss this as advocating the following: to know what you are doing and to persist in doing it in the hope that it will enable people to live better, although your study of history—from which you derive your hope for the future—also teaches that from the new perspectives which you will have helped others to attain, your contribution, and even your motives, will be known to be very different from how you have known them.

NOTES

1. "The Peculiarities of the English" (1965), responding to Perry Anderson, "Origins of the Present Crisis" (1962), in E. P. Thompson, *The Poverty of Theory and Other Essays* (New York and London: Monthly Review Press, 1978), 245–301.

2. This essay was originally drafted for a conference organized by Fredric Jameson on "Narratives of the History of Theory."

3. Jonathan Arac, *Critical Genealogies: Historical Situations for Postmodern Literary Studies* (New York: Columbia University Press, 1987).

4. Alexandre Kojève, *Introduction to the Reading of Hegel*, trans. H. Nichols, Jr., ed. A. Bloom (New York: Basic Books, 1969).

5. "A Genealogy of Morals: From Clapham to Bloomsbury," in Gertrude Himmelfarb, *Marriage and Morals among the Victorians* (New York: Knopf, 1986), 37. The essay first appeared in *Commentary*.

6. Raymond Williams, "The Bloomsbury Fraction," in *Problems of Materialism and Culture* (London: Verso, 1980), 156.

7. Jane Marcus, *Virgina Woolf and the Languages of Patriarchy* (Blooming-ton: Indiana University Press, 1987).

8. Perry Anderson, "Components of the National Culture," in Alexander Cock-burn and Robin Blackburn (eds.), *Student Power: Problems, Diagnosis, Action* (Harmondsworth: Penguin, 1969), 214–84.

9. Karl Popper, *The Open Society and its Enemies* (Princeton: Princeton University Press, 1950) and *The Poverty of Historicism* (London: Routledge & Kegan Paul, 1957).

10. I develop this point further in *Critical Genealogies*, 293–94.

11. Richard Rorty, "Posties" (review-essay on Jürgen Habermas), *London Review of Books*, September 3, 1987, 11. My understanding of Rorty has been sharpened by Nancy Fraser, "Solidarity or Singularity: Richard Rorty between Romanti-cism and Technocracy," in Jonathan Arac and Barbara Johnson (eds.), *Some Consequences of Theory* (Baltimore: Johns Hopkins University Press, forth-coming).

12. "Joubert" (1864), in *The Complete Prose Works of Matthew Arnold*, ed. R. H. Super (Ann Arbor: University of Michigan Press, 1960–77), 3:210.

13. "Sir William Temple" (1838), in Lord Macaulay, *Literary Essays* (London: Oxford University Press, 1913), 424.

14. The fame may best be illustrated by citing "Macaulay's New Zealander," an entry in the *Oxford Companion to English Literature* (2nd ed., 1937), along with "Macaulay's Schoolboy."

15. See particularly the complex pressures surrounding government legislation for emancipation of West Indian slaves in July 1833, in George Otto Trevelyan, *The Life and Letters of Lord Macaulay* (London: Oxford University Press, 1932), 1:282–86.

16. "Lord Bacon," in *Literary Essays*, 373. Further references to this essay will appear parenthetically in the text.

17. "Milton," in *Literary Essays*, 15. Further references to this essay will appear parenthetically in the text.

18. Minute no. 10 [1836], in C. D. Dharker (ed.), *Lord Macaulay's Legislative Minutes* (Madras: Oxford University Press, 1946), 179–80. Macaulay's current eclipse may be suggested by the borrowing history of the volume from which I quote: I was the first to take it from the Columbia University Library since its ac-quisition in 1948.

19. Letter of December 15, 1834, in Trevelyan, *Life and Letters*, 1:396. Further references will be given parenthetically in the text.

20. "Minute on Indian Education" (1835), in Thomas Babington Macaulay, *Selected Writings*, ed. John Clive and Thomas Pinney (Chicago: University of Chi-cago Press, 1972), 241.

21. "Alexander Pope," in Thomas De Quincey, *The Eighteenth Century in Scholarship and Literature* (Boston: Houghton Mifflin, 1877), 382–83.

22. "Lord Bacon," in *Literary Essays*, 399.

The Old Right and the New Jerusalem: Elizabeth Barrett Browning's Intellectual Practice

Deirdre David

Materialist / The age's name is.

Aurora Leigh

In these days of a developed feminist perspective on theory, when we realize that celebratory analysis of women's experience and an undoubting acceptance of its unmediated transmission into literary form elide problematical relationships between gender, social power, and cultural production, we need, as Chris Weedon puts it, to ask "how and where knowledge is produced and by whom."[1] In considering these questions, the work of women intellectuals, in nineteenth-century Britain in particular, possesses a special resonance: frequently articulating resistance to prevailing ideologies of sex and gender, they found themselves situated within (and authorized by) male-dominated structures of cultural production. Producing knowledge that frequently reproduced patriarchal privilege, they were, more often than not, engaged in attempts at radical social transformation, in efforts to diminish the patriarchal privilege that afforded them their own privileged status. The career of Elizabeth Barrett Browning, undoubtedly the most renowned woman/intellectual/poet of the nineteenth century, was, however, peculiarly deviant from this pattern of resistance. Her politics (sexual and other), although sometimes engrossingly radical, are for the most part profoundly conservative. Unambiguously affiliated with a male poetic tradition and forthrightly promoting a female independence that acknowledges hierarchical male supremacy, her intellectual practice reveals much about the conflicted situation of a supremely well-read, unusually privileged upper-middle-class woman who felt herself to be without poetic "grandmothers" yet determined to make her female mark.

In the preface to her four-book, 1,462-line poem "The Battle of Marathon," of which fifty copies were privately printed by her father, Elizabeth Barrett announces that the time in literary history has arrived when a woman "may drive her Pegasus through the realms of Parnassuss." She was hardly a woman—in fact, she was only thirteen years old—but her precocious learning licensed this female intrusion into traditionally male territory: the writing of epic poetry. Paying filial homage to her father-publisher in the dedication and literary homage to her idol-model Alexander Pope in a dashing display of heroic couplets, she proceeds to saturate the poem with evidence of her quite astonishing intellect. In a way, "The Battle of Marathon," which she later termed "a curious production for a child," was a kind of ceremonial exercise in the restricted, yet privileged education she enjoyed by virtue of her gender and her social class. As Robert Browning observed in a prefatory note to poems he collected after her death, she was "self taught in almost every respect."[2] Reading assiduously in her father's library, and assisted by her brother's tutor, she applied herself to classical literature, philosophy, and political economy, mastered seven languages, translated classical and Byzantine Greek, and made an intense study of English and Greek prosody. She relished Samuel Johnson, Walpole, Kant, Berkeley, Hume— and, of course, Milton, essential study for any ambitious poet. As a studious girl, she regularly composed Greek odes for her parents' birthdays and from the age of eleven corresponded daily with her mother in French. As a young woman, she read classical Greek at the rate of a hundred lines a day, writing to a friend in 1843 that at Hope End (the comfortable Herefordshire country house where she lived until the age of twenty) she studied "as hard under the trees as some of your Oxonians in the Bodleian."[3] In sum, Elizabeth Barrett's claim to intellectual fame, first displayed in the "curious" juvenilia of a thirteen-year-old girl and later manifested in all her literary production, was as strong, if not stronger, than most male intellectuals of her time. Her reputation in literary history rests upon powers that were judged by *Black-wood's Edinburgh Magazine* in 1844 "to extend over a wider and profounder range of thought and feeling, than ever before felt within the intellectual compass of the softer sex" (56:621–39).

If it was an "astonishing range of thought and feeling" that distinguished her "within the intellectual compass of the softer sex," then it was the sentimental narrative of frailty, marriage, and motherhood that gave her a different, less studious kind of celebrity. In popular myth, Barrett Browning became the revered "poetess," the soft speaker of sonnets to her husband that count the ways in which she loves him and rejoice in the radiant security of her marriage. She is the poet-mother who writes heartrendering ballads about the untimely death of children ("Isobel's Child"), the sensitive recluse who renders the pain of sisterly self-sacrifice ("Bertha in the Lane"). Sequestered in darkened rooms and tyrannized by a possessive father who forbade any of his children to marry, in the drama of Wimpole Street Elizabeth Barrett is carried off to Italy by an impetuous poet whose first letter to her ardently began, "I love your verses with all my heart, dear Miss Barrett." Adored and protected by Robert Browning, the frail woman who blossomed in the Italian sunshine and became strong enough to have a child at the age of forty-three is mythologized in the popular imagination is delicately emotional rather than aggressively intellectual.

It is only since her work has become the subject of feminist criticism that Elizabeth Barrett Browning has ceased to be understood primarily either as anomalous intellectual in a male-dominated culture or as feminine heroine of a suspenseful family romance. Understandably, Barrett Browning's self-termed "novel-in-verse" *Aurora Leigh* (published in 1856) is the key text for feminist critics. Narrated by its eponymous heroine, a scholarly poet who initially rejects but eventually finds happiness with her cousin Romney (an idealistic socialist converted by the end of the poem to Aurora's vision of the New Jerusalem), *Aurora Leigh* contentiously addresses some controversial issues: the rape of working-class girls, the sexual appetites of the aristocracy, the provincial narrow-mindedness of the gentry, the impoverished education offered middle-class women—and, in a sustained gesture of authorial self-examination, the place and function of an intellectual woman poet in Victorian culture and society. The poem is punctuated by Aurora's lengthy meditations upon art; it contains a startling amount of erotic and brutal imagery; and by the time of Barrett Browning's death in 1861 it had gone through five editions.

When it was first published *Aurora Leigh* was greeted by a volley of negative reviews. Critics denounced Barrett Browning's lavish metaphors, eccentric rhymes, abandoned meter, and, most generally and peevishly, her "unfeminine" poetic performance. But the astonishing achievments of *Aurora Leigh* did not go unremarked by Barrett Browning's fellow writers. George Eliot, for example, wrote of a "sense of communion" with the author.[4] Dinah Craik saluted Barrett Browning's specifically female achievement by saying that *Aurora Leigh* "has proved that we can write as great a poem as any man among them all."[5] And John Ruskin bluntly judged *Aurora Leigh* "the greatest poem which the century has produced in any language."[6] Needless to say, feminist critics have found themselves more in agreement with Barrett Browning's fellow writers than with her shocked and predominantly male reviewers.

Cora Kaplan, for example, in her introduction to *Aurora Leigh*, sees Barrett Browning's self-termed "novel-in-verse" as a revolutionary text contributing to a "feminist theory of art" in the way that it speaks "all that is repressed and forbidden" in patriarchal culture;[7] Sandra M. Gilbert and Susan Gubar also see *Aurora Leigh* as revolutionary, as an intense articulation, rendered in bold metaphors derived from female experience, of the woman poet's struggle for intellectual autonomy.[8] Sandra Donaldson, Barbara Charlesworth Gelpi, Delores Rosenblum, and Virginia V. Steinmetz, among others, have paid close attention to the imagery of suckling and motherhood that scandalized contemporary reviewers;[9] passages like the following, an evocation of Aurora Leigh's Italian childhood, led to charges of "unchaste" writing: "And now I come, my Italy, / My own hills! Are you 'ware of me, my hills, / How I burn toward you? do you feel tonight / The urgency and yearning of my soul, / As sleeping mothers feel the sucking babe / And smile? . . . "[10]

Yet the legends of intellectual industry and of delicate sensibility, the feminist recoveries of gynocentric themes and language in *Aurora Leigh*, tend not to stress one aspect of Barrett Browning's literary production: her political writings. To be sure, Sandra Gilbert has forged perceptive connections between Barrett Browning's artistic search for identity and the political struggles for unity that defined Italy's risorgimento; and Helen Cooper, Dorothy Mermin, Ellen Moers, and Patricia Thomson have made supple, suggestive analyses of the powerful verse concerned with social issues and the sonnets addressed to George Sand and to Robert Browning.[11] But many aspects of Barrett Browning's intellectual production are difficult to reconcile with the fervent gynocentricism and radical articulation of class suffering to be found in her poetry; consequently the contradictory aspects of her cultural practice get smoothed over, pushed to the side, or simply ignored.[12] My aim in this essay is to foreground the political writings (often contradictory) that participate in the Victorian discourse seeking significance for intellectual practice in an increasingly secularized and materialistic society, that denounce English middle-class liberalism and glorify France's Second Empire, and that elaborate political conservatism and sometimes advocate an androcentric sexual politics. It seems to me important to do this not only because the patronizing nineteenth-century dismissal of Barrett Browning's views (which I shall discuss in a moment) does a historical disservice to a woman who boldly entered the public sphere, but also because her irregular feminism becomes that much more interesting in the context of her mostly patriarchal politics.[13]

G. K. Chesterton's remark that "many modern blunders could be corrected" by a reading of Barrett Browning's political poetry would have shocked her nineteenth-century readers.[14] And in all probability Chesterton's contemporaries would have been more inclined to agree with Henry James, who, writing in the same year as Chesterton (1903), declared that "the cause of Italy" in Barrett Browning's poetry was "as high aloft as any object of interest could be; but that was only because she had let down, as it were, her inspiration and her poetic pitch."[15] Nineteenth-century critics dismissed the political poems as deformations in the work of a woman they considered temperamentally unsuited to the public sphere, charging her with harmful political meddling, just as they had accused her of "unchaste" writing in *Aurora Leigh*. The reception granted *Poems before Congress*, for instance (published in 1860 shortly before her death), signalizes the horrified response to verse that hails Napoleon III and curses American slavery. This slim volume, perceived by most reviewers as polemical pamphlet rather than as serious peotry, was greeted by the anonymous reviewer in *Blackwood's Edinburgh Magazine* with the announcement that "for the peace and welfare of society, it is a good and wholesome rule that women should not interfere with politics" (87:490). Barrett Browning's demands that Napoleon Bonaparte be "honoured in his grave" for the "genius" he possessed in life, her praise of his nephew Louis Bonaparte and the coup d'état in December 1851, her indictments of English "self-praise, self-interest"—these were political positions that led *Blackwood's* (and its francophobic readers) to declare its disgust with the spectacle of "an apparent female lecturing for the avowed purpose of providing funds for furnishing insurgents with spikes." *Poems before Congress* was termed "oracular raving."[16]

There is, in fact, something to offend almost everyone in Barrett Browning's political writings. Her thought is religiously conservative, quirkily revolutionary, adamant in a hatred of socialism, contemptuous of the liberal ideologies of competitive individualism and material progress cherished by the Victorian middle class, and smugly scornful of the intellectual capabilities of women unlike herself ("I believe that, considering men and women in the mass, there IS an *inequality* of intellect."[17] In her letters, she positions herself against Parliamentary measures that would admit women to the House of Commons ("there *is* a natural inferiority of mind in women")[18] and in *Aurora Leigh* stations her heroine in hopeful anticipation of a New Jerusalem where a patriarchal God demands hard work from his women poets. It seems to me, however, that in order to understand properly Barrett Browning's career as intellectual poet (or the career of any intellectual for that matter) we need to confront every aspect of that career, whether we find it congenially consistent or not. As a way of better comprehending the intellectual performance of someone who connected herself so strongly with a conservative tradition in politics and poetry while at the same time assuming transgressive attitudes in relation to a male-dominated middle-class culture, I have found Antonio Gramsci's ideas about intellectual practice particularly helpful. In his writings about the social function of intellectuals, Gramsci distinguished between two groups: the organic and the traditional. Organic intellectuals accompany any social group in its rise to power: "Coming into existence on the original terrain of an essential function in the world of economic production, [the ascendent social group] creates together with itself, organically, one or more strata of intellectuals which give it homogeneity and an awareness of its own function, not only in the economic but also in the social and political fields."[19] Traditional intellectuals already exist when the emerging social class and its attendant group of intellectuals rise to political prominence. These intellectuals, according to Gramsci, *seem* "to represent an historical continuity uninterrupted even by the most complicated and radical changes in political and social forms . . . they thus put themselves forward as autonomous and independent of the dominant social group."[20] Barrett Browning's political writings disclose a firm self-distancing from "the dominant social group" in English culture and society in the middle of the nineteenth century: the rapidly increasingly and politically powerful middle class. Self-tutored in a traditionally male classical education, feeling the absence of a sustaining female literary tradition, and barred by illness from public participation in any female or feminist community, Barrett Browning associated herself with a line of male poets ministering to a secular society. In almost all ways, her intellectual practice displays a strong affinity with that defined by Gramsci as traditional.

Believing that the quality of Victorian life was being vitiated by greed and political disorder, she seeks to remedy cultural and social malaise, wishfully separating herself from the practice of organic intellectuals who are defined, according to Gramsci, by their function of giving "homogeneity" and "awareness" to the dominant social class and by creating and elaborating the defining ideologies of that group. Mythologizing herself as an intellectual

at home in a world thought to have existed before the middle
class solidified its political power, she joins the "secular clerisy,"
the group that Ben Knights usefully describes as believing that
historically "there has been or that there ought to be a group in
society which sees more clearly, describes the permanent and truly important behind the ever-shifting, untrustworthy phenome-
na, and consequently knows society's needs better than its osten-
sible rulers."[21] Confident she saw more clearly, Barrett Browning
uncompromisingly set her vision before her reader.

The most important of the many metaphors of writing to be
found in *Aurora Leigh* is that deployed likening the human soul
to a thickly encrusted and inscribed text, so defaced that only a
poet called to the "secular clerisy" can divine and perhaps recover its original meaning. Aurora describes the soul in this way:

> A palimpsest, a prophet's holograph,
> Defiled, erased and covered by a monk's—
> The apocalypse, by a Longus! poring on
> Which obscene text, we may discern perhaps
> Some fair, fine trace of what was written once,
> Some upstroke of an alpha and omega
> Expressing the old scripture. (i:826–32)

Revealing Barrett Browning's enduring poetic preoccupation
with the traditional Christian myth of lost unity, these lines liken
man's soul to a scripture that once possessed its own perfect form
and its own internal coherence. Christ announces in Revelation
21:6, "I am the Alpha and the Omega, the beginning and the
end"; in an ideal analogue to this unity, man once (mythically)
possessed a unified soul-text. But the soul-text that resembled the
holograph inscribed by a prophet, who was, in his turn, inspired
by the original inscriber of all things, has been defiled by later
writers and the primary meaning of man's original soul-text has
been corrupted, transformed from oracular revelation to pastoral
romance (the apocalypse inscribed by a Longus). Proclaiming herself as God's new (and female) inscriber of the ideal world that
will replace the present one defaced by materialism, Barrett
Browning inserts herself into the conventionally male tradition of
biblical prophecy. In *Aurora Leigh*, in fact, in virtually all her political writing, she assumes a didactic role, aiming to instruct her

readers in reclamation of the metaphorical "original" text, or at least traces of it. If soul, text, and form have been corrupted through inscribed interpretation, erasure, and deformation, so, too, the alpha and omega of Victorian life have become obscured by ideologies of material progress. "When we drive out, from the cloud of steam, majestical white horses, / Are we greater than the first men who led black ones by the mane?" (2:207–8) asks a poet in one of Barrett Browning's early ballads, "Lady Geraldine's Courtship." According to her censure of England's vaunted technological supremacy, clearly not.

Undeniably, most of the political poetry that interrogates English material achievment is more overtly concerned with Italy than it is with England. For example, as an impassioned partisan of Italian nationalism, Barrett Browning mourns and celebrates Italian heroism in the two-part *Casa Guidi Windows* (published in 1851), a self-described "simple story of personal impressions" of Italian culture and politics derived from the fenestrated seclusion of her protected existence. Yet *Casa Guidi Windows* also expresses strong political criticism of English culture and society. Essentially it dramatizes Barrett Browning's response to a question she asks of herself and fellow poets at the beginning of Part II of the poem: after the defeat of risorgimento dreams of unification, "What now remains for such as we, to do?" (3:2.250). In 1848, that tumultuous year of political upheaval almost everywhere in Europe, Italian unification had seemed possible. However, the conflict between different revolutionary factions had undermined the struggle and the restoration of Austrian military rule demolished all hope for Italian nationhood by the end of 1849. Barrett Browning's poetic and political action in the face of risorgimento defeat is to indict England for glorification of mercantilism and indifference to Italian struggles for liberation. Rather than making a noble stand against Austrian aggression, England parades her trophies of trade and imperialism at the Great Exhibition of 1851:

> But now, the world is busy; it has grown
> A Fair-going world. Imperial England draws
> The flowing ends of the earth, from Fez, Canton,
> Delhi and Stockholm, Athens and Madrid,

> The Russias and the vast Americas,
> As if a queen drew in her robes amid
> Her golden cincture—isles, peninsulas,
> Capes, continents, far inland countries hid
> By jasper-sands and hills of chrysopras,
> All trailing in their splendours through the door
> Of the gorgeous Crystal Palace. . . . (3:2.577–87)[22]

The omnipotent territorialism of "Imperial England" is imaginatively (and quite daringly) likened to the acquisitiveness of its queen in the image of a "golden cincture" that encompasses the entire earth, drawing in the spoils of empire that are then metonymically displayed in the brilliant light of the Crystal Palace. But there are no "gifts for Christ" at the dazzling Great Exhibition, no remedies for eradicating the dark miseries endured by the industrialized poor. Implicitly, Barrett Browning points to an absence of "womanly" sympathy that should, by rights, come from England's queen:

> . . . no light
> Of teaching, liberal nations, for the poor,
> Who sit in darkness when it is not night?
> No cure for wicked children? Christ—no cure!
> No help for women, sobbing out of sight
> Because men made the laws? no brothel-lure
> Burnt out by popular lightnings?—Hast thou found
> No remedy, my England, for such woes? (3:2.634–41)

Never reluctant to censure male complicity in the social evil of prostitution, Barrett Browning scathingly attributes England's "woes" to spineless liberal politics and unbridled lust for profit.[23] Her voice in these passages of *Casa Guidi Windows* may be characterized as radically conservative: positioning herself to the left of laissez-faire economics and to the right of liberal politics, she occupies a position consistent with her implicit self-mythologization as a member of the "secular clerisy"—and as a Gramscian traditional intellectual.

In the preface to *Poems before Congress* (that volume termed female "oracular raving" by her male critics) she sardonically envisions an English politician saying, "This is good for your trade;

this is necessary for your domination . . . [but] it will profit nothing to the general humanity; therefore away with it!—it is not for you or for me" (3:315). At this point, I want to emphasize that Barrett Browning's notion of what might be good for "the general humanity" does not shut out the lower classes. Her distaste for middle-class values is, in fact, partly governed by what she sees as the neglect of this group by those in possession of cultural and social authority. Barrett Browning's conservatism, sympathetic to lower-class hardship, evokes a utopian society purged of the conflict that, in her view, is rooted in lower-class suffering. And in terms of the gender and class-specific nature of her political discourse, she speaks as an upper-middle-class woman whose indictment of bourgeois materialism implies the traditional attendance by the upper classes and women to the suffering of the poor. In her utopian society (to whose identification with the vision of a New Jerusalem I shall return at the end of this essay) the ruling classes do not neglect their responsibilities to the lower orders. And it is a conservatism coherent with the beliefs informing traditional intellectual practice as theorized by Gramsci. The traditional intellectual believes (or wants to believe) that there is a "historical continuity uninterrupted even by the most complicated and radical changes in political and social forms" (7). As I have argued, this structure of feeling causes nineteenth-century intellectuals like Barrett Browning to advance themselves as "autonomous and independent" of the "changes in political and social forms" brought about by middle-class hegemony. Her conservative politics are expressed in her self-created didactic mission to instruct her readers in recovery of their now corrupted but once noble culture and in her abhorrence of the industrial achievments created and celebrated by the "Fair-going" group that thronged the Crystal Palace in 1851. Moreover, she holds this group directly responsible for social misery.

In the two poems that powerfully present the suffering of children she charges commercial greed with the misery documented in the many Blue Books of the 1840s. In February 1843 she read the entire Report of the Commission on the Employment of Children and Young Persons in Mines and Manufactories; as a consequence, she was compelled to write her first poem of social protest, "The Cry of the Children," which appeared in *Blackwood's* in August of that year. The monotonous rhyme and meter make the reader experience the dizzying effects of the factory, force us to feel the dull clack of machinery that drowns out the sobs of child-workers. The children's hearts turn to the turning of machinery and all movement in the poem is generated by the droning movement of iron wheels:

> For all day the wheels are droning, turning;
> Their wind comes in our faces,
> Till our hearts turn, our heads with pulses burning,
> And the walls turn in their places:
> Turns the sky in the high window, blank and reeling,
> Turns the long light that drops adown the wall,
> Turn the black flies that crawl along the ceiling:
> All are turning, all the day, and we with all.
> And all day the iron wheels are droning,
> And sometimes we could pray,
> "O ye wheels" (breaking out in a mad moaning),
> "Stop! be silent for to-day!" (3:78–89)

The poem concludes its indictment of the factory system and those who profit from it with an accusatory lament from the children: how long, they cry, "Oh cruel nation / Will you stand, to move the world on a child's heart?" (152–53). How long will England stand (endure) a culture of mercantile profit that stands upon (rests upon, depends upon) exploitation, and how long will it figuratively stand with its crushing weight upon the heart of a child?

In the second of her poems of social protest dealing with children, "A Song for the Ragged Schools of London," written in 1854 for a charity bazaar organized by her sister, Barrett Browning relies upon the familiar association of the Roman and British empires in order to make the song an unsettlingly didactic one. Listening in Rome to hymns of praise for Britain's imperial power, her rich natural resources, her morally impeccable middle class, the speaker warns, "Lordly English, think it o'er, / Caesar's doing is all undone!" Defying the injunction of her male critics that "poetesses" should shun reference to sexuality, she insists that the English see their mother's breasts in those of the prostitutes thronging the London streets. England should remember that she already has "ruins worse than Rome's" in her "pauper men and women":

> Women leering through the gas
> (Just such bosoms used to nurse you),
> Men, turned wolves by famine—pass!
> Those can speak themselves, and curse you.
>
> But these others—children small,
> Split like blots about the city,
> Quay, and street, and palace-wall—
> Take them up into your pity! (3:41–48)

Prostitutes can curse, but children cannot. They remain disfiguring blots, spilled about the city in a kind of Blakean staining of the metropolis, their cries issuing from the center of his "London," where the speaker hears "mind-forg'd manacles" in every cry of every man and every infant. The most exhortative of her political poems, Barrett Browning's "Song" asks her "sisters" in motherhood whether they can bear "The sweet looks of our own children, / While those others, lean and small, / Scurf and mildew of the city, / Spot our streets, convict us all / Till we take them into pity?" (88–92). The poem demands that England not affirm the weary assumption that "Every nation's empery / Is asserted by starvation" (95–96).

If readers were offended by unseemly references to sexuality in political poems about the poor, by persistent reminders of the urban juxtaposition of "merchant's homes" and "ragged children," then just as troublesome were the writings that saluted France's love for Napoleon Bonaparte and welcomed the notorious coup executed by his nephew Louis Napoleon in December 1851. Better the autocratic heroism of Napoleon Bonaparte than the "shame" England should feel for the way she bound and vexed his conquered "Heart" on isolated St. Helena: better France in 1851 rejoicing in her release from disorder than England in 1851 relishing the achievements of her "Fair-going" culture—these are the opinions that inform Barrett Browning's poetry dealing with nineteenth-century French politics. Scorning the cosy celebrations of domestic wealth that pervaded English society, she rejects a "Peace that sits / Beside a hearth in self-commended mood" (*Casa Guidi Windows* 3:2.407–8). She prefers the dramatic swagger of Napoleon Bonaparte, which she ambiguously saluted at the beginning of the 1840s, to the self-satisfied complacency of English merchants, relieved that their nation escaped revolution in 1848, and, according to Barrett Browning, insisting "that for the ends of trade / And virtue, and God's better worshipping, / We henceforth should exalt the name of Peace" (*Casa Guidi Windows* 3:2.374–76).

In "Crowned and Buried," which was published in *Poems of 1844* after first appearing as "Napoleon's Return" in the *Athenaeum* in July 1840, she contemplates the removal of Napoleon's ashes from St. Helena to Les Invalides. Declaiming the name "Napoleon," "that great word," she traces its meaning for dying soldiers who "Near their last silence uttered it for God's," for "sages, with high foreheads dropped" who "Did use it for a problem," for priests who "blessed it from their altars," for widows who spoke it "with a moan" (3:1–18). He "who owned the NAME which vibrated / Through silence" is, of course, inevitably defeated by "God's thunder" (if not by England and her allies at Waterloo). What is interesting about the poem is that while Barrett Browning carefully declares "I do not praise this man: the man was flawed" (157), she also salutes his heroic energy, the glorious verve that embraced the French people: "He ruled them like a tyrant—true! but none / Were ruled like slaves: each felt Napoleon" (155–56). For her, the English return of his ashes to the French is the return of "Orestes to Electra" (114). Through this imagery she imbues England's enemy with the doomed but magnificent desire for revenge that invests Orestes with tragic meaning. Her transgressive praise of Napoleon Bonaparte stands in significant contrast to her lacerating scorn of the English bourgeoisie whose desire for peace originates primarily in a desire for what is good for "trade."

At the time of Louis Napoleon's coup on December 1, 1851, Elizabeth and Robert Browning were living in Paris at 138 Ave. des Champs-Elysees, well situated to observe events. The regime established by Napoleon Bonaparte's nephew was strongly authoritarian, concentrating power in the new emperor and licensing him to appoint all ministers and governing officials. The legislature, although elected by universal (male) suffrage, could not initiate bills, and its debates were published in censored form. Barrett Browning wasted no time in recounting her impressions of what to Karl Marx was not liberty, equality, and fraternity, but the transformation of these revolutionary ideals into "calvalry, infantry and artillery."[24] To her old friend Anna Jameson she wrote on December 10, "There has been *no resistance* on the part of the real people. . . . To judge from our own tradespeople: 'il a bien fait! C'est le vrai neveu de son oncle!' " (*Letters* EBB 2:33). On December 11 she reported that five days previously she and Browning had driven "down the boulevards to see the field of action on the terrible Thursday." Promenading jolly crowds assured her that all was normal and that the coup had been for the best: "The situation was in a deadlock, and all the conflicting parties were full of dangerous hope of taking advantage of it; and I don't see, for my part, what better could be done for the French nation than to sweep the board clear and bid them begin again" (*Letters* EBB 2:35). What she seemed to admire most of all was Louis Napoleon's theatrical panache. Claiming that she had "artistical admiration for the consummate ability and courage" displayed in his seizure of power, she pronounced the coup an aesthetic event, "a grand thing, dramatically and poetically speaking" (*Letters* EBB 2:42). This admiration did not diminish, and she wrote to John Ruskin in November 1855 that at the time of the coup she was "not sorry" and "since then I have believed in him [Louis Napoleon] more and more" (*Letters* EBB 2:219).

Initially expressed in her correspondence, the approbation of France's Second Empire and its leader later became a subject for her political poetry. For example, the concluding two lines of almost all the nineteen stanzas of "Napoleon III in Italy" (included in *Poems before Congress*) are a simple repetition of the jubilant cry "Emperor Evermore," shouted by the emperor's supporters "From the Seine back to the Rhine." France symbolically unearths the "old regalia" from the first Napoleon's grave, and partisans of the risorgimento (an eager Barrett Browning among them) await his nephew's help in their fight for liberation from Austrian imperialism. "Though the merchants persuade," this emperor does not find his country "in trade" (3:366–69); instead, he comes across the Alps to help Italy, welcomed by Barrett Browning in her vocation as poet "of the people" (77). On the day of the coup, she recalls, she "did not hate / Nor doubt, nor quail nor curse. / I reverencing the people, did not bate / My reverence of their deed and oracle, / Nor vainly prate / Of better and of worse / Against the great conclusion of their will" (41–47).

Perhaps the most arresting aspect of "Napoleon III in Italy" lies in Barrett Browning's deployment of conventional metaphors of the body-state, in her virtual literalization of traditional analogues between a leader and a nation:

> Autocrat? let them scoff,
> Who fail to comprehend
> That a ruler incarnate of
> The people must transcend
> All common king-born kings;
> These subterranean springs
> A sudden outlet winning
> Have special virtues to spend.
> The people's blood runs through him,
> Dilates from head to foot,
> Creates him absolute,
> And from this great beginning
> Evokes a greater end
> To justify and renew him—Emperor
> Evermore. (3:292–307)

"Incarnate" of the people as he is, Louis Napoleon almost *is* the body-state. The "subterranean springs" of the people's desire course through his body, their "blood" "runs through him," dilating him "from head to foot," making him metaphorically larger than he is, so that he is created, justified, and renewed as "absolute" ruler. Also writing about this "autocrat" who seized power in 1851, Karl Marx deploys metaphors of body-state in a very different manner and to a very different end from those displayed by Barrett Browning.

Marx wrote about the coup in a series of weekly articles under the title "The Eighteenth Brumaire of Louis Bonaparte" from January 1, 1852 to mid-February (the articles were actually published in the spring of 1852). For Marx, the monstrous, deformed Second Empire festers in an infected body-state (the chaotic parliamentary republic): a bayonet thrust from Louis Napoleon's soldiers bursts the "abscess," and "the monster" is made "to spring forth before our eyes."[25] Marx imagines the immense bureaucratic and military organization of the Second Empire as a "frightful parasitic body, which surrounds the body of French society like a caul and stops up all its pores" (237); so grotesquely deformed is the Second Empire that it seems to reproduce itself in a parastic growth that, in a stifling web formed of its own cells, creates its own self-destruction. And in an image familiar from *Capital*, where he writes that capital is "dead labour, that vampire-like, only lives by sucking living labour, and lives the more, the more labour it sucks" (volume I, part iii, chapter X, section 1), he declares that the "new bourgeois order" of the nineteenth century "has become a vampire that sucks out . . . the blood and brains [of the state] and throws them into the alchemist's cauldron of capital" (242). If body-state metaphors took us from Barrett Browning to Marx, from "Napoleon III in Italy" to "The Eighteenth Brumaire," then the language of "blood and brains," of festering abscesses and parasitic growth, will return us to *Aurora Leigh*.

Early in the poem a woefully misguided Romney Leigh attempts to reconcile political theory with political action. A dedicated Christian socialist (at this point), he plans to marry a working-class girl in a gesture that will close the symbolic "gaping wound" of Christ's body and of class division. Awaiting his bride in a Mayfair church he witnesses with his guests the arrival of a troop of London's poor that seems to issue from Hogarth's *Gin Lane*. This is the sort of language that astonished and puzzled Barrett Browning's Victorian critics: how could a revered, secluded "poetess" conjure up such a vision?

> . . . Faces? . . . phew,
> We'll call them vices, festering to despairs,
> Or sorrows, petrifying to vices: not
> A finger-touch of God left whole on them,
> All ruined, lost—the countenance worn out
> As the garment, the will dissolute as the act,

> The passions loose and dragging in the dirt
> To trip a foot up at the first free step!
> Those, faces? 'twas as if you had stirred up hell
> To heave its lowest dreg-fields uppermost
> In fiery swirls of slime, . . . (iv:579–89)

This is language partly derived from Barrett Browning's reading in the uncensored reports of testimony before the various Parliamentary committees investigating conditions in the factories, mines, and slum areas of the poor. The reports reveal a hellish world of stench, squalor, and disease, of open privies, of prostitutes and beggars living in dens that resembled animal lairs rather than human dwelling—and Barrett Browning's vision of the infernal poor is surely derived from her readings. But this is also language reminiscent of the important imagery deployed elsewhere in *Aurora Leigh*—that of the corrupted soul-text of Victorian life, the defiled alpha and omega obscured by ideologies of material achievment. If Marx sees the French body-state as infected by Louis Napoleon's monstrous Second Empire, then Barrett Browning sees the English body-state as infected by a diseased lower class whose condition is the direct responsibility of a middle class devoted to self-congratulation for its commercial supremacy. What is more, if Marx's remedy for the deformations of the Second Empire is revolutionary (as we know it is), then Barrett Browning's remedy for the deformations of English culture and society is also revolutionary—but of a very different order from Marx's. Marx envisions a New Jerusalem of the left; Barrett Browning envisions a New Jerusalem of the right.

The closing lines of *Aurora Leigh* suggest a useful conclusion to this discussion of Barrett Browning's political poetry. They are a densely allusive hymn to work, sexual love, and the vision of new city built from the consummation of man and woman, from inspirational vision and chastened experience. Aurora is instructed by Romney (he returns to her after the failure of socialist schemes inspired by the French doctrines that crossed the Channel in the 1830s) to become the privileged, witnessing poet of Barrett Browning's aesthetic discourse:

> . . . Art's a service,—mark:
> A silver key is given to thy clasp,

And thou shalt stand, unwearied, night and day,
And fix it in the hard, slow-turning wards,
To open, so, that intermediate door
Betwixt the different planes of sensuous form
And form insensuous, that inferior men
May learn to feel on still through these to those,
And bless thy ministration. The world waits
For help. (ix: 915–24)

The artist must work to unlock the doors of perception, must mediate between material and spiritual "planes," and the term "wards" not only indicates the mechanisms of a lock but also implies places of confinement of the individual to the stifling ideologies that Barrett Browning despised. The woman poet's taxing function (remember that Romney instructs Aurora in her duties) is to trace the first writings of that "old scripture" which inscribe a more spiritual, less materialistic existence. The "world" (and also English culture and society) "waits / For help."

Aurora is urged by Romney "to press the clarion on thy woman's lip . . . And blow all class-walls level as Jericho's" (ix:928–32). Sandra Gilbert and Susan Gubar read these closing lines as a revolutionary fantasy too inflammatory to be articulated by Aurora, and they suggest Romney's sanctification of revolution through marriage is a severe compromise of Barrett Browning's own politics: the "millenarian program Romney outlines is not, of course, his own; it is the revolutionary fantasy of his author—and of her heroine, his wife-to-be, discreetly transferred from female to male lips." That the program is revolutionary is undeniable, and Gilbert and Gubar are surely correct in noting that all must be made new, even though "a divine patriarch, aided by a human patriarch and his helpmeet," is doing the renovation (579–80). Yet what is to be made new, and the means of making it new, are imagined in highly traditional, even reactionary terms that, if placed in the context of Barrett Browning's androcentric sexual politics (at least as expressed in her letters), make the ending of *Aurora Leigh* less a compromise than a realization of her "revolutionary fantasy." We must examine the lines that follow Romney's call for Aurora to level class barriers: she must do so in order that all men and women may be flattened to an equality of subjugation to God's will so they might ascend to an unsexing of their incarnate state. Men's souls "here assembled on earth's flats" must "get them to some purer eminence":

> . . . The world's old,
> But the old world waits the time to be renewed,
> Toward which, new hearts in individual growth
> Must quicken, and increase to multitude
> In new dynasties of the race of men;
> Developed whence, shall grow spontaneously
> New churches, new oeconomies, new laws,
> Admitting freedom, new societies
> Excluding falsehood; He shall make all new. (ix:941–49)

New churches precede new economic systems and new laws in this hymn of Christian revolution, this refutation of the socialist programs for reform previously advocated by Romney. Having realized the futility of social reform predicated only on material change (and having received a symbolic punishment for his views through being blinded), he decrees that there must be "Less mapping out of masses to be saved / by nations or by sexes! Fourier's void, / And Comte absurd,—and Cabet puerile" (ix:867–69), a political statement fully coherent with Barrett Browning's views of socialism. It was a poltical system thoroughly repugnant to her and was the enemy of individualism, or at least the individualism she mythologized in contrast to prevailing middle-class ideologies of competitive individualism: "I love liberty so intensely that I hate Socialism. I hold it to be the most desecrating and dishonouring to humanity of all creeds. I would rather (for me) live under the absolutism of Nicholas of Russia than in a Fourier machine, with my individuality sucked out of me by a social air pump" (*Letters* EBB 1:452). In a virtual literalization of individualism (an essence that can be "sucked" out of the body) that reminds us of the metaphors of the body-state in the writings about Louis Bonaparte, she forcefully favors the absolutism of tyranny over the dehumanization (as she sees it) of socialism.[26]

To prefer the absolutism of a tyrannical czar to the socialist direction of a secular state and to call the first "liberty" and the other not seems somewhat contradictory. But then, in many ways, Barrett Browning's intellectual career and political practice are deeply marked by inconsistency. Let me give two summarizing examples. First, in February 1845 she wrote to Mary Russell Mitford that "I am *not*, as you are perhaps aware, a very strong partizan of the rights-of-woman-side of the argument—at least I have not been, since I was twelve years old" (235). When she *was* twelve years old she was busy writing "The Battle of Marathon," getting ready to drive her juvenile female chariot through the realms of Parnassus. She drove so well, was often so transgressively intrusive into male-dominated areas of cultural life, that she has become celebrated as a feminist poet, despite what seems to me, at least, to be the dedication of a woman poet to a patriarchal New Jerusalem at the end of *Aurora Leigh*. Second, her hatred of the middle-class ideologies elaborated and legitimated by organic intellectuals and her affiliation with a conservative political tradition did not preclude her felt indictment of exploitation of the poor, even if we see this indictment as legitimation of the class myth that the gentry attends to those less fortunate than itself and the gender-specific myth that women's hearts are more open to suffering than those of men. Her poems about suffering children and slavery, the moment in *Aurora Leigh* when Marian Earle, the working-class girl, observes that she belongs to the "Remainders of the world" (iv:261)—all this bespeaks an awareness that would seem to contradict the harsh criticism of a desire for money in middle-class men and the calculated indifference to the struggles for cultural and social equality in women. In sum, it seems to me that the inconsistencies in Barrett Browning's career express the anomalous position of a woman poet who resisted prevailing ideologies of sex and gender. Not to examine all her politics, not to see the unappealing conservatism of some of her views, is to relegate her to a category she would have fiercely resisted—that of intellectual "Remainders of the world."

NOTES

1. Chris Weedon, *Feminist Practice and Poststructuralist Theory* (Oxford and New York: Basil Blackwell, 1987), 7.

2. Robert Browning, Prefatory Note to *Poems by Elizabeth Barrett Browning* (London: Smith, Elder, 1899).

3. *Letters of Elizabeth Barrett Browning to Richard Hengist Horne*. With a preface and memoir by Richard Henry Stoddard (New York: Worthington, 1889), 127.

4. George Eliot, *The George Eliot Letters*, ed. Gordon S. Haight. 9 vols. (New Haven, Conn.: Yale University Press, 1954–78), 3:342.

5. Dinah Mulock Craik, *A Woman's Thoughts about Women* (London: Hurst & Blackett, 1858), 50–51.

6. John Ruskin, "Things to Be Studied," in *Elements of Drawing*, vol. 15 of *Works*, ed. E. T. Cook and A. Wedderburn (London: George Allen, 1903–12), 232.

7. Cora Kaplan, Introduction to *"Aurora Leigh" with Other Poems* (London: The Women's Press, 1978), 11.

8. Sandra M. Gilbert and Susan Gubar, *The Madwoman in the Attic: The Woman Writer and the Nineteenth-Century Literary Imagination* (New Haven, Conn.: Yale University Press, 1979), 578–80.

9. Sandra Donaldson, "Motherhood's Advent in Power: Elizabeth Barrett Browning's Poems about Motherhood," *Victorian Poetry*, 18 (1980), 51–60; Barbara Charlesworth Gelpi, "Aurora Leigh: The Vocation of the Woman Poet," *Victorian Poetry*, 19 (1981), 35–48; Dolores Rosenblum, "Face to Face: Elizabeth Barrett Browning's *Aurora Leigh* and Nineteenth-Century Poetry," *Victorian Studies*, 26 (1983), 321–38; Virginia V. Steinmetz, "Images of 'Mother-Want' in Elizabeth Barrett Browning's *Aurora Leigh*," *Victorian Poetry*, 21 (1983), 351–67.

10. *The Complete Works of Elizabeth Barrett Browning*, ed. Charlotte Porter and Helen A. Clarke. 6 vols (New York: Crowell, 1900; facsim., New York: AMS, 1973), v:1267–77. All references to the work of Elizabeth Barrett Browning are to this edition; citations are by volume and page or line number(s), except in the case of *Aurora Leigh*, where citations are by book and line number(s), and book numbers are indicated by roman numerals.

11. Sandra M. Gilbert, "From *Patria* to *Matria*: Elizabeth Barrett Browning's Risorgimento," *PMLA*, 99 (1984), 191–211; Helen Cooper, "Working into Light: Elizabeth Barrett Browning," in *Shakespeare's Sisters: Feminist Essays on Women Poets*, ed. Sandra M. Gilbert and Susan Gubar (Bloomington: Indiana University Press, 1979), 65–81; Dorothy Mermin, "The Female Poet and the Embarrassed Reader: Elizabeth Barrett Browning's Sonnets from the Portuguese," *ELH*, 48 (1981), 351–67; Ellen Moers, Literary Women (New York: Doubleday, 1976); Patricia Thomson, *George Sand and the Victorians: Her Influence and Reputation in Nineteenth-Century England* (New York: Columbia University Press, 1977).

12. For example, Angela Leighton's recent study concentrates upon Edward Moulton Barrett as the determining influence in Barrett Browning's career, an approach that tends to reduce her writings to symptoms of a troubled family life. For a comprehensive study of Barrett Browning's life and work see my *Intellectual Women and Victorian Patriarchy: Harriet Martineau, Elizabeth Barrett Browning, George Eliot* (Ithaca, N.Y.: Cornell University Press, 1987). For a perceptive discussion of Elizabeth Barrett Browning as political poet, see Marjorie Stone, "Cursing as One of the Fine Arts: Elizabeth Barrett Browning's Political Poems," *Dalhousie Review*, 66 (Summer 1986), 155–73.

13. In her introduction to The Browning Institute edition of *Casa Guidi Windows* (New York, 1977), Julia Markus is one of the few critics to take note of the dismissive neglect of Barrett Browning's political poetry. She observes that this two-part poem is still regarded as "written by an unknowledgeable and hysterical

female. Neither *Casa Guidi Windows* nor the remaining corpus of Mrs. Browning's political poetry will be reevaluated until she is exonerated from these false assumptions" (xix).

14. G. K. Chesterton, *Robert Browning* (London: Macmillan, 1903), 177.

15. Henry James, *William Wetmore Story and His Friends*, 2 vols. (Edinburgh and London: Blackwood, 1903), 2:55.

16. In a useful examination of how Victorian critics responded to the problematic nature of Barrett Browning's talent, Kay Moser points out that a few reviewers disagreed that political matters were inappropriate poetic topics for Barrett Browning. See "The Victorian Critics' Dilemma: What to Do with a Talented Poetess?" *Victorian Institute Journal*, 13 (1985), 59–66.

17. *The Letters of Elizabeth Barrett Browning to Mary Russell Mitford 1836–1854*, ed. Meredith B. Raymond and Mary Rose Sullivan. 3 vols. (Winfield, Kans.: Armstrong Browning Library of Baylor University, The Browning Institute, Wedgestone Press, and Wellesley College, 1983).

18. Elizabeth Barrett Barrett, *The Letters of Robert Browning and Elizabeth Barrett Barrett 1845–1846.* 1 vol. (New York: Harper, 1899).

19. Antonio Gramsci, "The Intellectuals," in *Selections from the Prison Notebooks of Antonio Gramsci*, ed. and trans. Quintin Hoare and Geoffrey Nowell Smith (New York: International Publishers, 1971), 5.

20. Ibid., 7.

21. Ben Knights, *The Idea of the Clerisy in the Nineteenth Century* (Cambridge: Cambridge University Press, 1978), 6.

22. Let me emphasize here, incidentally, that Barrett Browning never engages in an interrogation of imperialism as a rapidly developing structure of English exploitation and control. Her indictment is always of secular materialism, not imperial expansion.

23. During the Crimean War, Barrett Browning wrote to an old friend that "there are worse plagues, deeper griefs, dreader wounds than the physical. What of the forty thousand wretched women in this city? The silent writing of them is to me more appalling than the roar of the cannons." Elizabeth Barrett Browning, *The Letters of Elizabeth Barrett Browning*, ed. with biographical additions by Frederic G. Kenyon. 2 vols. (London: Macmillan, 1897), 2:213. Abbreviated *Letters* EBB.

24. Karl Marx, "The Eighteenth Brumaire of Louis Bonaparte," in *Surveys from Exile*, ed. and intro. David Fernbach (New York: Vintage Books, 1974), 184.

25. Ibid., 235.

26. Her hatred of socialism was so strong, in fact, that her deep sympathy for Margaret Fuller as a wife and mother and fellow exile from her native country was overcome by the repulsion she felt for Fuller's politics. On hearing of Fuller's death, she declared that "it was better for her to go" as "only God and a few friends can be expected to distinguish between the pure personality of a woman and her professed opinions," opinions that Barrett Browning believed were "deeply coloured by those blood colours of Socialistic views" (*Letters* EBB 1:460).

From Political Dissent to Intellectual Integration: The Frankfurt School in American Government, 1942–49

Alfons Söllner

Translated by Capers Rubin

I

Exile research, the long neglected stepchild of German contemporary history, has been, and will continue to be, regrettably one-sided insofar as it retains a nearly exclusive focus on literary and political exiles at the cost of studying immigrant scholars. But exile research is also threatened by a new developmental delay, one it has brought upon itself and that thus far resists internal criticism.[1] The problem becomes clear when a practical question, "Where was Germany going?," is posed. This question is inseparable from another, namely, "What could the exiles have done?" But then, given the familiar postulate of a unity of thought and action, too much has already, and systematically, been demanded of the refugees.[2]

Exiles have never been able to achieve such a unity of thought and action, and especially not when their native land, Germany in particular, has become a military enemy. If this *negativum*, this *severed* connection of theory and practice, is not methodically acknowledged, scholarly reconstructions will obliquely repeat the exiles' fate of expulsion, while any revitalization of the refugees' ideas will become a mere project in sentimentality, and so will fail

---

First published in Thomas Koebner et al. (eds.), *Deutschland nach Hitler* (Opladen: Westdeutsher Verlag, 1987), 136–50. Translated by permission of the publisher.

to show the solidarity with the refugees that is as necessary now as ever.

American interest in the history of those who fled Hitler illuminates the defects in German exile research all the more clearly. This scholarship, and particularly its early form (never taken up in Germany), characteristically proceeded from the abstract opposite of what would later become the perspective of exile research. It absolutized the category of assimilation, equating it, not without discomforting undertones of national pride, with Americanization, and obscuring the problems that preceeded and outlasted integration.[3] Insofar as it could be shown that the refugees from Hitler, especially those professionals of bourgeois origin, were integrated with less friction and greater rapidity than earlier immigrants of peasant-proletarian stock, there appeared to be a simple but radical solution to the problems of exile: they disappeared into the normal paths of a society that in any case derived a good part of its historical identity from the fusion of immigrant groups.

Probably not coincidentally, it is in the context of the history of science that a correction of *both* research emphases initially becomes possible, for here attention is turned to exiled scientists and academics in general. To a far greater degree than the history of literary and political refugees, the history of refugee scholars shows the intimate connection between the two faces of exile, between exclusion and integration. Whereas for political refugees, Germany continued to be the—mostly antifascist—point of orientation, and for literary refugees, artistic survival demanded retention of the German language, for scholars in exile, rapid orientation to the host land was far more typical. Any intentions of having repercussions on Germany, or of actually returning, largely presupposed more or less successful integration into the land of refuge.

This complex process may be understood using categories drawn from social anthropology, among which acculturation is the most important. Discussing immigration as an acculturative process brings the long, contradictory fusion of home and host milieus to the fore. Neither exile (as in exile research) nor integration (as in assimilation research) is the norm against which the other is measured and evaluated. Instead, the possibility and process of achieving such a synthesis are studied empirically. The new, third and independent identity this synthesis produces must be delineated by future immigration research.[4] But such a study will only be possible if the concept of acculturation becomes sufficiently flexible and descriptive to apply to the complicated, highly cultural amalgamations intellectual immigration entails. The modifications I will propose here are schematic, but by way of compensation, they are applied to a concrete, if restricted, example.

In distinguishing scholars' experiences of immigration from those of other exiles, the aspects common to them all ought not be overlooked. The expulsion of scholars was no less ruinous and no less politically determined than the expulsion of other figures. While the effects of measures aimed at scholars, such as the "Restoration of the Civil Service," may have been easier to foresee than the actions of the SA mob, which initially struck political dissidents, they too were merely the pseudolegal preparation of a development that finally culminated in the genocide of the Jews.[5] The unconstitutional totalitarian state is defined by the inseparability of political, cultural, and "racial" motives for persecution. If the exile groups had different experiences, this was because the earliest relief organizations to form in host countries were for scholars.[6] But even where these organizations were most effective, in the United States, England, and Turkey, it was natural that at first, only the prominent found rapid professional accommodation; moreover, considerable social and psychological insecurity remained when purely material cares were laid aside. Thus, an emphasis on acculturation, transfer of knowledge, and integration should not simply cover over the negative side of exile. Rather, it means examining more closely than before the full duration of a process that began with expulsion—a process that, at least among exiled scholars, eventually resulted in cultural synthesis.

Analysis might proceed on three levels. Since it may be assumed that exile politicized understandings of self and profession, even among those expelled "only for racial" reasons, the first level concerns the problems of political identity. This encompasses seemingly trivial, but actually often very dramatic, problems such as obtaining immigration permits and new citizenship, as well as questions of political orientation and activity in the host land and of the normative prerequisites of the scientific world. A second level may be distinguished from the first, this one concerned with the loftier, internal problems of scholarship —differences and agreements in theories, methods, and fields of study, including the more practical dimensions of research and teaching. Finally, there is the third—and, for an analysis of acculturation, decisive—level of social relationships. Formal relationships must be distinguished from informal ones, work relationships distinguished from contacts through religion, neighborhood, or friendship. Because this last dimension is all-encompassing, it is the one that finally determines whether or not an effective long-term cultural synthesis is achieved. Only when such a constellation has become stable is it accessible to sociological or culture-theoretical consideration, and this stability is attained only when acculturation preserves the identities it transforms, rather than simply extinguishing them. This normative premise underlies an empirical theory of identity that could be described in Benjaminian terms as a "rescue of the past."[7]

II

This theoretical model will be tested on an episode from the history of German immigration to the United States, an episode that combines experiences of political and intellectual exile in a characteristic manner. Moreover, it shows that at a certain level, integration into the host land may seem to provide a chance to alter that disunity of theory and practice so typical of exile life—in this case, German democrats and antifascists sought to influence America's policy toward their native land. The fact that their hopes were frustrated may disappoint historians interested in exile as a potentially political topic, but the other side of the exiles' story should not be overlooked: their long and painful path of disappointment served as a means of integration into American scholarship, and so led them to an enormous and unique cultural achievement, albeit in an area other than that of immediate political influence.

An account of this dialectic might begin with the first of the three levels I have distinguished, namely, the political possibilities open to exiles in America during the 1940s. In 1942, just as America entered the Second World War, a group of German immigrants was hired by the newly formed Office of Strategic Services (the OSS) or more precisely, by its Research and Analysis Branch. There were three members of Horkheimer's Insitute for Social Research: Franz L. Neumann, the labor lawyer who had just published a voluminous account of National Socialism, *Behemoth*; Otto Kirchheimer, the constitutionalist; and Herbert Marcuse, the philosopher. The group also included John H. Herz, a jurist and later internationalist; Hans Meyerhoff, a philosopher; Felix Gilbert, a historian; Oskar Weigert and Robert Eisenberg, former Prussian ministerial officials; the Austrians Robert Neumann and Henry Kellermann; and several other free-lance collaborators.

The reason for placing these "enemy aliens," as some were still classified, in sensitive positions was clear: the American government needed German experts to evaluate the enemy's situation and resources. They could do no better than to make use of men who could be trusted to combine a strong antifascist stance with a highly specialized competence in the Weimar Republic and its transformation under the Hitler regime. On the dependent end of this political working relationship, the immigrants had their own complex reasons for taking on this research and consulting work. By constructing and substantiating a certain image of Germany, they intended to influence the policy America would adopt toward the country, once Hitler's troops were defeated.

The details of what emerged from this, so to speak, skewed political interest group are beyond the scope of the present discussion. However, a look at the functional changes in the immigrant group's research and consulting assignments shows that they reflected American political developments of the 1940s.[8] The entry of the United States into the war brought intelligence assignments in the narrow sense, espionage and evaluation of the social and political strengths and resources of Hitler's Germany. With the foreseeable end of combat, questions about (negative) occupation and disciplinary processes came to the fore, in other words, the planning of the occupation government. Finally at the end of 1945, the research group was transferred to the State Department, where, with mixed emotions, they followed the (positive) reconstruction of Germany, a reconstruction that from the very beginning, and with great clarity after 1947, aimed at the reerection of a capitalist democracy in West Germany and assumed the existence of an East-West partition.[9]

The German immigrants worked in American government for half a decade and sometimes—Kirchheimer and Marcuse come to mind—far longer. But with what political results? Because the documentary material that might answer this question is both voluminous and remarkably ambiguous, interviews I conducted with some of the participants will be used instead. Here too, there is a certain ambiguity around the political convictions and goals of the immigrant group. This is not least due to the fact that prima facie, their work was value-free information gathering, and only implicitly aimed at the development of a political perspective.[10]

Nevertheless, there is no doubt that the research group had its own political goals and identity. These hovered between democratic socialism of continental European provenance on the one hand, and American individualistic liberalism on the other. Eugen Anderson, the immigrant group's American superior in the OSS, believes he remembers that the theoretical Marxism of Neumann's *Behemoth*, and of the Institute for Social Research in general, was transformed into an American concept of democracy.[11] Stuart Hughes, the group's American chief in the State Department, remembers otherwise. Hughes, whose political sympathies increasingly lay with the immigrants, insists on the dominance of a democratic socialism to the left of the SPD either during the Weimar period, or as reorganized à la Schumacher.[12] The key words were: democratic socialism for a nonaligned Germany and above all, "anti-anticommunism."[13]

The truth probably lies somewhere in between, as John Herz, one of the group's most productive members, recalls. His look back is all the more worth quoting since he takes a position on current histories of the epoch.

In discussing American occupation policy—the very term is problematic because the actual goal was the erection of a new democratic regime in Germany—two opposing tendencies are generally to be distinguished: one that sought to ally Germany with America against the Soviet Union as quickly as possible; and the other, which—à la Henry Morgenthau—sought to punish, destroy, "pastoralize" Germany. But even German research ignores a third trend, which lay between the first two and which at that point may even have been the dominant one among the immigrants in any case, but also in the American government. This view emerged from a liberal democratic perspective and entailed belief in the possibility of creating a democratic Germany beyond agrarification, but also beyond Western capitalism—a Germany with a democratic constitution that would temporarily leave all options open. At first there was to be no socialism; however, a basis would be created for other things, possibly including democratic socialism. I believe . . . Neumann, Marcuse, and Kirchheimer also took that position. I would emphasize . . . that they advocated a social democratic-reformist position and not so much a Marxist one. They inclined toward a democratic (in the broad sense) constitution in Germany, which was first of all to eliminate the effects of authoritarian, illiberal tradition at all levels in German life. It was a position with which I, as a non-Marxist, could agree: a kind of Anglo-Saxon democracy, but one from which socialist measures could arise when conditions were right.[14]

Of course it must be remembered that this characterization of the immigrants' collective politics comes from the group's decided liberal, and may not be harmonizingly generalized. The group from the Frankfurt Institute, particularly Franz Neumann, who as head of research planned and dominated the work, was committed to an explicitly socialist political theory. Its position was indeed democratic rather than communist, but it was uncompromising, for example, in the question of rapid socialization of key industries, and thus, of a socialist foundation for democratic reconstruction. Moreover, they believed that measures like de-Nazification and reeducation could succeed only on condition of extensive structural changes in the economic and education systems. If the group's expert reports were hesitant rather than aggressive in expressing a position to the left of any liberal-democratic consensus, this may be understood as part of their

own, possibly covert, political strategy to indirectly bring socialist immigrant ideas to bear despite increasingly conservative
American policy.

Whatever their internal conflicts, there was clearly a wide gap
between the research group's image of Germany and actual
American policy after 1945. The differences increased until in the
end, the immigrants' ideas became obsolete. There is no ambiguity in John Herz's assessment of his experiences from 1942, when
he optimistically joined the OSS, to 1948, when he left the State
Department.

> You have to make a distinction: in the beginning we were ob-
> sessed with the idea of being able to do something. The defeat of
> fascism and the defense of the democratic system were of world-
> historical importance. . . . Particularly because America had ac-
> cepted me as an immigrant, I felt a moral duty to do something
> to prevent fascism from taking over the world. Naturally, step by
> step, one grew disillusioned, that's quite true. . . .
>
> I would put what you said before about resignation much
> more strongly: we submitted memorandum after memorandum—
> and the desk officers, the decision makers in the rest of the State
> Department, just threw them away. We never got any reactions,
> never had the feeling that any of our recommendations or warn-
> ings were noticed. In 1945, there were already hints about build-
> ing Germany up into an ally as quickly as possible, and this line
> was adopted in 1946/1947. To summarize our experiences after
> 1945: we immigrants were all so disappointed about our lack of
> influence, about the ineffectuality of what we had worked on for
> years, that one after the other got the feeling: there is nothing left
> for us here. [15]

Without going into detail, the turning point is clear. It was condi-
tioned by the anticommunist swing in American policy, which itself was partially a reaction to the intensification of the East-West
conflict, but also partially responsible for it. With the announcement of the Truman Doctrine and the Marshall Plan in the spring
of 1947, America's German policy was expanded to a European,
and finally a world policy directed at containing communism and
solidifying the Western alliance. Securing the capitalist world
market and building a military block became the preeminent
means of accomplishing this.[16] There was a corresponding de-
emphasis on the concerns that motivated the immigrants'

plans—thorough de-Nazification, far-reaching political reeducation, and transfer of the future affairs of state to a democratically
reliable, untainted civil service. Given these aims, in which the
immigrants were united and uncompromising, their efforts at political intervention can only be described one way: they failed.

III

At this point, traditional exile research would break off, since
analysis only seems once more to confirm what was already
known; namely, that exile did not permit a genuine unity of theory and practice. However, for research into acculturation, it is
here that the problematic begins: how could this primarily negative, politically discouraging side of exile metamorphose into a
difficult but eventually successful process of social integration
with extraordinary intellectual results? In the case of the German
immigrants, virtually all the members of the research group began
astonishingly rapid and productive careers as academic researchers and teachers immediately on leaving government service.
Franz Neumann and John Herz became professors of political
science at prominent New York universities; Marcuse went first
to a Russian research center and then to Brandeis; Kirchheimer
taught at the New School for Social Research and later at Columbia; Hans Meyerhoff became a professor of philosophy in California; and Felix Gilbert made his name as a Renaissance scholar.

It would be an exaggeration to claim that these academic
careers, which began in the late 1940s and early 1950s, were immediately and causally connected to the fact that the immigrants
had participated in the American war effort. While conservative
colleagues may have interpreted their work for the OSS and State
Department as proof of national loyalty, anyone—McCarthy-era
university boards, for example—who looked more closely would
have learned, if not the opposite, at least that the group had a leftist slant.[17] What made the difference was a factor specific to scientific theory and practice. The task of defining this brings us to the
second of the levels of analysis I distinguished earlier in this essay.

Our example will show that in the course of the immigrants'
progressive political disappointment, opposing tendencies were

at work, ones that would not be apparent on first glance. These tendencies dated from the beginning of the seemingly precarious employment of enemy aliens in American intelligence and thus can hardly be considered accidental. There is no doubt that Franz Neumann's prominent role in the immigrant group—although responsible to an American administrator, he directed research— was linked to the high respect scholars accorded *Behemoth*. The first edition of Neumann's book appeared in 1942, and a new, expanded edition was reprinted two years later.[18] This prominence is puzzling, for author and work were not only the products of Teutonic scholarship, but overtly and traditionally Marxist. In the strategic last chapter of *Behemoth*, Neumann went beyond simply arguing for the necessity of America's entry into the war against Hitler: only on condition of internal reform could the Western democracies morally and psychologically convince the German people of these democracies' superiority.[19]

However, Neumann's prominence cannot be explained solely by the progressive element in American politics of the early 1940s, which had emerged from Roosevelt's New Deal with its accompanying swing toward liberalism. A closer connection becomes apparent in a memorandum by William Donovan, the founder of the OSS. Donovan argued for the necessity of harnessing scientific or, more precisely, social scientific intelligence for strategic planning of the war on Hitler. A passage such as the following converges unintentionally but substantively with *Behemoth's* theoretical perspective, that is, with a Marxist sociology of modern warfare.

> In modern war the traditional distinctions between political, economic and military data have become blurred. Enemy armament production or military transportation are not things apart, but are aspects of the total economic picture, which in turn reflects manpower problems, administrative machinery and the general state of morale.[20]

What Donovan, founder of the United States' first integrated secret service, had designed as a strategy for convincing the politicians in charge was actually carried out by the German immigrant group in the Research and Analysis Branch. The following account was supplied by Eugen Anderson, who strongly denied any relation between the research methods of his immigrant group

and an orthodox Marxist theory with political pretensions. As becomes clear, Anderson could identify unconditionally with the
group's scholarly ethos, because in his perception, it corresponded entirely with his own understanding of social science research:

Our specialists were so well educated that most of them could
work in several areas, and were able to handle each field with a
perspective I would describe as integral, totality oriented, or collective. Marcuse, for example, was as competent in German
forms of thought as he was in what the Nazis made of them;
Franz was expert in work organization, but also in theories, economy and social structure, etc. Each of us was more or less familiar with, but certainly interested in, all aspects of German society.
So . . . you specialized in unions, education, etc., but you did it
considering all the other influences and aspects. And when that
did not happen and the paper was presented—Neumann went
through it alone, or called a group together—then it had to be re-
worked. . . . This work process expressed an entirely new way
of thinking. . . . This had already been done in the Institute for
Social Research, but now in America, they saw that there really
was something like *the* social sciences. Not only social psychology and sociology, but population structure and economy as well,
were only aspects of a whole, so that an analysis of unions, for
instance, had to consider all these different social influences.
They got away from the German tradition—Max Weber never
had real influence on German social science. The Germans valued *Staatswissenschaft*, we Americans had political science—that
was an enormous difference, and I am not sure they had already
been familiar with something like that in Weimar.
Question: That was certainly the case . . .
Anderson: Probably from their study of Marxism . . .
Question: . . . In which the concept of totality, of the structured whole is central.
Anderson: Exactly, but they dropped Marxist dogmatism and determinism and the dictatorship of the proletariat, and replaced it
with what I call the social scientific perspective.[21]

Such accounts highlight the extremes of two different and
thoroughly contradictory networks of scientific theory that inter-
meshed in the day-to-day work of the OSS and State Department.
A process of compromise began and eventually led to the amalga-
mation of German and American scholarly traditions. The extent
and duration of this process may very well have been one of the
prime forces behind the German social scientists' later academic

careers in America. The process could not have been without disappointment and loss for the immigrants, but it must also have demanded learning of the Americans. In short, it must have entailed all the contradictions, blocks, and breakthroughs of acculturation. And perhaps it was above all the sublimated and rationalized form of conflict resolution typical of scholarly debate that made productive development possible.

Again, it is not possible to describe fully the intellectual results of this compromise process. Nonetheless, there were a dozen highly qualified specialists who worked together uninterrupted for years. The countless expert evaluations, longer research reports, and shorter planning papers, even if read only with the interested eye of an intellectual historian, merge into a kind of apocryphal encyclopedia of German development in the 1940s, a collection unparalleled among exiled scholars. The refugee social scientists produced a wide variety of reports on their homeland. They dealt with themes ranging from the German resistance movement through Nazi cartel politics to de-Nazification lists, including exacting depictions of left-wing parties and unions, empirically rich surveys of de-Nazification and reeducation policies, and analyses of nationalist tendencies prior to the founding of the Federal Republic of Germany.

But the immigrant group's research reports are also interesting for the very specific theoretical perspective they offer on the German situation. This perspective, or "immigrants' view,"[22] acquired some diagnostic acuity from the political concerns that, however unsuccessfully, motivated their research. But the decisive element was a structural and theoretical knowledge of the deep social, economic, and political roots of National Socialism, combined with an awareness that occupation rule—which necessarily constituted a new authoritarian regime—was a defective instrument of democratization. With both empirical density and unsparing judgment, the group's skeptical reports stand up to today's histories of postwar development. They are the archaeological monuments of German democracy,[23] in many respects superior to the affirmative self-representations of the early Federal Republic (slogan: "Zero Hour of Democracy"), as well as to later critiques (slogan: "Capitalist Restoration"). This is all the more notable since the immigrants had virtually none of the temporal distance on which historical judgment rests. Were it not easily misunderstood as a cynical addendum to the familiar West German postwar repression of the immigrants' view, it could almost be said that what their American employers denied them in political power, the refugees gained in critical understanding of the ambiguous years of upheaval before and after 1945. It would seem that for the exiled social scientists, the relation between knowledge and power was dialectical. With time, a dramatic disparity between intellectual competence and political power became a positive quality, though not of course in an immediately political arena.

IV

At this point, we arrive at the third level of analysis I distinguished ealier: how the problems of social identity—here, those presumably inherent in the exile of scholars—affect integration and acculturation. However, some qualification is needed, for our inquiry will be restricted to the social conditions of scholarly communication and work, rather than encompassing the full breadth of social life. Eugen Anderson's formulation, cited in the preceding section, is particularly informative on just this topic. It shows the almost naive immediacy with which an assumption-laden theory of knowledge—the integration of different social sciences into the totality of social theory—seems to have been applied to the practice of research.[24] Anderson was well aware that the integration of German scholars involved transplanting entire intellectual cultures that differed in theories, methods, and above all, practices. Problems were inevitable.

For an account of their solutions, the memories of Stuart Hughes, the group's State Department superior, seem more realistic than those of his OSS predecessor. Anderson saw only harmony based on a liberal democratic, antifascist consensus between the immigrants and their American employers, whereas Hughes stressed the differences. His memories are also worth citing extensively, because they touch on the sociology of knowledge, and on institutional and organizational factors that once again changed drastically after 1945. The context is the incipient Cold War, with its characteristic dovetailing of domestic and foreign policy.

Let me distinguish three dimensions that explain the lack of influence: an organizational, a personal, and an ideological dimension.

I will begin with *organization*: the long-time officials of the State Department could absolutely not reconcile themselves to the fact that such a large number of people had come over from the OSS; we did not come from the diplomatic corps, but from an academic background, and we just happened to land in the State Department. At that time, the official units of the State Department for the then current areas were fairly small—there were maybe three or four people working on Middle Europe. We, however, arrived with 15 or 20 people and represented an organizational threat, at least for the traditional diplomatic service. . . .

The *personal* question concerned problems of ethnic and class origin. The people in the foreign service normally came, to put it bluntly, from the WASP upper class. . . . Their knowledge of Europe and foreign languages came from Swiss boarding schools —I am talking about a kind of ideal type. They found the specialists from the R. and A. Branch exotic, peculiar, probably threatening, because they were foreign, had an accent and were in large part Jewish. In the diplomatic service, it was the other way around: very few were Jewish. . . .

And with this, I come to the *third dimension*. . . . From the beginning, the problem was that my friends and I did not think in national interest categories—I still cannot today, I just do not know what it would be; to us, the important thing was the well-being of the people in the country we were researching. . . . it was completely obvious to us that we had to see the country we were to understand through the eyes of its inhabitants. That was already enough to violate conventions. Added to that was the fact that we were on the left, in the sense of socialism.[25]

Hughes refers to the prepolitical, structural dimensions of the integration process. These were partly organizational, partly class structural and partly emotional. But although they meant that the immigrants were even less likely to influence America's German policy, there is another aspect of the story. This other aspect was linked to the informal structures that could be set up in the OSS and State Department, despite the control these established institutions exercised when formal and political differences arose. Stuart Hughes addressed this elsewhere and—confirming our hypothesis of the dialectic of knowledge and power—actually came to a conclusion that almost contradicts what he said in the preceding quotation:

> There was time, however, for conversation—fleeting, fragmentary, inserted once again in the interstices of the job. The subculture of the O.S.S.'s Research and Analysis Branch took the form of an ongoing if ever-interrupted seminar. The Americans might [have] listen[ed] more than they spoke, but they were seldom deferential. They even gently teased the emigres about central European mannerisms and complained about the opacity of Teutonic prose—something that I find difficult to imagine happening in a psychoanalytic institute. Thus on the one hand, the Research and Analysis Branch provided free of charge a second graduate education to young political scientists, historians, or sociologists who were to go on to become professors at major universities. On the other hand, the emigres who worked with them enjoyed a rare opportunity to familiarize themselves with American manners and values under conditions that minimized occasions for wounded sensibilities or hurt pride. The interchange succeeded for the very reason that it was unintended: neither side needed to be self-conscious about a process that occurred so naturally that only long after the fact did its importance become manifest.[26]

This description centers on the Research and Analysis Branch's social history and, not by accident, was the product of a long term perspective. In fact, informal relationships were probably more decisive than the political and intellectual identity problems heretofore stressed, and although they are hard to document, research on the acculturation of immigrants should focus as much on them as on formal ties. In so doing, it is important to remain aware that informal communication processes often have their own logic, without being rigidly separable from the formal structures in which they develop. Based on his own experience with immigrants, Stuart Hughes offers an abstract model of the process, which, however general, still seems capable of further development.

Hughes names three conditions for successfully negotiating the immigrants' precarious route from an old identity to a new one: first, from the start, the immigrants had to be very open to the new culture; second, the receiving institutions had to explicitly need new impulses; finally, and most important, the right people (immigrants and natives alike) had to be in the right place at the right time.[27] The OSS and State Department episodes were the real counterparts to this ideal construction. As the preceding analysis stresses, only under such conditions would it be possible to resolve conflict productively, only then could political failure be transformed by means of (social) acculturation into long-term intellectual success.

Careful generalization of individual immigration experiences confirms this pattern, which could be described as cultural synthesis with resistance. Franz Neumann's 1952 attempt to determine the influence of German immigrant social scientists on American scholarly culture is a case in point. Neumann named three possibilities for coping with the differences in the German and American traditions:

> Exiled scholars may abandon their previous intellectual positions and adopt the new orientation without reservation; they sometimes did this de facto. They may adhere closely to the old way of thought and either see their mission as completely remodeling the American pattern of thought or retreat to an island with scorn and contempt; both happened. But the third possibility is to try to combine new experiences with the old tradition. This, I believe, is the most difficult, but also the most meaningful solution.[28]

It is clear that Neumann preferred the third attitude, even if he considered it the most difficult to realize. Surely this ambivalent appraisal expresses his own experiences in American government, as well as those of the other immigrants. His attempt to work through this ambivalence indicates the social and psychological problems of cultural synthesis, and is at the same time its most definite result, the immigrants' contribution to American scholarship. Thus, he opposes the "German" tradition of theory and historical perspective to the notorious American tendency toward optimism and scientism, but also concedes that the pragmatism and empiricism of American social and political science are necessary correctives to German idealism and legalism.[29] The keynote is skepticism, a precise middle position that unites optimism and pessimism with an attempt at rational mediation.

V

Only recently has the history of scholars-in-exile been the subject of genuine research interest. This area offers a double corrective for the focus of so-called exile research on politics and the arts—a corrective not only of subject matter but also of time. Exile researchers must become aware that their topic does not end in 1945, for often the results of exile only appear much later, and in forms as various and contradictory as exile itself. Indeed, the skepticism expressed in the passages quoted earlier is the most valuable tool the history of exiled scholars can provide. With this skepticism, the categories of acculturation theory allow identification of the overwhelmingly positive results that immigration, understood as a process of cultural synthesis, has produced in large part and over the long run. Immigration emerges as one of the most important factors in the transition from a limited European national consciousness to a full cosmopolitanism. To assert this is not to deny the immigrants' suffering, as the autobiography of John Herz, one of the research group's last survivors, shows: Herz sees skepticism as the basis of his life and the origin of his worldview. Skepticism defines the character of intellectual immigration to America: the unmistakable, historically reflective profile of a progressive and at the same time critical cosmopolitanism.[30] It remains to be seen whether Germany, the land from which the immigrants so negatively departed, has realized enough of what they wanted return to it.

NOTES

1. Manfred Durzak competently summarizes the field's internal criticisms in "Deutschsprachige Exilliteratur," in Manfred Durzak (ed.), *Die Deutsche Exilliteratur 1933–1945* (Stuttgart: Recclam, 1973), 9ff.

2. As, for example, in Joachim Radkau, "Das Elend der Exilpolitik 1933–1945 als Spiegel von Defiziten der politischen Kultur," in *Gegenstrom. Für Helmut Hirsch zum Siebzigsten* (Wuppertal, 1977), esp. 130.

3. For example, Stephan Duggan and Betty Drury, *The Rescue of Science and Learning* (New York: Macmillan, 1948), and particularly Donald Peterson Kent, *The Refugee Intellectual: The Americanization of the Immigrants of 1933–1941* (New York: Columbia University Press, 1963).

4. Cf. Herbert A. Strauss, "Changing Images of the Immigrant in the U.S.A.," in *Amerikastudien*, 21 (1976), esp. 129ff.; Herbert A. Strauss "The Migration of Academic Intellectuals," in *International Biographical Dictionary of Central Eu-*

ropean Emigres 1933–1945 (Munich, New York, London: K. G. Saur Verlag, 1983), vol. 2, LXVII; Marion Berghahn, *German-Jewish Refugees in England* (London: Macmillan, 1984), esp. 9ff.

5. [The Law for the Restoration of the Civil Service (Wiederherstellung des Berufsbeamtentums) was promulgated on April 7, 1933. It provided for the firing of political undesirables and non-Aryans from the civil service, which in Germany also includes the university system.—Trans.]

6. Cf., for example, Maurice R. Davie, *Refugees in America* (New York: McGraw-Hill, 1947), pp. 93ff.; Norman Bentwich, *The Rescue and Achievement of Refugee Scholars* (The Hague: Nijhoff, 1953).

7. This theoretical model derives from the research project "Wissenstransfer durch Emigration" (The transfer of knowledge through immigration), in which the author participates under the direction of Herbert A. Strauss at the Zentrum für Antisemitismusforschung, Technische Universität, Berlin.

8. Alfons Söllner (ed.), *Zur Archäologie der Demokratie in Deutschland*: *Analysen politischer Emigranten im amerikanischen Geheimdienst 1933–1945*, vol. 1 (Frankfurt, 1986); *Analysen politischer Emigranten im amerikanischen Aussenministerium 1946–1949*, vol. 2 (Frankfurt: Fischer Verlag, 1986).

9. The best overview is still John Gimbel, *The American Occupation of Germany* (Stanford: Stanford University Press, 1968).

10. Bradley F. Smith, *The Shadow Warriors. The O.S.S. and the Origins of the C.I.A.* (New York: Basic, 1983), 368. Cf. Barry M. Katz, "The Criticism of Arms: The Frankfurt School Goes at War," *Journal of Modern History*, 59 (1987), 439–75.

11. Söllner, *Zur Archäologie der Demokratie*, 2:29–30.

12. [The SPD is the Social Democratic Party. Traditionally the party of the working class, after the Second World War it attempted to broaden its political base with a platform of democratic socialism, nationalization of large-scale private enterprise, anticommunism, and nationalism directed against the Allies. Kurt Schumacher led the party during the Weimar Republic and again after the war.—Trans.]

13. Söllner, 2, *Zur Archäologie der Demokratie*, 2:50–53.

14. Ibid., 37.

15. Ibid., 43–45.

16. Cf. Thomas G. Paterson, *Soviet-American Confrontation* (Baltimore and London: Johns Hopkins University Press, 1973), esp. 235ff.; on the scholarly controversy of realistic and revisionist appraisals of the Cold War cf. Wilfred Loth, *Die Teilung der Welt, 1941–1945*, 4th ed. (Munich: Deutscher Taschenbuch Verlag, 1984), 9.

17. The extent to which German scholars were actually affected by the Communist witch hunts of the early 1950s is still to be fully investigated—those in the universities were surely less affected than those in the civil service.

18. Cf., for example, C. Wright Mills's emphatic review, "Locating the Enemy: The Nazi Behemoth Dissected," in *Partisan Review*, 4 (1942), 432ff.

19. Franz Neumann, *Behemoth* (Toronto and New York: Oxford University Press, 1942), 476.

20. William Donovan, "Functions of the O.S.S." (1942) in *O.S.S.—War Report* (Washington, DC 1949), 2:343.

21. Söllner, *Zur Archäologie der Demokratie*, 2:24–26.

22. Cf. my essay "Emigrantenblicke: Westdeutschland im Urteil von Franz Neumann und Otto Kirchheimer" in Wolfgang Lutheralt and Alfons Söllner (eds.), *Verfassungsstaat, Souveränität, Pluralismus: Otto Kirchheimer zum Gedächtnis* (Opladen: Westdeutscher Verlag, 1989), 101–11.

23. Cf. esp. the introductions to chapters 3–5 in Söllner, *Zur Archäologie der Demokratie*, vol. 2.

24. Cf. Helmut Dubiel, *Wissenschaftsorganisation und politische Erfahrung* (Frankfurt: Suhrkamp Verlag, 1978), 135ff.

25. Söllner, *Zur Archäologie der Demokratie*, 2:48–49.

26. H. Stuart Hughes, "Social Theory in a New Context," in Jarrell C. Jackmann and Carla M. Borden (eds.), *The Muses Flee Hitler* (Washington, D.C.: Smithsonian Institution Press, 1983), 118.

27. Ibid.

28. Franz L. Neumann, "Intellektuelle Emigration und Sozialwissenschaft" (1952), in *Wirtschaft, Staat, Demokratie* (Frankfurt: Suhrkamp Verlag, 1978), 417.

29. Neumann, "Intellektuelle," 420–21.

30. John H. Herz, *Vom Überleben: Wie ein Weltbild Entstand* (Düsseldorf: Droste Verlag, 1984).

New Brooms at Fawlty Towers:
Colin MacCabe and Cambridge English

David Simpson

The fight within the Cambridge English faculty that centered upon the firing of Colin MacCabe, an assistant lecturer, in 1981, was the subject of national and even international attention. It was a regular feature of the British national newspapers for a number of weeks, culminating in the *Guardian*'s front page story reporting the discussion of the "state of the faculty" in the University Senate House (February 4, 1981). It was also the subject of various radio interviews, of a thirty-minute television report, and of articles in several periodicals, in *Newsweek*, and in the *Boston Globe*. "Angry flow the dons," proclaimed the *Daily Telegraph* (January 18, 1981), in one of the better headlines. For a while, literary critics and their doings seemed to matter to the media. Despite the predictably disgruntled assertions by Mac-Cabe's opponents that the whole affair was merely a piece of contrived sensationalism, the evidence suggests that the press tried assiduously to get the facts straight, and to provide some honest account of the intellectual differences involved in the quarrel. Where they did not get the facts straight—particularly those of the bureaucratic and procedural sort—one is less inclined to blame the press than the facts themselves, which were rather crooked. In a situation where the King Edward VII Professor himself, Frank Kermode, the senior professor in the department, spoke credibly of the Faculty Board as "a forum for the display of stubborn self-regard, and occasionally as the instrument of mischief,"[1] and where most members of the faculty themselves could not get an

245

honest account of what had happened, it could hardly have been expected that the newspapers should provide an exact history.

They tried hard, nonetheless. Names like Saussure, Barthes, and Heidegger began to appear in the editorial sections, and strangers would want to know who was and who was not a "structuralist," this being the term that the "business as usual" faculty majority chose as their *omnium gatherum* definition of the enemy. While no newspaper produced anything like a definitive or greatly complex summary of the intellectual implications of the dispute, the attempt was certainly made, and it was not always wholly wide of the mark. As a member of this particular intellectual subculture, the Cambridge English nonconformists, it was hard not to feel a bit more important than one had felt before, hard not to see in the proverbial dreaming spires some faint resemblance to the topless towers of Ilium, hard to refrain from thinking of the whole affair as another of the great lost causes that had changed the course of history.

If Colin MacCabe had been fired from Leeds or Lancaster, there would probably have been very little fuss (although, as I discuss later, he would probably not have been fired from those universities). But Oxford and Cambridge, popularly conflated as "Oxbridge," are England's oldest and most prestigious universities, outstripping the rest by a much larger margin than do Harvard, Yale, and Princeton in their control over the education and production of the nation's ruling class, and in their exceptional and very visible attachment to traditional pageantry and to the academic good life. They are, for the British public, objects of both fantasy and scorn, of both fetishism and detestation. One goes to and from the other universities, but *up* to and *down* from Oxbridge. British culture, and especially English culture, is founded in a highly sophisticated class consciousness pervading every point in the social hierarchy. Oxford and Cambridge, with their disproportionately large upper- and upper-middle-class student populations, and their earnest openness to (highly selected) students from less privileged backgrounds, are exemplary microcosms of British social life, and are seen as such by all who contemplate them from the outside. Not surprisingly, then, Oxbridge has a long tradition of providing good newspaper copy, and endless material for novels and films, mostly based on the irresistibly fascinating conjunctions of privilege and corruption, decadence and high seriousness, public virtues and private vices. Since the individual colleges are almost all several hundred years older than the university, and are separately endowed, they have been able to maintain highly diversified traditions and to resist the vicissitudes of state support. As viewers of *Glittering Prizes* and *Brideshead Revisited* will be aware, they are miniature emblems of the national culture, refigured in such a way that it is the "working class" that appears as the minority. In *The Prelude*, Wordsworth recounts his own college career very much in these terms:

> 'tis enough to note
> That here in dwarf proportions were expressed
> The limbs of the great world—its goings-on
> Collaterally pourtrayed as in mock fight.[2]

And Wordsworth too found much wanting, saw

> Feuds, factions, flatteries, Enmity and Guile,
> Murmuring Submission and bald Government
> (The idol weak as the idolator)
> And Decency and Custom starving Truth,
> And blind Authority beating with his staff
> The child that might have led him.

> (III, 636–41)

For every earnest grammar-school boy (now an extinct species) seeking and often getting a first in mathematics, there is an idle scion of the monied class propping up the bottom end of the law or history class lists (that is what the published examination results are called; they are a symbolic reclassing). And of course there are many in between, doing their best or a little less, mostly seeking to reenter the middle class on slightly better terms than they left it. The students play out their rituals—May Balls, athletics, parties—very much in the public eye. The debates of the Oxford and Cambridge Unions are reported in the press, and often televised. Very distinguished speakers are willing to appear for little or no remuneration, since they themselves have often been through the same rites of passage. And a high proportion of student politicians become real politicians, haw-hawing in the House of Commons in very much the same tones that they have practiced at university.

For many students, Oxbridge is either a route into the political and economic ruling class, or a reaffirmation of membership for those already there. The making of contacts is often as or more important than the achievement of a good degree. This sense of the student body as a disproportionately influential group of young people is shared by the public and by those who teach them, the so-called dons. Many of these are ordinary, decent people, conscientious and even modest. But the temptations to grandiose self-importance are considerable, and to the public eye they live a life very different from that enjoyed by their peers in other universities. This life has the name and all the addition of aristocracy: beautiful old buildings, feasts, fine wines and furred gowns. Few are immune to at least some of the gratifications of this way of life (I myself plead guilty to three of the above four). That this theater is maintained by professional intellectuals who themselves emanate largely from the middle and lower middle classes lends it a deliciously paradoxical identity much loved by the English in their tendency to both indulge in and ironize the delusions of class mobility. Regardless of their individual preferences and political convictions, fellows of Oxbridge colleges operate within an anthropological anachronism that they will find either charming or absurd, and often both at once. They in turn are uncomfortably differentiated from an underclass of porters, maintenance workers and cleaning women, largely non-unionized, and cast in a role somewhere between that of wage laborer and loyal retainer, often with the disadvantages of both. It is still common, even in the more liberal colleges, to hear these people referred to as "servants," and it seems impossible to cure some of them of the habit of addressing the male fellows and undergraduates, in tones that vary between sarcasm and sincerity, as "sir."

The general atmosphere of Cambridge life has thus always been conservative, though often more in appearance than in fact. Cambridge does its bit, along with Oxford, the trooping of the colour, and the Tower of London, for a British tourist industry founded in the inspection of feudal antiquity followed by refreshments at

Ye Olde Tea Shoppe. But in the academic and pedagogic sense, the state of affairs from which Colin MacCabe was dismissed was a schismatic and incoherent muddle whose reliance upon conventions rather than methods had been severely tested by the events of the years 1968–78, which it could not ignore even as it tried to. The English faculty had, since the late 1960s, been expanding at an unprecedented rate in terms of student numbers, but it continued to operate a teaching system, based on single or paired supervision (called at Oxford the "tutorial"), that derived from the leisured days when students were few and largely grateful or indifferent. Although the English faculty was uniquely disadvantaged in terms of its staff-student ratios, it was also, thanks to a peculiar blend of self-interest and the ideological blindness that persuades us to perpetuate the very terms of our own discomfort, particularly resistant to change. English at Cambridge was and still is taught by three kinds of persons: by lecturers paid by the university, whose job it is to give forty lectures a year; by lecturers paid by the colleges, who are primarily responsible for the supervision system; and by a sizable army of others, who teach on a wage labor basis, as and when needed, at so much per student-hour. In practice these categories overlap considerably, as they have to if the system is to function. But none of these factions has any real interest in changing that system. Consequently the forty lectures given by the first group are only loosely (if at all) coordinated with college teaching, which they often indeed repeat, the same person frequently wearing both hats. There is no syllabus, though there are broad period and topic requirements. And, astonishingly, attendance at lectures is strictly optional. Not surprisingly, they are attended by a small proportion of the students, though fashions change from time to time.

All of the participants in this "more or less perpetual disarray," to quote Frank Kermode once again (*Reporter*, 333), complain bitterly of overwork. But they had, as of 1981, done nothing to change the system that overworks them, either by reform or by revolution. Self-interest, parochialism, and sheer inability to cooperate help to explain why. But one must add in here the respect for a tradition in which the teachers themselves had almost all been students. Like a number of self-important institutions,

Cambridge hires dominantly from among its own graduates. And it continues to sponsor (though not without distinguished exceptions) a large number of teachers who regard research and publication either as a symptom of vulgar professionalization or as something one should not have time for if one is doing a proper job in nurturing the student mind. Brilliant teachers and students continue to survive almost unscathed, because Cambridge gets a very high proportion of the best students who want to study English, and because the environment is so uncoercive as to prove a virtual paradise for the confident autodidact. This is the student for whom the university is often thought to exist; but there were never very many of them, and the recent changes in British secondary education have ensured that there will be even fewer, and those, moreover, from an ever-narrowing range of mostly private schools. For the rest, the teaching system has simply not adapted to the fact that today's students are less well prepared than they were twenty-five years ago. There are more of them, they have not read the whole of English literature and much of the classics besides, and many of them are poorly trained in the basic skills of argumentative writing and logical thinking. They arrive at Cambridge in the 1980s to a setup that assumes that they can already do these things, and which is reluctant to change its habits to meet their needs. It was no surprise to hear an anatomy lecturer and college tutor stand up in the Senate House and ask, as his question about the "state of the faculty," why it should be that so many students of English suffered mental stress and breakdown (*Reporter*, 351).

A few students, of course, did have all the talents, enough of them to enable those intent on "business as usual" to conclude that nothing much needed changing. These students tended to come from the "better" schools. Up to 1981, when I was following the statistics, the widening gap between private and public education in Britain was appearing in Cambridge entrance figures, very predictably, as an increase in the (already unbalanced) proportion of students coming from the private sector. Many of these students could already do what the university would pretend to teach them; they had the confidence to survive the "hazing" system of a separate entrance examination and a mythologically intimidating interview; and they could thus be more or less relied upon to make it through three years on their own, or with a little help from their teachers. It is hard to believe that ten more years of Thatcher's policies have done anything to expand the social base of the Cambridge student body.

Such, briefly outlined, were the local conditions surrounding the scandal of Colin MacCabe's dismissal. And scandal it was, since MacCabe was by any publicly recognized standard spectacularly overqualified for tenure. Much of what I will have to say will concern itself with the arguments about British education that devolved around the MacCabe affair. It must first be said, however, that to those of us on the spot, the whole business was an object lesson in the degree to which the discourse of intellectual dispute—all too prone to assume heroic dimensions in the rhetoric of all parties—serves as a mask for political dispute; and both in turn are mediated through the most petty pathologies and paranoias, individual and collective. It is hard to say what proportion of the events can be ascribed to the tides of history and to high-minded principle, rather than to the rag-and-bone shops of certain academic psyches. But these psyches cannot be written about, except in novels and under false names, without incurring the revenge of the libel laws. Moreover, the power of these motivations is not so much at odds with as assisted by the objectively describable differences of opinion over the teaching of English at Cambridge. That these differences could be invoked and attended to is strong evidence that they were real.

Pitching the discussion, then, at this most serious of levels—a level at which one risks taking oneself far too seriously—why was MacCabe fired? And why, beyond the level of the public appetite for scandal in high places, and for what HRH Princess Margaret was reported to have called a "spanking good row," should anyone outside Cambridge have cared? The answers to these questions tell us much about the perceived and actual roles of the Oxbridge intellectual in British culture, and about the peculiar (if largely self-appointed) place of literary criticism within that culture, both very different from the analogous functions in the United States. We must ask how intellectuals matter in Britain; whether they matter as much as they would like to, or in the ways that they think that they do; and we must understand that doing something at Cambridge is very different from doing exactly the same thing at Keele or Kingston Polytechnic.

The study and teaching of English at Cambridge has always been very different from the same activity at other universities, including Oxford. The Cambridge English faculty was a late arrival, by British standards, but it has always made up in zeal and intensity for what it lacks in sheer longevity. Through control of a major examining board in the secondary schools, and by sending generations of "trained men" (as they mostly were) into those same schools to preach the gospel of the best that has been known and thought in the world, the orthodoxy in English (though not Scottish or Irish) literary education has been a creation of the Cambridge school. This school was founded with a strongly utilitarian motivation, which grew even stronger with the passage of time. For I. A. Richards, perhaps the most important founding father of Cambridge English, the study of literature, and of poetry in particular, was the central ingredient in a psychologically polymorphous education conceived as a humane alternative to the threatening hegemony of the scientific worldview. Neither philology, classics, nor history could do the work of poetry. Taking on the mantle of Coleridge and Arnold, and armed with a theoretical language derived from recent initiatives in philosophy and psychology, Richards set out to construct a university education that might hope to produce in those who went through it a sympathy for irony and ambiguity and a habit of suspending belief and doctrinal conviction that could, in the best of all worlds, preclude the sort of intellectual passivity that had brought about the horrors of the Great War. Patriotism would succumb to internationalism as literal meanings gave way to complex ones, reconstituted into inclusive rather than exclusive explanations. It was a noble ambition, even a moral one, entirely coincident with Richards's hopes for the future of basic English, and with the whole political project of the League of Nations. Richards wanted intellectuals to matter, and applied his entire and phenomenal energy, between the wars, to devising ways in which they might matter. If we laugh at this response to the casualty figures of the first day of the Somme offensive, then it is up to us to do better.

Arnold had found his preferred alternative to the limitations of modern life in the classics, and in a non-Christian culture. Richards directed the attention of readers to their own language. A major and crucial specification of this shift was enacted, beginning in the 1930s, by F. R. Leavis, through his own books, through his journal *Scrutiny*, and through his immense personal influence upon generations of secondary school teachers. There is no figure in American literary criticism who stands with Leavis in either influence or ambition. One has only to compare the shrunken notoriety of a Paul de Man, who specified the appeal of the American university as a place where the literary critic has "no cultural function,"[3] and for whom the power of intellectualism consisted precisely in its ability to turn us away from the world. Not surprisingly, Leavis has aroused little curiosity in the United States, for his work has no context here. But it was Leavis, more than anyone, who set out the guiding preoccupations of Cambridge English, and identified its mission within the national culture.

Leavis himself was a ferocious nonconformist, antagonistic to what he regarded as the Cambridge literary establishment of upper-middle-class belle lettrists and Bloomsbury types (gathered in the fashionable colleges whose thresholds he never crossed), and a constant critic of the scientific and mathematical priorities of the university as a whole. The English faculty of his time was, as usual, more than happy to respond by excluding him from as much as it decently could, and then a bit, in the manner of what Raymond Williams has described as the "easy habits of a culture steeped in personal disparagement" as a way of "evading radical arguments."[4] Leavis's particular hatred of the Bloomsbury ethos was founded in differences of doctrine, class, and institutional prestige. He stood, above all, for a lower middle (never a working) class ethic of vital human nature that, ever since the Augustans, he thought, had been disclaimed and displaced by polite culture and polite conventions. Leavis's preferred authors now seem somewhat blandly canonical: Jane Austen, George Eliot, the high modernism of T. S. Eliot and of the early Pound (before the *Cantos*), Lawrence, Shakespeare, and the metaphysical poets. Against Bloomsbury common sense and Fabian humanist-socialism, he offered the challenges of difficult texts and the emotionally demanding vitalism of D. H. Lawrence. These challenges, tame as they must now seem, were real at the time. It was not, after all, until the 1960s that *Lady Chatterley's Lover* was freed from the restraints of the obscenity laws in Britain. And from my own schoolboy days I well remember the forceful example of teachers for whom all literature led to Lawrence, and to an ideal freedom from inhibition, whether sexual or social.

The Leavis view of literature became, ironically, something of an orthodoxy in Cambridge, and it remained so into the 1960s, deprived, inevitably, of its original force and timeliness and become little more than a habit of intense behavior and a notional positioning of literature in the context of historical "life and thought." Its limitations, in view of what would next appear on the horizon, were as obvious then as they are now. The Leavisite attitude had never encouraged much self-consciousness about its own purposes and origins. There had always been a pronounced tendency to publicize an ideal lower-middle-class nature as "human nature," and to characterize the bourgeois tradition as the great tradition, or the common pursuit. Much was excluded from the canon of "great" literature. Milton and Shelley were found guilty of failing to write the common language, and their political babies went out with the stylistic bathwater. Blake's prophetic books, the *Cantos*, and *Finnegans Wake* were also found far too obscure, thought to appeal only to a minority, elite culture and thus cut off from the common reader. That common reader was not truly common, however. Leavis had no time for truly radical literature, or for popular culture, which for him was merely the opium of a corrupted readership able to manage only a passive response. Nor was he at all interested in setting out a properly thorough analysis of the historical conditions producing the negative aspects of the modern world. The romantic primitivism that informed Lawrence's analysis of the demise of English culture was never held up for skeptical attention. It is at least arguable that Leavis's attachment to the notion of a vital human nature recoverable through reading great literature was popular partly because it offered a moderate alternative to the Marxist view of life. Certainly, before the 1950s, British literary criticism had not developed a significant Marxist or leftist dimension.

Leavis thus bequeathed a rather narrow definition of what was essential to English culture. For the production of a civilized society, he posited the absolute superiority of an education based on reading English literature. Many senior Cambridge figures find it hard to forget these hubristic habits. At the same time, Leavisism excluded a good deal of English literature from that education, and it further asserted that the procedures of the literary education should be announced in intuitive rather than in methodologically sophisticated terms. Edmund Burke, rather than Tom Paine, lies behind Leavis. Cambridge English had from the first defined itself less by what it was than by what it was not. It was not classics or a foreign language; hence it did not need to teach grammar or tend toward a comparative approach. It was not philology; hence it did not teach the histories of words. It was not history, and thus did not need to set the authority of facts against the authority of feelings and responses. And above all it was not science or philosophy, and thus did not require for its pursuit either a complex analytic vocabulary or a commitment to consecutive reasoning. What is left, alas, is very little—a terminology trading heavily in tautology and assertion, and making a great deal of use of the language of the "vital," the "concrete," of the "embodiment" of "feeling," and of "human" nature.

Of course, not all Cambridge literary critics were unmodified Leavisites. But the foregoing summary seems to me to describe the general disposition of the faculty rank and file into the 1970s, and even into the 1980s. Given this conjunction of a high degree of self-importance with a relative poverty of conceptual language —the sort of language that can be publicized and made intelligible to others—one can see why the English faculty was the object of a good deal of scorn in the university at large, and also why it could not withstand the challenges of its own dissidents. In 1976, Colin MacCabe was appointed to an assistant lectureship, and to a Fellowship at King's College, very definitely a "fashionable" college and, as it happens, a particular object of scorn for F. R. Leavis himself, thanks to its Bloomsbury traditions. During the 1960s, however, King's became the most avant-garde intellectual community in Oxbridge. Provost Sir Edmund Leach, indeed, was a principal mover in the introduction of Lévi-Strauss, and thus of "structuralism," into British intellectual life. While "structuralism" does not account for what was going on in the English faculty in the late 1970s, it had certainly initiated the challenge to the nationalistic, antitheoretical majority within the humanities faculties, well before MacCabe and others like him came along. Left-wing economists, historians, and social scientists also gathered in King's, as did a flamboyant and vocal generation of students. The college was something of a haven for those in antagonistic relationships to their various faculties and was, according to my own happy recollections, a genuinely liberal, tolerant, and exciting intellectual community. In 1976, English at King's was taught by Frank Kermode, Tony Tanner, John Barrell, Norman Bryson, Colin MacCabe, and myself—a group diverse enough, indeed, but sharing a common distance from the mainstream of the faculty. As we surely created that distance, so more distance was thrust upon us.

The *Guardian* (January 17, 1981) described MacCabe's dismissal as setting off "Cambridge's biggest academic row since the bitter days of Dr. F. R. Leavis a generation ago." Such indeed it was. But a couple of years before MacCabe's appointment in 1976, the English faculty had experienced some more nasty moments over the nonappointment of George Steiner to a university lectureship, resulting in Steiner's departure for Geneva. The major problem about Steiner was that he was the most popular lecturer in the faculty, perhaps in the university. He had a magisterial acquaintance with *Weltliteratur*, and an extraordinary talent for putting it across. Steiner's enthusiasm was distinctly un-British, as were many of the names he came out with: Homer, Virgil, Goethe, Mann, Spitzer, Jakobson, and so forth. His enemies complained that he never answered the questions he asked, never attached more than a string of luminous adjectives to any of these proper names. For the students, however, these names and these questions were not even to be heard elsewhere. Above all, Steiner insisted that we read and know about more than just English literature—indeed, about more than just literature. "Human nature" did survive in his vocabulary, but only as besieged by a host of difficult names, and framed within a tragical view of Western culture that did not, finally, endorse the saving functions of the literary experience as a secure place to hide.

Why should popularity, and the ability to rouse large audiences —the lecture hall was the largest the university could offer, and it was still hard to get a seat—to ask questions that they probably could not answer have been regarded as a threat in Cambridge in the early 1970s? In those days, there was something in the sight of large numbers of students doing anything at all that was threatening to many of the guardians of the culture. Cambridge never witnessed student activism as extreme as that at Essex or at the London School of Economics. When it came, it came rather late, and was about different issues (the Greek junta, unjust disciplinary procedures, and so on). But the previous nonappearance of a major explosion over general educational issues made it all the more likely, in the eyes of many, that such might occur. Students had occupied the Senate House in the spring of 1971, and memories were fresh. At this point, it is important to undertake a brief review of the state of the student body in the early 1970s.

Between 1960 and 1970, according to a UNESCO report of 1975, there was a worldwide explosion in student numbers, from eleven to twenty-seven million.[5] Britain was well behind the trends set by other countries. As late as 1977, only 15 percent of the age group entered degree-level higher education, as compared to 29 percent in France and Italy, and 57 percent in the United States.[6] Nevertheless the perceived effects of this expansion on a traditionally static British society were quite considerable. The increase in student numbers in Britain in the years 1962–67 was greater than it had been in the previous twenty-five years.[7] There were more young people than ever before, and the mood was still positive enough in 1969 for Layard, King, and Moser to declare that "apart from electronics and natural gas, higher education has grown faster than any major national enterprise in the 1960s" (13). The famous Robbins report of 1963— about the time of the Beatles' first album, as Philip Larkin might have reminded us—was the first attempt ever to plan higher education on a predictive basis. Robbins, who was committed to the idea that all who might make good use of a higher degree should have the chance to obtain one, got some things right and some things wrong. He overestimated student numbers, so that the expansion of the mid-1960s would inevitably be followed by cuts, and he predicted a fall in arts (humanities) enrollments—exactly the opposite of what happened, so that the arts were underfunded from the start. Britain never, moreover, unlike many other countries, planned to absorb the majority of the new students into the universities. Instead—how typically British—it decided upon a "binary" system, expanding the polytechnics, technical colleges, and colleges of further education (this last for the training of teachers), at a faster rate than the universities, which thus tended to remain centers of academic research for a chosen few, albeit a few more than before.

Robbins did, however, recommend an increase in interdisciplinary as opposed to single-subject options for the bachelor's degree, somewhat on the American model. And the new universities that were set up after 1961—Keele, Sussex, East Anglia, York, Kent, Essex, Warwick, and Lancaster—did offer courses very different from the traditional single-subject concentrations offered at Oxbridge and most of the civic universities (in the humanities). To Cambridge faculty members, the interdisciplinary approach would thus inevitably smack of the fashionable education being offered in the new (and thus less serious) universities. (I speak only of the humanities, for the strength of Cambridge science had always depended upon its willingness to ignore the traditional boundaries between subjects.) This alone would probably have been enough to prompt many English dons to say no to any comparatist or theoretical initiatives in their own faculty. But between the Robbins report of 1963 and the dismissal of MacCabe in 1981, three other things happened: the student disturbances of 1966–74; the decline in student numbers; and the election of Margaret Thatcher's Conservative government.

Cambridge was not the center of the British student movement, but it did have its moments, and Colin MacCabe had a good deal to do with them. MacCabe was no Dutschke or Tariq Ali, but he had been a member of the British Communist Party, and a regular speaker at meetings and demonstrations. As a graduate student, he had also taken steps to set up an alternative seminar system, outside the regular faculty operation, and focusing on topics of agreed mutual concern. These were the days when the university buildings bore graffiti declaring that "the tygers of wrath are wiser than the horses of instruction." Cambridge tigers never quite took over, but there were growls from the thicket. Conservative morale was not much assisted by Raymond Williams's agreeing to accept German student radical leader Rudi Dutschke as a graduate student—an arrangement finally revoked, amid some controversy, by no less an authority than the Home Office. Williams himself, Britain's leading leftist literary figure, had been teaching at Cambridge since the 1950s. In his edition of the *May Day Manifesto, 1968* (Harmondsworth: Penguin, 1968), he had analyzed very precisely and prophetically the underlying causes of the present discontents. Against the rosy view of the world economy that had governed the thinking of the early 1960s, Williams predicted increased poverty, the spread of American cultural imperialism, and incrementally negative social consequences emerging from modernization and technological progress. Growth would come to a halt or regress (121), and against such changes conventional Labour Party politics had already proved themselves helpless and hopeless, indeed corrupted apparently beyond rescue. Faced with the "deadening language of a false political system" (13), Williams predicted and endorsed some radical alternative to the old two-party establishment. He was not suggesting that politics be taken out into the streets; much of the text of the manifesto had been written before the spring of 1968, which made it possible for the first time to speak of an international student movement. But neither was he inviting the formation of the present-day Social Democratic Party. Having Raymond Williams in the English faculty in the late 1960s and 1970s seemed to many of the students to hold out hope for change. Presumably the faculty conservatives felt the same prospect as a threat. It was bad enough to be advocating "cultural materialism" as a model for reading literary texts, but Williams did far more than this. A long-standing spokesman for film and television studies, for the study of popular culture, and for an interdisciplinary humanities school, he was also both willing and spectacularly able to pronounce upon the political and class struggle outside the university. By 1968, Williams was aware of the dangers of the "authoritarianism of the sixties," one that "does not segregate dissenters in concentration camps, but allows them to segregate themselves in little magazines and sectarian societies" (*Manifesto*, 149–50). Something more seemed to be required. In the mid-1970s, others were trying to work out the terms of an alternative literary education along lines very much inspired by Williams's objections. Stephen Heath and John Barrell were already calling for changes on recognizably political grounds, and MacCabe, tenured, would have made a fourth in a faculty where three was a crowd.

Student unrest in Britain was on a much smaller scale than that in Paris, Prague, Berlin, and Berkeley. But Britain is a small country, where even small vibrations are felt far and wide. Nor did the disturbances *seem* minor at the time. A parliamentary select committee traveled up and down the country to try to sort out the mess, and produced a two-hundred-page document that now makes for hilarious as well as serious reading. On the hilarious side, there is the standard academic compulsion to place everything within a tradition: "The history of mediaeval universities reveals many examples of student unrest."[8] At Essex University, the committee heard its evidence against "a fairly steady background of abusive comment" (7). The report also quotes a repentant Lord Robbins, regretting the increase in size that had made the modern university a place where a student becomes "apt prey for any articulate neurotic who happens to come along and find his spiritual compensation in working on the emotions of others" (39). But the same report, in the classic British reformist tradition, notices the need for the universities to question their "long standing assumptions" and set about "re-appraisal and reform" (40). Of the Cambridge students, in particular, it cites the opinion that "a lot of these people say that what they are being taught in English, History and economics is irrelevant" (87).

Cambridge in general, and in particular its English faculty, did little or nothing in response to this report. Following the exclusion of George Steiner, an unofficial working group, chaired by Frank Kermode, spent many hours during 1976 drawing up proposals for the rationalization of the teaching system and the curriculum. Despite the group's painstaking attempt to include representatives of every shade of opinion, its recommendations were unambiguously thrown out by the faculty at large. Normally intellectuals love to discuss change. It is, according to the most cynical interpretation, the one sure thing that prevents them ever bringing it about. But the English faculty members were so traumatized by the debate over the working group's proposals that they voted—pure Monty Python, this—for a two-year moratorium on the *discussion* of change, except as it pertained to the teaching of Shakespeare, American literature, and literary criticism (this last a rather narrower concept in Cambridge than it might sound to the outside reader).

By the mid-1970s, moreover, change was becoming less and less of an obligation in any sector of British higher education, owing to the fall in student numbers, both actual and projected. In 1971, Britain had estimated a student population of 825,000 by 1981. By 1975, that estimate had been revised downward, to 600,000. In 1974, only 450,000 were already enrolled (and most of these, as I have explained, in institutions other than universities).[9] The founding of the Open University in 1971 was followed by 194,000 applications in its first four years of operation (ibid., 2085). A large body of potential students could thus be expected to stay at home and acquire a part-time education through radio and television; no new buildings need be paid for, and the few could teach the many. For purely demographic reasons, then, retrenchment was in the air by the mid-1970s, and everyone was becoming aware of the shrinking job market. Cambridge English responded to the challenge not by reorganizing its ever more limited resources but by digging in and refusing to discuss change.

I come, at last in some detail, to the case of Colin MacCabe, appointed in 1976. His mandate was to devise some new approach to the teaching of the English language in a way suited to the needs of a literature department. It was something of a surprise that he was appointed at all. If not quite as un-British as Steiner, he was, however, an Irishman. His major work had been on Joyce, and on *Finnegans Wake* in particular, and it was work that had not only swallowed but to an impressive degree digested the lessons of poststructuralist Paris, where MacCabe had himself studied for a while. He also minced few words about the status of Joyce's Irish English as a colonized language implicated in a political and psychological struggle for identity. Now you would not expect an ex-Communist Irishman who had studied in Paris and been active in student politics to come out with any blandly reassuring version of the history of the language. But in fact MacCabe labored long and hard at the traditional tools of the discipline, and qualified himself to lecture very ably about the great vowel shift and the pronunciation of Shakespeare's English. He did his job, and more; none of those competent to judge his efforts here argued against his tenure. But this did not seem to matter, for, soon after 1976, "the faculty"—new faces, different votes—decided that it did not after all require anyone to teach the history of the language, thank you very much. And, by 1981, the election of the Thatcher government gave an enormous boost of confidence to the intellectual right wing, which no longer felt obliged to parade the values of liberal tolerance. Fewer teaching jobs, they thought, would surely mean fewer jobs for leftists, since much of the previous fifteen years' expansion had been associated with nontraditional teachers and courses. This reaction, if such it was, completely misunderstood the nature of the Thatcher government's contempt for intellectuals in general—a lazy and unproductive bunch if ever there was one—rather than simply for leftist ones. (MacCabe himself would go on to chair a department at Strathclyde, and raise funds for new posts from the corporate sector!)

When the CV hit the table, moreover, it became clear that MacCabe was not only doing his job but a good deal more besides. A book on Godard, a collection of essays on psychoanalysis, continuing extracurricular efforts at teaching film, television, and even rock and roll, a promised book on Milton that proposed to put politics together with linguistic and historical scholarship, bringing forward to unarguable prominence the great figure of English literature excluded from the Leavisite canon . . . and, finally, membership in what was coming to be perceived as a King's-Jesus faction, all rendered him vulnerable to the changing times. The argument was not about structuralism, although that term served as a useful mnemonic for the collective paranoia. It was about the promising conjunction of Marxism with psychoanalysis and literary criticism that MacCabe was developing, and about the prospective collapsing of all boundaries between high and low culture, and between the study of literature and the study of culture as a whole. The Open University had begun its integrated humanities course with a study of the Yoruba of Nigeria. MacCabe, and those who were aligned with him, seemed to many to be beating the same drums. Straight structuralism was never a threat to the English faculty, which had always made room for young, artfully casual lecturers in jeans and turtlenecks sounding off about Lévi-Strauss and yet another ingenious way to read a text. The *Sunday Times* (January 25, 1981) noted the apparent paradox of the conservative Christopher Ricks lecturing about Bob Dylan to anyone who would invite him, while the radical MacCabe was "banging on about the need of Eng Lit students to know grammar." In fact, MacCabe had things to say about rock music too, and they were not just about crafty half-rhymes and the clever subversion of the cliché. And grammar, for MacCabe as for Cobbett before him, was an important tool in the training of logical thinking and in the breakdown of class boundaries.

The ambitions of Colin MacCabe and his allies thus went beyond simply reading literature in different ways, or reading different literatures. They were groping toward some practical implementation of Williams's "cultural materialism," but by including rather than excluding the traditional scholarly aptitudes. The real threat of this program was not just that it proposed some alternative within a range of alternatives; nobody minds that. It was that it promised to put things together in a new way. It would not be a choice between approaches but an approach that set out to incorporate all others into some synthetic analysis —political and social history with linguistics, philology, close reading, psychoanalysis, and so on. This wholeness has always been a goal of Marxist methodology, and it makes others uncomfortable because it threatens to make choices and find some things more important than others, even as all things are considered and explored. In this way it disfigures the uneasy pluralist alliance that governs the ethics of agreeing to differ. It antagonizes liberals as well as conservatives—in fact, it is more threatening to liberals, who usually cannot bear the aspiration toward objectivity from either left or right.

I hope I can pass over all but the bare details of the firing itself. The exact bureaucratic moves are probably of interest only to the protagonists themselves, and they were seldom clear even to them. Academics love secrecy; it allows them to perpetrate squalidly personal policies under the guise of professional confidentiality. A few telling citations from the newspapers will tell enough of the story. Christopher Ricks told the *Sunday Times* (January 18, 1981) about the unfortunate influence of "a particular radical, Marxist, semiological clique"; George Watson, always ready to be quoted, told the *Guardian* (February 2, 1981) that Marxism is "a stale superstition" and that recent events merely showed once again that "the sixties avant-garde, egg on face, needs a better act and knows it." Howard Erksine-Hill, one of the more histrionic of MacCabe's opponents, spoke passionately on BBC television's "Newsnight" (January 26, 1981) about the cancer growing within his faculty, formed of those who denied "the significance of the ideas of evidence, probability, and truth," and whose students would "lose their capacity to argue cogently" and leave Cambridge "in a state of total confusion." What he meant, of course, is that these students were graduating, often with very good degrees indeed, but with a cynical or skeptical view of the world they were about to enter, one in which the evidence for certain truths and probabilities was all too clear and cogent. Quite a number of these students, moreover, had told Erksine-Hill exactly what they thought of his view of life and literature, and in no uncertain terms, cogently enough to persuade him to take the highly unusual step of moving from a progressive to a more comfortably conservative college. It was not uncommon, in those days, that such events would emerge refigured into the rhetoric of high-minded concern for the future of literary criticism.

The Senate House discussion, predictably, produced nothing beyond a public display of the grievances: no action on the part of the university came out of it. There was some wrangling about just how bad the staff-student ratio really was, and much appeal for more teaching positions—an argument that must have looked to the assembled outsiders like a plea for good money to be sent after bad. There was a plug for the faculty library budget, and there were several assurances that business as usual was flourishing, and a good thing too. MacCabe's supporters made their cases, backed by the details and the statistics that so often announce defeat, convincing though they may be. The others merely blustered, since the details would not have flattered them. The students who got up to speak complained bitterly, and to a person, about the kind of education they were experiencing, but students who complain are always said to be unrepresentative. Perhaps the last word on the public discussion should rest with one Dr. M. D. Long: "I see no point in even *trying* to advance things until a decent interval has elapsed, lest anyone should run away with the idea that this episode has somehow galvanized us usefully. It hasn't" (*Reporter*, 344).

As far as I know, that "decent interval" has still not elapsed, so reluctant is the English faculty to give the impression that it might have learned something from having its dirty linen displayed in public. Bad enough for Dr. Long and his colleagues, worse still for their students. Most of the defeated faction in the MacCabe affair have left, and are happier elsewhere. Looking back, it is tempting to focus on the funnier moments. The *Times Higher Educational Supplement* (January 23, 1981) published photographs of "two revolutionaries," Karl Marx and I. A. Richards, but labeled them the wrong way round. *Private Eye* weighed in with its own unique contribution. The locally printed *Quarto* published a brilliant rewrite of the whole affair as if it were a row over how to coach a football (American "soccer") team. Titled "Early Barthes for MacCoy," it concluded that most of the team "just want to get on with playing the game."

I began by saying that MacCabe would not have been fired from Leeds or Lancaster, places that might well have appreciated what he was doing. Energy, intelligence, and initiative are not disadvantages everywhere, even when devoted to radical causes. In the less prestigious and poorly funded polytechnics, where "that sort of thing" is the norm, MacCabe would have been a hero. Being hired or fired in those places does not attract national attention; but nor does working in them stand any chance of effecting changes in the education of the economic and intellectual elite. One is allowed to preach disaffection twenty hours a week in the polytechnics, within the wisdom of the "binary system" of higher education. Intellectuals of MacCabe's sort thus "matter" in Britain rather more in some places than in others, although they have mattered rather less than before, everywhere, since Margaret Thatcher's election. Even the conservatives are beginning to cross the Atlantic, not so much out of greed but out of sheer frustration at the unremitting erosion of the university system from the outside, and its total inability to change with the times from the inside.

In a sense, the saga of Colin MacCabe and Cambridge English was an object lesson in what happens when the times change, and when an articulate student movement becomes adult and starts to seek to change the system from within. MacCabe was not given to personal abuse and private vendettas; he was too busy for that. But it is not to be supposed that those who preferred the old ways did not perceive which way their votes ought to go. And the spectrum of those who were felt to rock the boat was astonishingly broad. Frank Kermode and Raymond Williams have very little in common, politically. But they were both perceived as threats by the old guard of all ages, because they were interested in change, and because Kermode, in particular, had the imagination and professional integrity to support the tenure of a colleague with whom he did not simply and in all ways agree. MacCabe has had the last laugh, several times over. He left Cambridge for a chair at Strathclyde, where he laid the foundations of a department of cultural studies, concentrating on the study of film and television. Scotland, fortunately, has always been a foreign country. Now MacCabe holds two jobs, reaching one semester a year at the University of Pittsburgh and heading production at the British Film Institute. Exciting things are happening in both places. Quiet flow the dons.

What conclusions can we come to? Some are already apparent. There is little point in speaking of a class or subculture of intellectuals as a whole, without factoring in the objective functions of the institutions to which they do or do not belong. Time and place must matter a great deal to any theory that seeks to describe their behavior. Britain is not the Soviet Union, where intellectuals have tended to matter quite critically to the various administrations since 1917. MacCabe did not go to Siberia, or to prison, did not have to wait for the sunshine of *glasnost* to filter through the windows, did not have to publish in the underground press or write under a pseudonym. Nor is Britain quite like the United States, where it appears for the moment as if many more things can be said and done without interference, on the understanding that none of them really matter. Certainly, after Cambridge, most American universities are paradises of tolerance and openness. But one must be careful with this assumption. Things were very different here in the 1950s, in the days of the House Un-American Activities Committee. And just recently, there have been at least three denials of tenure to Marxist or proto-Marxist professors, two at Princeton (David Abraham, Thomas Crow) and one at Northwestern (Barbara Foley). I do not have enough information to comment on what may be common between these three cases, nor can I speculate in any detail about whether a national trend is operating here. But I do know that the dismissal of Foley was on clearly nonacademic grounds, and indeed was carried out by overturning the positive decisions of all the appropriate academic review committees. Princeton and Northwestern also share with Cambridge an overactive sense of self-importance, but I do not have the competence to assess its credibility. These cases have aroused some small interest outside academia—there have been short reports in the *New York Times*, at least of the Foley case. But none of them has provoked the response generated by MacCabe's dismissal. There is not, in the United States, a small, literary coterie of the sort that exists in England, and the public perception of the "great" universities is also very different. Intellectuals in the United States are much more widely separated from national politics than they traditionally have been in Britain. Nor does the American press seem to have any interest in creating the taste by which it would be enjoyed. They have little interest in intellectuals in general, and none at all in defending the "left." The MacCabe affair was reported most intensively in the *Guardian*, England's major left-of-center national daily. No such newspaper exists here. Despite the post-Watergate mythology of the press as heroic watchdog of the public interest, it is perfectly clear that many things are not said or pursued, and that a Democrat has to be a good deal more careful than a Republican if he or she is to survive its attentions.

But what about Britain or, more specifically, England? Despite a wider than usual gap between Parliament and the universities, intellectuals still get some attention. When E. P. Thompson gave up teaching history to work for European nuclear disarmament, people did take notice; that is, the press gave them the information they would need to be able to choose to take notice, or not. Left-leaning governments in Britain have generally been more solicitous of the participation of intellectuals than have right-leaning governments. (At least in appearance, the same distinction would seem to characterize the difference between the Kennedy and Reagan administrations.) This may suggest that there is something in the intellectual disposition that makes it tend toward the extension of particulars to generals, in the manner of Tom Paine rather than of Edmund Burke. Intellectuals theorize, mostly, and the left has always had more use for theory than the right, which has tended to prefer the language of special cases and unpredictable instances. Or, more cynically, it may suggest that different political positions require different legitimating rhetorics, which are not to be assumed to be in organic relation to what is actually brought about by those positions. Williams's *May Day Manifesto* announced a schism between the official Labour Party and the prominent faction in the left intelligentsia, one that has still not healed and shows no signs of healing. I know a good deal about what happened to and around Colin MacCabe in 1981, but I am not sure that the conclusions one might draw from these events can be extended beyond particular individuals in particular institutions at a specific time. Even Oxford, "the other place" that shares with Cambridge the higher education of almost the entire British ruling class, would probably not have seen the need to fire MacCabe. Its appointments are structured differently, with a higher degree of college autonomy and a less collective faculty mentality, and English at Oxford has never set itself up as the arbiter of the national literary culture. It is hard to predict what might have happened to MacCabe had he been an assistant professor in an American university. My own experience since 1982 suggests that literary criticism in the United States functions as a remarkably monolithic discourse whose disputes cover a very small part of the political (as opposed to the rhetorical) spectrum. If feminist criticism currently holds the most promise for broadening this spectrum, it has not yet achieved a coherently political identity: it too has its own left- and right-wing devotees. The MacCabe affair was so rooted in a particularly English, and Cambridge English quarrel, that it is hard to imagine an exactly parallel case in the United States; trying to turn English at Yale into a department of comparative cultural materialism might come as close as any. This might well get an assistant professor fired, but it would probably not get the same attention in the national media.

MacCabe and his supporters were, thanks to a high level of student support, within an ace of making changes that seemed to be of real importance. We will never know whether they would have been truly effective, though we may debate whether they should have been, that is, whether even a progressive version of Oxbridge hegemony is a good or ideal thing. The paranoid reaction to Colin MacCabe proves only that he and his kind were felt as a threat; it does not enable us to predict exactly what would have happened had he been successful. One more member of what was already a small, if very visible and vocal "Marxist semiological clique," to cite Christopher Ricks once more, would probably not have changed the deadening bureaucratic structures and intellectual conservatism of the English faculty. It would, however, have meant that a certain kind of teaching would have been much better represented than it is now. Most of MacCabe's allies have left, and the few (two or three) who remain have, not unreasonably, given up. A department whose most exciting work was being done in the mode of an inclusive cultural materialism would have been an exciting place. It might have functioned as a focus for kindred spirits in history, classics, anthropology, and political science (not at that time a full-fledged faculty in Cambridge, but staffed with some brilliant people). If it had lasted, it might have provided a genuine test case, given Cambridge's prestige, resources, and the quality of its students, for the possibilities of the kind of education that is to this day still limited to the poly-technics and to some of the "new" universities. My advice to to-day's eighteen-year-olds would be to go to Sussex or Strathclyde rather than to Cambridge.

Even if the MacCabe faction had survived early opposition, it might well not have survived. At the present time of writing, May 1987, Britain approaches another election. In a country with three million unemployed, with certain inner city areas destroyed probably forever, with increasing racial tensions, and tensions be-tween all sectors of the young unemployed and the police (Tot-tenham, Brixton, Toxteth), and, indeed, with the most polarized relations ever between the government and the universities, all the polls predict another Thatcher victory. Despite civil war in Northern Ireland, the unemployment problem, and the increas-ing class division that has resulted from the Thatcher govern-ment's aggressive redistribution of wealth (the "haves" now have even more), Britain still seems a long way from radical change. It is hard not to agree with John Dunn's diagnosis of a "massive in-stitutional continuity" (*Times Literary Supplement*, April 24, 1987, 442) wherein riots substitute for revolutions and little real change occurs. Business as usual may indeed be the battle cry of modern Britain. But it is too easy to cast gloom from a distance, too easy to chronicle, with every annual visit, yet one more nega-tive development in the general decline of everything. I remem-ber the years 1976–81 as, basically, hopeful ones, at least ones during which a good deal of time and energy was spent working for what one felt to be progress. In 1970 I was in my first year as an undergraduate at Cambridge. I remember sitting in a somewhat sparsely attended public lecture given by a senior member of the faculty of English, during which he remarked, quite without irony —as if irony would have helped!—that "the trouble with Hitler was that he made intelligent anti-Semitism impossible for ever af-ter." John Cleese, in his role as Basil Fawlty, image of the paranoid English lower bourgeois, brim full of bigotries and prejudices designed to keep the world at bay and Manuel in his place under the stairs, might *just* have tried this one, but I doubt it. A bit strong, even for *Fawlty Towers*. While this lecturer is not at all typical of his colleagues in the English faculty, he is tolerated, and he is at this moment still employed there. It is a pity that the students can no longer compare him with Colin MacCabe. But MacCabe was, basically, the wrong sort of chap. He is also one of the most energetic, honorable, and intelligent people I know. I hope, and trust, that he will have several more last laughs.

NOTES

1. *Cambridge University Reporter*, no 5108 (February 18, 1981), 334.

2. *The Prelude*, eds. Jonathan Wordsworth, M. H. Abrams, and Stephen Gill (1805; New York & London, 1979), III:615–18.

3. Stephano Rosso, "An Interview with Paul de Man," *Critical Inquiry*, 12 (1985–86), 790.

4. Raymond Williams, *Writing in Society* (London: Verso, 1984), p. 214. For a comprehensive history of Leavisism, see Francis Mulhearn, *The Moment of "Scrutiny"* (London: New Left Books, 1979).

5. Gareth Williams and Tessa Blackstone, *Response to Adversity: Higher Education in a Harsh Climate* (Guildford: Society for Research into Higher Education, 1983), 1.

6. The figures are less dramatic, but still dramatic, if one takes the figures for universities strictly defined: 9.4% in Britain, 27% in the United States.

7. Richard Layard, John King, and Claus Moser, *The Impact of Robbins: Expansion in Higher Education* (Harmondsworth: Penguin, 1969), 13.

8. *Report from the Select Committee on Education and Science: Student Relations* (London: Her Majesty's Stationery Office, 1969), 12.

9. Figures are from *The International Encyclopaedia for Higher Education*, ed. Asa S. Knowles; 10 vols. (San Francisco, Washington, London: Jossey-Bass, 1977), 4139.

Espionage as Vocation:
Raymond Williams's Loyalties
Bruce Robbins

The secret revealed at the end of Raymond Williams's fifth novel, *Loyalties* (published in 1985), is espionage on behalf of the Soviet Union. The topic is not exotic. Williams was writing the novel in the period just after the revelations about Sir Anthony Blunt, the Cambridge colleague who was the "fourth man" in the spy group of Burgess, Maclean, and Philby; to some extent *Loyalties* may be a *roman à clef*. The subject may also have appealed to Williams for less topical reasons. There are significant parallels between Blunt and Williams himself. Both were leftist students at Cambridge during the thirties, both later became Cambridge dons, both were professionally concerned with the criticism of art, and for both there was some question about the fit between politics and profession. These parallels suggest a sense in which the spy comes still closer to home for Williams: as a figure for the political-intellectual-as-academic. I want to argue that through the spy, which has become an especially important figure of political imagination in the postwar period, and through the political thriller, with its formulaic distance from the semiautobiographical realism of Williams's Welsh trilogy, Williams found a new and liberating way of speaking about a problematic that, from the beginning of his writing career, has bothered both his other novels and, less obviously, his critical writing: the problematic of his own working life and how it fits into the larger politics of society—his moral, political, ideological "take" on his role as an intellectual, his career as an academic.

In brief, my thesis is that the figure of the "intelligence agent" belongs to the problematics of postwar professionalism. I can introduce this idea by quoting the essay on Blunt written by George Steiner, entitled "The Cleric of Treason," which came out in the *New Yorker* in 1980.[1] Steiner writes: "I would like to think for a moment about a man who in the morning teaches his students that a false attribution of a Watteau drawing or an inaccurate transcription of a fourteenth-century epigraph is a sin against the spirit and in the afternoon or evening transmits to the agents of Soviet intelligence classified, perhaps vital information given to him in sworn trust by his countrymen and intimate colleagues. What are the sources of such a scission?" (191). To pose the issue in terms of the working day, setting an evening of treason against a morning of scholarship, is to suggest that its hidden referent is the problematic of work. In fact, Steiner goes on to offer the scholarship as the cause of the treason, which thus becomes a sort of professional deformation. "Obsessive scholarship," he says, "breeds a nostalgia for action" (199). The nostalgia for action and utility that leads to espionage stems from the absolute uselessness of the "absolute scholar," or of research as a vocation.

This view of *Wissenschaft als Beruf* becomes more interesting when one recalls that the portrait of Blunt is a retake of the figure that first made Steiner's reputation, the concentration-camp-torturer-who-goes-home-and-reads-Goethe, a figure we can call the *cultured Kommandant*. This figure should be familiar; Steiner has been playing variations on the theme since the late fifties. "We know now that a man can read Goethe or Rilke in the evening, that he can play Bach and Schubert, and go to his day's work at Auschwitz in the morning." The names change, along with the times of day, but the "scission" remains the same. In January 1986, Steiner wrote in the *New York Times Book Review:* "Too many are the butchers and clerks of totalitarian rule who, in their personal and private lives, respond with cultured delight to the claims to fiction and the arts. We know now that a man can torture in the afternoon and be moved to truthful tears by Schubert or Pushkin at nightfall."[2] The cultured Kommandant clearly represents a major chapter in our recent moral history—but perhaps, as with the Holocaust itself, we have been too close to it to see which chapter. The juxtaposition of this figure with Steiner's portrait of Blunt suggests that the former was not simply, or perhaps even primarily, a representative of the moral burden of the Holocaust, as we tend to think. More precisely, it translated that burden into a domestic American dilemma of public life versus private life—that is, the problematic of postwar *work*.

This problematic results from one of the same developments that help privilege espionage as a postwar theme. With its civilian bombings, its Occupation, and its Resistance movements, the Second World War was characterized by an extension of hostilities into the domain of civil society. The Resistance, for example, politicized, or rather polemicized, the routine of everyday life. This is why, as James Wilkinson writes, there was a "general tendency among Resistance intellectuals to reduce political questions to the level of personal conduct" and why "the distinction between public and private spheres of action became blurred."[3] This invasion of the everyday (extending the penetration of capital into previously protected areas of life) certainly has something to do with postwar spy paranoia; in the same way, it has to do with a new consciousness of the shifting relations between work and nonwork. Many of the major figures of the postwar imagination can only be understood in these terms. Steiner's cultured Kommandant belongs together with Sartre's café waiter in *Being and Nothingness* who is playing a café waiter, a figure of professional identification offered as a paradigm of inauthenticity. It also belongs with Camus's Sisyphus and the hero of *The Plague*, a functionary who "asked only to make himself useful in small tasks" and who bears an interesting relation to how Foucault is being used these days.[4] On the level of popular sensibility, one thinks of the Alec Guinness character in the film of Pierre Boulle's *Bridge over the River Kwai* (1954), a British colonel so intent on being "happy in his work" that he betrays his country in the interest of efficient bridge building. If work already served as the hinge between the immanent and the transcendent, as Franco Moretti puts it, the point at which the dialectic of history stooped to illuminate everyday reality, the trials of the Nazi war criminals (who were "just doing their job") touched the same point with a transcendent horror.[5]

I call this motif a problematic because a clear or unproblematic response to it was beyond the postwar range of ideological possibilities. The result of the trials could not be a consensus of humanistic or humanitarian antiprofessionalism, as one might expect, for the simple reason that the *excuse* given by the executioners, "I was just doing my job," was also the ideological *solution* offered by postwar "end of ideology" thinking. The "just" in "just doing my job" meant not being personally involved in any political program, but extracting oneself from politics by simply fulfilling one's duties in a given area of specialization or competence. Work was outside ideology. To speak of war criminals, so the defense went, would be like speaking of *work* criminals, as difficult to conceive as to pronounce. In effect, postwar ideology accepted the absurdity of such a notion. At the same moment when professionalism was being labeled collaboration with the enemy, neutral technical expertise was also being celebrated as the replacement for any political taking of sides. The ideology of privatization, which removed morality and politics from the workplace and consigned them to the home, shrugged off accountability for the meaning and consequences of one's work. It positively welcomed the split between home and work on which the defense of the war criminals rested.

The best example of this contradiction in the postwar problematic of work is the lesson Steiner himself drew from his cultured Kommandant. He offered this figure as a challenge to the belief "that culture is a humanizing force," and thus that the work of scholars and humanists is socially meaningful. Contemplating his Kommandant, Steiner said he could no longer believe, with Matthew Arnold and F. R. Leavis, that the humanities humanize. And yet Steiner almost immediately backs down from his challenge (perhaps under pressure from the "engagement" of Sartre, the postwar voice who took the same challenge in the opposite direction) and retreats to the Arnoldian humanist position, with its immense nostalgia for Europe's lost cultural splendors. The logic of his retreat is as clear as it is paradoxical. What he wants is culture in privacy—or rather, culture *as* privacy. Since public life has proved a nightmare, let us withdraw into the patient, self-sacrificing, apolitical work of cultural transmission—even if (here is the paradox) the *capacity* of culture to remain apolitical, its *in*-capacity to prevent or even resist the horrors of the war, is what has thrown what we mean by culture into question, and even if the contiguous but separate coexistence of high culture with the horror of the camps has been (for the cultured) the greatest horror of all. In short, the solution repeats the problem. This explains why Steiner's fascination with the cultured Kommandant has been capable of reproducing itself over and over for thirty years: the figure represents at the same time what most horrifies Steiner in the Nazi period and what Steiner now urges intellectual work to become.

On this point one would expect a clear contrast between Steiner and Raymond Williams. But that is not what one finds. Like Steiner, Williams establishes a hidden equation between intellectual work and treason. Throughout his trilogy of semiautobiographical Welsh novels—which are all about the choice and the politics of vocation—intellectual work is what makes the protagonist leave Wales and what keeps him from coming back to it, and is thus a betrayal of his most fundamental loyalty. As the Welsh protagonist of *Second Generation* (1964) says of his presence in Cambridge, "a people had conceived its own liberation as training its sons for the enemy service."[6] In his own eyes, he is *in* the enemy service. (Later, when he is offered a chance to go to the United States for reasons of work, he frames his refusal as agreement with an African statesman's discourse on national liberation.) Doing intellectual work means being a traitor to his nation in much the same way that Blunt is a traitor to his.

Hence, as the interviewers of *Politics and Letters* remark, academics—and especially leftist academics—replace capitalists as the villains of *Second Generation*, and are treated with barely concealed fury, although (or perhaps because) they represent nothing more or less than Williams's own vocation.[7] Williams's painful unease with this logic makes itself felt in his treatment of the materials of family romance. The academics of *Second Generation* are surrogate fathers of higher station, produced in order to legitimate the young man's independence or "upward mobility." But identification with these surrogates is experienced as an unendurable, sexually doubled betrayal of the original, Welsh, working-class father. In *Second Generation*, as in *Loyalties*, the *Adam Bede* motif of an upper-class man who seduces and abandons a working-class woman is transmuted into the still more charged tableau of the Other Man as Leftist Academic who takes or tries to take the working-class Mother away from the working-class Father. *Loyalties* conceals this structure somewhat by spreading the story out over more than one generation, so that mother, son, and academic interloper do not occupy the narrative stage at the same time. In *Second Generation*, on the other hand—which is, as one critic says, a "deeply vocational" novel—the structure is openly visible.[8] The married working-class mother of a grown son has an affair with a (personally unappetizing) leftist academic on the son's faculty. The structure brings out Williams's intention to condemn and reject this intellectual, but it also highlights his failure to carry that intention through. Williams does not know quite what to convict the academic *of*, beyond his upper-class accent and (like Norman in *Loyalties*) his not being good in bed. The disparity between the thinness of the character and the intense desire to repudiate the position he occupies leads the novel to fill up that position with a second academic villain. This second villain, the protagonist's academic adviser, is also the professional model whom he will finally and rather harshly reject ("you're the enemy"), just as his mother rejects her lover. But here too the case against the academic is strangely insufficient. When the adviser reappears in the later novel *The Fight for Manod* (1979), this time working for the government and unquestionably one of "them," it is as if Williams were trying to blacken the earlier portrait, realizing it was not as critical as he had wanted it to be.

The structural problem is of course that Williams cannot repudiate the erotic interloper without repudiating the mentor, since they are the same figure. Which is to say that he can neither accept nor repudiate himself as he has been constituted by the vocational aspirations that lead away from Wales and from the working class. Work is the locus of equal and irreconcilable loyalties; family romance is thus transmuted into vocational tragedy.

To be fair, Williams does not let the matter go at that. If the Welsh trilogy establishes a clear equation between intellectual work and treason, it does not accept this vocational tragedy as inevitable. While Williams is condemning himself and his vocation, he is also trying to *redefine* his work so as to resolve the conflict of loyalties. In *Second Generation*, the hero concludes, "What I shall try to do, here, is a new kind of inquiry, with ourselves involved in it. And for our own understanding, not just for report . . . not a survey. That's just what's been wrong" (344). Yet even reconceptualized, his work still looks to his father like the enemy's hostile observation: "From what I can see he's in the same trade. And it makes no difference, that he happens to be born here. He wants the same, just to measure and see what we're good for" (344–45).

More or less the same conclusion is reached in *Border Country*, Williams's first published novel (before it came out in 1960 he had written three unpublished novels). On its first page, we find the lecturer-hero's "anxiety about his work," which is research "on population movements into the Welsh mining valleys in the middle decades of the nineteenth century. But I have moved myself, he objected, and what is it really that I must measure?" (9). This turn of the content of his research toward himself puts a great deal of weight on his work. It is in the name of his work that he refuses the offer of a lucrative job that would allow him to return to Wales, so his work bears the burden of not being mere money making, while it is also not solidarity with his people. The role assigned to work is to resolve the (personal) contradictions between going and staying, family and militancy, upward mobility and local solidarity. He leaves the community, then seeks to come back on the level of his work: " 'He's studying Wales,' Eira said, 'and he goes to London to do it' " (271).

In short, work is required to function as a synthesis. But this is not to say, as the ending indicates, that synthesis is or can be achieved on that level. What the protagonist has really wanted, it seems, is for his father to tell him he's doing the right work (rather than work like his own, as a railway signalman, which the father has dramatically refused to leave for a chance to go into business), or that it is all right for him to be doing it. Just before dying, the father does accept the son's work, but only in unacceptable terms: "You're working for your boys" (279). The real "structure of feeling" is total intransigence, and that is expressed over and over; in the structure that associates the son's work with the father's death, and again in two key scenes. In the first, news of the father's fatal attack is given to his son on a railway platform as he is about to return to Cambridge. He is "hailed" by a colleague of his father's who recognizes him by resemblance—a classic scene of ideological interpellation in which he is recognized as his father's son and becomes the subject who returns to Wales. The second is at the father's deathbed, when the father, in delirium, denies in effect the separate pressure of work over love. "Only the one trade to get into and that's a wife to love you." The father remains an unbending ideal, condemning his son's work, and work thus remains betrayal, treason. It is a vocational form of modern tragedy: he is "blamed for something that is quite inevitable" (279).

This vocational impasse is in fact what defines the concept of "tragedy" that Williams develops in his first major piece of criticism. The first chapter of his first published book, *Drama from Ibsen to Eliot* (1952), offers a revisionary reading of Ibsen's career in terms of "vocation," described as "the most persistent single theme in Ibsen's whole work." [9] What is this "vocation" that Williams substitutes for the usual reading of Ibsen in terms of 'the destruction of an idealist"? It is more than an ideal in that it is a specifically *individual* call to idealism—that is, a call to a *feasible mode of individual activity*, to a *career*—and at the same time its idealism is *more* than individual: he speaks of vocation as aimed at "the restoration of wholeness" (29) and at "liberation" (34). This is why, as Williams insists, vocations cannot be, as Ibsen's idealists appeared to Shaw, objects of satire. Yet if Williams takes a more sympathetic view than Shaw, his view is sympathetic to both sides in what we quickly see is a tragic sense of vocation. Perhaps "the fundamental statement . . . in the whole work of Ibsen," Williams writes, is the absolute impossibility of answering the call to vocation. "The call is absolute; so are the barriers" (29).

What creates the vocational impasse of Ibsenite tragedy, and how does Williams find himself sympathizing with both sides of it? He summarizes the conclusion of *Brand* as "the impossibility of fulfilling the vocation of the ideal under the load of 'inherited spiritual debt' " (28), and he defines "debt" (still according to *Brand*) as the taking over of parental sins and responsibilities. In other words, in his first piece of sustained critical writing Williams frames the theme of vocational tragedy in Ibsen so as to reproduce, or rather anticipate, the generational conflict and vocational impasse of his first two Welsh novels. Like those novels, it attempts to resolve this impasse by allowing vocation to be brought into synthesis with the world of the parents. Invocation of the parents can sacralize even ordinary, politically quiescent work: "Brand's mission can no longer be the reform of the world, but the actual, limited sphere of 'daily duty, daily labour, hallowed to a Sabbath deed' " (31). Again as in the novels, this solution is judged impossible. The claims of vocation and inheritance are equally peremptory: this is "the essential tragedy of the human situation" (32). Moreover, here Williams adds an ironic twist that is not in the novels. The real vocational tragedy, he suggests, is less the impossibility of fulfilling one's vocation than how *the ideal itself comes to be changed*, under pressure from other loyalties. The tragedy is, in particular, how vocation comes to be redefined "not as social reform, but as the realization of the actual self"—how "social reform" is diminished to "self-fulfilment" (30).

In responding to the interviewers of *Politics and Letters*, Williams makes it clear that vocational tragedy is his description of the postwar situation, both for himself as a would-be militant-academic and in general. He can only assent to their question: "You felt that the hope of a kind of fusion of your personal work as a writer with the general activities of a political militant in the thirties had been frustrated—hence you were in a situation like that which is at the centre of Ibsen's work?" (63). Yet in devoting the postwar years to the (academic) work of laying out this dilemma in Ibsen, he had done something more than define the tragic need for an impossible fusion between large political goals and daily vocational routine; he had done more than displace and contain the impasse within his academic work (as one might say I am here trying to contain my own). His account of tragedy already points beyond the impasse. What is opposed to vocation, what produces tragedy, is "inheritance," in other words, the father's intransigence. But the father's intransigence has to be understood generously here: not as private psychological materials that have not been worked through, but as an insistence that redefinition *within* the work, the effort to displace the conflict *into* his work and to present work, reconceived, as the synthesis between leaving Wales and staying, as a way of returning to Wales on a higher level, cannot take him very far. The reason is that it is still self-regarding, in two senses: it sacrifices Wales both to self-interest and to self-reflexivity. Thinking about himself in relation to his subject is good, but it is no more effective than doing the usual sort of "objective" survey. Neither sort of work produces action in and on the world. What is needed is a new relation *between* work and the world: specifically, some mode of acting on the distant forces that have been working against Wales.

It is precisely an emphasis on action that permits Williams to keep the concept of tragedy alive. Here contrast with George Steiner is again useful. Steiner's position inheres in the title of his book *The Death of Tragedy* (1961): there is no modern tragedy. Williams disagrees, above all because he refuses Steiner's Arnoldian premise that significant action is impossible in the postwar world. There *is* significant action, Williams insists in *Modern Tragedy* (1966). (In fact, Williams sees the denial that tragedy exists as a professional deformation of academics influenced by their training to value the past over the present, and to neglect present action [46].) And thus there is tragedy, as he had already shown in Ibsen. But in order to support the belief that tragedy is ordinary, just as "culture is ordinary," Williams must be willing to discover and acknowledge new, postwar genres and resources of action, especially collective, collaborative action, at points where others will see nothing happening, and must demonstrate their political vitality. Again as he had shown in Ibsen, one such point was the vocation, which has its own tragedy, at least the tragedy of not being the collective revolutionary action it wants to be. Through his work, if not in full consciousness, Williams could be said to have assumed the task of making moral room for action that our professional deformation would invite us to condemn out of hand—including, or perhaps especially, our own.

One unusual place Williams is willing to countenance professional action is in the political thriller, and in espionage. Williams's first political thriller, *The Volunteers* (1978), introduces the spy as something approaching a positive professional model. Narrated by a journalist, once a leftist militant, who is assigned to cover an act of "terrorism" carried out by people like his preprofessional self, the novel pivots on the question of his commitment. On the most obvious level, this means his eventual refusal of the role of "the watching devil, the staring professional intruder" and his volunteering for extraprofessional action.[10] But what is more interesting than this conventional moral frame is the other sense of the title term "volunteers." The "Volunteers" are a group of Fabian-style professionals whose political program is infiltration of the bureaucratic system, using the usual weapons of careerism. Instead of entry only into leftist organizations, or entry anywhere but always identified as leftists, they attempt a hidden permeation of the modern state apparatus, a very "long term" gambit. "To work normally, to attend to their careers, to show no traceable interest in anything else . . . But still they've made their commitment." This gambit is subjected to scrutiny: "a commitment to nothing. A commitment that will never be called," the narrator says when he uncovers their secret. By the time it is called, he goes on, "they'll have become their offices . . . Haven't you watched your friends growing up? Haven't you seen what happens to people?" But this belittlement cannot overbalance the weight of the thriller's form, which goes with rather than against their politicized professionalism. The head of the "volunteers," Mark Evans, is presented to us as another figure of the successful, hateful careerist, despised by "the committed" (67). Moreover, he is despised as a Welshman who has sold out. And yet he is the figure the reader will be taught, if not to admire, at least to see, against first and second temptations, as a principled radical, one who has the power to threaten real damage—"the system will lose its confidence. Who can we trust, they'll all ask . . . "—and who has in fact accomplished something: "not much perhaps but enough" (179).

In *Loyalties*, Williams does not much like his upper-class Cambridge spy. The spy's name, Norman, already says enough about which side he's taken to be on. In fact, Williams concludes the novel with a rather grand denunciation of Norman and his espionage, put for greater effect in the mouth of Norman's natural son, whom he abandoned and who was raised in the Welsh working class. Yet the thriller form again works in the spy's favor. Norman's transformation into a spy is located at a very strange point: it coincides with his jilting of the Welsh working-class girl he has seduced and made pregnant. For most of the novel the reader is encouraged to take this as the usual pattern of male upper-class behavior—the *Adam Bede* motif of the gentleman who uses class privilege to seduce and then abandon a working woman, as in the family romance of *Second Generation*. Williams saves until quite late the news that Norman in fact had a *principled* motive all along, but one that had to *remain secret*: his intelligence work. Thus, as in *The Volunteers*, Williams makes the spy's principled motives look very much like the "point" the novel has been building up to. More generally, this is the effect of working within the pre-Le Carré conventions of the political thriller, and allowing Norman's spying to function less as a moral issue than as the novel's mystery, obliquely hinted at but revealed only relatively late in the novel. The reader follows what seems to be both Norman's abandonment of his Welsh lover and his abandonment of his political commitment, a slow turn to the right that coincides with his rising professional career in the government bureaucracy, and develops a bad opinion of him—so bad that it can only change for the better. Thus the revelation of his spying, coinciding with the revelation that he never *did* abandon his radical ideas, makes the point that, whatever else has happened to him, pursuing his professional career was not in fact selling out.

Loyalties clearly locates espionage as a subset of the general category of professionalism. Norman is first and foremost a "serious professional" (133). He speaks of others as amateurs (193); he himself deals with matters "too complicated for any amateurs to touch" (373–74). He has only contempt for his sister's "amateur" spying (133). His sister chides him for leaning his politics too heavily on his profession: "You think your professional *couche* is a viable political alternative. But it isn't and it can't be" (168–69). In the view of a Cambridge friend, "He had become used to living in a consensual professional world." But neither the friend nor the sister knows his secret. In fact, Norman's professionalism takes him far outside consensus, and in terms of the novel, at least, his mode of action would seem to be the most efficacious, if not the most acceptable "political alternative" around. Williams seems to be asking us to consider whether this is not what action has come to require. "It's a skilled professional world," Norman tells his sister, "and becoming more so every year, every day" (176). This is what another old friend and fellow Cambridge spy explains to his son, Gwyn, who has accused his father: "Why do you not act as you believe? . . . Did you fight in Normandie? Did you fight the fascists anywhere?" (268). As opposed to those working openly in the Party, on the one hand, and those fighting in the trenches, on the other, he says, "ours was a different choice, neither political nor military. What we were doing, indispensably, was operational" (318). It was "a special case: one in which others, however brave, could not volunteer." Although it was specialized, moreover—"a dynamic conflict within a highly specialized field"—this professional narrowing down was not a treasonous withdrawal from broader loyalties but on the contrary an extension of loyalty outward: one's first loyalty, the fellow spy declares, had to go to the "human species" (316).

In the later confrontation scene, *Loyalties* reverses the earlier alignment; here it is an intransigent son who accuses his intellectual father. But the accusation is in the name of the same values: Wales and the working class, "shared existence and shared knowledge." "No authentic act for socialism can distance itself, let alone hide, from these ties of its own people" (358). The son's words echo the socialist humanism of E. P. Thompson, or of Williams himself, while the father's answer, in the mode of professional expertise, accepts an Althusserian "distance" from "experience" that is seen as largely error: "That I should be loyal to ignorance, to shortsightedness, to prejudice, because these exist in my fellow countrymen?" (360). Judging from the keywords, one would have to place Williams on the side of the son and closely shared ties as against distance and longsightedness.[11] But Williams introduces a symbol that mediates between the two positions. The novel's major metaphor is a pair of binoculars, emblematic of the tactical power of longsightedness (itself Williams's continual metaphor for academic work). The binoculars first belong, appropriately enough, to a Cambridge student. But distance also means, here, the commitment that sends this student off to Spain to fight for the Loyalists. When he is killed, this double emblem of intelligence at a distance is carried home by the hero's adoptive working-class father. Thus it is passed on, or back, to the Cambridge-educated son. It is Williams's one *acceptable* symbol of Cambridge, which is to say of action involving (like the railway where his father worked) distance as well as closeness.

Here, as so often, the issues of professionalism and internationalism overlap. Like Steiner, Williams locates the far-seeing spy as a figure of and after the Second World War. Norman becomes a spy in the course of the antifascist struggle in Spain. But unlike Steiner, Williams takes Spain and its antifascist alliance as the war's central meaning: a moment of "temporary fusion" drawing together otherwise irreconcilable social classes and groups in a common struggle, sending Welsh miners and Cambridge undergraduates off together to fight a distant enemy who would ordinarily be invisible. This is something like what David Hare (who was tutored by Williams at Cambridge) was suggesting in the play and film *Plenty*, the war (and, coincidentally, undercover resistance work) as a sort of Golden Age of significant collective action, in relation to which the self-seeking routine and compromises of postwar work seem mean and meaninglessness. At the end of the war, the world falls back into its usual national rivalry, and according to the logic of Williams's narrative (though not according to his explicit commentaries), the opprobrium that is then heaped on spies would result from the sudden and arbitrary criminalizing of what had been the war's international solidarity. In this sense, the spy is keeping the "fusion" of the war alive into the fallen postwar period. Put in terms of the problematic of work sketched out earlier, the spy (or professional) would be the figure who, continuing to respond to solidarities that have grown distant or invisible, continues to invest work with public, political meaning, to hold public and private together. Or, more exactly, whose problematic loyalty and moral status registers the strain of holding them together.[12]

The political thriller thus offers something beyond the range of the Welsh trilogy. There, community meant closeness, and action was enclosed by the community. Here, imagining that the stuff or substance of community can be spread more widely, can be distributed differently, Williams seizes the possibility of action at a distance, and solidarity at a distance.[13] He tries to grasp a solidarity that would not only be to him (and others) what Wales is, but would help him and them to act upon the forces working against Wales, as working *within* Wales might not allow them to do. I hope it is clear that I am not speaking—as I think Williams is not speaking—of the peculiarities of espionage, but rather of professional work in general. Like professionalism, espionage involves professional secrets, a monopoly of information and control over its flow, a narrowing down of community that paradoxically also claims to expand or universalize loyalties. It also represents a professional ideal: political activity in the midst of what appears to be political quiescence, or acquiescence.

Like espionage, professionalism more frequently appears to Williams as a variant of rootless cosmopolitanism. In his capsule history of "Cambridge English" in *Writing in Society*, for example, he refers to literary study, as it has emerged from its origins in modernist "estrangement," as "the profession of a stranger."[14] It is statements like these that permit Terry Eagleton, in a moving obituary, to affirm that Williams "had little or no sense of himself as part of a 'profession.' "[15] And again: "What some left academics sometimes like to feign—that they are merely passing through the system, dipping in and out, fundamentally detached—was in his case oddly true" (7). What is oddest here, however, is not Williams's very real loyalties outside his profession, which are shared in kind if not in the same degree by many of his professional colleagues, but rather the profession's general eagerness both to "feign" such detachment from itself and to praise, as Eagleton does, those who seem genuinely to achieve it. To see detachment from the profession as a persistent convention of professional eulogy is to see Williams's ambivalence, which he himself saw in class and national terms, as an ambivalence that is also intrinsic to the profession itself, at least in its recent historical form. Eagleton more or less admits as much when he describes Williams as "always haunted by the border he had crossed from the 'knowable community' to the life of educated intelligence" (6). Put in these terms, the haunting (which is what Williams's fiction is all about) seems not a quirk of Williams's autobiography but a general phenomenon of professionalism. And perhaps what is most frightening in it, both for Williams and for Eagleton, is the implication that the "life" of "educated intelligence" is not after all a privilege of the newly isolated individual but a "community" in its own right—that one may have joined a new, less "knowable" community in the act of (or without) leaving another behind, and that the two communities may share common loyalties. If for Williams the lives of intelligence agents, like those of other professionals, seem to hover near tragedy, in that they transgress or threaten to transgress a very powerful loyalty, at least *Loyalties* comes closer to a successful reconciliation of loyalties than any of Williams's previous writings (except perhaps *The Country and the City*, which works hard to relativize the story of the lonely urban intellectual's departure from a rural home). At any rate, it is certainly a large step away from the inchoate self-hatred of the autobiographical novels, a step toward consciously inhabiting one's professional life rather than pretending it is someone else's, and toward seeing even the academy not as, like Steiner's extraterritoriality, an excuse for nonaffiliation, but as a place where new affiliations can (and must) come into being.

NOTES

1. *New Yorker* (December 10, 1980). There is more to say about parallels and intersections between Steiner and Williams beyond their common proximity to Blunt and their common interest in spies. (Steiner's novel *The Portage to San Cristobal of A. H.* is overrun with secret agents.) Both writing careers began in the years after the Second World War, both began with specifically international books (Williams on Ibsen, Steiner on Tolstoy and Dostoevsky), and both turned very quickly to the question of whether, after the war, the concept of tragedy retained its usefulness. Their clandestine debate over tragedy was indirectly about the meaning of the war. The present essay points toward another, still more clandestine debate between them about internationalism and intellectuals.

2. Steiner, *New York Review of Books*, January 12, 1986.

3. James Wilkinson, *The Intellectual Resistance in Europe* (Cambridge, Mass.: Harvard University Press, 1981), 74–75.

4. Ibid., 76.

5. Franco Moretti, *Signs Taken for Wonders* (London: Verso, 1983), is interesting on work as immanence and transcendence.

6. *Second Generation* (London: Chatto & Windus, 1964), 138. Further page

references will be given in the text. Williams's novels have recently been reissued in paperback by Hogarth Press. For further readings on Williams, see Jan Gorak, *The Alien Mind of Raymond Williams* (Columbia: University of Missouri Press, 1988); Alan O'Connor, *Raymond Williams: Writing, Culture, Politics* (Oxford: Basil Blankwell, 1989); and *News from Nowhere*, 6 (February 1989).

7. Raymond Williams, *Politics and Letters: Interviews with New Left Review* (London: Verso, 1979).

8. J. P. Ward, *Raymond Williams* (University of Wales, 1981), 42. Since his death in 1988, Williams and his work have become the objects of increasing critical attention. Notable are Gorak, *The Alien Mind of Raymond Williams News From Nowhere*, 6 (February 1989), and a forthcoming volume by John Higgins.

9. *Drama from Ibsen to Eliot* (London: Chatto & Windus, 1952), 27.

10. *The Volunteers* (London; Chatto & Windus, 1978), 136. The remainder of the discussion will concern *Loyalties* (London: Chatto and Windus, 1985). Also relevant to the theme of professionalism is *The Fight for Manod* (London: Chatto & Windus, 1979).

11. In *Border Country* (London: Chatto & Windus, 1960), Williams contrasts the "longsightedness" of the view from the mountains with "things close-up," which "are all to difficult" (p. 244).

12. Professionalism seems to have become a major concern of the political thriller genre specifically in the postwar period. Before the war, according to Myron J. Smith in *Cloak and Dagger Fiction* (Santa Barbara, Calif.: ABC/Clio, 1982), in its "Innocent Age," the spy thriller pitted upper-class amateurs against clearly defined national enemies. After the war, in the "James Bond" era, professionals of dubious morality or problematic loyalty, like Le Carré's heroes, tend to be set against other professionals, elite against elite, with no clear national enemy. Jerry Palmer's *Thrillers: Genesis and Structure of a Popular Genre* (London: Edward Arnold, 1978) presents a similar argument: "Professionalism is a feature of all thriller heroes" (211). In Forsyth's *The Day of the Jackal*, for example: "The world in which the Jackal himself moves is entirely dominated by professionalism. Amateurs who impinge on it are victims" (207). More specifically, Palmer sketches out a dealectic of isolation (individual freedom) and participation or allegiance which casts the professional ("capable of membership in a group" [14]) in the role of synthesis. See Tony Barley, *Taking Sides: The Fiction of John Le Carré* (Milton Keynes: Open University Press, 1986), for Le Carré's reading of espionage in the postwar context: spies like Philby were just what "the Establishment deserved. Philby is a creature of the postwar depression, of the swift snuffing out of the Socialist flame, of the thousand year sleep of Eden and Macmillan" (85).

13. Istvan Ronay's suggestion that realism and nationalism are deeply implicated in one another is one context for Williams's turning from realist autobiographical fiction to the thriller. Another is Williams's military service. His own experience of the war, which *Loyalties* brings to articulation, seems to have encouraged Williams's opening up to professionalism via internationalism. In *Loyalties* he gives that experience to the working-class Welshman (the adoptive father of Norman's son) who, having barely survived Spain, is horribly wounded in a skirmish between tanks in Normandy. Armor, artillery, mechanized mobility: the constellation of terms characteristic of tank warfare leads away from the language of rootedness, openness, and proximity we have been led to associate with

Williams. And the experience does seem to have marked Williams in an unfamiliar direction. His brief discussion of his military experience in France, in *Politics and Letters*, includes uncharacteristic praise of specialization. As an officer commanding a crew of five in his tank as well as three other tanks, he found that because each had "technical jobs to do," relations were "not so hierarchical." Specialization creates social cohesion without hierarchy; within its limits, it is egalitarian. Moreover, its efficiency contrasts with Williams's rage at the "incompetence" of his leaders (55).

14. On *Writing in Society* (London: Verso, n.d.), see my "English as a National Discipline," *Harvard Educational Review*, 55 (February 1985), 129–30. For Williams on work in general, see his "The Meanings of Work" in Ronald Fraser (ed.), *Work: Twenty Personal Accounts* (Penguin in association with New Left Review, 1968) and *Towards 2000* (London: Chatto & Windus/Hogarth Press, 1983), 85–87.

15. Terry Eagleton, "Resources for a Journey of Hope: The Significance of Raymond Williams," *New Left Review*, 168 (March-April 1988), 9.

The Scholar-Warrior versus the Children of Mao: Conor Cruise O'Brien in South Africa

John Higgins

Introduction: University Activism and the de Klerk Regulations

On October 19, 1987, new regulations concerning state funding of the South African universities came into operation. These regulations—commonly known as the de Klerk regulations after their prime architect, F. W. de Klerk, minister of education responsible for the universities—claim to have as their aim the safeguarding of academic freedom on university campuses.[1]

The year 1986 had been a troubled one on South African campuses as students responded to the increasing pressures of what even the state acknowledged to be a revolutionary situation. At the University of Cape Town, one of South Africa's largest desegregated universities, two events stood out. The first was a student protest against South African military intervention in neighboring states and the killing of striking miners in Johannesburg. A peaceful placard protest on De Waal Drive, the major motorway link between the center of Cape Town and the white suburbs, turned to violence as police pursued protesting students onto campus. The second was what has become known as the "O'Brien affair" in which a visiting lecturer, Dr. Conor Cruise

I should like to record my thanks to Eve Bertelsen, John Coetzee, Dorothy Driver, and Frances Long-Innes for their critical comments on an early draft of this essay.

O'Brien, was forced to cut short his stay at UCT when students, infuriated by his repeated attacks in the South African media on their calls for progressive education and an academic boycott, disrupted two of his lectures and staged a sit-in at the Political Studies Department. The new regulations attempt to bring an end to such expressions of political dissent by threatening the universities with subsidy cuts in the event of further campus activism.

The government claims that the new regulations are only designed to enable the unhindered running of the universities on a day-to-day basis, and such a claim, seen in isolation, might seem reasonable. But it is likely to be treated with some skepticism in the light of the increasing number of new regulations that aim to stifle dissent by criminalizing any "left-wing" opposition to the policies of the ruling National Party. Important new restrictions on the press had been announced two months earlier under which the Minister of Home Affairs, Mr. Stoffel Botha, can close for up to three months any publication he finds offensive.[2] These new measures have been imposed in addition to the already powerful array of new state powers contained in the State of Emergency regulations. Under these regulations, an officer may judge whether a particular person is a threat to the state, and place that person in detention for an indefinite period. The officer's judgment need never be tested in court. Thousands of people have been imprisoned in this way since the regulations came into force in 1986.[3]

As a piece of legislation, the de Klerk regulations share the totalitarian paradox of these other recent rulings. Through the due process of law that is legislation, the new regulations effectively do away with that due process of law. In its place, an arbitrary and absolute power is vested in the agents of the state. Just as it is Stoffel Botha's opinion that is the sole criterion for whether a publication is offensive or not, it is entirely in the hands of Mr. P. J. Clase, minister of education and culture, whether or not a university is judged to have offended the new regulations.

A glaring example of the entirely subjective nature of the minister's exercise of judgment in this regard can be found in Clase's reply to the objections the universities made to the initial draft of the regulations:

> I would like to stress that the obligation to report on incidents
> and occurrences as set forth in paragraph 2 of the conditions
> does not mean that your Council has to report to me on, for in-
> stance, typical student pranks, horseplay or similar trivialities.[4]

Paragraph 2 of the conditions makes a university responsible for
"any incident of unrest or disruption or any other occurrence
against the happening of which the preventive measures . . .
are directed." The minister's qualification, which in any event as
correspondence and not legislation does not have the force of
law, betrays what it seeks to conceal. Under the new rules, it is
entirely up to the minister to determine whether or not an "occurrence" constitutes a triviality to be ignored or an infringement
of the rules that will result in a subsidy reduction. Will the Day of
Protest against the imposition of the regulations be counted as a
"typical student prank" by Minister Clase, or will some or all of
the universities observing the Day of Protest be penalized?[5]

The simple and central criticism of the de Klerk regulations is
that they are *ultra vires*: in the sense that they both extend the
jurisdiction of Minister Clase beyond its natural boundaries and
seek similarly to overextend the jurisdiction of the university
authorities over their own members. The draft regulations sought
to make the university responsible for disciplining "any student
or staff member who conducts himself [sic] in a seditious or riot-
ous manner within a radius of two kilometres from the perimeter
of the campus" while the equivalent section in the imposed regulations extends that responsibility to "any place"! As UCT pointed out in its reply, the state is attempting to make the universities
responsible for the activities of its members as members of civil
society rather than of the university, to hold it responsible, in effect, for policing the politics of its constituents.[6]

Decisive Images

It is in the context of this substantial attack on the autonomy of
South African universities that I wish to address some of the issues
involved in the questions raised by concepts of academic freedom in the South African context. I take as my starting point an
article published in the *Cape Times* by Professor Andre du Toit

of UCT's Political Studies Department.[7] In this article, Professor du Toit examines what he sees as the dynamics of public support for the government's new repressive measures.

Du Toit writes, "The idea that firm action is necessary to restore law and order on the campuses is a very popular one," and he seems to suggest that this popularity—the basis of public support for the de Klerk regulations—is the natural response to a number of what he terms "decisive" incidents. I want to begin here by questioning this assumption and to argue instead for a recognition that the interpretation of such incidents as "decisive" is, rather, an ideological operation. I intend this to be taken in the classic sense of the term in which a biased and selective account of events is passed off as a complete understanding of them. Let us examine a crucial passage in du Toit's argument:

> It is the Conor Cruise O'Brien incident, the stoppage of traffic on De Waal Drive due to student demonstrations, the refusals to let Helen Suzman or Chief Buthelezi speak on campus, the images of students in violent confrontation with the security forces or toytoying in protest which continue to be decisive. And these popular feelings are then harnessed to such liberal values as the need to protect academic freedom and freedom of speech.

What is it that makes an image—the mere likeness or representation of something—decisive? What can lend to humble appearance the incontestable status of the conclusive or the determinative? Perhaps an image becomes decisive only when there is something to supplement that appearance. The process of representation transforms the raw material of an incident into the smooth-surfaced commodity of the image, and it does so by fixing the meaning of the image. An image is decisive when one interpretation of an incident is fixed upon as the meaning of that incident, when one point of view is selected as the frame for the whole incident.

Two examples from du Toit's own account will suffice to illustrate this force of representation in which the language of the description is always at the same time the language of the explanation of events. When he writes "the stoppage of traffic on De Waal Drive due to student demonstrations," the responsibility for this stoppage is placed entirely on the students. It is an interpretation of the event that neglects that it was the decision of the security forces to close De Waal Drive to rush-hour traffic. Such a closure would be guaranteed to make the placard demonstration unpopular with commuters, and unlikely to be the aim of the demonstrating students themselves. The police claim that the closure was due to fear of stone throwing needs to be assessed in relation to the apparent role of police agents provocateurs in the one outbreak of stone throwing in the three days of demonstrations.[8] And again, when du Toit offers the image of "students in violent confrontation with the security forces," it locates the students as the prime agents of that violence. The explanatory surplus of this description can easily be grasped if one reverses the grammar of agency and produces as "decisive image" "the security forces in violent confrontation with the students."[9] Description, which may on the surface appear neutral, is always bound up in representation with explanation.

The O'Brien Affair

In this essay I want to examine the representation of what has become known as the "O'Brien affair" at the University of Cape Town. In particular, I want to examine the deployment of notions of academic freedom and freedom of speech in the representation of that affair in the news media. I write "deployment" here in order to emphasize the ideological meaning of that "harnessing" that du Toit describes, and in order to emphasize that even "eternal values" (of which more later) are given a particular meaning by their expression in a particular time and place.

The title of my essay points to what might be called the "narrative image" given to the whole affair by the press accounts.[10] As the "Warrior-Scholar." Dr. O'Brien is the hero of the story. His heroism, in this case, lies in his fearless defense of the liberal values of academic freedom and freedom of speech. The villains of the piece are the "children of Mao"—a phrase that refers to the students who protested against O'Brien's presence at UCT by disrupting two of his lectures.

What is the main effect of representing the protesting students as "the children of Mao"? I believe it blocks any attempt to understand the motives of the protesting students by offering the reader a position from which the events can be immediately understood. We might say—to invert a favorite term in the vocabulary of Russian formalism—that it *familiarizes* the reader with the students in such a way that an investigation of their particular motives is made unnecessary. A great deal is *understood* or rather, appears to be understood, once the protesting students are seen as "the children of Mao." They are represented by others, and not allowed to represent themselves, in Marx's telling phrase. We shall see that this structure of repressive representation is a central characteristic of the reporting of the O'Brien affair.

Before examining some of the media reports of the events, let me begin by offering an account of the events drawn from the Commission of Enquiry Report. This report has, of course, its own bias; it too attempts to frame an understanding of the events. But whatever the agenda of its own interpretation, its ninety-eight pages at least fulfill the discursive obligation proper to the report of a commission of inquiry, and contain the fullest account of the events and the background to them.

Dr. Conor Cruise O'Brien had given two lectures in the Department of Political Studies at the University of Cape Town in 1985. No protests or disruptions occurred during this visit, though the notorious "academic boycott" was still in operation. Dr. O'Brien was invited to return in 1986 to participate in a series of lectures entitled "The Politics of Siege Societies" with Professor Heribert Adam of the University of Vancouver. Professor Adam (one of many overseas visitors to UCT in 1986) completed his course of lectures without disruption, while two of Dr. O'Brien's lectures were disrupted, resulting in the cancellation of the remaining three.

These disruptions and the final abbreviation of Dr. O'Brien's visit were widely reported in the press, and stimulated a lengthy debate on questions of freedom of speech and academic freedom in South African universities, as well as spirited discussion of the academic boycott tactic. UCT ordered a full inquiry into the whole affair, and this report was itself the object of further controversy.[11]

Dr. O'Brien had made clear his opposition to the academic boycott in a letter to the *Times* on September 6, 1986.[12] He arrived in Cape Town on September and continued to make public his opposition to the boycott and to calls for a program of progressive education in the local press and on the state-run radio and television networks.

The first expression of student dissension took place on October 2 during a lunch-hour meeting with students organized by the Social Science Students' Council. According to the Commission of Enquiry: "No real debate took place. Dr. O'Brien was apparently subjected to a series of repetitive and rhetorical questions which attacked his position on the academic boycott and questioned his sincerity. Apparently he lost his temper as a result of the attack."[13] It was this exchange that led to a lunchtime mass meeting on October 7. After this meeting, the students marched to the main administration building to demand an end to Dr. O'Brien's stay at UCT. In the evening, a public lecture was disrupted after eighty to a hundred protesting students who had been refused entry to the lecture forced their way in. A second lecture was disrupted the following morning, after a meeting between students and administration had been unable to reach any immediate solutions. Students staged a sit-in demonstration at the Political Studies Department on October 9 and 10. Dr. Stuart Saunders requested Dr. O'Brien to cancel his remaining lectures. Dr. O'Brien agreed, having been warned that further lectures might lead to an escalation of the disruptions. Dr. O'Brien left South Africa shortly after.

"They're Debating Freedom of Speech"

I want to examine in some detail a few sections of the BBC "Newsnight" report of October 8 in order to demonstrate the workings and dynamics of representation.[14] My principal criticism of the BBC report concerns what I see as a structured complicity between Dr. O'Brien's own account of the events, and the account offered by the BBC report. I shall examine some of the ways in which the report positions its viewer so that he or she is likely to accept and to endorse Dr. O'Brien's own interpretation of the events.

The BBC report begins as follows:

Recorded visual image: students scuffling in a corridor with security guards.
Recorded noise: indistinct shouts and chanting.
Recorded phonetic sound (voice-over): In Cape Town's college cloisters they're debating freedom of speech.

The phrase "college cloisters" sets the British home viewer at a comfortable distance from the events depicted. One of the narrative logics of the report becomes that the events that took place at the university of Cape Town would not take place in an English university. Just as Cape Town does not have college cloisters because it is not organized on the "Oxbridge" model, neither does it have a debate on freedom of speech, but instead scuffles, violence, transgressions. Indeed, I do not think it would be too exaggerated to suggest that one of the major issues involved in the whole O'Brien affair is prejudged by the very logic of this opening sequence. The question of whether or not the university should be an ivory tower, cut off from the struggles of the rest of South African society, is already resolved here. The disruptions at UCT are "explained" by "saying" that UCT is not that ivory tower: its "cloisters" are visibly *not* quiet. This is what happens if you bring politics into the university.

This first sequence is followed by some footage and some discussion of student politics in South Africa as background to the events. But what is crucial is that the third sequence of the report offers O'Brien's own words in the place of the authoritative or narrating voice-over. His words begin and carry the viewer over a cut in the visual sequence from students scuffling in a corridor to O'Brien addressing an audience and picking up his words. He speaks at this point from two positions in the report: as the informing voice-over and also as Dr. Conor Cruise O'Brien:

Can anyone imagine that my presence on this campus has anything to do whatever with either fomenting or averting civil war?

This question is rhetorical and invites a negative response. What is occluded here is that this rhetorical question is given as an answer to a question from a student—an answer to a question from a student, moreover, in a debate on academic freedom and freedom of speech! As a reply, it is impatient and evasive, displaying the anger and frustration that apparently characterized the whole debate between O'Brien and the students on that Tuesday afternoon. In a sense, this omission of the question to which O'Brien's question is an evasive response reflects the structure of omission in the report as a whole. For what is omitted is precisely the voice and viewpoint of the protesting students.

A second—and perhaps even more important—delegation of the narration occurs at the end of the report. The closing sequence is introduced by the following voice-over:

> *Recorded phonetic sound (voice-over):* Dr. O'Brien had come to Cape Town to deliver a series of lectures comparing South Africa to Israel and Ireland . . . "Societies under Siege.' "

What is emphasized here is O'Brien's essential *innocence*. There is an echo of an earlier description of him as "an unlikely target . . . supporter of sanctions." This innocence is crucial to the establishment of his identity as the "Warrior-Scholar," thrust by circumstances beyond his control into a courageous confrontation with the forces of chaos represented by the "children of Mao." Any of the more complex problems regarding his stance as a liberal opponent of apartheid are left unmentioned: the debate between O'Brien and Neil Ascherson, the anti-apartheid movement's disapproval of his visit to UCT, the problematic relations with the *Observer*, in brief, his whole status as a *controversialist.*[15]

The narration, having identified O'Brien as the innocent and courageous hero of the story, delegates the narration to him. He is given, quite literally, "the last word":

> It is a determined challenge from a determined minority—and whether that kind of thing—the shouting down of teachers—shall be prevented at a university or not. What is challenged here is the freedom to teach and to learn—values that are absolute and eternal—important from the days of Socrates and Plato and whose value will still be here long after apartheid has vanished into the garbage can of history.

This "last word" operates a crucial shift of emphasis in the report as a whole, which began with the question of freedom of speech ("In Cape Town's college cloisters they're debating freedom of speech"). At the end of the report, the focus is on academic freedom: "What is challenged here is the freedom to teach and to learn." What are the effects of this shift?

The concepts of academic freedom and freedom of speech share what might be called, to borrow Wittgenstein's term, a "family resemblance."[16] In Western liberal discourse, the two are associated as values and ideals belonging to the notion of democracy. In South Africa, as practices rather than ideals, the two are in very different positions. Freedoms of speech and association are severely restricted in South Africa, with further restrictions being added almost every day;[17] and, as we have already seen here, the autonomy of universities is under threat from the de Klerk regulations. The easy conflation of the two for the BBC audience does not stand serious scrutiny in the context of South Africa. The report's equivocation on whether academic freedom or freedom of speech was at stake in the O'Brien affair serves to obscure, as we shall see, the case against O'Brien. The conflation works to make O'Brien's defense of the "absolute and eternal values" of academic freedom a defense of O'Brien's own exercise of his personal freedom of speech. In an important sense, the report makes O'Brien represent the values of academic freedom and freedom of speech. He is their embodiment, and any attack on him is thus an attack on those values.[18]

Let me try to clarify why I see this conflation of the two as so important. I want to say that the real stakes of the O'Brien affair should not be understood as a conflict about the abstract principles of academic freedom and freedom of speech, but rather as a conflict concerning the practical exercise of those freedoms in a particular time and place. The conflict that interests me here is between an idealist view of such freedoms and a materialist analysis of them. What is ignored in the BBC report is exactly a sense of the particular time and place of the events, the context necessary for a fuller understanding of them.

The Debate

The coverage of one particular incident in the report can serve to illustrate this in an especially striking manner, and at the same time display the extent to which the report acts to endorse

O'Brien's own interpretation of the affair as the correct one. It is the reporting of the debate that took place—or did not take place—between Dr. O'Brien and the members of the Social Science Students' Committee. It is worth noting that the Commission of Enquiry assigned an important causal role to this encounter:

> The overwhelming view of those who gave evidence before us was that the "debate" and Dr. O'Brien's response to the students on that occasion was in fact the trigger which set off the subsequent disturbances.[19]

The commissions's view of the debate emphasizes O'Brien's "response to the students" as a crucial factor. In their view, it was the tone adopted by Dr. O'Brien in his response to his questioners that infuriated students enough to begin protesting against his presence on campus. The report gives the following account of his own immediate reflections on the lunchtime debate:

> I was insulting and condescending. I did not follow my own standards. I was guilty of an error of judgement.[20]

It is important to note that Dr. O'Brien has since stated that he never made such a statement, and strenuously rejects the way in which the report made him at least partly responsible for the disruptions.[21] Once again, I wish not to attempt to adjudicate between two different interpretations of what happened but only to show the way in which the interpretation of the BBC report itself decides the issue. The "story" (itself a revealing term in news reporting) is constructed so as to represent O'Brien as the heroic Scholar-Warrior in conflict with the forces of evil represented by the children of Mao.

The BBC report gives a number of sequences from the debate, and in all but one of them, only Dr. O'Brien's reply is heard—a fact of some importance in itself. In the instance in which both the question and Dr. O'Brien's response are shown, I want to examine particularly the structures of representation at work.

Dr. O'Brien described the event in the *New Republic* (October 27, 1986):

> On October 2, at the university, I had my first serious encounter with the militant students. I had accepted an invitation from the Social Science Students' Committee to take part in a debate on the subject of the "academic boycott." When I showed up and

asked who would present the case for the other side, I was told, "Nobody. You are to speak for about five minutes, and then it's questions."

It began to dawn on me that I had been set up. By accepting the invitation, I had let myself in, not for a debate, but for an organized grilling. It was a neat trap. Saving what I could, I told them I didn't accept their "five-minute" ordinance, but would speak as long as necessary to present my case. Then they could put their questions. This was agreed.

One might question whether being given the opportunity "to speak as long as necessary to present [his] views" constitutes a very formidable trap; but the crucial point is O'Brien's sense of the existence of a trap and who was responsible for setting it up. For Dr. O'Brien, the trap was constituted by the form of the debate. In his view, the absence of a single other debater was a clear departure from the rules of civilized debate: "I had let myself in, not for a debate, but for an organized grilling." In his interpretation of the event, the very aim of the "debate" was to make a "neat trap" for him.

There is a striking similarity in the way in which the BBC report begins its main coverage of the debate. These are the words that introduce this sequence:

And he fell into the trap, agreeing to take part in a debate with them only to find himself in a rhetorical shooting match with him as the target.

The report also sees the debate as Dr. O'Brien was to see it in hindsight, as an "organized grilling," "a rhetorical shooting match with him as the target." It is important to note that an alternative explanation of the structuring of the debate does exist. The Commission of Enquiry reported as follows:

The evidence before us clearly suggests that whatever Dr. O'Brien's prior expectations might have been, there was no scholarly debate concerning the merits of the academic boycott. The students believed *with justification* that they were prohibited by the Emergency Regulations from advancing the cause of the academic boycott. This seems not to have been adequately explained to Dr. O'Brien.[22]

My point here is not to adjudicate between these two explanations of the particular form the debate/grilling took, but simply to note that the BBC report chooses to endorse Dr. O'Brien's in-terpretation. Like him, the report ignores or appears to be ig-norant of the prohibition of any public endorsement of boycott strategy to which the commission refers. O'Brien's account and the BBC report share an important emphasis on the Western ideals of debate and freedom of speech; but it is an emphasis made at the expense of attention to the material realities of state repres-sion of just those issues in South Africa today.

Questions of Rhetoric

There are further important connotations at work in the way in which the BBC report represents the event as a "rhetorical shoot-ing match with [Dr. O'Brien] as the target." A shooting match is usually thought of as a competition between two or more oppo-nents in which the skill of each is tested. The weapons of this match are words—it is battle of rhetorics, or persuasions. But once again, Dr. O'Brien is given an ambiguous position. He is seen at the same time both as one of the opponents in the shooting match, and as the target in the match. The force of this is strength-ened or made clear by the quotation of O'Brien's own view of the debate, which immediately follows. "Are—These questions ap-pear to me quite frankly rhetorical. They are not questions designed to elicit information. They are questions designed to make ideological points."

I shall come back to the concept of communication that is im-plicit in the notion that questions should be asked only to elicit information (it is the status of communicator or teacher that is im-portant). For the moment, I only wish to note the way to which rhetoric—here a pejorative term—is assigned solely to O'Brien's questioners. In this representation, only Dr. O'Brien's opponents employ rhetoric; only the have "ideological points" to make. The implication is that Dr. O'Brien's own responses to the questions are free of rhetoric; the assumption is that he had no desire or need to make "ideological points."

The exchange is closed/framed by the following commentary:

The liberal at bay, surrounded by young radical opponents deter-mined not to accept his arguments, driven to the edge of anger.

Why describe his opponents as "young" and "radical"? Radical here takes its meaning in opposition to liberal. The information that his opponents do not share his liberal views is perhaps superfluous; but the connotation of radical, particularly when linked to young, suggests that the opponents of Dr. O'Brien's views are wrong. The implication is that they lack the experience and authority conferred on Dr. O'Brien by his status as a teacher and internationally known figure. What is described as their *determination* not to accept his arguments is then understandable. It is not that they have rational grounds for rejecting those arguments, but that they simply are determined—by their youth, their inexperience, their very radicalness—not to accept them. Once again, the children of Mao. And once more, the heroic Warrior-Scholar, "surrounded" by opponents (in fact, facing them from the authority of the podium), "at bay." Why describe O'Brien as "driven to the edge of anger"? This implies that he did not in fact become angry. Why should he become angry? Because his opponents would not agree with him? But then this would suggest too strongly that he was *their* opponent, and equally determined not to accept their arguments. So, "driven to the edge of anger" only. My own reading of what is shown does not fit the interpretive frame offered by the commentary. To my eyes, Dr. O'Brien is visibly upset and angry in this sequence, driven over the edge, and the narration is here attempting to occlude that visible upset.

Let us now turn to the actual verbal exchange that is framed in the manner described earlier:

Anonymous questioner: To what extent and in what particular ways are you advancing your struggle against apartheid by being here?

Dr. O'Brien: I'm not a soldier in a revolutionary movement, nor am I playing at being a soldier in a revolutionary movement. And I don't intend to do that or be that. And I don't accept the right of these people or any people to dictate to a free scholar when he should teach or what he should teach. And I don't think that principle should be accepted by any university [boos from the audience]. Nobody who is a liberal could endorse an academic boycott—it is anti-liberal in the extreme. And I am not going to have the framework of my liberalism set for me again by other people with whom I don't agree.

O'Brien's answer seems to read the question as asking him why he has broken the academic boycott. His reply is that he does not agree with the academic boycott. What is occluded in that reply is the relation between his principled opposition to the tactic of academic boycott and his struggle against apartheid. The questioner seems to interpret O'Brien's breaking of the boycott as being in contradiction to his opposition to apartheid. O'Brien's response evades or refuses that contradiction in the name of maintaining his individual identity as a liberal.

A response to this exchange would be unlikely to accept the interpretation offered by its framing in the report—namely, that Dr. O'Brien had no ideological points to make and did not employ rhetorical, persuasive or emotive language. It would be difficult not to hear the strains of rhetoric in O'Brien's opening statement "I'm not a soldier in a revolutionary movement, nor am I playing at being a soldier in a revolutionary movement." Surely the coordinate clause is highly emotive, and suggests precisely the aggressive condescension O'Brien was later, in some accounts at least, to admit and then later still to deny? It is also difficult to see how a statement such as "Nobody who is a liberal could endorse an academic boycott" is not asserting an ideological point! The whole effort and effect of the representation of the event are working against such perceptions as these, and toward a view of Dr. O'Brien as innocent of any political intentions, the innocent victim of the political intentions of others—a claim that, as we shall see later, is directly controverted by an untelevised portion of the interview footage.

"You Guys Don't Know What You're Doing"

In this report, the viewer is engaged in a relay of points of view in which he or she is addressed either by the voice of the narrator or by the voice of Dr. O'Brien. What is strikingly absent in the report is any direct representation of the views of the protesting students. They are represented usually in the third person, outside the "I-you" circuit that links the viewer to the narrator and/or O'Brien. For only one shot in the report is someone critical of O'Brien allowed to speak directly to the camera. For some seven seconds an anonymous student is interviewed on the steps of Jameson Hall. The content of this student's remarks endorses the interpretation of events offered by the Commission of Enquiry, but the way in which the viewer is positioned by the authority of the narration works against such an interpretation. This is what the student says:

> He seemed somehow contemptuous of the efforts people are making here to bring about change and he seems to come in as an outsider and say, "Well look, you guys don't know what you're doing. I know what I'm all about—I have my individual rights and therefore I'm here." It's a sort of contempt for what people here are doing.

There are two main aspects to the narration's refusal of this point of view. The first is the choice of venue for the interview. It is an informal interview, on the steps of the university's Jameson Hall. Its casual nature contrasts strongly with the interview accorded to Dr. O'Brien in the garden of a Cape Town house. Its informality detracts from the authority of the statement made in the same way that the anonymity of the interviewee also detracts from the authority of the statement. The informality and the anonymity work together to suggest that it is not a considered opinion—not the opinion of an expert like Dr. O'Brien—at all. The better to grasp my point here one only has to ask what difference it would have made to identify the student as Patrick Bulger, the chair of the debate, a person who certainly thought through the issues involved as much as O'Brien did, and if the interview had been conducted in the quiet of an office rather than in the bustle of the campus.[23]

More telling still is my second point, the sequence that precedes Bulger's remarks:

> *Recorded visual image:* Students marching on UCT campus carrying a banner marked GO HOME O'BREIN.
> *Recorded phonetic sound (voice-over):* Left-wing students may not be able to spell his name, but they see him as the overriding issue of the moment. An unlikely target . . . supporter of sanctions . . .

Here the "spelling mistake" (it has been suggested that it could be the equivalent of a bad Shakespearean pun) is used to prepare the viewer to accept the contention "You guys don't know what you're doing." The narration says that O'Brien is an "unlikely target" and claims that he is seen by the protesting students as "the overriding issue of the moment." The convergence of the two suggests quite simply that the students are wrong in regarding O'Brien as the "overriding issue of the moment." Once again, the narrative of the report works to make O'Brien's own interpretation the preferred reading of the events for the television viewer.

"I'm Not Just a Scholar . . . I Have to Go Public"

The crux of the matter came to be O'Brien's notorious attack on the academic boycott strategy, and its widespread dissemination in the local and international press, as well as on the state-run radio and television networks:

> It [the academic boycott] exerts no effective pressure on the regime in Pretoria where I believe it is good for a laugh. It actually damages the anti-apartheid cause by the conjunction of conspicuous silliness with overt bloody-mindedness. In all its aspects and its supposed political objectives, the academic boycott is Mickey Mouse stuff.

This is not, surely, the language of temperate academic debate —qualified and polite in its detailing of an opponent's arguments as it is rigorous and implacable in its arguments against them. It is rather the language of provocative polemic and ridicule: the journalistic style of an upmarket *Sun* leader. It is worth noting that these challenging words are addressed not to a present equal, who would have the right to reply in kind, but to the absent and disempowered "third person," who, according to the Emergency Regulations, would not even have had the right to reply in public.

I think my principal criticism of the BBC report is probably clear by now. The report tells the story of the events from the point of view of the Warrior-Scholar himself—seeking all the time to maintain his status as the hero of the story. In so doing, it is content to cast the protesters in that most clichéd of roles—that of mindless left-wing activists, the children of Mao. For all its apparent endorsement of the liberal values of free speech, the report chooses to ignore what that champion of free speech, John Stuart Mill, regarded as *sine qua non*: the granting of an equal degree of rational motivation to each side in any dispute.[24] The report consistently focuses on the expression of O'Brien's arguments and ideas at the expense of any exploration of the views of those who grew to oppose his visit to UCT.

Of course the complicity of the BBC report with O'Brien's views need not be seen as a conscious strategy. Rather, O'Brien has the "natural" privilege accorded a "public" figure: the right to direct address, to a relatively unmediated expression of his views. O'Brien's very status as that public figure empowers him in a way that is denied to his absent, third-person opponents.

It is worth quoting from an untelevised section of the final interview in which O'Brien identifies himself as just that kind of public figure, and at the same time acknowledges what is strikingly absent from the televised BBC account: the intentionally provocative nature of his visit to UCT. He is replying here to a question as to whether or not he was surprised by the disruptions:

> I was expecting something of the kind. I went public breaking the academic boycott because I'm not just a scholar. I'm a journalist and a communicator, so I have to go public.

This acknowledgment of his particular status as a journalist and communicator gives a context for understanding an earlier remark. "They are not questions designed to elicit information" was his complaint about the questions thrown at him by the social science students. That particular complaint sheds light on the kind of power O'Brien is used to having as a public figure. It is a power that has been admirably described by Suzanne Kappeler in her essay "Communication":

> In the domain of public communication . . . "to communicate" means speaking in an amplified voice to a silent mass audience. The contributors are monologuers, their contributions are monologues, their need to communicate is a monologue. Communication has become a one-way process, a transitive transfer of information, "facts" and opinions (representations). The term "communication" is most inappropriate and should be replaced by "self-expression" if not "monologue," although both these terms fail to make explicit the coercive aspect of the process with regard to the receiver group—the "general public" or, as it is known among the professionals of the media, "the target audience.[25]

It is this coercive aspect that needs to be attended to in order to understand the full effects of that conflation of academic freedom and freedom of speech I began by pointing out. The real stakes of the O'Brien affair were never the abstract rights of academic freedom and freedom of speech, but the material embodied of those rights in existing South African society. The core of the O'Brien affair was never O'Brien's right to hold the opinions he had on those issues, but the political questions raised by his "going public" with them in the South Africa media in October 1986.[26]

Opinion and Nuisance

Once again, it is worthwhile returning to some of the detail of John Stuart Mill's arguments in favor of free speech in order to grasp what was consistently evaded in the BBC coverage—the politics of the O'Brien affair. It is my belief that these can best be understood as the politics of speech as a particular form of action or agency.

Mill's essay *On Liberty* (1859) is justly famous for its defense of freedom of speech. Perhaps the most widely quoted section is the following:

> If all mankind minus one were of one opinion, and only one person were of the contrary opinion, mankind would be no more justified in silencing that one person, than he, if he had the power, would be justified in silencing mankind. . . . We can never be sure that the opinion we are endeavouring to stifle is a false opinion; and if we were sure, stifling it would be an evil still.[27]

Above all, it is proper that a university should seek to defend that essential liberty. But a less cited passage contains a distinction that is crucial to an understanding of the O'Brien affair. It is the distinction Mill makes between holding and expressing opinions. According to Mill, there are certain circumstances in which expressing an opinion counts as an action; and, as he puts it, "No one pretends that actions should be as free as opinions." He continues:

> Opinions lose their immunity when the circumstances in which they are expressed are such as to constitute their expression a

positive instigation to some mischievous act. An opinion that corn-dealers are the starvers of the poor, or that private property is robbery ought to be unmolested when simply circulated through the press, but may justly incur punishment when delivered orally to an excited mob assembled before the house of a corn-dealer, or when handed-out among the same mob in the form of a placard. . . . The liberty of the individual must be thus far limited; he must not make himself a nuisance to other people.[28]

O'Brien's case differs in important respects from the ones imagined by Mill, but I think that the central principle is the same. It was precisely O'Brien's desire to "go public" and to "make himself a nuisance to other people" that places his case beyond the bounds of any real possible defense in terms of freedom of speech or academic freedom. Going public in the way in which O'Brien did in South Africa constitutes rather a direct political challenge to the majority of the progressive movements in the country.

By locating speech as a kind of action, Mill brings to our attention the fact that language is not simply the neutral medium of expression it figures as in liberal idealist arguments. Rather, language itself is both the stake and site of political and ideological struggle. In that struggle, it seems rather absurd to seek to defend O'Brien against an attack he both expected and provoked. Nevertheless, it is as the innocent victim of the "children of Mao" that O'Brien is represented in the report. What this representation refuses is any explanation of the events that would see them as ones in which a directly political challenge was met by a directly political response; where public provocation was met with public reaction; where the context was between the political force of coercive monologue and the political force of mass protest.

It is a commonplace of television criticism that its newscoverage represents the outside world as hostile. In the pseudodialogue that takes place between the television report and the television viewer, that hostility is likely to be embodied in the bearer of the third-person address, the dialogue's "other." The commercial pressures under which television "coverage" is produced are unlikely to foster any serious understanding of the complex realities that form the raw material from which the commodity (i.e., news) is produced. The general case is, I think, all too well illustrated by this particular instance.

I have tried to emphasize here precisely what is involved in the deployment of a "universal value" such as freedom of speech and academic freedom in a particular—and particularly complex—material context. The obvious question raised by such and emphasis is, Why bring this "universal value" to bear on only one particular incident and not on others?[29] Surely such a selective use of a supposedly universal concept only destroys its claims to any ethical force? It is for this reason that I have tried rather to evaluate the rhetorical force of this deployment of the concept, its force as representation.

Conclusion: Local Coverage, the Questions (Not) Asked

In conclusion, I should like to add a few points concerning the particular effects of that deployment in the South African coverage. It might be thought that the local coverage would be able to go beyond the simple "Warrior-Scholar versus the children of Mao" narrative that structured the BBC coverage. Anthony Heard's article, "But Why Do Students Act Like This?", did make a number of points that would be essential for a deeper understanding of the whole affair—but this belated coverage was only to appear as late as October 18, when the structure of the dominant representation was already firmly in place. Heard's own frustration is evident:

> What makes students disrupt meetings and break down doors to stop a world figure, who incidentally favours economic sanctions and intervention, from merely speaking?
>   If this question is not asked, the matter is not remotely addressed, because something must drive otherwise normal students to such behaviour.
>   The answer, it would seem to me, is simply that black bitterness has grown so exponentially that there is, currently, little room for traditional reason.
>   The classic statements in favour of free expression and academic inquiry, however noble, are seen to be meaningless in a country under a state of emergency, indeed close to military rule, where freedom is denied.

The local press reports ignored these questions just as much as did the BBC report, preferring to offer Dr. O'Brien's account of the incidents rather than explore the motives of the protesters. But there are two important and related differences in the local coverage. There is an emphasis on the necessity for adopting punitive measures that is absent from the BBC coverage, and a related definition of the object of such punitive measures. It is this dual response that was crucial in the imposition of the de Klerk regulations.

The first of these differences can be gathered from the initial report of the disruptions in the *Cape Times* for October 8, 1986. Once again, it is Dr. O'Brien's account that is offered as the major interpretive context for the reader's understanding of the disruptions. He is quoted as follows:

> Universities are about communication and freedom of intellectual communication—not about having people shouted down. Those who do try and do this must be resisted and discouraged and I think in the end there should be no place for people who do that on a university campus if they persist.

Here the need to defend academic freedom is given a particular emphasis that is absent from the BBC account. It is an emphasis on the necessity for a punitive response to the disruptions of lectures: "There should be no place for people who do that on a university campus if they persist," I find it difficult not to see this kind of response—the denial of the right to a university education to protesting students—as a special kind of "shouting down" of people in itself. Such a response does not seem to me to meet the standards of equal and rational exchange proposed by Mill, but rather to be a mirror image of the "violence" of the disruptions themselves.

The second difference is in the identification of the object of that punitive response. This is a more complex matter. The *Cape Times* again differs from the BBC in offering a second interpretive context—though still not that of the protesting students themselves. This is the one offered by UCT's Moderate Student Movement (the MSM is a right-wing student organization usually associated with the policies of the ruling National party):

> Once again left-wing students have demonstrated their intolerance of views with which they disagree. They have once again

displayed their total disregard and contempt for the principles of academic freedom and freedom of speech which they claim for themselves.

The object of that punitive response can here be read as students who represent the forces of anti-apartheid activism. It was precisely this dissatisfaction that was behind the government inquiry into the "breakdown of law and order on campuses" reported on by *Sunday Times* October 9, 1986.[30] What was to be most important in the accounts to follow was the ways in which those forces were themselves represented, not as anti-apartheid forces, but as antirational. What we can see is a "shouting down" of opponents no less violent than that decried by O'Brien himself, a "shouting down" that takes the form of equating the disruption of a lecture with the familiar forms of state terrorism and the most brutal and terrifying forms of township violence.

I offer two quotations in support of this, the first from the editorial in the *Cape Times* for October 10, 1986:

The gross discourtesy shown to Dr. Conor Cruise O'Brien was as symptomatic of mindless left-wing zealotry as police sjambokking of peaceful protestors is illustrative of right-wing ideological obsession.

The second is taken from a letter in the *Cape Times* for October 15 from N. Harris of Noordhoek:

These tub-thumping trendies have no solution to offer and their anarchism strikes one as being very close to the mindlesness of the necklace murders of the townships. . . . I am deeply ashamed of the bad manners of these culpable radicals.

The language here betrays the strains of trying to equate the discourtesy of disrupting a lecture with the physical violence of sjambokking or necklacing, but it also serves to reveal a third central component of the local coverage. A great deal of the local coverage dwells on the "mindlesness" of the protesters, seeing their actions as an attack on the standards of Western rationality itself. In a letter to the *Cape Times* (October 15, 1986), Eve Bertelsen commented on the oppositions set up between the dissenting students ("mindless intellectual terrorists, bigoted zealots") and the supporters of O'Brien (the "civilized community, reasonable, scholarly, in the Western tradition"):

It does not require a Sigmund Freud to piece together from this series of verbal slippages the most shameful set of racial stereotypes. For what the *Cape Times*, of course, is talking about (although the words themselves are never voiced) is black students and black resistance politics in South Africa today.

What is largely absent from the BBC coverage—the representation of the views of the protesting students—is also absent from the local coverage; but in the local coverage that absence in itself is represented in a particular way. The figures of the "children of Mao" are crayoned in with the violent colors of white minority fear.

In liberal discourse, the concepts of academic freedom and freedom of speech may well be used to refer to a timeless realm of universal values. But the decision to bring those values to bear on a particular situation at a particular moment in time is likely to be worthy of analysis. As Kenneth Burke remarked long ago, "All questions are leading questions. . . . Every question selects a field of battle, and in this selection it forms the nature of the answers."[31] The decision to focus an account of the O'Brien affair on the concepts of academic freedom and freedom of speech had, in the BBC report, the effect of making it difficult to examine the motives of the dissenting students. In the South African coverage, it had the effect of blackening their motives, making it—consciously or not, which is to say *ideologically*—near-perfect propaganda material for the National party's attempt to discipline the universities through the de Klerk regulations. Perhaps the proper defense of ideals requires a more scrupulous materialism than any liberal would be likely to dream of.

NOTES

1. Cf. The *Guardian Weekly* (November 8, 1987): "The government claims to be acting for the taxpayer. But the universities have amply demonstrated in their PR campaigns that their public money is efficiently used and that student activism has little effect on academic standards, and is probably beneficial. . . . The minister of education responsible for the universities, F. W. de Klerk, is leading contender in the presidential succession stakes. 'Dealing' with the English language campuses boosts his image as 'tough man' of the Nationalist party."

2. The *New Nation* is the first newspaper to be banned under the new regulations, though several other publications have been warned. As the *Sowetan* March 23, 1988) notes: "With all the laws at its disposal, the government is not prepared to test the cases it has made against newspapers in a court of law and outside the

media regulations. We challenge the minister to do just this." The *Weekly Mail*, also under threat, observed that "the purpose of issuing a warning must be to enable the newspaper to avoid falling foul of the minister's opinion again. . . . [the editors] could discern no rational criteria for what the minister accepted and what he objected to and no way of infering such criteria" (January 15–21, 1988).

3. The *Weekly Mail* (March, 18–24) reports, for example, that a total of 1,338 youths aged seventeen or under had been detained under the emergency regulations in 1987, and 234 are currently in detention. A number of respected lawyers such as Raymond Suttner have been in detention without trial since June 1986.

4. Letter from Minister Clase to the chairman of council dated October 13, 1987. The extremely condescending tone of the letter as a whole is also evident in the misspelling of the chairman's name: L. G. Abrahamse is given in the reply as Abramhamse.

5. On October 19, a day of protest against the imposition of the regulations was observed at the universities of Witwatersrand in Johannesburg, at Western Cape, and UCT in Cape Town. A group of students and staff also held a protest meeting at the University of Stellenbosch, long-regarded as the "think tank" of Afrikanerdom. The University of Natal and held an earlier meeting and the University of the North staged a one-day boycott in sympathy.

6. See the letter from the chairman of the University Council to Minister Clase, August 27, 1987, page 11: "Staff and students are citizens. The university has limited jurisdiction over them. . . . Council is required to act in respect of acts undertaken by staff or students off the campus. In many or all of such cases such offenses, if proven, would be outside the university's jurisdiction." The regulations have now (March 1988) been successfully challenged as *ultra vires* by UCT and the University of the Western Cape in the Cape Division of the Supreme Court and by the University of Natal in the Natal Division.

7. *Cape Times* (December 1, 1987): "Open Universities Face State Threat without Support."

8. Daniel Pretorius, a member of the Students' Representative Council, the Social Science Students' Council (which organized the crucial Tuesday debate with O'Brien), confessed to being a police spy in August 1987. UCT's *Monday Paper* (August 17–24, 1987) reported that Mr. Pretorius "said he was convinced there was an overall plot to undermine 'progressive' organisations in South Africa. Dr. Saunders [the vice-chancellor of UCT] was regarded as a liberal and an 'enemy' by the security police and that it was his perception that the security police would make use of organisations such as the National Students Federation to provoke incidents on campus. These incidents were designed to give the Minister of Education, Mr. F. W. de Klerk, ammunition with which to take action—particularly in terms of the proposed regulations on which the Vice-Chancellors of universities had to report-back [*sic*] on August 31. And Pretorius claimed there could be 'another three' campus spies at UCT. . . . His involvement with the police was subsequently confirmed by Minister of Law and Order Mr. Adriaan Vlok." A series of descrations of campus mosques at UCT and the universities of Durban and the Witswatersrand suggests that such destabilizing activities continue to be a tactic in 1988.

9. See my analysis of the *Cape Times* report of the incident in "Throwing Stones: The Rhetoric of Objectivity" (forthcoming).

10. "Narrative image" is the term used in film criticism to designate the ensemble of effects by which an anticipatory image of a film is offered to its potential audience. By using it here, I wish to emphasize the ways in which the language describing the events of the O'Brien affair constantly prefigures an interpretation of those events. The two terms of the title were never, as far as I know brought together elsewhere. They figure separately as the title of an important *Sunday Times* editorial November 19, 1986), and in the *Business Day* report of September 22, 1986, "A Warrior-Scholar busts the Academic Boycott on South Africa." O'Brien himself used the comparison; see, for example, the *New Republic* (October 27, 1986, 10): "What was being conducted in South Africa under the name of an academic boycott seemed to be a sort of creeping form of the Cultural Revolution, which had wrecked the universities of China and which the China of today had repudiated with abhorrence."

11. The *Report of the Commission of Enquiry into the Events Which Occurred on the Campus of the University of Cape Town on 7 and 8 October* (University of Cape Town, December 18, 1986). For a spirited but confused attack on the report itself, see Charles Simkins's article in the *Cape Times* (March 31, 1987). "UCT Report on O'Brien Is Flawed." UCT's publication, *Forum*, devoted a special number to the whole issue of academic freedom in the South African context in 1987. An early version of the "Opinion and Nuisance" section of the present essay appeared there as "Freedom or Nuisance?: Some Notes on the O'Brien Affair."

12. The letter attacked Neil Ascherson's endorsement of the academic boycott in relation to the World Archaeological Congress at Southampton. Ascherson's own reply can be found in the *Argus* (September 19, 1986).

13. *Report of the Commission of Enquiry*, p. 17. It was this accusation that most angered Dr. O'Brien in the later controversy with the University of Cape Town over the report. See the correspondence between Dr. O'Brien and the vice-chancellor of UCT, Dr. Stuart Saunders, published in the *Cape Times* (March 7, 1987).

14. I should like to thank Cliff Bestell for his generous co-operation in the use of this material; and Craig Matthew and Joelle Chesselet of Doxa Productions for the use of their videosuite in my repeated viewings of the material.

15. Neil Ascherson's reply to O'Brien's letter to the *Times* (September 6, 1986) was reprinted in *Argus* (September 19, 1986). The *Weekly Mail* (September 26, 1986) reports the anti-apartheid movement as saying O'Brien's "is an open and shut case. He is totally out of step and misguided in breaking the academic boycott." Bill Buford's editorial in *Granta* 13 (1984) examines some of the contradictions in O'Brien's relation to the *Observer* and "Tiny" Rowlands's interests in Bophuthatswana. Tom Paulin's essay, "The Making of a Loyalist," examines the contradictions in O'Brien's opinions on Northern Ireland. Paulin's contention that "the dazzling light of 'international attention' transformed him into a personality . . . his authorial personality owes much to his sense of his audience's expectations" (*Ireland and the English Crisis* [New castle upon Tyne: Bloodaxe Books, 1984], 29–30) throws some light on O'Brien's status as a media personality, a question we shall return to later.

16. Wittgenstein discusses the notion of "family resemblance" several times in the *Philosophical Investigations* and *The Blue and Brown Books*. The particular emphasis I wish to make is that concepts derive a great deal of their meaning from

the circumstances in which they are used. Wittgenstein decisively abandoned the notion of context-free concepts in his later work.

17. The latest prohibitions include the severe restrictions imposed on seventeen organizations, and the prohibition of the committee formed to protest against those restrictions, the Committee for the Defence of Democracy.

18. This line of thought is most clearly expressed in the letter from Charles Simkins to the *Cape Times* mentioned in note 11.

19. *Commission of Enquiry*, 44–45.

20. *Commission of Enquiry*, 17.

21. See the correspondence between Dr. O'Brien and the vice-chancellor of UCT, Dr. Stuart Saunders, published in the *Cape Times* (March 7, 1987). Dr. O'Brien writes: "I invite your attention to the statement in the report (p. 17 thereof) that I admitted that my attitude to students on a particular occasion had been 'insulting and condescending'. The statement is false. I never said anything of the kind, and I do not accept these words as an accurate description of anything I said or did while on your campus."

22. *Commission of Enquiry*, 43–44. My italics.

23. Patrick Bulger's account of the affair, "A Strange Democracy," can be found in the *Sunday Star* (October 12, 1986). As many readers may not have access to the original report, I have omitted detailed discussion of the ways in which the visual rhetoric of the the report also empowers and endorses O'Brien's own interpretation of events.

24. Mill notes the difficulties of this in his essay "On Liberty," and notes, "With regard to what is commonly meant by intemperate discussion, namely invective, sarcasm, personality, and the like, the denunciation of these weapons would deserve more sympathy if it were ever proposed to interdict them equally to both sides; but it is only desired to restrain the employment of them against the prevailing opinion: against the unprevailing they may not only be used without general disapproval, but will be likely to obtain for him who uses them the praise of honest zeal and righteous indignation. Yet whatever mischief arises from their use is greatest when they are employed against the comparatively defenceless; and whatever unfair advantage can be derived by any opinion from this mode of asserting it, accrues almost exclusively to received opinions. The worst offence of this kind which can be committed by a polemic is to stigmatise those who hold the contrary opinion as bad and immoral men" (*Utilitarianism*, ed. Mary Warnock [Glasgow: Fontana, 1962], 181–82). The coverage of the O'Brien affair displays these features to the full.

25. See Suzanne Kappeler, *The Pornography of Representation* (London: Polity Press, 1986), 188.

26. Cf. Eve Bertelsen's account in an unpublished paper for UCT's African Studies seminar, "The Unspeakable in Pursuit of the Unbeatable": "A visitor arrives at UCT. He not only breaks a boycott which these students respect (others have come and been politely received), but he does so militantly and defiantly, throwing out a challenge from the day of his arrival to all comers. In the name of 'free speech' he uses platforms such as the SABC and SATV to discredit the peoples' organizations and their allies abroad. He is given column inches *ad lib* to pursue these themes in the daily newspapers as well. Under the circumstances it would not be too difficult to construe this degree of calculated insensitivity as

deliberate political incitement. At any rate this is clearly the way it was read by the students. They responded with indignation and anger staging several lively protests'' (19).

27. John Stuart Mill *Utilitarianism*, ed. Mary Warnock (Glasgow: Collins, 1964), 142–43.

28. Ibid., 184.

29. Carla Sutherland, president of UCT's Students' Representative Council, noted in the *Cape Times* (October 13, 1986): "If we are talking about an issue of academic freedom, or freedom of speech, then why did UCT academics and students not quiver with the same outrage, as they do now over the O'Brien affair, when SADF troops invaded and occupied schools in black townships or when the University of the North is held under military siege? UCT's senate recently passed a motion stating that there is no academic freedom in South Africa. Nor will there be until apartheid ends. Yet that same body refused to endorse the section of the University Assembly statement that called for the removal of troops from the townships, the lifting of apartheid and security legislation, the unbanning of political organizations and the release of all political prisoners including Nelson Mandela. All of these infringe an academic freedom and freedom of speech, and yet there is no similar sense of outrage at their continuation."

30. The leader of the National Students' Federation (the parent body of the Moderate Students' Movement at UCT), Mr. Philip Powell, is quoted as making the following protest: "In the past year, we haven't managed to hold one speaker event, man one information table or organise any public activity on campus." Once again, to selectively deploy the "universal value" of freedom of speech for the protection of the National Students' Federation would seem to me to destroy the apparent ethical force of such a value.

31. Kenneth Burke, *The Philosophy of Literary Form* (New York: Vintage, 1957), 56–57.

Making the Difference: Paul de Man, Fascism, and Deconstruction
Christopher Prendergast

I

In Paul de Man's literary and philosophical writings (what, in the current controversy, has come to be referred to as "late Paul de Man"), there appears to be a "linguistic" version of the doctrine of the Fall: "What stands under indictment is language itself and not somebody's philosophical error."[1] Geoffrey Hartman (in an article to which I shall return in detail later in this essay) glosses this claim as meaning that something called Language is the site and source of an "essential failure" and an "original fault."[2] Language (as distinct from the specific uses to which it is put by human speakers and writers) is intrinsically and "originally" duplicitous, and hence the belief that error can be corrected by truth, that enlightenment can come from reflection and criticism, is a delusion. I leave on one side here the paradoxical point that, if this argument is held to be true (a clearing away of erroneous conceptions of language), it is self-defeating from its own premises. I want rather to draw attention to the fact that this represents a curiously theological notion of language (doubly curious when we recall that deconstruction is expressly devoted to ridding philosophy of theological metaphysics, what Derrida has resumed in the category of the "ontotheological"). I want further to invite readers to consider what kind of "duplicitousness," if any, they might see in the following passage. It is the opening paragraph of de Man's article entitled "Les Juifs dans la Littérature actuelle" and published in the Belgian newspaper *Le Soir* on March 4, 1941.

This is one of the articles recently uncovered by Ortwin de Graef, and—as its very title indicates—it is at the heart of the current debate about de Man's life and work. I quote it in the original French:

> L'antisémitisme vulgaire se plaît volontiers à considérer les phénomènes culturels de l'après-guerre (d'après la guerre de 14–18) comme dégénérés et décadents, parce que enjuivés. La littérature n'a pas échappé à ce jugement lapidaire: il a suffi qu'on découvre quelques écrivains juifs sous des pseudonymes latinisés pour que toute la production contemporaine soit considérée comme polluée et néfaste. Cette conception entraîne des conséquences assez dangereuses. Tout d'abord, elle fait condamner a priori toute une littérature qui ne mérite nullement ce sort. En outre, du moment qu'on se plaît à accorder quelque mérite aux lettrés de nos jours, ce serait un peu flatteuse appréciation que de les réduire à être de simples initiateurs d'une culture juive qui leur est étrangère.[3]

Let us suppose we come to this paragraph as "innocent" readers (in the sense of being unencumbered by any fore-knowledge of the de Man affair). The first sentence might well strike us as a gesture of dissociation from the ideology and cultural politics of fascist anti-Semitism, although the role of the word "vulgaire" in the sentence is ambiguous: it is either anti-Semitism as such that is being rejected (as "vulgaire"), or it is a particular form of anti-Semitism that is being rejected (the vulgar sort, as distinct from some other, more respectable sort).[4] Similarly, the third sentence ("Cette conception entraîne des conséquences assez dangereuses") could be read as a warning about the dangers of anti-Semitism, at least in the field of "culture." But the second, fourth, and fifth sentences tell us that the "dangers" de Man has in mind are quite other. The second sentence (particularly its second clause) is slightly odd, but the fourth and the fifth show that what de Man is objecting to here is not "discovering" (and presumably denouncing) "quelques écrivains juifs sous des pseudonymes latinisés"; he is objecting to the theme of guilt (or rather, pollution) by association: a few Jews here and there do not make a difference; they do not entail the claim that "les phénomènes culturels d'après-guerre" are to be seen as "dégénérés et décadents, parce que enjuivés." De Man is thus indeed concerned with refuting an "error," the erroneous belief that modern literature has been contaminated by a Jewish influence. But, as the fifth sentence makes clear, the error in question is not the view that a Jewish influence or presence in modern literature contaminates; it is the view that there *is* a significant Jewish influence in modern literature.

The argument, then, is that modern literature has been mercifully spared pollution by the Jews (though Kafka is cited as one of the exemplary moderns, without, however, any reference to the fact that Kafka was a Jew). Jewishness is indeed alien, carries the threat of infection, but, as we learn later in the article, such is the healthy vitality of Western culture that its representatives have been able to resist infection ("Qu'ils ont été capables de se sauver de l'influence juive dans un domaine aussi représentatif de la culture que la littérature, prouve pour leur vitalité"). Nevertheless, de Man goes on to add, in the light of "l'ingérance sémite dans tous les aspects de la vie européenne," it might not be a bad idea if the Jews were to leave European soil (whether voluntarily or coercively is not made clear): "En plus, on voit donc qu'une solution du probleme juif qui viserait à la création d'une colonie juive isolée de l'Europe, n'entraînerait pas, pour la vie littéraire de l'Occident, de conséquences déplorables." It is to be noted that de Man does not explicitly commit himself to this as a "solution" to the "Jewish problem"; the tense of the main verb is the conditional ("entraînerait"). Furthermore he takes care not to engage with the politics of anti-Semitism; his concerns are purely "literary." Moreover the purpose of such a solution is left peculiarly vague: it is not offered as a prophylactic measure, designed to protect Western literature from infection (how could it, since de Man has been at some pains to stress the imperviousness of literature even when the Jews are in our midst?). Rather it is simply that the disappearance of the Jews would be no great cultural loss. The status of the "donc" in that sentence is therefore unclear. Although not entirely discrepant with the major premises of de Man's argument, this recommendation (if that is what it is) seems illogical, or at least redundant: if Western ("Occidental") culture continues on its healthy way notwithstanding the presence of the Jews, what specific purpose is usefully served by getting rid of them?

Perhaps the unacknowledged answer to that question, in the terms of de Man's article, is political after all. For while it is true that European *literature* has survived intact "malgré l'ingérance sémite," the same cannot be said of European civilization generally: "Les Juifs ont, en effet, joué un rôle important dans l'existence factice et désordonnée de l'Europe depuis 1920."

This I call duplicitous writing, though not by virtue of some "original fault" inscribed in Language as such. I gather that some people have taken the view that it is duplicitous in the sense of being *ironic*, that de Man does not mean what he says, though I have not yet encountered this view in print and see no evidence in the article itself to substantiate such a view. Others have claimed that the article needs to be seen in "context." Restricting myself to Hartman's article, at least three such contextual candidates are on offer. The first is quantitative: de Man's anti-Semitic remarks, "though ugly," are "infrequent"; scanning the corpus of wartime articles unearthed by de Graef, Hartman tells us: " I have found *only* one other prejudicial reference to Jews by de Man" (my italics). But suppose we remain unimpressed by the quantitative argument, and address ourselves to the question of the quality of these "references"? Palliation is to hand by virtue of the other two contexts. One is stylistic. Echoing de Man's talk of "antisémitisme vulgaire," Hartman says of the article: "This is not vulgar anti-Semitism"—on the contrary, the "formulations" are "polished"; later they are "mild," then "very general," and finally "polite." Polished, mild, very general, and polite—perhaps I am mistaken, but this surely must represent a whole new dimension in the characterization of 1940s anti-Semitic discourse. Finally, there is the "historical" context, broadly the claim—to which I shall return—that very many Europeans were at the time more or less all in the same boat, victims of the anti-Semitic *Zeitgeist*, as a distortion of what originally was a "common sort of nationalism."

Hartman also says other, far more censorious things (often within the same sentences) about de Man's anti-Semitism. And entirely legitimate considerations of "context" require that much of what I have already quoted be restored to those sentences, though whether syntax and logic work together in the interests of intelligibility, whether the censorious and the palliative easily coexist, remains to be seen. But I have to say that most of what I have so far taken from his text strikes me as pitifully inadequate to the issue before him, a "failure" not of some primally flawed thing called Language, but of argument, of moral imagination and historical sense. I shall explain why I hold to this view in more detail later. For the moment, however, I want to agree—the agreement will be already implicit in aspects of my own prose style—with Hartman's statement that "it is hard to be dispassionate" about all this. There are clearly many personal and contingent reasons why this might be so. Before the revelations of his record as a wartime journalist, de Man's work inspired both fierce loyalties and strong antagonisms, particularly in the literature departments of certain universities in the United States. The unfolding of the story here has inevitably got caught up in relations of friendship and emnity. And no doubt strictly professional interests involving careers and reputations have also played their part; as almost everywhere in contemporary academic life, there are "territories" to be defended, crowns to be grasped, ambitions to be satisfied, and all the rest of the normal yet unpleasant undergrowth of the groves of academe. Much of this doubtless explains—though does not excuse—why the weave of much of the debate has come out as a hopelessly tangled skein of confusion, contradiction, evasion, special pleading, and sleight-of-hand. Whatever the motives, the outcome, in my view, has been pretty disastrous, whether in the form of paranoid defensiveness or holier-than-thou sanctimoniousness.

The facts of the matter so far documented appear to be straightforward and shocking: under the Nazi occupation of Belgium, de Man wrote articles for a newspaper controlled by the occupiers until the end of 1942, when, as Hartman puts it, "all but the deliberately ignorant would have known that the persecution of the Belgian Jews begun before the end of 1940 had taken a drastic turn"; or, in his somewhat puzzling formulation of the same point, when "an ideological figure of speech became literal and lethal" (does this mean that as figure of speech, anti-Semitism is relatively harmless, mere "literature"?). In other words, unless we are to classify de Man among the "deliberately ignorant" (whatever that might mean), he must have known of some of the dreadful things that were going on. If these are the facts, then the notion that there is something to be "done" about them—that they have to be "interpreted," "contextualised," and all the rest —seems quite preposterous, just as it is equally preposterous to be now organizing a kind of "trial." The debate about collaboration has been going on since the end of the war; the literature on the subject is extensive; and the argument over whether Error or Sin is the appropriate category of interpretation and judgment has been at the heart of the debate from its very beginnings. There does not seem to be anything discernible in the basic facts of the case of de Man that would call for special treatment, and hence justify all the nervous energy and high passion that have been expended.

II

And yet there is. The distinctive feature of de Man's case is that, in later years, he came to be the foremost representative in America of a style of critical thought called "deconstruction." In this connection, the substantive intellectual issue has been whether or not there is any significant relation between de Man's involvement in the terms of fascist thinking and his elaboration of the terms and strategies of deconstructive thinking. This issue has cropped up again and again in discussion, but has also tended to disappear beneath the weight of the more personal and parochial passions the case has aroused. Although the issue has constantly come into view, the furor has ensured that the view remains blurred; none of the parties to the discussion, whether shell-shocked or gleeful, seems able to get a proper handle on it. Yet for those of us who did not know de Man personally, or who have no vital professional stake in the fortunes of deconstruction, this is indeed *the* issue. One intellectual collaborator more or less makes little or no difference to our understanding of the phenomenon of collaboration. But does it make a difference to our understanding of deconstruction? Hartman says that the "discovery of these early articles must make a difference in the way we read later de Man." What, then, is the nature of that difference, and what are its implications and consequences? Hartman never gives us a clear answer, and that lack of clarity is both instructive and, I would maintain, symptomatic of the more general intellectual disarray into which the whole discussion has tended to collapse. For this reason, I propose to confine myself here for the most part to a more detailed analysis of the arguments and the mode of writing informing Hartman's contribution, more or less in the spirit of the activity of "close reading" that Hartman associates with the enterprise of deconstructon itself. My title, moreover—"Paul de Man, Fascism and Deconstruction"— echoes one of the titles given to his *New Republic* article. That title represents what for me is the central intellectual issue (as distinct from speculations of a purely biographical character); I initially assumed that this title also carried the same meaning for Hartman, since it is difficult to see what other meaning it could bear.

Sustaining that assumption in the actual reading of Hartman's text does, however, turn out to be rather hard work, and notably at the key moment of encountering the claim that "the discovery of these early articles must make a difference in how we read later de Man." I take it that the phrase "later de Man" is a metonymy referring to de Man's later writings, and hence to the critical enterprise of which those writings were, in America, the outstanding example, the enterprise of deconstruction. The revelations are thus problematic for deconstruction as such (and not just Paul de Man's private relation to it). Elsewhere Hartman says that it is the "purity of deconstructive thought that can now be questioned" (not just de Man's involvement with deconstructive thought, but deconstructive thought *tout court*). Yet the sentence that immediately follows the one about making a difference makes clear that the primary concern is in fact of a biographical order, not with the later writings as such, but with their relation to a biographical drama: "The new disclosures imbed a biographical fact in our consciousness, a fact that tends to devour *all* other considerations" (my italics). In important senses, the whole of Hartman's article converges on this sentence. But "converge" is scarcely the right word. In a parody of deconstruction's love of self-unstitching and self-dispersing textual forces, Hartman's text falls apart at exactly the moment it promises to deliver. The result is an incoherence so deep and so pervasive that it is difficult to know where to begin in the effort to sort the mess out.

But let's have a shot at this by starting with some of the features of this extraordinary and bewildering sentence. Let us even try to take some of its major terms at face value, and see where they lead in relation to some of the other statements in the article. Hartman speaks of a "biographical fact" so overwhelming that it "tends to devour all other considerations." It is unclear what "tends" means here, in particular which and whose tendency is envisaged. Is it a tendency generated by the disclosures in Hartman's own thinking about later de Man? Or is it a tendency of others where the verb "tends" is to be understood in the sense of "in danger of being," thus designating a tendency to be resisted and avoided? Neither the sentence nor the paragraph in which "tends" appears does much to help us get at the relevant sense. If it is the former (the biographical fact tends to devour all considerations for Hartman himself), this sits impossibly with what he says elsewhere: "What is neglected by some of de Man's critics, who are in danger of reducing all to biography again, is the intellectual power in his later work." If, on the other hand, it is the tendency of others (and therefore a danger to be avoided), he clearly cannot mean that either, since the biographical fact that tends to devour all other considerations has imbedded itself in "*our* consciousness" (my italics)—the implied "we" necessarily contains an "I." But this cannot be where Hartman stands, since he is also at pains to dismiss those who hold exactly the view he is here describing, namely, those critics of deconstruction who "have seized on the revelations" to discredit deconstruction itself: "Their (the critics') sense of deconstruction as morally unsound and politically evasive seems to stand confirmed." But, according to Hartman, appearances are deceptive: "Such a judgment is superficial, and divorces deconstruction from its context in the history of philosophy." Quite so. I agree entirely, certainly in the sense that the stridently polemical innuendo implying that there is some intrinsic link between deconstructive thought and fascist ideology is both blatantly false and entirely disreputable. But, in that case, what does Hartman mean when he says that *all* considerations regarding the status of the late de Man texts (presumably including—by definition from the force of that "all"—considerations regarding their intellectual status) tend to get devoured by the biographical fact? Where, in relation to that "tends," that "devoured," and that "all," does Hartman stand?

In immediate context we simply cannot tell. We do, however, get some (very limited) sense of what Hartman means when he goes on to talk of the later works in terms of what he describes as a reactive endeavor. In the light of the revelations about early de Man, we are now obliged to read later de Man as reaction against that murky past, to see his reflection on the unbridgeable gap between intention and language, action and art, figure and letter as "a deepening reflection on the rhetoric of totalitarianism," a "belated, but still powerful, act of conscience." So, the late writings not as compromised (in that sense of "devoured") by the wartime episode but as a form of private atonement and confession: "It may turn out that in the later essays we glimpse the fragments of a great confession," something in the tradition of Goethe perhaps.[5] Well, not quite. For we also learn that "there is nothing of a confessional nature in de Man," and indeed Hartman himself is quick to condemn de Man's silence about his past ("One crucial and hurtful problem is that de Man did not address his past"). But the condemnation just as quickly evaporates when Hartman turns to the problematic status of the category of "confession" itself in de Man's own theoretical and critical writings. Deconstructed in the context of an analysis of Rousseau's *Confessions*, the project of self-disclosure is presented by de Man as irredeemably caught up in the duplicitousness of Language, in narratives of self-exculpation. Hartman summarizes these views for us, with apparent approval or at least with no acknowledgment that these views are scarcely compatible with his own criticism of de Man for having maintained silence over his wartime activities; instead we are steered toward the idea of a suffering that is "specifically linguistic," a "linguistic pathos" that is the "painful knowledge" of having been "trapped by an effect of language." This is the Language-as-original-fault hypothesis being wheeled on stage at a crucial point, along with some grotesque irrelevances about the need to avoid "nostalgia" for a lost past and the futility of

"mourn[ing] the past as lost in order to guarantee ourselves an unencumbered future." But nostalgia and mourning have nothing to
do with the issue of early de Man—there is nothing there to be
nostalgic about; shame and regret would be the more appropriately relevant terms. But these are exactly the terms that the
deconstructive reading of Rousseau treats with a large dose of
skeptical suspicion. And out of this incredible mess of "argument," there somehow emerges an image of a tragic figure grap-
pling with "painful knowledge": refusing to do a Rousseau on his
own past, de Man both avoids the narrative-linguistic traps of confession, but at the same time also manages—obliquely, abstractly
—to confess, and so register "disenchantment" with the "errors"
of the past (in the form of a "turn from the politics of culture to
the language of art"). We appear therefore to have two kinds of
confessions, the Rousseauist and the de Manian, the explicit and
the tacit. One mentions specifics, real or imaginary ("even where
there is no discernible fault or error"), and, by that act, gets
caught up in narratives of self-justification; the other does not
mention anything at all (other than the "original fault" of Language), and thus escapes the dangers that beset the former enterprise. But, if this distinction between kinds of "confession" is to
be taken seriously, why then does Hartman reproach de Man for
his silence, why is the silence about the past a "crucial and hurtful
problem"? Of what is that silence a *crux*?

I imagine my reader is by now as bewildered as I am in trying
to hold the twists and turns of all this in my head—confession that
is not confession (which makes no mention of the specifics of the
past, the "exceptional Nazi years"), but which still remains an
"act of conscience." But the real question buried in these tor-
tured to-ings and fro-ings is: outside the hothouse of a certain
branch of the academy and its internecine rivalries and obses-
sions, who cares? I can well see why it matters to people who, like
Hartman, were in personal relationship with de Man. But for
those of us who were not, there is no strong reason why we might
be specially interested in the private *motives* behind the arguments developed in the later writings, as distinct from the arguments themselves. This, ultimately, seems to be all Hartman has
in mind when he says that "the discovery of these early articles

must make a difference in the way we read later de Man." The difference they make to our reading is indeed of a purely biographical sort, a matter of a "personal history," a "reflection by de Man on de Man"; the conjunction of early and late enables us to read the story of an individual spiritual journey from complicity to renunciation, and in which the elaboration of the deconstructive project served as an intellectual instrument to help effect the journey. As for the standing of the arguments themselves, and in particular their difficult relation to questions of politics and history, Hartman has nothing to say beyond the assertion that the "epistemological hassles" we all face, and which deconstruction addresses in its accounts of philosophical and literary texts, reveal the terms in which these questions have been raised by the opponents of deconstruction as superficial ("Such a judgment is superficial").

Thus, the attack elsewhere in Hartman's article on the "reduction" of the intellectual issue to biography is flatly contradicted by the *ad hominem* terms of his own approach. But this is rapidly becoming par for the course. Although the terms vary, the basic principle of *ad hominem* procedure has also characterized the essential moves of the opposition in the controversy. One of these moves turns on an interpretation of a theme (a "trope") that de Man took from Nietzsche and discussed in an essay in *Blindness and Insight*—the theme of "forgetting." De Man's comments on Nietzsche's claim that we seek "the destruction and dissolution of the past in order to be able to live" have now been read (notably by Frank Lentricchia in remarks quoted in the *Nation*) as rationalization of the desire to bury his own wartime past: "Anyone who thinks that he left this all behind him, that it did not motivate the life and career that followed, is crazy. . . . He didn't just say 'forget history'; he wanted to paralyze the move to history."[6] We thus have two conflicting interpretations of the function of deconstruction for Paul de Man. Where Hartman sees de Man using deconstruction to confront the past, Lentricchia sees it as serving the end of forgetting that past. There is nevertheless fundamental agreement between Hartman and Lentricchia on at least one point: if one sees the later writings as atonement and the other sees them as repression, they both agree on psychobiographical explanation as the relevant frame of reference. The problem with Lentricchia's way with this form of explanation, in terms of any useful critical statement about deconstruction as such, is that it is both highly speculative and excessively generalized. There is nothing in the syndrome of "forgetting" that is unique to either deconstruction or fascism. There are many kinds of painful pasts other than fascist ones that people wish to repress; and there are many ways of repressing a painful past (just as there are many ways of indicting such a past) other than deconstructive ones. The thesis about repression does not therefore supply any useful insight concerning the intellectual structure of deconstruction as a body of thought; it merely psychoanalyzes one practitioner of it.

III

As I have already said, I for one am not particularly interested in the question of late de Man's motives for writing, but do wish to know more about the relation, if any, implied by the title of Hartman's article, between fascism and deconstruction. But perhaps on this front there is in fact nothing to learn. The absurdity of the notion that there might be some significant substantive link is indeed instantly revealed if we take out the proper name Paul de Man and substitute that of the other outstanding proponent of deconstruction, Jacques Derrida. The structure of Derrida's thinking inflected by some relation to fascism, or indeed any brand of authoritarian ideology? The notion is laughable. The question of the "politics" of deconstruction remains, of course, what it has always been, extremely controversial. As Richard Rorty has pointed out, it is impossible to *infer* any determinate political position from deconstruction. Accordingly, its political incarnations and appropriations have been various—on a spectrum from feminism and Marxism to anarchic libertarianism and quietistic pluralism, tolerant of multiplicity but uninterested in concrete change, talking a lot of "empowerment" and the like, deconstructing fixed systems of "meaning," while leaving actual arrangements more or less as they are. The most cogent and probing formulation of this aspect of the matter that I know of is Stephen Heath's. Heath gives us, on the basis of reviewing two books by Jonathan Culler and

Terry Eagleton, respectively, a wide-ranging review of the literature, history, and institutional settings of deconstruction. Noting
that Derrida "produces a strong deconstruction that overturns
and displaces, that undermines," he goes on to pose and pursue
the following central question:

> But in relation to what project? Other than simply the project of
> deconstruction, in which case it merely turns in the void, an end-
> lessly repeated gesture, a set of themes and style of writing, a
> continual recycling of the demonstration of the terms of the
> "metaphyics of presence" and its "foundations," again *not mak-
> ing much difference* [my italics]. Reliable guides to deconstruc-
> tion do indeed often come out at this point with a kind of ratio-
> nal limitation of deconstruction—"don't do it all the time!". Thus
> Christopher Norris in his "New Accents" *Deconstruction: Theory
> and Practice*: "Deconstruction is . . . an activity of thought
> which cannot be consistently acted on—that way madness lies—
> but which yet possesses an inescapable rigour of its own." The
> madness of words becomes the madness of deconstruction's
> knowledge of that madness; one had better go about one's busi-
> ness, texts can still be interpreted . . . Culler also has an in-
> teresting comment in this connection, an interesting image: "One
> can and may continue to sit on a branch while sawing it."
> Presumably if we then say that, however that may be, one can*not*
> continue to sit on the branch once it has been sawn, the answer
> will be that it never will be since deconstruction is a constant, an
> operation that will never be over. But this just brings us back to
> turning in a void, makes deconstruction into some universal
> mode, Norris's "activity of thought" that you acknowledge now
> and then for its own "inescapable rigour" while getting on with
> things as usual. Culler, however, develops his image: "If 'sawing
> off the branch on which one is sitting' seems foolhardy to men
> of common sense, it is not so for Nietzsche, Freud, Heidegger
> and Derrida; for they suspect that if they fall there is no 'ground'
> to hit and that the most clear-sighted act may be a certain reck-
> less sawing, a calculated dismemberment or deconstruction of the
> great cathedral-like trees in which Man has taken shelter for
> millennia." This flourishes rhetorically, but leaves everything un-
> suitably vague (to say the least), precisely rhetorical—calculated
> *for what?*[7]

Calculated for what?—This is indeed a pertinent question. Seen
in relation to the idea of a *project*, deconstruction can appear doubly pointless: doing it *all* the time risks turning in the void of

deconstruction's endless self-reproduction (and going mad); doing it *some* of the time means that the rest of the time will be business as usual. Either way, nothing much happens (beyond a certain "activity of thought"), nothing gets changed. For a project implies both values and commitments, on the one hand, and, on the other hand, a set of strategies designed ("calculated") to secure the ends sponsored by those values and commitments. Although outcomes can never be guaranteed, are intrinsically uncertain, this is the only sense of the word "calculation" that is properly relevant to the business of having a project. From the way it is internally constructed, deconstruction seems unable to deal with these kinds of considerations. It shies away from values and strategies, ends and means, commitments and calculations because it fears that this is to restore a metaphysical language of grounds and foundations. Whence the dilemma. One may turn elsewhere for values and the rest, for somewhere to "stand" (Marxism, feminism, etc.), and try to harness the "undermining" force of deconstructive analysis as a strategy, practical and intellectual, in the name of those values. But this is vulnerable to the charge of self-contradiction, since it is precisely the "elsewhere," the anchoring or "grounding" elsewhere, that deconstruction forbids—what it requires you deconstruct in turn. Deconstruction does not allow you to stand anywhere, only to sit on the branch while sawing it. The alternative, then, is to abandon the idea of standing anywhere and of being able to give cogent reasons for those choices. But, as Heath says, what then is the point of deconstructive work, why bother—what *difference* does it make?

All this is relevant to de Man's reflection on the problematic relations between thought, language, and action. But the terms of that reflection are not the only ones for engaging with these problems, although they are the only terms that Hartman allows into the field of discussion (with what results I shall presently consider). The unavailability of an ultimate "ground," an absolute foundationalist move in which to anchor ethical and political life (what Derrida calls the "ethico-political") is a familiar theme of contemporary moral philosophy. It is, for example, central to Bernard Williams's argument in his recent *Ethics and the Limits of Philosophy.*[8] But this does not prevent Williams from arguing for the ethical life (for the relevance of what he calls ethical "considerations"), nor from claiming that rational-critical thought (what Hartman, summarizing de Man, defines as the illusions of "enlightenment") has a key place in such considerations. This is not a return to foundationalist thinking; on the contrary, it emphasizes the social and historical situatedness of the projects we construct and the decisions we make. The fact that there is no philosophical calculus for our decision making does not exempt us from having to make them and live by them, including decisions of the ethico-political sort.

Decision-making is in fact one of the key issues in the whole debate about the politics of deconstruction, and turns on what has arguably become its most notorious category, the category of the "undecidable." In its journeys around the intellectual marketplace, this word has come to mean so many things that it now probably has no more useful intellectual life left in it. As I understand its operation in Derrida's work, however, it has essentially two contexts. One is strictly formal, a somewhat obscure attempt to apply Gödel's undecidability theorem in mathematics to the interpretation of texts. The other concerns the question of decision making in the more "ordinary" senses. In this context, the undecidable is not meant as a recipe for passivity and opting out. It stresses two aspects of decisions: first, that to decide for one possibility always and necessarily entails the repression of other possibilities; second, that we cannot know fully in advance what the outcomes of our decisions will be; if we could, they wouldn't be decisions but something else (something that robots or computers do). In other words, the undecidable does not represent a rejection of decision, but is one of the very *conditions* of making a decision.

Neither of these two emphases (on repression and unknowability) is particularly novel (they are, for example, at the very heart of the representation of the problem of decision in tragedy). I certainly see nothing in this use of the "undecidable" that is incompatible with Williams's approach to the question of ethics. Everything thus depends on how the point about the absence of secure foundations is made, and how its implications are handled. In that regard, Hartman's performance is nothing short of lamentable, as at once an account of deconstruction and a demonstration of it in action. Hartman's way with the undecidable is for the most part to avoid decisions, to hop first on one foot, then on the other. I said earlier that his use of such adjectives as "polished," "very general," and "polite" with reference to de Man's anti-Semitism needed to be put back in context, in particular into the sentences that condemn de Man. Here is some of that context: "But the fact remains that, however polished de Man's formulations are, they show *all* the marks, and the dangerous implications, of identifying the Jews as an alien and unhealthy presence in Western civilisation" (my italics). "There is, clearly, an accommodation, *but* it remains very general, without recourse to the usual 'virile' invective" (my italics). "But I cannot ignore these expressions of anti-Jewish sentiment, *even* if they remained polite" (my italics). This is all over the place. Hartman condemns, initially in no uncertain terms ("all the marks"), yet retracts condemnation. He says that "the *destruction* of European Jewry" was "*abetted* by such [i.e, Paul de Man's] propaganda" (my italics). That is a very strong statement, a statement about causal and moral responsibility for decisions in history. And yet he cannot follow through; the judgment fades away into the vagueness of phrases like "perhaps culpably blind" and so forth. What on earth can we do with these endless backtrackings and proliferating qualifiers, phrases, and sentences that take away with one hand what they give with the other? I do not mean by this that a decision on the de Man affair is required. One might prefer the stance of irreducible ambivalence. But if that is the preferred response, it should be explicitly and scrupulously represented as such, and not be confused with flailing indecision or with rhetorical gestures toward decisions that are then undermined the moment they appear to arrive somewhere. Certainly, explicit and scrupulous ambivalence is not compatible with the claim that de Man's anti-Semitic formulations "show all the marks, and the dangerous implications, of identifying the Jews as an alien and unhealthy presence in Western civilisation"; and by the same token I see no plausible sense in which, under that description, the formulations can also be described as "polite."

IV

There is, however one area in which Hartman does make what appears to be a series of moderately clear decisions, and it calls for special comment. It is, surprisingly, in the form of an appeal to that category which has come in for quite a lot of heavy deconstructive treatment (and notably in de Man's writings), the category of history. "In the light of history, de Man's article become[s] more than a theoretical expression of anti-Semitism." I'm not quite sure what this means, especially the phrase "more than a theoretical expression." However, the phrase that interests me here is "In the light of history." History? Light? The possibility, then, is of enlightenment in and through history. But "enlightenment" is exactly what Hartman, summarizing de Man, is skeptical about ("enlightenment as such cannot resolve error, and even *repeats* it"; my italics). If we cannot learn from history, learn historically in the sense of being able to mount rational interpretation and criticism of past events and actions, why then the appeal to history, what sort of light can be said to come out of history?

Nevertheless, let us persist with the metaphor of light, and see where it takes us in terms of Hartman's further speculations about history, both particular and general. The sentence I have just quoted might lead us to believe that historical enlightenment in the case of the de Man affair consists in seeing just how dangerous and culpable the anti-Semitic intervention was. But this is not at all the theme of what elsewhere in the article Hartman has to say about history. Three points in particular stand out. The first is Hartman's injunction that "it remains important, however, to place oneself into that era, into its motives and attitudes." This is an odd injunction, given deconstruction's criticism of that branch of empathetic hermeneutics that believes you can recover the intentions and meanings ("motives and attitudes") of historical actors, grasp the past from the point of view of the past. This, however, is what Hartman says we must try to do. What kind of recovery does he have in mind? It turns out to be the frame of mind of what he calls the "common sort of nationalism" in Europe of the period (though exactly what period is left vague), and in particular the "cultural" nationalism to which de Man ("this Flemish sympathiser") was drawn. "Nothing in this common sort of nationalism," writes Hartman, "had to result in anti-Semitism." As a historical claim, this is dubious, but no matter. The real point is that the frame being set up here is deeply misleading. It may or may not be true that, prior to the Nazi occupation of Belgium, there was a form of nationalism that did not "have" to result in anti-Semitism. But Hartman is not talking about de Man's position on nationalism *before* it "turned into" anti-Semitism. He is talking about, trying to "explain," texts written in the 1940s, that is, in Hartman's own words, "well past the time when all but the deliberately ignorant would have known that the persecution of the Belgian Jews begun before the end of 1940 had taken a drastic turn." A teleological red herring (nationalism, at least of the "common sort," did not "have" to result in anti-Semitism) is thus laid across the path of the argument, and yields the following wit-less question (to which, moreover, no clear answer is given): "Was it youthful inexperience, then, or a broader acceptance of fascist ideology that made de Man write an anti-Semitic piece?" "Youthful inexperience" may be relevant, but on its own its ex-planatory power is zero; lots of foolish things come out of youth-ful inexperience, but the task to hand is to explain why *this* partic-ular thing might have come out of it. As for "broader acceptance," I do not know what "broader" means here (as dis-tinct from simple "acceptance"). But in any case, acceptance (broader or otherwise) does not explain much either in any rele-vant sense of historical explanation. What then is the point of re-quiring us to place ourselves "into that era, into its motives and attitudes"? The effect is a discreditable one; it puts in place a smoke screen made from some notion of a relatively harmless "common nationalism" that has nothing to do with the particular historical facts of the matter at hand.

The second point is even more discreditable. This is Hartman's serving up of historical "context" in the form of the appalling in-the-same-boat hypothesis. In the last paragraph of his article, Hartman rehearses his feelings of moral indignation at de Man's anti-Semitism (with talk of "accuse," "abhor," and "feel betrayed"). Then comes the following (with the customary back-tracking "however"): "The accusations we bring, however, are a warning to ourselves. They do not justify complacency about the relation of political ideas to moral conduct." All too true. But what has this to do with the specifics of the history of the Nazi period? What it has to do with it is specified in the following two sentences: "Many on the left also welcomed what Kenneth Burke called 'sinister unifying' and succumbed to xenophobic and anti-Jewish sentiment. De Man's 'dirty secret' was the dirty secret of a good part of civilised Europe." Yes, many on the left did succumb, and I suppose not too many questions are begged in saying that "a good part of civilised Europe" was caught up in anti-Semitism. Certainly, no one, to my knowledge, is claiming that de Man was *alone* in expressing anti-Semitic sentiments. But, as the deconstructionists are the first to insist, we should also attend to the rhetorical force as well as the factual claims of statements of this type. The rhetorical effect of Hartman's statement is obvious: it evokes a generalized culpability enveloping the Europe of the period, touching left and right, barbarian and "civilised" alike. It is code for saying guilt was everywhere. As "history," this is somewhat breathtaking. It "forgets" or evacuates from the historical picture what crucially makes the difference: the fact of sustained, articulate, and determined opposition to the obscenities of anti-Semitism. There was not some unspeakable *Zeitgeist* irresistibly seducing everyone into passive or active collaboration. And if Hartman were to object that, of course, he has not forgotten this, the important point remains: why does he not mention it? I make this point not just for the sake of something called "balance," nor simply out of personal loyalty to the memory of my father (who fought in wars against fascism in both Spain and Germany), but because it shows that at the time there were other options, from silence to departure to active resistance.

Resistance, however, would not seem to be a particularly meaningful category for Hartman. This brings me to the third point of his way with history. We have seen Hartman rehearsing de Man's view that enlightenment can never correct error, and "even repeats it": "Enlightenment as such cannot resolve error, and even repeats it, if one is deluded into thinking that the new position stands in a progressive and sounder relation to language, that it has corrected a historical mistake once and for all." Repetition thus emerges as the commanding figure of this theory of history. We can never accede to the dignity of rational self-understanding; we cannot correct the past. All we can do is repeat it. But in which case how do we know that it is error? This way with the past and its interpretation collapses vitally important distinctions into simpleminded and question-begging equations, in particular the equation between, on the one hand, thinking that a later position is "sounder" than a previous one and, on the other hand, supposing that a historical mistake has been coerrected "once and for all." The latter idea might just be associated with certain versions of enlightenment or progressivist hopes. The former is associated with there being any hope at all. The shift from the latter to the former—assisted by the intellectually opaque conjunction "progressive *and* sounder"—implies that unless one accepts some vast and vastly optimistic rationalist program one cannot get a sounder understanding of anything.

Does Hartman believe that, and, if so, how does his own article stand to that belief? Is he saying that this is what de Man said, and that he himself agrees? How can he, since he berates de Man not only for his "error," but also for not having disclosed it? Yet here he is moving toward a description of de Man's work as "a deepening reflection on the rhetoric of totalitarianism" in the following terms: "There cannot be, he [de Man] suggests, a future that will not prove to have been a past like that." Like what? Like that *wartime* past? Hartman continues: "His [de Man's] essay on Benjamin envisages a temporal repetition that subverts the hope in new beginnings, in a New Era: it subverts a hope, ultimately messianic, that always revives." Messianic hope can be plausibly represented as a dangerous animal, but was it messianic to hope, and to act on the hope, that Europe might be liberated from fascism? Were those actions simply repetition of the same sort of thing? I apologize to my reader for having to put these silly questions. But they arise inevitably from the encounter with Hartman's text.

What are the implications of this account of "history," and where do they leave us with the question of the "politics" of deconstruction? From the terms of the account, they leave us essentially with the politics of the bystander, with the flight from decision, out of the political arena, and into what? The "literary." Hartman tells us that "the only activity that escapes the immediate

ideological pressure is art itself whose deeper tradition de Man often cites as able to resist the pressures of the purely contemporary
(*l'ingerence* [sic] *de l'actualite*)." This was the mode of de Man's
gesture of atonement, of his "act of conscience." The relations
between the key terms of this statement ("activity," "immediate
ideological pressure," "art," "tradition," "the purely contemporary") are indeed difficult and complex. Hartman's formulation
(in particular that question-begging metaphorical "deeper") simply elides these difficulties and complexities, in a reduction of
"art" to the idea of an "escaping." Art or "literature" thus appears
as a privileged term in the construction of a generalized skeptical
attitude to the category of action itself. As a strategy for questioning primitive conceptions of "action" (those impossibly paradoxical efforts to conceive action as emptied of the reflective, of that
which is both the curse and the blessing of all active human
projects), such skepticism can be immensely salutary, and in the
detailed analyses and arguments of de Man's work was often just
that.

The problem with Hartman's representation of this position is
that it is made to look paralyzingly indiscriminate. Action is im-
perfect and incomplete; disaster is always attendant upon the
move from language into praxis; change is impossible, we are all
in the same boat, condemned to repeat (though we can also
atone). This generalized skepticism Hartman particularizes by seeing it as a critique of totalitarian programs of action originating in
de Man's disillusion with the fascist version of action. But how,
in the terms of this account, do we get from particular to general
and back again to other particulars? Is it that the fascist compromising of action taints all action, including the action that
sought to rid Europe of fascism? Does Hartman believe that? Did
de Man? Is that the "lesson," that ultimately nothing makes a
difference? If so, it is indeed a recipe for passivity, not only
saturating the field of action with skeptical agonizing but also
homogenizing and equalizing all practical endeavor under the law
of eternal repetition. It implies taking and leaving the world as
you happen historically to find it, since the attempt to change it
succeeds only in repeating the errors you sought to correct. It is
not, then, that the intellectual structure of deconstruction has any

intrinsic link to fascist ideology (a nonsense), but that, in Hartman's version of it (and his version of de Man's version of it), it would seem inevitably to entail detachment from, and hence acceptance of, anything that happens to be the case, including—if that happens to be the case—fascism.[9] If that is what deconstruction is all about (I myself, from the terms of other accounts, would wish to believe otherwise), then, to coin a trope, forget it.

NOTES

1. Paul de Man (summarizing his interpretation of Rousseau), "The Rhetoric of Blindness: Jacques Derrida's Reading of Rousseau," *Blindness and Insight: Essays in the Rhetoric of Contemporary Criticism*, rev., 2nd ed. (Minneapolis: University of Minnesota Press, 1983), 140.

2. Geoffrey Hartman, "Paul de Man, fascism, and, deconstruction. Blindness and Insight," *New Republic*, March 7, 1988. Since this essay went to press, Hartman has published another article ("History and Judgment: The Case of Paul de Man," *History and Memory: Studies in Representation of the Past*, vol. 1, no. 1. [Spring/Summer 1989], 55-84). This is a far more measured and coherently reflective commentary than the earlier piece. However, as "event" (intervention), it is of course of secondary importance alongside the first, which was one of the earliest published reactions to the "affair," appearing, moreover, in a widely read journal. In any case, my views of the substantive claims of the first piece remain unaltered by my reading of the second.

3. Paul de Man, "Les Juifs dans la Littérature actuelle," *Le Soir*, March 4, 1941, 10.

4. This essay was written before the appearance of Jacques Derrida's article, "Like the Sound of the Sea Deep within a Shell: Paul de Man's War," *Critical Inquiry*, (Spring 1988). A belatedly added footnote is clearly not the place to address the range of complex argument presented in Derrida's essay. I do, however, feel it is necessary to register my disagreement with him over the crucial question of how to interpret the artcle "Les Juifs dans la Littérature actuelle" (and in particular the context, significance, and implications of the phrase "antisémitisme vulgaire"). Derrida remarks that the phrase is irreducibly ambiguous between the two senses I have noted (ether anti-Semitism as such as "vulger," or there are two kinds of anti-Semitism, the "vulgar" and the "distinguished"). Derrida also says that, if it was the former de Man intended ("a possibility I will never exclude"), then "he could not say so clearly in this context." That is the crux of the difference between Derrida and myself. Whereas Derrida sees the context as placing limits on what, in other respects, he in fact reads as an "anticonformist" statement with regard to prevailing anti-Semitic notions, I see the context as fatally compromising; or at least I cannot see how a document of this sort can be reasonably described as anticonformist when the "context" prevents it from being clear on the one point that is vital to the anticonformist stance. Furthermore, there is, as I see it, no sense whatsoever in which the one explicit and unambiguous argument of the article concerning the Jews—namely, that Western literature has healthily resisted contamination by Jewish influence—could be seen as anticonformist. It

simply registers a disagreement with those who hold to the opposite view, but as a disagreement within a shared universe of discourse (the dominant assumption of which is that Jews are indeed an alien presence in Western culture, whether or not they have succeeded in contaminating it). I am, morever, perplexed by what strikes me as inconsistent observations in Derrida's text. In respect of the most disturbing moment of de Man's article (when he refers to a "solution to the Jewish problem" in terms of "the creation of a Jewish colony isolated from Europe"), Derrida speaks of the "*unpardonable* violence and confusion of these sentences" (Derrida's italics). Yet he also says that he does "not understand" these references to a "solution" and a "Jewish colony." If he does not understand them, why are the sentences in which they appear "*unpardonable*" (as distinct from being that on which judgment should be suspended until the references are understood)? And if they are unpardonable, do they not undermine the claim that the article is anticonformist (in the sense of anticonformist that counts, as more than simply a disagreement with a majority view *within* the prevailing discourse of anti-Semitism)? Finally, "unpardonable" is a word that, as far as I can recall, has not been used in any of the published remarks on the affair that I have read. It is a very strong, perhaps the strongest possible, term of condemnation available in the language. For someone who like Derrida, weighs his words and those of others with such scrupulous care, I take it that he is fully alert to the massive weight of this word. What are the implications, then, for the rest of the article of a view that describes the relevant sentences as being beyond pardon? These are issues that will have to be taken up in more detail elsewhere.

5. Jon Wiener, "Deconstructing de Man," *Nation*, January 9, 1988.

6. Ibid., 7.

7. Stephen Heath, "Literary Theory, etc.," *Comparative Criticism*, 9 (1988) 301.

8. Bernard Williams, *Ethics and the Limits of Philosophy* (Cambridge, Mass.: Harvard University Press, 1985.

9. This is one respect in which there may be a relation of continuity between "wartime" de Man and late de Man. Christopher Norris—whose book on de Man appeared after this essay was written—alleges of the wartime journalism that "the practical upshot of de Man's arguments is always a counsel of non-resistance: that the ultimate lesson to be drawn from events in France is the pointlessness of presently standing in the way of German political and cultural supremacy. Nobody who reads these lines can remain in any doubt of his defeatist attitude." "Postscript," Paul de Man, *Deconstruction and the Critique of Aesthetic Ideology* (London and New York, 1988), 185. In fairness to Norris's argument, however, I have to add that the last sentence in the above quotation is followed by a sentence beginning with "But," inaugurating a statement that effectively cancels the force of the previous one: de Man wasn't defeatist after all since apparently he could also "imagine an alternative future." This is typical of Norris's mode of argumentation, as it is of Hartman's (whose article Norris cites approvingly), and the cumulative effect is exactly the same.

The Spectacle of Intellect in a Media Age: Cultural Representations and the David Abraham, Paul de Man, and Victor Farías Cases

Dana Polan

In the mid-1980s, a young concept named "postmodernism" began to appear in theoretical conferences and to draw a perplexed attention to itself. Although we have had endless discussions of the supposed objects of a postmodern condition, I want to detour the usual discourse of/on/in postmodernism—a discourse so often given over to deciding whether this or that phenomenon is "postmodern[1]—by looking at the implications of the "appearance" itself of the concept: why in the eighties, how in the eighties does one talk in and of postmodernism? And I want to do this by tying the appearance of the "postmodern" to another phenomenon of appearance: what I would call the mediatization of the intellectual (or spectaclization, as I have referred to it elsewhere).[2] This phenomenon may lead us to analyze less what intellectuals can teach us about postmodernism (or other contemporary practices) than what conditions the teaching of intellectuals operates within.

I will comment in particular on a phenomenon around intellectuals that seems to repeat itself every several years in intriguingly symptomatic ways: namely, a scandal or debate about the truthfulness or not of some historical documents and about the relationship of an intellectual's career to those documents, and finally the entrance of the debate, which is often fairly obscure in its academic details, into the public realm through its reportage in such arena as *Time*, *Newsweek*, and the *New York Times*. For all their highly important differences—differences that are often intensely political and historical in their implications—these cases are given a surprising regularity by processes of mediatization: an intellectual claims falsifications or distortions in the work of another intellectual; debate rages, is reported on in one or another of those periodicals that belong to what Fred Pfeil terms the professional-managerial class—for example, the *New Yorker* or the *New York Review of Books* or even the *Nation*[3]—and resolution of this *différend* (Jean-François Lyotard's term for incompatible and conflictual discourses)[4] becomes increasingly difficult as archives get closed off, information retreats into arcania; finally, a mass media periodical reports on the debate, usually leaving it in irresolution (the resolution of the matter being one that the periodical ultimately seems to feel is best left to the very intellectuals who made a murkiness of it in the first place) and usually giving a rendition of it that few intellectuals accept as accurate and usually representing the drama of the debate through closeup photographs of the protagonists (more about this later). With this appearance in the media, the debate vanishes from critical priority so as to allow attention to ready itself for the next scandal or controversy.

Part of what is so regular about such events is precisely their representation as *events*, punctual instants of momentous and spectacular import—intellectual debate transformed into breathless fashion, a cult of the critically new. Indeed, my own opening line, about the sudden and momentous appearance of the postmodern in the 1980s, intended a pastiche of this mediatic kind of conversion of the asynchronicities and the *longues durées* of history into Event, a happening. It seems predictable that postmodernism—although ostensibly concerned with what Lyotard terms the breakup of *grands récits*, master narratives—becomes itself the object of history writing as *narrative* form, specifically, of narrative as exciting punctuation. Hence the frequent desire among critics to assign a date to postmodernism: not so far from Virginia Woolf's modernist dating of modernism "on or about December 1910," there is an apocalyptic dating of postmodernism—1939 or 1945 (and there the choice is Auschwitz or Hiroshima as the decisive happening); or, as in the opening line of Charles Jencks's *The Language of Post-Modern Ar-*

chitecture, "July 15, 1972," date of the dynamiting of the Pruitt-Igoe (modernist) housing project in St. Louis.

Deliberately, then, my opening line tried to parody this evenemential quality by which we put forward intellectual representations insofar as it was a transformation of the opening to Janet Malcolm's *In the Freud Archives*: "In the mid-seventies, a young man named Jeffrey Moussaieff Masson began to appear at psychoanalytic congresses and to draw perplexed attention to himself." In the media age, concepts (like postmodernism) and people (like Jeffrey Masson) undergo a similar fate: a burst of notoriety, a productive explosion of discourse, and then a fall into obscurity, the replacement of what had seemed pressing debate by another fashionable debate (one could argue, for example, that the term "postmodern" comes so often in the mid- and late eighties to substitute in the field of literary criticism for the Bakhtinian term "dialogic" of the early eighties—and to be applied to comparable objects: for example, "Chaucer and Postmodernism," as one article in *Chaucer Studies* is entitled).

We can see the process of mediatization of intellectuality—of concepts and people alike—quite explicitly in three of the most prominent debates about American intellectual practice in the 1980s: the battle around Freud archive director Jeffrey Masson's charges of falsification in Freud's rethinking of the seduction theory, reported on by Janet Malcolm in the *New Yorker* (and picked up by other magazines and papers); the controversy around David Abraham's *The Collapse of the Weimar Republic*, the challenges to its scholarship by senior historians, the challenge to the senior historians' handling of the case, all of this reported in the *New York Times*, the *Nation, Time*, and so on; and, of course, most recently, the scandal around revelations of Paul de Man's involvement in collaborationism and anti-semitism, again reported on in many mass circulation week lies. And, to remind ourselves of a certain internationalness of the mediatization of practices of everyday life, we might note one further example: the debates that began to rage at the end of 1987 in France (and to a lesser degree, Germany) around Victor Farías's *Heidegger et le nazisme*, mediatized even more perhaps than American controversies by its appearance on several nights of primetime French television.

It is not accidental that so many of the controversies take place in relation to questions about a German or Germanized thought. Of course it is essential to insist on differences among the various cases: I do not at all want to suggest any possible similarity in content between the work of a David Abraham, dedicated to his Jewish parents who went through the hell of Auschwitz, and that of a Paul de Man, who seems to encourage the very sending off of the Jews to an elsewhere. The similarity I am interested in is a similarity in the ways these quite diverse and even opposed approaches to a German question got reported on in the media, get transformed into media events. In a media age where we seem to be fascinated equally by what Jean Baudrillard analyzes as simulacra (the recessions of the Real behind an empty play of signifiers, of symbolic forms) and by what Susan Sontag terms "fascinating fascism" (the harnessing of the glittery, sleek simulacral surfaces to spectacles of might, the materiality of bodies tied to power), the question of Germany becomes the very question of the referent, of the possibility indeed of reference, of the Real. As Jon Weiner and Jane Caplan suggest in their *New Statesman* article on the David Abraham case, "It is doubtful that the case would have become so public—with articles in the *New York Times* and *Time* magazine—had it turned on events less prominent in the American public mind than the rise of National Socialism. . . . Every contribution to the history of Modern Germany is potentially part of the chronicle of this monstrous and uniquely execrated event" (May 3, 1985, 27).

Not surprisingly, the media endlessly return to the question of Germany. It is almost as if there is the sentiment that if a show can be made even of this horror, if the Holocaust can become *Holocaust, the mini-series*, then the media will have proved their ultimate simulacral power, will have shown that no real is too real to resist becoming spectacle. If, as a whole series of philosophers from Adorno to Lyotard contend, Auschwitz might seem to be the last unassimilable Real, the last materiality beyond discourse and representation, then it is here precisely that the media *have* to venture, *showing* that all is representation, that all is good show. As film critic Thomas Elsaesser puts it in the case of contemporary German cinema's look (specifically, in Syberberg and

Fassbinder) at the fascist past, "The cinema can deal with history only when and where history itself has acquired an imaginary dimension, where the disjunction between sign and referent is so radical that history turns on a problem of representation and fascism emerges as a question of subjectivity within image and discourse." But equally unsurprisingly, if the name "Auschwitz" is the ultimate stake of the media, it has become one of the ultimate stakes in philosophy and especially in philosophizing on postmodernity, on the possibility or not of a ground in our historical moment.

Hence, the stake of Jean-François Lyotard's *Le différend* (1984), his first full-length work since *La condition postmoderne* (1979) with its sense that narrative reference has been broken up by the multiplication of agonistic language games. *Le différend* is paradigmatic of the problems facing any critical analysis today: as a text coming after what we can call the "linguistic turn" in the human sciences, *Le différend* wants to say that we are only in representation, that we have no guaranteed absolute ground. On the other hand, its ability to say that, to declare undeniably this situation, depends on a faith, a hope, that undeniable declaration is still possible. For Lyotard, then, the problem becomes one of saying that everything is language while guarding the sentiment (his word) that "Auschwitz" has an irreducibility that should make it resist the revisionist attempts of a Faurrisson or a Rocque (two extreme right-wingers intent on denying the existence of extermination camps). Lyotard's solution, not so far from Fredric Jameson's political unconscious in which every present narrative gives utopian glimpses of a future narrative that is logically necessary and inevitable,[5] is to narrativize the two positions of nominalism and realism: navigating between his acknowledged masters, Wittgenstein and Kant, Lyotard represents the *present* as the site of language games, the battle of *différends*, and the *future* as a sublimity of totalized human history projected, imaged, imagined, by the present—future history as unified by the Kantian expectation, enthusiasm, for a shared rationality of human subjects.[6]

But, as I will suggest, Lyotard's politics—the present as a game of language giving only a sentiment of future engagement and enthusiasm—may be only partially satisfying. Like Jameson's, Lyotard's engagement, insofar as narrativized, remains an aesthetic form of engagement, and the present becomes inaccessible to any analysis of its materiality and direct material effects. As Meaghan Morris declares in her critique of Lyotard's sublime, one of the "petrifying and formidable complex of elements" in Lyotard as his "increasingly explicit and insistent Kantianism in both aesthetics and politics, and here it is easy to imagine a fairly ordinary art world-drift (a *dérive*) away from the details of Lyotard's argument and towards something that might well accommodate a vogue for kitsch landscapes, a space of ersatz transcendentalism with 'sublime' for its buzzword and for its content a re-discovery of the unspeakable, the ineffable, the mystic catatonics of art. And thence . . . to declarations of distance between politics and art."[7]

For a poststructuralist thinker like Lyotard, German history has to do precisely with our ability to still imagine history, to still think commitment within the heart of representation. And yet it seems to me necessary to raise questions, as Meaghan Morris does, about the very representation of the Holocaust within a framework devoted to a sentiment of historical ineffability. Too often perhaps, discussion of the German question as a question of the Holocaust leads to a thinking of history in terms of exceptional events, losing sight of the ways that events, under capitalism, may be anything but exceptional, may in fact be nothing but an expression of certain structural tendencies of capitalism per se (I refer here to all the debates on whether fascism is an aberration within the modern age or a potentially logical outcome or later stage of the age's capitalism). What may be lost in an emphasis on the exceptionality of an Auschwitz is the potential historical continuity of a case like the Holocaust with everyday forms of politics, ordinary enactments of power. Indeed, much of the interest of David Abraham's *Collapse of the Weimar Republic*—despite its dedication to Auschwitz survivor-parents and its epilogue on Nazism and big business—lies in Abraham's attempt to write the history of Weimar as if Nazism were not the necessary teleology of Weimar; Abraham's structural model intends to look at the specificities of Weimar Germany that suggests historical regularities

and continuities in Weimar and fascist capitalism without suggesting that one had automatically to lead to the other.

Even the Jeffrey Masson case—Austrian, not German—finally is
a case of guilt and responsibility, the question of the relation to
a Real of the body (and we might remember that Janet Malcolm
reports on a cocktail party where Masson cites the Holocaust as
example of a Real that is too real to become fodder for psychoanalytic symbolization): not merely a question of falsification per se,
where the content of this falsification would be unimportant or
irrelevant, the question of the Masson case has to do once more
with a blaming of the victim, the question indeed of deciding who
the victim is. In Masson's reading, Freud moves from a conception of the girl's body as a passive one, pure object of the man's
aggression, to the body as active, the girl as traversed by unconscious desires—the girl, to be sure, not intentionally *responsible*,
but responsible at some level nonetheless. It is part of the complexity of such a case, of the ambiguity surrounding any notion
of the Real and of responsibility in today's critical context that the
Masson controversy seems finally to end in a literal and direct
recession of the Real: as a consequence of debate and media
coverage, the Freud archives become fully closed to research. It
is also part of the complexity of the case that it ends furthermore
in a weird, parodic, postmodern confusing of terms and positions: hence, Masson, a man whom Malcolm describes as a veritable playboy, a ladies' man (one hesitates in this context to say
"seducer") now declares himself to be a "feminist" while a
poststructuralist-inspired feminist like Jacqueline Rose in *Sexuality in the Field of Vision* critiques Masson for not recognizing the
role of fantasy and desire on the girl's part.[8] But the complexifica-
tion of positions here—what is real? what is it to be a feminist?
what, to use the title of a recent book, are "men in feminism"?—is
not simply a reversal in which a fixed real becomes threatened by
simulacra, Masson standing in for a principle of reality as against
some sort of investment by Rose in a principle of phantasy. Rather, between positions, blurring their clarity, there is the emphatic
role of media, converting all clarities into spectacle, the battle of
politics as good show where belief and commitment on the intellectual's part can come to seem less important than the intellec-

tual's ability to perform well, to be a good performance. It seems predictable, then, that when Masson spoke on the childhood-seduction theory at Marin College in California in 1985 (a speech I attended), the event was advertised primarily in the Sunday entertainment supplement (commonly known as the "pink section") of the *San Francisco Chronicle*, advertised in a style no different from that of the *Chronicle*'s ad for the next concert of this or that rock singer with a studio glossy of Masson in close-up, tickets available for seven dollars at "Bay Area Ticket Outlets."

Certainly, we might be all too easily tempted to dismiss such a spectacle as a mere epiphenomenon hanging over the "real" work of "serious" intellectuals (indeed, Masson's very lack of an academic affiliation seems to render his controversy less serious for many academics). But I would want to argue that it is precisely such mediatization, such conversion of intellectual practice into good show endlessly superseded by other good shows, that is both a central part of the work of intellectuals, part of what they *do* (even if they do not know or admit that their "job" is to put on a show for the media) *and* something that intellectuals might make an object of their own critical interrogations. Too often, it seems to me, we conceive of the intellectual's position as one of a relation to a pristine truth, independent of all spectacle, all rhetoric of the presentation and the displaying of that "truth." In other words, we assume that truth exists (somewhere) and that the intellectual's role is to find it and transmit it, his or her language and mode of self-presentation as an intellectual interfering not at all in the successful transmission of that found truth.[9] To take one example of this assumption, Lyotard's *Le différend* seems to abandon the earlier *La condition postmoderne*'s sense of irreconcilable language games within which all action occurs to imagine instead an extra-mediatic situation in which the philosopher directly faces games while not being implicated in them, while remaining safely outside them. Hence, the overeasiness of Lyotard's distinction between philosophers (good guys) and intellectuals (bad guys): "There's a responsibility in thought to detect *différends* and to find the impossible idiom that can express them. That's what the philosopher does. [In contrast,] an intellectual aids in the forgetting of *différends* by favoring this or that genre to the benefit of political hegemony.''

Broadly, there are two versions, one relatively optimistic, one relatively pessimistic, of this notion of the intellectual as philosopher-hero able to express the inexpressible, the intellectual as figure in an immediate or potentially immediate relation to truth, rather than a mediate or mediatized one. Both versions, significantly, *can* acknowledge the force of media, the power of spectacle, but only as epiphenomena that cover a preexisting and fully constituted truth and block, perhaps only temporarily, the intellectual's access to that truth. In the optimistic version of intellectual truth, there is an everyday world of media lies, of popular culture, of the doxa of ordinary experience, but the intellectual can break through this, not only to capture the truth for himself or herself but to offer this truth to those everyday people caught in media lies and thus help them move out of the darkness of their Platonic cave (and, as an aside, we might note that a dominant motif in recent film theory has been the comparison of the myth of Plato's cave to the myth of cinema as ideological apparatus, the passive spectators of mass art immersed in a darkness that only the philosopher's knowledge might deliver them from).

As I argue in another essay, one of our most prominent current representatives of this position may be Edward Said, especially in a book like the significantly titled *Covering Islam*.[10] If, as I argue, certain of Said's other works, like *The World, the Text, and the Critic* with its structuring of argument around a montage of critical essays (essays in the literal sense of tactical forays), suggest that Said sometimes imagines critical practice less as a capturing of a truth than as a combative production of positions, nonetheless *Covering Islam* can seem highly classical, highly traditional, in its title: the media as an external force that covers over, blankets, a Real; the intellectual as that traveling figure who sees what those under the sway of media can only miss. It is not surprising to find Said giving the title ''Ending Ambiguity'' to one of his articles on Palestine and going so far as to make a distinction between pseudotruth and truth serve as the center of his intervention.

Significantly, this conception of the intellectual as bringer of truth into a world of media lies seems to be a dominant one in much of the discourse of/on postmodernism where one of the central lessons of postmodernity—namely, that new forms of mechanical and electronic reproduction lead to confusion over truth and simulacra—seems to be ignored for the case of the intellectual him- or herself who is imagined (or who imagines him- or herself) as someone who can cognize the postmodern condition from without, without being affected by it, and can even intervene in and on that condition, without being affected by it. Significantly, the work that appears to represent the first important American use of the term "postmodern"—architect Henry Hudnut's essay "The Postmodern House," published in 1945—already invokes a strict binary opposition between the architect as knowledgeable hero and the masses as blinded prey of the mass media. Facing the moment of postwar suburbia, Hudnut figures modern architecture as the bland anonymity of the prefab house of mechanical reproduction and poses against this the possibility of a "postmodern architecture" (which, for him, means a return to a naturalist architecture responsive to biological needs of "man" in all his existential richness).

Even when a postmodernist discourse works to abandon Hudnut's naturalism and yet to still imagine architecture in the service of everyday needs, the discourse seems to give in to the temptation of a binarism that imagines those everyday needs as dominated by a blindness that only the privileged and knowledgeable figure (the architect or the architectural theorist) can really know. Hence, the ambiguity of a supposedly paradigmatic postmodernist architecture theory like that of Robert Venturi that, on the one hand, devotes itself, as in the title of his (coauthored) 1972 book, to "Learning from Las Vegas," but only to create systems of popular allusion "glued" decoratively onto the surfaces of buildings and, on the other hand, imagines that the masses are so lost in media passivity that nothing should be celebrated but their own passivity. Hence, then, the argument against open space in the (in)famous terms of Venturi's 1962 *Complexity and Contradiction in Modern Architecture:* "The open piazza is seldom appropriate for an American city today. . . . The piazza, in fact, is 'un-American.' Americans feel uncomfortable sitting in a square: they should be working at the office or home with the family looking at television."

What I term the "pessimistic" version of intellectual truth guards the same binarism of active intellectual and passive masses but assumes simply that these two inhabit fully different, fully incommensurate worlds with no contact, no communication of truth, between them, the intellectual as producer of knowledge in an ivory tower. The paradigmatic fictional representation of this model might well be David Lodge's novel *Small World*, where virtually the only reality for the intellectual is the reality of conferences and endless movement from one conference to the next. Significantly, though, for all of its projection of intellectuality as a world apart, a world whose positions have no claims on an everyday world of everyday people, Lodge's novel cannot prevent itself from engaging on its own in some of the oldest projections and stereotypes as to what that everyday world is all about: for all its playful deconstruction of the importance of intellectual "work," Lodge's novel falls for one of the most traditional and undeconstructed representations of the nonintellectual as a femininity caught up in enslavement to mass cultural ideology.[11] One of the very few figures in the novel outside the intellectual world is the airline clerk, Cheryl, caught up in her dreams of romance offered by Harlequin novels, and only able to imagine academic knowledge as a fixed set of messages to be learned by rote (as when she begins to read Northrop Frye, quoting him but not understanding what she is quoting).

But for its representation of Cheryl, *Small World* imagines the world of the intellectual as one ignored by the discourses of everyday life (who but Cheryl could ever care a whit about Northrop Frye?). And this might be one of the appeals of the novel (for its typical reader, the university professor who gleefully recounts its anecdotes to colleagues who have experienced similar stories in their own "real" academic lives): the novel appeals in its seeming reconfirmation of splits between intellectual production and material production that intellectuals endlessly worry about (hence, one of the great self-comforting affectations of academics is to refer to everything outside the university as the "real world" as in the phrase, "I'm going back to the real world now" [said when one's day of teaching and committees is over]), its confirmation of the intellectual's simultaneous hope and fear that nothing he or she does matters to the world "at large." And yet, I would want to argue that intellectuality is far from ignored in the mass media and popular mythology. Quite the contrary, an image of the intellectual is endlessly played out in the media, massively solicited, actively produced. Instead of worrying about the ways they are ignored, or instead of luxuriating in their supposed isolation from the supposed trivialities of the "real world," intellectuals might do well to examine how that world anticipates them, figures them, positions them, and thereby frames and influences the kind of work they can do. Controversies like those around Masson or Abraham or de Man attract because they easily fit into two seemingly opposed, but actually complementary, images of the dangers of the intellectual: on the one hand, the intellectual as dangerous because he or she produces something, but a wrong something, a bad knowledge; on the other hand, the intellectual as dangerous because he or she produces nothing, wastes energy.

We can see these two representations and their similar work in the mass media representation of the *Marxist* intellectual. On the one hand, the Marxist is condemned for a dangerous influence, a potential to mislead ordinary people. This representation reaches an extreme in *Newsweek*'s report on the Paul de Man case, where Marxism is singled out for commentary at the end of the article (despite the potential incompatibility of de Manian deconstruction and materialist analysis; despite the possibility, as I have argued elsewhere, that de Man's approach in a work like *Allegories of Reading* may flounder precisely in its inability to imagine a materiality of oppression other than linguistic in form);[12] as *Newsweek* has it (February 15, 1988), "Opponents of deconstruction think the movement is finished. . . . What's next? Berkeley professor Frederick Crews sees the rise of 'the new militant cultural materialism of the left' That school prescribes the study of books not because of their moral or esthetic value but because they permit the professor to advance a political, often Marxist agenda. Crews contends that there's more than a trace of deconstruction in 'the new historicism'—which is one reason traditional humanists hope that it, too, will self-deconstruct in the wake of the de Man disgrace.''

On the other hand, the Marxist will be condemned for the *failure* of his or her influence, as in *Time*'s one and only discussion of Louis Althusser, an article entitled "The God That Failed," and concerned predictably with announcing links between Althusser's Marxism and his killing of his wife.

In other words, then, the intellectual as dangerous because effective; the intellectual as dangerous because ineffective. On the one hand, the standard image of Heidegger in the Victor Farías debate: Heidegger in Nazi uniform, arm outstretched in Nazi salute. On the other hand, the standard image of the academic in the ivory tower: photographed in a nondescript suit, the intellectual as a figure either gesticulating madly (and futilely) *or* fixed in pomposity in front of row after row of books, sign of a character lost in a knowledge that is abstract, the intellectual as lost in words. (A perfect example of both positions is the *Chronicle of Higher Education* article [February 6, 1985] on the David Abraham case: both men in front of their book cases, the younger man [Abraham] a little wild in his demeanor, the older man [Henry Turner, one of Abraham's most virulent opponents] solemn and portentous [and photographed even in imposing shadow]).[13] A systematic and insistent media representation will then distinguish between *teachers* and *professors*. Teachers—those figures who avoid the artificialities of the university for the gritty reality and realism of high school: if university professors are endlessly photographed against books, the iconography of the high school teacher portrays him or her against a blackboard or in the battlefield of the school's hallways (for example, Joe Clark with his baseball bat), the teacher in direct and earth-shattering confrontation with students (as in the recent film *Stand and Deliver*, where everything is defined in relation to a direct effectivity of teaching, the end title a chronicle of the increasing number of students at Garfield High who pass advanced placement math). Two sets of images are paradigmatic here. On the one hand, the *Daily Princetonian*'s iconography for its article on David Abraham (then still teaching at Princeton): the subject being a university professor after all, the article gives us one page where the three inserted pho-

tos are all of Abraham filmed head-on and gesticulating or thinking abstractly, the three shots all taken at the same moment, at the
same angle and distance and in front of the same row of books,
the intellectual debate as that which takes place in word-filled
offices where men gesture in seemingly meaningful but ultimately
meaningless expenditures of energy. On the other hand, the
newspaper ad for *Stand and Deliver:* on the left, the teacher
(played by the tough cop-boss from "Miami Vice") also filmed
head-on but this time with a look of determination (no vague abstraction here!); on the right, the student leaning slightly back in
his chair and thus contrasting with the uprightness of the strong
and committed professor, the student as resistant in-itself that the
good educational system (or, rather, the good individual in a
generally bad system) must make into a for-itself, a good member
of society, a teenager knowledgeable in calc, trig, and geometry.

All too often, professors arrive in the classroom assuming that
their function for students is to impart knowledge, communicate
a truth, when much of that function may be to perform a role, to
play out a spectacle, to conform to an image. One demonstration
of this might be the *Yale Daily News*'s April Fools parody of the
David Abraham case, where it is announced that Henry Turner
(one of Abraham's attackers and a senior professor at Yale, and
again photographed in front of his books) has gone after an undergraduate who dared offer a Marxist interpretation of Nazism: "It's
just another witch hunt," [Farnam Professor of History] David
Montgomery complained. 'If this keeps up I'm going to quit my
job and go back to work as a machinist.' Sterling Professor of History John Morton Blum was skeptical of [student] Gerger's claims.
'In all of *my* conversations with Hess he never once mentioned
having coffee with Rathenau,' Blum said. 'Of course, Joe Stalin
used to tell me quite frequently that he saw a connection. . . .
That reminds me of a conversation that I once had with Eleanor
Roosevelt. . . . ' Adjunct Professor of History Wolfgang Leon-
hard, seen escorting a freshman woman into his Davenport apart-
ment, said, 'Go away—don't bother me.' John Musser Professor
of Economics William Nordhaus, Gerber's advisor, was away lob-
bying for the Nobel Prize. . . . '' What most strikes me here is
the sheer way in which each of the Yale professors is named, cata-

logued, fit into his clichés, independent of any knowledge he
might have to teach, any difference he might have hoped to make.
What can the academic do in response to such mediatization?
I don't want to present here full answers or prescriptions so much
as to offer suggestions for further discussion. Most immediately,
it seems to me possible to imagine as a critical tactic of the intellectual the tactical reinsertion of a *reference to history* into intellectual discourse. Mass culture, I would argue, works most ideologically (as does high culture) not by creating mythic distortions, a false
consciousness, of history, but by confusing all consciousnesses
whatsoever, by offering no stable set of ideological values. Too
often, work inspired by the Althusserian conception of ideology
—ideology as the work of representation—reduces representation to the offering of myths or messages and by that falls into a
traditional conception of ideology as simple untruth. I would argue, instead, that so much contemporary culture works not by
offering messages but by offering no positive knowledge whatsoever, by breeding a confusion that is meaningless, that offers no
hold on the history of the world we live in. Hence, despite what
I said about media attacks on Marxism and the possibly "dangerous" effect of the intellectual, it is not really necessary for a journal like *Time* or *Newsweek* to address the question of intellectual
effectiveness: an article like *Time*'s on the David Abraham case or
Newsweek's on Paul de Man seems to work not by giving the reader enough clear information to decide the cases one way or the
other but, rather and quite the contrary, to so blur things, to so
pile up names and twists and turns of academic maneuvering, that
academic debate comes to seem so much the irrelevant outpour-
ing of words that popular cliché would often imagine it to be (I
wonder, for example, what anyone might make of *Newsweek*'s
explanation in the de Man case of what "deconstruction" is all
about). The effect of *Time*'s presentation of the Abraham case—a
liberalist presentation where one decides not to decide one way
or the other—is little different from that of the American Historical Association's ruling: in deciding not to investigate charges that
Gerald Feldman had exceeded professional responsibility by
writing unsolicited letters and by calling search committee members about Abraham, the AHA claimed that the academic profes-

sion itself provided an open forum for the working out of grievances, that claim thereby occulting all the operations that work to prohibit a constitution of academia as open and liberal forum.

Time does not need to attack one position or another, since its confusing neutrality is itself a powerful position that evacuates commitment and encourages the reader toward cynicism. As Raymond Williams argues for the specific case of television, mass culture's meanings come not so much from the sense of its discrete bits, its individual shows, as from a *flow* that slides one show into the next and evacuates history in the process. Now, while I do not want optimistically to overestimate the power of any intellectual discourse to resist mediatization, it seems to me possible to imagine discourses that might emphatically disturb the indifference of flow by insisting on practices, on flows of history, that are less easily assimilable to media flow. History, here, would not be imagined as an object of truth that cuts through falsehood but, rather, as the object of a rhetorical practice that, in Frank Lentricchia's nice pun in *Criticism and Social Change*, "forges" connections— that is, makes links across the indifference of flow, but does so in full awareness that such links are political fictions, rather than inevitable and final truths. History writing then becomes itself a montage that conjoins elements, that for every show offered by our Society of the Spectacle offers in return an insistence on the political investments behind spectacle, the material forces and means of spectacle's production. Against the in-difference of flow, a conjoining montage insists on difference, specifically on the difference of politics as that which reists, as that which can never be just a Happening or Event or Spectacle. History here is a tactic that mediates realism and nominalism by arguing that in an age in which everything is potentially linguistic, some things may take longer to become so, certain things do not yet have a full mediatic expressibility and speaking of them can therefore perhaps give them a forceful power against mediatization.

But this is to suggest that academics have to engage more fully and frequently in an analysis of media and popular culture and refuse a process that within academia seems as frequent and as regularized as the mediatization of the intellectual and that often works to the same end of disengagement of the intellectual from the critique and analysis of everyday culture: namely, the reconversion of concepts geared toward the analysis of everyday life and mass culture into concepts most appropriate for the analysis of high culture alone. This seems to me, for example, to be the case currently with the concept of postmodernism. There is a conceptual battle to be fought over the field of application of such a concept: on the one hand, the postmodern as a term for a blurring of high and popular culture, an understanding of today's cultural practice as beyond those binary oppositions that (1) take high culture to mean difficulty, antinarrativity, the critique of simple pleasures and so on, and (2) takes mass culture to mean simplicity, narrative, mythicality, celebration of simple pleasure, and so on; on the other hand, the postmodern (as in the criticism of Ihab Hassan) as precisely a reinvestment in the traditional opposition of mass and high, a reinvigoration of canons by now referring to works as "postmodern" where one formerly called the "complex" or "rich" or "ironic" or "dialogic." If intellectuals so often ignore the force of media and popular culture, this ignoring or ignorance can go hand in hand with a high art elevation of certain concepts like the postmodern away from the masses, away from the popular.

Significantly, although I singled out Edward Said's *Covering Islam* earlier as an example of an intellectual division of the world into intellectuals and masses, it seems to me that Said's career (to use a word that he himself often uses in his criticism to suggest the political contradictions of a life situation) is often exemplary in its positive recognitions of the needs for intellectuals not only to engage with, but engage in, media and popular culture. Hence (and here I simply rephrase my *Critical Exchange* article), if a fairly late text like Said's review of John Berger and Jean Mohr's *Another Way of Telling* seems to revert to an existential(ist) myth of pure selfhood undone by discourse (including the "bad" discourse of Modern media—Said speaks here of "monopolistic systems of order, all engaged in the extinction of privacy, subjectivity, and free choice"),[14] it is as possible to read the essay in another way as a recognition that political struggle means not a return to a pure space of existential inviolability but rather an attempt to rework the restrictions of a current space in new directions, new permutations. Indeed, Said's essay suggests that what most interests him in Mohr and Berger's blending of text and image is not some process by which all this representation would give us back a truth of the land, of the peasant, that we have lost beneath the alienations of modernity. Quite differently, Said's essay seems very attuned to the ways in which Berger and Mohr are themselves using modernity (photography, the mass-market book) to reconstellate some of the arrangements that modernity commonly establishes. The politics of *Another Way of Looking* lies not so much in a referent of the words or the photos as in the montage between word and image, and the new and productive reading that that montage encourages. Indeed, Said himself seems quite attracted to this notion of a productive montage that does not so much reflect a world as add a new praxis to it: he has expressed great admiration for the strategy of Mallek Alloula's *Colonial Harem* where postcards of Occidental imperialism are altered by a graffiti-like writing (and for his own part, in an essay on life in exile, Said has called for a politics of "contrapuntal" practice); he has produced a BBC program that is less a document on Orientalism than an active confrontation of different words and images to direct a particular new representation of thinking on the Orient; and his most recent book, *After the Lost Sky*, juxtaposes text against Jean Mohr photographs precisely to engage in the same sort of creative and popular intervention in mass culture as John Berger with Mohr.

The very fact that someone who conceived the media as a covering can also think of ways to work at reconstellation is heartening for the cultural analyst. In fact, if we wish to analyze and understand contemporary culture—all the massive effects of mediatization, of spectaclization that I have described—it is also important to insist on the incompleteness, on the limits to effectivity, to covering or blanketing, of that culture's power. And some of these limits may come from the very nature of the dominant practices themselves: they structure reality in such a way that alternate structurations can sometimes have an earth-shattering effect. For example, if mediatization involves a regularized temporality of history as Event, the regularized temporality of the fad, of the conversion of all practices into fashion, then it might well be possible to imagine that some practices can offer or embody temporalities that extend beyond the boundaries of momentous spectacle or happening: they can have a durability that makes them refuse to go away. Indeed, it seems to me that it is precisely the threat of a temporality other than that of its own mediatizing that a journal like *Newsweek* is reacting to when it uses its de Man article to project a self-deconstruction of Marxism into the future: *Newsweek* (along with the Frederick Crews it quotes) is trying desperately to outrun Marxism, to anticipate it. It is important, then, for cultural critics to insist on those temporalities that refuse to disappear when fads change: for example, in a moment of multiplying post-Marxisms, of Marxisms in crisis, it may be of great tactical value to insist on the ways in which Marxism is not a "god that failed."

Indeed, we need to note that, in a certain modification of everything that I have said thus far, dominant power does not work only by the conversion of history into media event; there is a contrary tactic that involves the hiding of events that should have been noteworthy, a tactic well demonstrated by Todd Gitlin in his *The Whole World is Watching* on TV and the *New York Times*'s nonreporting of the Vietnam War. To take a more recent example, the very claim by the opponents of David Abraham that their opposition was a purely scholarly one, a matter of historical principles, appears in a different light when one learns of an interview granted by Henry Turner in 1986 to the extreme right-wing academic discipliner, *Accuracy in Academia*: with the case now fallen into relative obscurity, with its fading from public view, such an interview works differently than it might have in the heart of mediatized debate. It seems to me important, then, to resist the temporalities of media and dominant obfuscation by *going* back to controversies like that over Masson or Abraham or eventually de Man long after they have ceased to be spectacle (but while they are still functioning in the subterranean world of intellectuality, still relating to questions of reference and history that plague intellectual knowledge).

From the question of Auschwitz to the advertisement for a typical liberalist Hollywood movie; from philosophical debates on the question of the referent and the linguistic status of action to the antics of university professors as reported and misreported in the world of mass culture: we may seem to have moved in this essay around a number of postmodern themes that have no evident connection, no mediation. But the point may well be that their usual mediation is their potential for mediatization, the ability of all questions—from Auschwitz to a professor in front of his or her students—to become caught up in the flow of our society's spectacle. The role of the critical intellectual, then, might be to battle for other forms of mediation, to try to make the stories of history more gripping, more flowing, than any of the stories our culture usually tells.

NOTES

1. A computer search I conducted in 1987 (and an undoubtedly incomplete one) turned up over 1,500 items with "postmodern," or variants thereof, in the title.

2. See my essay, "A Vertigo of Displacement: The Sartrean Spectacle of *L'idiot de la famille*," *Dalhousie Review*, 64 (Summer 1984), pp. 354–75.

3. Fred Pfeil, "Makin' Flippy-Floppy': Postmodernism and the Baby-Boom P.M.C.," in Mike Davis, Michael Sprinkler, and Fred Pfeil (eds.), *The Year Left*, vol. (New York: Verso, 1985).

4. See Lyotard, *Le différend* (Paris: Minuit, 1984).

5. It is pertinent perhaps that it is Jameson who writes the preface to the American translation of *La condition postmoderne*.

6. On this point, see also Lyotard's *L'enthousiasme: la critique kantienne de l'histoire* (Paris: Galilée, 1986).

7. See Morris, "Postmodernity and Lyotard's Sublime," *Art & Text*, 16 (1984), p. 46.

8. Rose, *Sexuality in the Field of Vision* (London: Verso, 1986), pp. 12–14. See also her essay "Jeffrey Masson and Alice James," *Oxford Literary Review*, 8 (1986), pp. 185–192, which, among other things, includes useful references to Masson's declaration of his "feminism."

9. One exception to intellectuals' disinterest in the way their own "interest" may be reshaped, reframed, by contemporary media representations is Régis Debray's *Teachers, Writers, Celebrities: The Intellectuals of Modern France* (London: New Left Books, 1981). But it seems to me that Debray too falls for an either/or mythology: today's intellectual as totally caught up in the debilitating traps of modern media in contrast to yesterday's intellectual offered a freedom by the sheltered sanctity of a special realm of intellectual life (for example, the dialogue among the members of a classic literary or critical review). This either/or-ism has as its consequence that, but for a very few comments in the last pages on the need for intellectuals to outparody the clichés of the mass culture around them, Debray can offer no positive suggestions as to how intellectuals might work in and through their contemporary world.

A useful discussion of modern intellectuals' encounters with, and attitudes toward, mass culture is Andrew Ross, *No Respect! Intellectuals and Popular Culture* (New York: Routledge, 1989).

10. See "Worlds and Words: The Politics of Meaning and the Meaning of Politics in the Work of Edward Said," forthcoming, *Critical Exchange* (special issue on Said of the journal of the Society for Critical Exchange).

11. For an analysis of a similar process whereby the playful and deconstructive multiplication of positions seems to hesitate when it might be a question of deconstructing the association of woman and mass culture, see Teresa de Lauretis's analysis of Calvino's *If on a Winter's Night* in *Technologies of Gender* (Bloomington: Indiana University Press, 1987).

12. See my essay, "SZ/MTV," *Journal of Communication Inquiry*, 10 (1987).

13. This photographic convention is so strong that, as Abraham explained to me, when *Time* came to interview him at a conference of the American Historical Association, they dragged him from booth to booth of the book exhibit until they found an impressive array of books (including one with a swaztika on it) against which to photograph him (see *Time*, January 14, 1985, p. 59).

14. Said, Review, *Nation*, 235 (December 4, 1982), p. 595.

CONTRIBUTORS

Jonathan Arac is Professor of English at the University of Pittsburgh and an editor of *boundary 2*. He is the author of *Critical Genealogies* (1987) and *Commissioned Spirits* (1989), editor of *After Foucault* (1988), and a contributor to the Cambridge History of American Literature.

Stanley Aronowitz is Professor of Sociology at CUNY Graduate Center and an editor of *Social Text*. He is the coauthor, with Henry Giroux, of *Education under Siege* (1985) and *Postmodern Education* (forthcoming), and the author of *The Crisis in Historical Materialism* (1981) and *Science as Power* (1988).

Deirdre David, Professor of English at Temple University, is the author of *Fictions of Resolution in Three Victorian Novels* (1981) and *Intellectual Women and Victorian Patriarchy: Harriet Martineau, Elizabeth Barret Browning, George Eliot* (1988). Her current project, entitled "Grilled Alive in Calcutta: Victorian India, Victorian Women," examines ideologies of race and gender in the construction of the British Raj.

Barbara Ehrenreich's most recent book is *Fear of Falling: The Inner Life of the Middle Class* (1989).

John Higgins is Lecturer in English at the University of Cape Town and a member of UCT's Academic Freedom Committee. He is completing a study of Raymond Williams for Routledge's Critics of the Twentieth Century series, and is an editor of the new South African interdisciplinary journal, *Pretexts: Studies in Writing and Culture*.

Dana Polan teaches film and English at the University of Pittsburgh. He is the author of *The Political Language of Film and the Avant-Garde* (1985) and *Power and Paranoia: History, Narrative, and the American Cinema, 1940–1950* (1986) and articles in journals such as *October, boundary 2, Camera Obscura*, and *Enclitic*.

Christopher Prendergast is Distinguished Professor in French and Comparative Literature, The Graduate School, City University of New York. He is the author of *Balzac: Fiction and Melodrama* (1978), *The Order of Mimesis* (1986), and editor of *Nineteenth-Century French Poetry* (1990). As a member of the editorial collective of *Social Text*, he is currently assembling a collection of essays on the work of Raymond Williams.

R. Radhakrishnan teaches Cultural Studies and Critical Theory in the Department of English at the University of Massachusetts at Amherst. His essays on poststructuralism, theories of ethnicity, feminist historiography, critical theory, and so forth, have appeared and are forthcoming in *MELUS, boundary 2, Cultural Critique, Works and Days, Transition, Differences*, and a number of collections of essays. He is completing a book, *Theory in an Uneven World* (forthcoming from Basil Blackwell).

Bruce Robbins teaches in the Department of English at Rutgers University and is an editor of *Social Text*. The author of *The Servant's Hand: English Fiction from Below* (1986), he is at work on a book about professionalism and literary theory.

Andrew Ross teaches English at Princeton University. He is the author of *The Failure of Modernism* (1986) and *No Respect: Intellectuals and Popular Culture* (1989). He is also the editor of *Universal Abandon? The Politics of Postmodernism* (1988) and an editor of *Social Text*.

Edward W. Said is Old Dominion Foundation Professor in the Humanities at Columbia University, and his books include *Beginnings: Intention and Method* (1984), *Orientalism* (1979), *The Question of Palestine* (1980), *The World, the Text, and the Critic* (1983), *After the Last Sky* (1986), and the forthcoming *Culture and Imperialism*.

David Simpson is Professor of English at the University of Colorado, Boulder. His most recent books are *Wordsworth's Historical Imagination: The Poetry of Displacement* (1987) and (ed.) *The Origins of Modern Critical Thought: Germany Literary and Aesthetic Criticisms from Lessing to Hegel* (1988).

Alfons Söllner is Research Fellow at the Zentrum für Antisemitismusforschung. His most recent publications include *Peter Weiss und die Deutschen: Die Entstehung einer politischer Ästhetic wider die Verdrängung* (1988), (ed.), *Verfassungsstaat, Souveränität, Pluralismus: Otto Kirchheimer zum Gedächtnis* (1989), and numerous articles on the German academic emigration.

Gayatri Chakravorty Spivak was educated at Calcutta and Cornell universities and now teaches at the University of Pittsburgh. She is the translator of Jacques Derrida's *Of Grammatology* and the author of *In Other Worlds*, as well as the forthcoming *Master Discourse, Native Informant: Deconstruction in the Service of Reading* (Harvard University Press), *Feminism in Decolonization* (Verso), and *The Post-Colonial Critic*, a volume of interviews edited by Sarah Harasym (Routledge).

INDEX

DATE DUE			
DEC 21 '94			